The CORONATION STREET *Story*

CELEBRATING THIRTY-FIVE YEARS OF THE STREET

Daran Little

Based on an idea by

Tony Warren.

ROVERS RETURN INN
35

CELEBRATING
THIRTY FIVE YEARS
OF THE STREET

Daran Little

BOXTREE

Published in association with

GRANADA TELEVISION

This book is dedicated to the writers of Coronation Street:
Adele Rose, Patrea Smallacombe, Sally Wainwright,
Paul Abbot, Martin Allen, Frank Cottrell Boyce,
Tom Elliott, Barry Hill, Stephen Lowe,
Stephen Mallatratt, Julian Roach, John Stevenson,
Peter Whalley, Mark Wadlow and Phil Woods.

This paperback edition first published in 1996 by Boxtree Limited
First published in Great Britain in 1995

5 7 9 10 8 6 4

Designed by Maggie Aldred
Typeset by SX Composing, Rayleigh, Essex
Printed and bound in Great Britain by Bath Press Colour Books, Glasgow
for

Boxtree Limited
Broadwall House
21 Broadwall
London SE1 9PL

A CIP catalogue entry for this book is available from the British Library.

ISBN 0 7522 1019 X

Contents

Tony Warren

Introduction

Coronation Street is without doubt the most successful television programme in the world. It has run for thirty-five years, has been viewed in nearly every continent, has average viewing figures in the UK of 18-19 million per episode, and is studied by school pupils as part of the National Curriculum and undergraduates for degree dissertations. I first met Tony Warren, the genius who created the programme, and its original residents when studying for a degree at Manchester Polytechnic. I had been a fan of the programme for a long time and wished to devote my dissertation to Warren's original characters. He broke his own rule never to speak to students about his work because he thought the spelling of my name must be Armenian and his curiosity was aroused. If he was disappointed to find I was English he did not let it show, and kindly bought me dinner at Manchester's Midland Hotel. We talked for four hours about Esther Hayes, Christine Hardman, God and angels, and became firm friends. Within six months, I had been taken on by Granada Television as archivist on the Street, Tony Warren having convinced the new executive producer David Liddiment that I was worth employing.

I owe a lot to Tony Warren, as does Granada, everyone who works on Coronation Street and everyone who has ever watched an episode. I wanted to write this book so that all these people would know how this highly acclaimed, award-winning programme was created, and how it has changed and developed over the years. It soon became apparent to me that unless someone plotted the history of this remarkable programme soon then its origins could well be obscured by the dramatic and comic storylines of the present and future. In the last two years alone, the Street family have lost so many loved ones – the original producer, Stuart (Harry) Latham; one of the first directors and the producer of the show in 1961, Howard Baker; the Street's original archivist Eric Rosser; the longest serving producer, Bill Podmore; and the original Duchess of Weatherfield, Doris Speed M.B.E.

There is so much which could be (and has been) written about Coronation Street. For the purposes of this book I have had to look closely at each storyline and judge which should be included. Not all the major stories are retold and you may well be surprised at some of the seemingly minor ones. All the material presented in this book goes towards building, brick by brick, the structure of what is today the world's longest running drama serial.

I hope you enjoy reading how the programme was created, that you will be reminded of characters long ago overtaken in the memory by the likes of Raquel and Reg, and that at the end of the book, you will agree with me that Coronation Street is the most fascinating programme to exist in the history of television.

DARAN LITTLE
June 1995

Daran Little

'Mam, did yer know some o' them shows are watched by 20 million people?'

'Shurup Dennis an' eat yer dinner.'

In the Beginning . . .

In the beginning there was Ena Sharples, Annie Walker and Elsie Tanner. Three very domineering women, different in temperament and background, values and social standing, but all three living in the same grimy back street and all three created by writer Tony Warren. Warren was a child actor who outgrew his talent; as he puts it 'I got too tall'. Contrary to popular belief he was not brought up in a Coronation Street; his father was a Manchester Merchant and home was a semi in Swinton. He disliked the grammar school where he was sent and spent all his time reading plays and theatrical biographies at Manchester's Central Library. He joined Granada in 1958, aged 21, having been interviewed by casting director Margaret Morris. She recognized that he was at a difficult age: 'I was a beanpole with a baby face', but surprised him by saying she knew he'd been trying to write material for comedienne Avril Angers. Rather than giving him an acting job she suggested he talk to Canadian Harry Elton, a producer who was building up a band of contract writers. Tony discovered that Elton was producing a detective show called *Shadow Squad*, so he went home and wrote half an episode, sending it off to Elton with a note: 'If you want to know how this ends, telephone Pendleton 2437.' He then sat waiting for the phone to ring, but it never did. After a week, he called Granada and discovered the script had never reached the Canadian. 'About an hour later he rang back and said: "This is amazing; it's full of arresting material, I have to talk to you and fast." So I went in.'

Tony Warren was taken on by Elton and commissioned to write episodes of *Shadow Squad*. The first one he wrote was about a prostitute and was called *Streets of Gold*. It was designed by Denis Parkin and directed by Derek Bennett, both of whom were in tune with Warren's thoughts about the north and the social climate he wanted to present. Parkin would eventually design the original Street and Bennett direct the first Street episode.

Harry Elton felt that Tony needed to learn more about television and got him in a job in the Promotions Department, making trailers for Granada shows. The writers working there were a small band of like-minded souls. Jack Rosenthal had just left and Tony worked alongside Geoffrey Lancashire; eventually Rosenthal and Lancashire would join Warren as core writers of the Street. Tony found himself in the middle of a busy television network: 'It was very new and very exciting. We were making the rules up as we went along and the opportunities were endless.' Soon Tony was taken on as script-writer on a local show, *People and Places*; he recalls his favourite programme being one devoted to pantomimes. Executive Dennis Forman watched the rehearsal of the programme, read Tony's script and the next day he was given a year's contract to write exclusively for Granada, on £30 a week. During that year he wrote episodes of *Biggles*, but this made him incredibly unhappy and led to him perching on top of Harry Elton's filing cabinet yelling, 'Let me write what I know about.' Elton ordered him down and gave him twenty-four hours to come up with an idea that would 'take Britain by storm'. The idea became Coronation Street, the world's longest running television drama, now celebrating it's thirty-fifth anniversary.

Over the last thirty-five years several people have

'*Coronation Street* is more than a soap opera. It is a national institution which has won its way into the hearts of eighteen million viewers because of the virtues and values which it portrays and celebrates. In the North, 'quality' is an adjective of unqualified praise. *Coronation Street* is a quality programme.'

Roy Hattersley

'Ida Barlow is a kindly woman somewhere in her late forties. Her husband Frank is a little older. Once he might have been muscular but has now gone to seed. Their son Kenneth is twenty. He has little or no northern accent and looks faintly out of place in these surroundings.'

Tony Warren first introduces the Barlows in Episode One of *Florizel Street*.

laid claim to the creation of the format for the Street, and to influencing Tony Warren or helping him create the characters. The truth of the matter is that the Street came to life in Tony Warren's head and the only people who influenced the characters of Ena and Co. were the real-life characters of the northern back streets that he observed and put down on paper. The idea for *Coronation Street* did not come to Tony Warren overnight. Back in 1956 Warren, then an unemployed nineteen-year-old actor, wrote a script about a northern back street, called *Where No Birds Sing*. A year later he wrote a comedy version of the same script, called it *Our Street* and sent it off to Barney Colehan at the BBC in Leeds, who acknowledged receipt and said he would present it to the television board for their comments. Thirty-eight years later Warren is still waiting for their decision. When he was first commissioned by Granada (but not yet under an exclusive contract) he tried to sell the idea of *Our Street* to Olive Shapley, a producer at the BBC in Manchester (she created *Woman's Hour*). Olive Shapley remembers Tony's excitement at the time: 'We were on the sleeper train coming back from London, I'd been producing a television programme and Tony had been one of the actors – we worked a lot together. Tony woke me at 2am, and said "Olive I have to tell someone, I've a great idea for a television show. Picture a little street in Salford, with a pub at one end and all the lives of the people being shown", and I just said "Oh Tony, how boring" and went back to sleep! I didn't even listen to him!'

Although not brought up in back streets, Warren knew a great deal about the people living in them, his grandmother being one. When Elton gave him only twenty-four hours, his pen floated across the paper as he remembered character upon character from his childhood. As he told a reporter from the TV Times in December in 1960, 'I started with one household, that became two, then three, and then a whole street, and I had to add a pub, an off-licence and a place of worship.' Remembering his earlier attempts to harnessing stories about a street, Tony Warren knew that the format was viable.

Harry Elton was fired with enthusiasm for this script, called *Florizel Street* (there was a portrait of Prince Florizel hacking his way through the enchanted forest to get to the Sleeping Beauty hanging on Warren's office wall). He told Tony to write a second episode and a memo describing the series. The memo, he says, took longer to write than either of the episodes. The fading blue paper still exists in the Street archive. It starts with Tony's outline description:

> A fascinating freemasonry, a volume of unwritten rules. These are the driving forces behind life in a working-class street in the north of England. To the uninitiated outsider, all this would be completely incomprehensible. The purpose of *Florizel Street* is to entertain by examining a community of this kind and initiating the viewer into the ways of the people who live there.

The memo then goes on to explain the Street and the residents. In the original script the Corner Shop was an outdoor beer licence, or off-licence, there was no Albert Tatlock and the Barlows had a daughter, Enid, who was married to a fitter called Harold and lived at No. 7. Lucille Hewitt was then known as Janice, and the Walkers had three children – Joan, Billy and Norman. Norman, following in his father's footsteps was running a new pub on the main Manchester-Blackpool Road with his new wife Brenda, an ex-ballroom dancing teacher.

The episodes and memo were shown to Granada's executives, and although they were not as enthusiastic about the idea, they realized that the programme offered what Granada really needed. As Tony Warren puts it: 'Granada's licence to transmit in the north of England required them to provide employment for people in the north of England and to reflect the region. . . . They were providing very little work for northern writers and even less for northern actors; because the accent was totally unfashionable. But I knew there were great burning talents hanging around who just didn't happen to talk posh.'

In his autobiography, H.V. Kershaw, who would become writer, script-editor and producer on the show, recalled his first reactions to the scripts: 'You closed your eyes and you could see the pot flights of ducks, and the antimacassars, and the chenille tablecloths, and the newspapers stuffed under the cushion of the easy chair. You sniffed and you could smell the burning sausages, and the cheap hair spray, and the tang of bitter beer.' Kershaw was given the role of script-editor, working alongside Warren and Harry Latham, who was given the job of producing two pilot episodes.

Margaret Morris was given the task of casting the twenty-two characters who appeared in the first two episodes. She was assisted by José Scott, and, together with Tony, they took a ledger and wrote down in it all the names of every northern actor they could think of; from this they auditioned, using the pilots, or dry runs as they were called, to test actors who showed potential. William Roache remembers the pilots well, as all the actors were petrified: 'I remember being very impressed by what it was and the way it was written and the devotion of everybody to it. I remember Pat Phoenix very well as being the strong personality standing out, laughing a lot, being very confident.'

The episodes were not well received by the executives and directors, and the whole project would have been scrapped if Harry Elton had not put into operation a sensational piece of showmanship. Tony Warren recalls what happened next with admiration and glee: 'He had television sets, monitors, put all over the studio; he sent questionnaires to everybody – from the cleaners to visiting dignitaries – and said they would be showing these two episodes between one and two o'clock and that would they please look at them and fill in these forms. It was very odd, because the reaction, right at the very beginning, is what everybody's reaction to *Coronation Street* has always been: they either loved it or they loathed it, but there wasn't much in between.' These passionate responses caused the executives to think again and, on 25th August 1960, the decision was made to produce sixteen episodes of Florizel Street. By the middle of October the first six scripts were completed, two directors – Derek Bennett and Mike Scott – had been assigned, and Latham sent a memo to Margaret Morris: 'Final and approved casting for launching the serial needs to be completed the last week in November for Bennett to start rehearsing the morning of Monday, 5 December.

Meanwhile, designer Denis Parkin put the finishing touches to his designs. He had spent days touring round back streets: 'Tony and I used to go round Salford West, all the places that he knew, showing me streets of houses and pubs.' For the first two years every single scene was recorded, live, in Granada's Studio Two. That included parks, railway stations and all the Street exteriors. For some weeks the whole street, from the Rovers to the shop across cobbles to the back of Elliston's Raincoat Factory, all had to be fitted into the studio, along with interior sets. Parkin had the job of creating homes which reflected each family and the individual characters: 'The hard part was making them all look different in black and white, so we had long talks about characters. I decided there'd better be a variation in at least one of the houses, so No. 9 was given a sort of glazed lean-to built at the back. It was to make a difference. Seven houses in black and white; to make them all look individual was quite a job.'

Tony worked on thirteen episodes, the last three written by Kershaw. Producer Harry Latham sent copies of the scripts around the building, attaching a memo explaining the length of the cast list: 'Certain characters may emerge as having greater interest and appeal, but initially, no individual star parts are contemplated.' Company chairman Cecil Bernstein read the scripts and commented: 'Are there any really nice people in the street? Of course there must be all sorts but who are the ones which the audience are really going to feel an affection towards and switch on for.' In the same memo, he went on to say that the off-licence should be a grocer's shop.

In the last week of November, actors were found for the three remaining uncast characters – Dennis, Ida and Ena. Everyone looked forward to rehearsals on the following Monday; the first live transmission would be on the Friday of that week. The programme was still known as *Florizel Street*; from the start many people involved in the programme voiced doubts about the title, but it was only when Agnes the tea lady said it sounded like a disinfectant that Tony Warren was asked to come up with some alternatives. He suggested two names – 'Jubilee Street' and 'Coronation Street'. The final decision fell to the three Harrys – Kershaw, Elton and Latham. They locked themselves away one evening and debated the names before agreeing to cast votes, as there were three of them and there was bound to be an absolute winner. Kershaw takes up the story in his autobiography: 'The following morning copies of a memorandum from Harry Latham winged their way to every interested recipient in Granada announcing that the new serial was to be known as *Coronation Street*. One of the copies was waiting for me as I arrived and I immediately took it into Harry Elton's office on the sixth floor. He was sitting at his desk reading his copy as I walked in. His head lifted. "I'm pretty darned sure I voted for Jubilee Street," he said. "And I'm pretty darned sure *I* voted for Jubilee Street too," I added. And thus it was that our serial came to be known as *Coronation Street*.'

Casting the Net...

THE ORIGINAL CAST

The original cast came from varied careers and backgrounds. Casting for what was then known as *Florizel Street* had taken five weeks, with over 600 actors auditioned for the few available roles. Casting director Margaret Morris, her assistant, José Scott, and Tony Warren saw nearly every actor and actress known to have been born in the north of England. Some actors had been chosen before the decision was made to go ahead with the initial sixteen episodes, and these actors portrayed the characters in the two pilot shows (dry runs) shown to Granada executives. As Tony Warren later wrote in his autobiography, sometimes the casting was easy: 'A girl walked in, auditioned for us and maintains that I passed across a note which read: "She is very plain but when she smiles it's like the sun coming out." This was Christine Hargreaves who was eventually to play Christine Hardman. Christine had been born in a Salford street very much like Coronation Street, and trained at RADA, getting an Honours Diploma before touring as understudy with the Old Vic. Before joining the cast, Christine worked at Granada on the drama series *Skyport*, a programme in which many other Street actors had appeared.

Appearing in the dry runs with Christine was Doris Speed as Annie Walker. The character of Jack Walker did not appear in the pilots, but later Arthur Leslie was given the role. Doris Speed and Arthur Leslie had plenty in common as they settled down to play the Walkers behind the bar of the Rovers. Both were children of theatrical parents, both were born whilst those parents were on tour. As Doris recalled: 'I first went on the stage when I was five. As I grew up I had to attend a different school every week; it was shocking for my education, but good for my self-confidence.' Arthur Leslie started in rep in 1916, aged just sixteen. His future had always been mapped out: 'The whole family had a theatrical background. When I left school it was assumed I would enter the profession, too, which I did. My real name is Arthur Broughton, but I chose Arthur Leslie as my stage name. Over the years I have appeared in over 600 productions and taken every kind of part from Lancashire comedy to Shakespeare. But the real bread-and-butter work was repertory. I've twice managed my own company, once in the 1930s and the other in 1951-52.'

Doris Speed toured in rep, playing most of the classics, including Lady Macbeth, and in the 1940s turned her talents to radio. It was at Manchester's BBC Studios that she first met the twelve-year-old boy who would change the course of her life. Tony Warren, a child actor working under his real name Tony Simpson, performed on *Children's Hour* with Doris. When the auditions started for the Street, Doris was working on a play in Bristol. Warren pursued Doris because he felt she was exactly right for the part of Annie: 'From the word go, I had pencilled the name Doris Speed against Annie Walker, so that was all right, but we needed tit and glitter to bring Elsie Tanner to life.'

Patricia Phoenix, having just changed her name from Pilkington, landed the role after auditioning in a foul temper. In her autobiography, she recalls facing a panel of six, one of which was Tony

'A telegram arrived asking me to go for an audition. I replied, saying it was quite impossible. They called by telephone. Again I refused. That night an actress friend tipped me off that it might be something special. I turned up in a bad temper, and read a scene. For the first time in my life I knew I'd get the part.'

Doris Speed recalling her audition for *Coronation Street*

'I always thought that people looked at Swindley as such a monster and such a villain, but in his own right I always thought he was okay. I like people who are very definite, and Swindley was very definite. And I'd actually known people like Swindley. There was a draper's shop near to where I grew up and they used to say to you, "Mr Davies will attend to you." Mr Davies had an Adam's apple that bobbed up and down between a "Come to Jesus" collar and I knew nothing about him, but everyone I ever saw I imagined an entire life for them.'

Tony Warren recalls how he created Leonard Swindley.

Warren, who she thought was just a boy: 'They gave me a script folded over and asked me to read. . . . We were not used to television dialogue that sounded like real people in those days. Ladies on television then were "awfully naice" and had nicely rounded vowels to match. I could see if there was anything rounded about Elsie Tanner, it wasn't her vowels. After I had read for them, the blond youth asked me if I would mind standing up and removing my coat. "Cheeky young devil," I thought. "No," I said flatly. "You'll just have to guess at it, won't you?"'

During the 1960s, Phoenix allowed reporters to believe she had been born in romantic County Galway, Ireland, but she later put the record straight by saying she had been born Patricia Frederica Pilkington in Manchester in 1924. When the Street started it was thought she was too young to play Elsie Tanner and she wore body padding to make herself appear older. She soon developed a love for showbusiness: 'I was always dressing up and acting. My heroines were Ginger Rogers and Bette Davis. And I was going to be just as famous as they were some day, I told myself.' After trying an office job she joined the Manchester Arts Theatre. For the next eighteen years she toured in rep and worked in radio. She auditioned for the Street in August 1960 and played Elsie in both dry runs.

Someone who was not cast until after the pilot shows was Arthur Lowe. Unlike Pat, who did not appear in a major feature film until 1962 (when she played a prostitute in *The L Shaped Room*), Arthur featured in many films before the Street, *Kind Hearts and Coronets* and *The Spider and the Fly* to name only two. His Mr Swindley, a pompous self-important lay preacher, first appeared in Episode Three. Arthur had been brought up in Manchester but got his first taste of show business while organizing entertainment for the troops in the Middle East during the Second World War.

Jack Howarth spent the Second World War running a show at Colwyn Bay. 'It was the hardest work I've ever done. With the war and the shortage of men, I finished up doing almost the whole lot!' Rochdale-born Jack (he went to school with Gracie Fields), used to sell programmes after school in the auditorium at the Theatre Royal whilst his father, a comedian, trod the boards. After the First World War, in which he served with the Lancashire Fusiliers (like his Street character Albert Tatlock), Jack joined Leslie Henson's famous touring company and in 1935 formed his own company. In 1947 he entered the world of films, television and radio, and for fourteen years played the part of Maggs, in *Mrs Dale's Diary*. His son John went to boarding-school with William Roache, a fact which Roache recalled on Jack Howarth's *This Is Your Life*: 'I remember being seven years old and being sent to Rydall School in North Wales. On my first day at school I was crying my eyes out, and Jack came up to me and said, "What's your name?" I said, "Billy Roache." He said, "Where do you come from" and I said "England!" And he treated me like a kind old uncle, not a bit like Coronation Street.'

William Roache studied medicine but abandoned it to take a Regular Army commission, serving as a captain in Jamaica, British Guiana, Bermuda and Germany. He acted for the Foreign Office in Turcial Oman, attempting to keep the peace amongst seven tribes during the Suez crisis. After leaving the Army, he spent eight months looking for work, and realized that desperate measures were called for. 'I went to an agent, lied like a trooper, told him I had just finished two years with a leading seaside repertory company and got a job.' Repertory, film and television work led him, eventually, to Granada. Roache recalls in his autobiography, 'Apparently, while I was recording the play *Marking Time* at Granada, Tony saw me. He fetched the Street's casting director, José Scott, pointed me out, and said, "*That* is Ken Barlow". . . .' Bill was called for a Street audition which he did not really want, having just got his career starting in London: 'It wasn't an audition, it was an interview. They chatted away about my background, that I'd done rep and I'd done a bit of acting, so they were happy about that. I had a newspaper with me and they said would I read anything from the newspaper, starting in normal English and going into broad Lancashire, which I did. It happened to be a very funny article about Bessie Braddock the politician flicking inky pellets at a political opponent, and we all had a good laugh. I didn't want the job, and you're very confident when you don't want the job.'

Someone who *did* want a part in the new programme was Alan Rothwell, who was cast as Kenneth's younger brother David Barlow. However, his was one of the last characters to be cast as David was not in the original scripts and did not appear until after the dry run of the first episode. Tony Warren recalls: '[The producers] asked me to inject two characters. They said all the older characters were rather abrasive and critical; they

Monday 5 December 1960: the cast meet each other for the first time and line up for the first Coronation Street photograph.
Back row *(l to r) – Ivan Beavis* (Harry Hewitt), *Jack Howarth* (Albert Tatlock), *Ernst Walder* (Ivan Cheveski), *Philip Lowrie* (Dennis Tanner), *Alan Rothwell* (David Barlow), *Arthur Leslie* (Jack Walker), *Bill Croasdale* (appeared as a non-speaking policeman in Episode Two), *Frank Pemberton* (Frank Barlow), *Noel Dyson* (Ida Barlow), *Margot Bryant* (Minnie Caldwell). **Front Row** *(l to r) – Doris Speed* (Annie Walker), *Betty Alberge* (Florrie Lindley), *Anne Cunningham* (Linda Cheveski), *Patricia Phoenix* (Elsie Tanner), *Violet Carson* (Ena Sharples), *Christine Hargreaves* (Christine Hardman), *Bill Roache* (Ken Barlow), *Penny Davies* (appeared as a police woman in Episode Two), *Patricia Shakesby* (Ken's girlfriend Susan Cunningham) *and Lynne Carol* (Martha Longhurst).

Frank Pemberton, like the majority of the original cast, came from a background of weekly rep. His screen wife, Noel Dyson, was a successful West End actress who did not want to be typecast by the show.

wanted one of age, charm and dignity. Well, I was never very good at obeying orders, so I invented Albert Tatlock. And they wanted another, rather representative of the north of England teenager boy and that was David Barlow.' Because of the late injection of the character, Alan Rothwell did not even audition for the role: 'I played the son in *Love on the Dole* for television. And people at Granada saw it and offered me a part in *Coronation Street*. They offered me David Barlow straight from that.' Alan was born in Oldham and had started acting as a child in Children's House, alongside Tony Warren and Billie Whitelaw. He worked at Oldham Rep with Bill Roache, and spent a year training at RADA before doing his National Service.

Tony Warren thought that casting Ida Barlow would be no problem, as he had written the part especially for Betty Alberge. However, after Betty read for the part at the first auditions, everyone agreed she was better suited as shopkeeper Florrie Lindley, and it was as such as she appeared in the pilots. Betty's first taste of acting was at school in the play *The Death off Tintageles*, playing the sister of schoolfriend Pat Phoenix. After working in ENSA, Betty did radio work (including *Over the Garden Wall* and *Clitheroe Kid*)and plenty of television work. In the pilots, the part of Ida was taken by Ruth Holden, who eventually appeared as Vera Lomax, Ena's long-suffering daughter. She did not get the part of Ida as she was thought too young and, in fact, was given a special costume for the dry run: 'I was very slim in those days so the wardrobe department folded a towel, a sort of long bathtowel to make me look fatter, to pad me out and give me a middle-aged look.' When Ruth appeared as Vera in Episode 5 she was still regarded as too slim, so played all her scenes wearing a massive winter coat which hid her body completely.

Eventually, West End actress Noel Dyson landed the part of Ida. Manchester-born Noel was a well-known face from films such as *Carry On Constable* and *Stretched for Time*. She had left RADA in 1938 but was soon forced to give up the theatre because of thyroid trouble. She rested for four years, during which time she served as a VAD nurse. After the thyroid was removed she toured with ENSA: 'We were called Masks and Maids, and we had three of the most unsuitable one act plays,' she recalls now. 'We went round the hospitals and convalescent homes and we played on tables pushed together at the end of the ward. Our most difficult audiences were Canadians because if they didn't like you they rolled empty bottles down the aisles, and started fights. It certainly taught you audience control.' After the War Noel Dyson worked at Oxford Rep, before appearing in the West End and moving into television and films. Like Bill Roache, she did not really want to work on the Street because her family lived in the south. However she accepted the role as it was only meant to run to thirteen episodes.

The part of Ida's husband Frank was given to Frank Pemberton. Frank had served in the Royal Navy during the War, and on being demobbed in 1946 formed a repertory company with two partners: 'We played Birkenhead, Dunfermline, Falkirk, Cromer and Great Yarmouth and finally I decided there were less worrying ways of earning a living.' When he joined the Street in December 1960, Frank was already a veteran of films and television, appearing in programmes such as the BBC's *Champion Road* and ATV's *Emergency Ward 10*. His film credits included *Saturday Night Sunday Morning* and *David Copperfield*.

Dozens of actresses were auditioned for the parts of Ena, Minnie and Martha. Merchant Navy sweetheart Doris Hare MBE was approached to appear as Martha: 'Tony said, "I'm doing a new thing, it's called *Coronation Street* and there is a lovely part I want you to play." ' She agreed to play the part in a dry run to help Tony out. At the end of the dry run, Margaret Morris decided that Doris was wasted as Martha, then quite a small part, and offered her the role of Ena Sharples. Unfortunately, Doris Hare had commitments with the RSC and turned the part down.

The parts of Martha and Minnie eventually went to Lynne Carol and Margot Bryant. Lynne Carol first appeared on stage when she was nine days old, carried on by her actress mother Mina Mackinon. Years of theatre work, radio and television eventually led to Martha Longhurst. The costume was Lynne Carol's own idea; she bought the glassless spectacles, beret and rumpled mackintosh for a few bob in a jumble sale. She later told a reporter from *Weekend*, 'There are an awful lot of Marthas in the world. Some viewers used to tell me to mind my own business but most people could see that Martha was really a pathetic old dear.'

Margot Bryant was a trained dancer and had began her career in chorus work; in one West End show, *Stop Flirting*, she danced with Fred Astaire. She was often found on the Manchester stage, including a run in *Gay's the Word* at the Palace Theatre, and her voice was regularly heard on radio in favourites such as *Mrs Dale's Diary*.

Ivan Beavis was thrilled to land the part of Harry Hewitt. After serving in the Navy during the War he became an audit clerk, working in Northern Ireland

Doris Hare (left) as Martha appeared in a dry run of Episode 3 with Nan Marriott-Watson as Ena and Alison Bayley as Minnie. The roles eventually went to Lynne Carol, Violet Carson and Margot Bryant.

where he contracted TB. While recuperating in the early 1950s, he joined an amateur dramatics company and quickly found himself in demand on the amateur circuit. The story of how he joined Granada reads like a fairy-tale: "I was just passing Granada and said I'd like to see Margaret Morris. She saw me and said, "Oddly enough, we've got something going out tonight, how's your American?" So I read it. . . . I didn't get that part, but about four days later she rang up and gave me a part in *The Army Game*,and that was the start of it.' Five years later and with other Granada shows under his belt, Ivan was given the part of bus conductor Harry.

The part of Harry's eleven-year-old daughter Lucille was given to fifteen-year-old Jennifer Moss. Her career started with *Children's Hour*, in a play in which her brother was played by Davey Jones who appeared as Ena's grandson Colin in Episode 25. Tony Warren realized that Jennifer was going to need help to prepare herself for live television so

'Tony asked me to take off my shoes and I kicked them off. I'm four foot eleven so I passed as eleven years old. The scene I had to read was Lucille running away from the orphanage and she was supposed to cry. And I was so nervous I did cry; it was very, very easy. By the time I got home to Wigan, Granada had telephoned and I was in it.'

Jennifer Moss recalling her audition

invited her along to the first rehearsals and her voice was featured in the first episode – checking Elsie Tanner – and then in the second, as Martha Longhurst's complaining grandaughter Sandra.

Albert Tatlock had not been in the original scripts but, once created, became the person young Kenneth Barlow turned to for advice. Originally the role of adviser had belonged to Esther Hayes, the spinster from No. 5. She was played by London-born actress Daphne Oxenford, who never gave a thought to auditioning: 'My agent called and said Granada wanted to see me for this new series. And I said don't be silly, I couldn't do a Manchester accent. No, she said, they're seeing everybody who lives roundabout. So I came in and I was asked to read the part of the landlady Annie Walker, which I read very badly.' Needless to say Daphne did not get the part and happily carried on life as usual, working on *What the Papers Say*. That was, until the Thursday before the Street rehearsals started: 'Somebody got in touch and said would you do this part of Esther Hayes in Coronation Street, and we start rehearsals on Monday. I mean, I was the bottom of the barrel.' Daphne acepted the part but worried about the accent, 'They said, don't worry, Esther is better educated than some other people so we can get away with it like that.' It was the accent which Tony Warren thinks caused the character to not fit in with the others: 'She was the only one who was played by somebody who wasn't northern, and that camera is a great finder of truth.'

Daphne's theatrical career began at the age of nine, she trained at the Embassy School of Acting and made her first professional appearance at the Globe in London. She appeared in two Joyce Grenfell reviews and became a favourite presenter on *Listen with Mother*. She had worked with most of the cast of the Street in radio plays. One of Miss Oxenford's oldest friends is Joan Heath. Joan was cast as May Hardman, who died in Episode 7. Many of the younger actors were in awe of Miss Heath as she was leading lady at Manchester's Library Theatre and had trained in Sir Barry Jackson's repertory company in Birmingham. It was her agent who persuaded her to take the part of May: 'We did not want me to stay long in a television programme, but May seemed ideal; to go in, have a nice little build up, a good little flash death and come out of it.'

The part of Elsie's daughter Linda was given to twenty-three-year-old Anne Cunningham. Born in Leeds, Anne spent her childhood in South Africa. She came to England to train as a nurse but decided upon an acting career, training at the Bristol Old Vic. Orson Welles picked her for his Shakespearean company, to play Viola in *Twelfth Night*. Margaret Morris saw her in a production of *Grand Night Out* in Buxton and decided she would be perfect for Linda. Harry Latham did not believe she could do a Manchester accent: 'He said from now on just talk to me in a Northern accent. So I did. He asked me about a book I was reading so I had this bizarre conversation talking about a book by an Algerian French writer in this broad Yorkshire accent.'

The part of Linda's Polish husband Ivan was eventually given to Austrian actor Ernst Walder. He had arrived in England in 1952 on a work permit, working as a domestic servant. In his spare time he went to drama school and soon found himself cast as Nazis in war films, such as *Carve Her Name With Pride*. When he was given the part of Ivan, no one seemed to mind that his accent was not Polish: 'I haven't got a real German accent. It's being Austrian you see, it's a softer accent. But I had Polish people coming up to me in Manchester and blabbering away at me and I couldn't understand a word they were saying!'

One of the last characters to be cast was Dennis Tanner, a role that former child actor Tony Warren quite fancied for himself, 'It was a much better part than Ken, as originally written. There were infinite possibilities in Dennis that were never explored. The criminal side. In those streets there is always a bad 'un, a wrong 'un. And he was the wrong 'un.' After seeing many would-be Dennises and after the pilots, in which the two Dennises were unsuitable, Philip Lowrie and Kenneth Farrington were called for camera tests. Both had trained at RADA (Philip with Christine Hargreaves) and had appeared in television shows. Farrington was coming to the end of a year's solid television work when he was auditioned by José Scott: 'She said, can you do a north country accent. Well I'd only ever been up north for two weeks but I had been at drama school with Albert Finney so I copied his accent.' José Scott put Ken up for a camera test but warned him not to tell anyone he was not northern: 'I did a camera test with Pat Phoenix and did not get the part, but they told my agent they would write me in as another part.' That other part turned out to be Billy Walker, who appeared in Episode 15 and continued to appear for twenty-four years. As soon as she had finished camera-testing with Ken Farrington, Pat Phoenix did the same scene again with Philip Lowrie. He recalls the test being on a Thursday: 'I came back to London on the train on the Friday and when I got back to my flat the phone was ringing, and my agent said you'll have to go straight back because you start work on Monday, you've got it. So I went straight back and started on Monday, absolutely petrified.'

It has now become part of televison fable that the part of Ena Sharples was nearly cut from the series. Dozens of ageing character actresses were auditioned, two appeared in the pilots and some were even camera-tested but none were right. Tony Warren knew that what was needed was a woman of seventy with the vitality of a girl of seventeen. It was then that he remembered an actress who, as Auntie Vi, had dominated *Children's Hour*: 'I suddenly heard myself saying: "There's always Violet Carson."'

Violet Carson's career started when she left school in 1918, as pianist with the orchestra in Manchester's Market Street cinema, in the days of silent films. When the talkies started and cinema pianists were no longer in demand she turned to singing and with the advent of radio was greatly in demand as singer, pianist and actress. During the Second World War she worked at the BBC, playing the piano in an attempt to boost public morale. In 1946, she joined a programme that would make her a household name – she became the pianist in *Have A Go* with Wilfred Pickles. At the end of the run (six seasons) she felt the need to expand and took on heavy parts in radio dramas. Her sister Nellie told her about the Street and talked her into writing to the producers. The letter was never answered and weeks went by until Granada telephoned her home in Blackpool. José Scott recalls the audition: 'We had an awful job trying to find the right actress to play Ena Sharples. We couldn't sleep at night for thinking about her. Violet Carson was the last person to be auditioned, and by that time we had almost given up and were thinking of cutting Ena right out of the show. Actresses who seemed to fit the part just weren't interesting on the screen. Then Violet walked on, with that amazing face, and said her line: "Are these fancies fresh? I'll have half a dozen – and no eclairs . . . I said no eclairs"' The repeat of "no eclairs" was not in the script and everyone knew at once that Ena Sharples had finally come to life! The last part of the casting jigsaw had been fitted into place and rehearsals could finally begin.

Daphne Oxenford as Esther Hayes and Joan Heath as May Hardman rehearse Episode Five. They both auditioned on the same day and thought it odd they were being seen at all, as Daphne explains: '[Joan] said "I'm not from Manchester, I'm from Worcestershire," and I said "I'm not, I'm from London!"'

The First Week

'Then my agent rang again and said, "They're going to try the series for a thirteen-week run and want you to play Ken Barlow." I was still less than keen. But as he pointed out, "To do thirteen weeks of a twice-weekly serial has got to be an even better shop window for you than *Marking Time*." So I said, "Okay, but I'm only doing the thirteen weeks."'

William Roache

On the morning of Monday 5 December 1960 the cast of twenty-two nervously gathered at Granada and started to rehearse *Coronation Street*. The first two episodes were to be rehearsed until the Wednesday afternoon, when a 'producer's run' would take place – a run-through watched by the producer, the writer and all the technical crew. The Thursday and Friday would consist of camera rehearsals, some in costume. The episodes were to be recorded on the Friday night, and the first one transmitted live at 7pm. The second, recorded after a fifteen-minute break, would be treated as live but would not go out until the Monday night. Many of the actors were used to this sort of turn-around and did not seem that bothered by live television. However, for some the mere thought was a nightmare, as Philip Lowrie recalls: 'Harry Latham told us on the Wednesday, after the producer's run, that is was going out live on Friday at seven o'clock. It was the most frightening moment of my life ever, nothing ever to compare with it. . . . I was just a little actor who went on little plays on the stage, and suddenly it was all down to seconds and all these technicians and you had to stand with your weight on one foot so that you wouldn't shadow somebody else's face. You were literally thrown in at the deep end.'

Patricia Shakesby was used to live television, having appeared in shows such as *Emergency Ward Ten*. What troubled her during that rehearsal week were two other things. Firstly, to land the part of Kenneth Barlow's girlfriend Susan, she had lied to the casting director, saying she was nineteen when she was really eighteen. Everyone found out when she celebrated her birthday that week, but by that stage noone minded. What concerned everyone more was where Susan was lodging: 'I booked myself into a house of ill-repute. Violet Carson and Doris Speed realized where I was staying and marched me off between them, demanding that the place I was staying in returned my suitcase.' Susan had no idea what the problem was: 'In those days, at eighteen, you were quite innocent. I didn't know why they didn't take any money from me that night or why I was in a sort of wooden cabin. Doris and Violet were wonderful!'

'Those of us who were involved in it were very passionate about it,' recalls Derek Bennett, who directed the first episode. He knew that many of the Granada executives were worried about image and had attempted to make the programme more respectable, something which he and the production team fought against. 'The thing that appealed to me was that it was very much about the working class, and a very grotty working class at that. Here was something that was about back-to-back houses and people having loos at the bottom of the yard. I don't think that had happened before.' As Bennett gathered the actors together in the rehearsal room they all knew they were breaking new ground.

William Roache explains how the actors tried to relax during the rehearsals. This was rather difficult as there was no separate room for them to sit in. Their chairs were simply placed around the rehearsal room: 'It was a small room and we all sat round in a tight circle and they'd shove a table in the middle with the chairs around, we would come out and everybody was watching. It was very nerve-racking from the point of view that you were watched intently by your colleagues.' Anne Cunningham enjoyed working in this way, as it was so reminiscent of working in the theatre: 'Your emotions were involved with other people's scenes. It was all very exciting . . . there was a very strong bond amongst the actors to make this show a success. We quite quickly gelled in to a strong unit, because everybody was involved with everybody else. And because the story was in the street, and everybody was meant to be involved with everybody else, that quickly happened.' This way of involving all the cast in the rehearsals continued throughout the week. On the Friday afternoon, after running the two episodes in order, the cast were assembled to receive notes on their performance by the director. This was another experience Bill Roache will never forget: 'You took notes in front of everybody sitting round a table. Often the notes were quite intimate, but you were given them in front of everybody. It was all very public, though on the other hand, we were all in the same boat. The community feel was quite tremendous.'

On most counts the finished product was more or less identical to the script, but director Derek Bennett wanted to start Episode 1 with an ambitious

shot. The first scene was to be played outside the Corner Shop, which Florrie Lindley had just bought. The outgoing shopkeeper, Elsie Lappin, played by Maudie Edwards, was to speak the first lines: 'Now the next thing you want to do is get a signwriter in. That thing above the door'll 'ave to be changed.' Before Mrs Lappin delivered these lines, Bennett visualized the camera following a cat jumping out of a dustbin, walking around the Corner Shop and then entering the shop where the first scene would be played out. Richard Everitt was floor manager on that first week, looking after the smooth running of the Studio whilst the director sat watching the action on monitors. He remembers that, against all the odds, the cat actually performed on cue at the dress rehearsal: 'The cat was beautiful but on the take you never saw the cat at all. So that was the end of that rather beautiful kind of northern atmosphere that [Bennett] was hoping would start the show.' Instead of the cat, a couple of girls were brought in to play a ball game outside the shop and Mrs Lappin was brought outside to help a small boy put his money in the bubblegum machine by the door.

Doris Speed waits for her cue between shop and snug sets.

Coronation Street was transmitted live on Fridays at 7pm for the first six months. After this, the programme was moved to the 7.30pm slot on Mondays and Wednesdays. The reason for this move was that in May 1961 it became fully networked; prior to this, Tyne-Tees and ATV Midlands had opted out of showing it. So, on Friday 9 December 1960, not every house in the country was able to enjoy the new family drama series. The trailers for the show in the Granada region introduced the characters: 'Elsie Tanner, a bold-eyed woman, separated from her husband and with a son, Dennis, who is always in and out of trouble with the police. Young Kenneth Barlow, on the other hand, has won his way to university and is regarded by his neighbours as something of a snob. He, in turn, is a bit ashamed of living in CORONATION STREET.'

At 7pm that evening twenty-two actors waited in sets or on the sidelines as Eric Spear's haunting theme tune started up and the two girls started their schoolgirl chant. The cast had made sure they were certain of their lines, as Bill Roache explains: 'There was a tremendous atmosphere of caring, we had run our lines, run them and run them, quickly, slowly. Messed around with them anyway we could so we would remember them. And there was this feeling of being the condemned man, the awful inevitability of it.' The sets were incredibly close together, with actors able to touch other sets without leaving their seats. Again, Roache: 'You had to freeze, you couldn't cough or anything. Once your scene was finished you froze. It was the most terrifying ordeal.'

One actress who, despite years of live performances, was suffering from nerves was Noel Dyson. She nearly changed the whole course of the programme on her opening lines. She had to bring a teapot into the Barlow's parlour and talk to Frank Pemberton about 'their' son Kenneth. As she entered she knew something was not quite right: 'I nearly forgot Ken's name. He might have been called something quite different – George! Fortunately I remembered just in time.'

Daphne Oxenford did not have to appear in the first episode, but like the others who would be in the second episode, she sat out of vision in her set, willing her new friends on and trusting to their combined experience: 'You see, one was used to live television, so you knew that if anything went wrong, somehow people would get out of it. None of this being able to stop and start again and go back. That was a luxury.'

Philip Lowrie recalls standing at the top of a flight of stairs down which he was to storm, closely followed by Pat Phoenix. He remembers that, whilst he was terrified and nervous, she appeared quite calm: 'You see I tried to be a character, I was playing against myself. But it always seemed to me that she lived it, that the character was written for her. I knew that wasn't true, but she seemed to embody that woman from the word go.'

At the end of Episode 1, everyone had dinner before starting work on the second episode. This time everyone seemed more relaxed but, although it was not to go out live, it still had to be recorded as if it was. Alan Rothwell, as David, appeared in both episodes, and remembers how different they both were: 'If you look at those episodes I think you'll find that in the first one everybody's working on a great high level of energy. On the second one, everybody's relaxed and their eyes aren't quite open, and because they know it was recorded it wasn't all that desperate.'

Philip Lowrie agrees that everyone was more relaxed about the second episode. As Dennis Tanner was not in it he sat around and watched the episode being recorded: 'Nobody wanted to know about the second episode. So they had to drag it up again a quarter of an hour later, because the euphoria had died.' Lowrie recalls how he watched the second episode, thrilled at the thought that he was part of the whole thing. 'On that Monday, Pat Phoenix had taken me to Blackpool and we stopped at a pub. There was nobody in the pub, and she said to the landlord, can we watch the television set. So he put it on and it was seven o'clock and we were watching it and I was thinking "Oh, Pat's brilliantly good."'

Ernst Walder did not appear as Ivan until the last scene of Episode Two. He sat in the studio watching his colleagues in the first episode.

Thirty-five years on, with the Street going out in colour three times a week, with editing and locations all over the north-west, it is hard to imagine the tension produced by a handful of actors and technicians huddled together in and around sets in a comparatively small television studio. In a piece written to celebrate the twenty-fifth anniversary of the Street, Tony Warren tried to explain the atmosphere: Anyone who was working at Granada Television on Friday, 9 December 1960, remembers it with affectionate awe. The sort of night legends are made of. The show went out live, and there was an excitement around the building that I have never known before, or since. People remember it as belonging to an exclusive club. All along the line *Coronation Street* had been *ours*. We gave it to the world.'

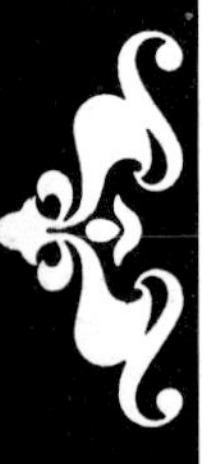

SIXTIES

·1960·

Mrs Elsie Lappin, a small bird-like woman with a faintly aggressive manner, is talking with Mrs Florrie Lindley, a kindly, altogether warmer woman than Mrs Lappin.

Mrs Lappin: . . . Now the next thing you want to do is get a signwriter in. That thing above the door'll have to be changed.

Episode One, ***Coronation Street***

Rovers Jack and Annie Walker • Concepta Riley

No.1 Albert Tatlock

No. 3 Frank, Ida, Kenneth and David Barlow

No. 5 Esther Hayes

No. 7 Harry and Lucille Hewitt

No. 9 *Empty*

No. 11 Elsie and Dennis Tanner • Linda Cheveski

No. 13 May and Christine Hardman

Shop Florrie Lindley

Shop flat Empty

No. 16 (Mission) Ena Sharples

Non-residents Leonard Swindley • Martha Longhurst • Minnie Caldwell

COMINGS AND GOINGS

Coronation Street was launched onto an unsuspecting world in December 1960 and although, there was less than a month to go to the end of the year, it was quite an eventful one! Elsie Lappin, who had run the Corner Shop since 1930, handed it over to ex-barmaid Florrie Lindley before retiring to Knott End. Next door to the shop, at No.13, May Hardman died from a brain tumour in the hallway on New Year's Eve. She was found by Florrie after she had banged for help on the adjoining wall. At No.11, Elsie Tanner was surprised when her married daughter Linda returned home after leaving husband Ivan in Warrington. He followed her, and they were reconciled when she announced she was pregnant.

BAN THE BOMB

Kenneth Barlow was extremely embarrassed when his middle-class girlfriend from university, Susan Cunningham, insisted on being shown round the Street. Ken had entered university on a scholarship and his father Frank disliked the way his twenty-one-year-old son thought himself superior. The first episodes saw Kenneth and Susan taking part in a 'ban the bomb' march, much to the horror of pro-establishment Frank. Actress Patricia Shakesby remembers rushing for the London train with Bill Roache one Friday night, 'We were waylaid by hundreds of students with banners, asking us to march from Manchester to Hull that weekend with them. They took it all terribly seriously.'

TROUBLE AT NO.13

Christine Hardman tried her best to cover up for her mother's absence from the Street. May, she told the residents, was resting in hospital. Florrie Lindley had her first taste of life in the Street when Christine tracked Ena Sharples down in the shop on Florrie's first day behind the counter. Christine's voice faltered as she asked caretaker Ena to stop saying nasty things about her mother. Ena was indignant: 'You don't want to be so touchy. Just because your mother's gone Pots-for-Rags there's no need for you to start accusing.'

Much to the interest of the locals, May Hardman returned home and Christine ignored her talk of stabbing pains in the head. She was at work at the end of the year, bending over her machine at the raincoat factory, when May died in the hallway.

DENNIS GOES STRAIGHT

Elsie Tanner was exasperated by her son Dennis; six weeks out of prison, he still had not found a job and showed no signs of mending his ways. When he turned up with

£25 she immediately thought he'd been up to his old tricks again and refused to believe that he'd won it on the dogs, until neighbour Harry Hewitt verified his story. As originally written Dennis was the bad boy, the local villain, but the actor cast in the role, Philip Lowrie, had immense charm and this bubbled over in Dennis. Lowrie remembers a conversation with Producer Harry Latham: 'He said, you played last night's episode well, you gave it some comedy. I'm very glad you did that because we've been considering writing Dennis out. And that's how Dennis Tanner became a little funny character.'

THE IRISH ELEMENT

One of Granada executive Dennis Forman's concerns about the programme was that viewers might find it hard to define characters if they all had Manchester accents. Warren had already installed Polish Ivan but Forman suggested a 'relief' accent – Irish or Cockney. Coincidently, Warren was already creating an Irish character. Concepta Riley was to be resident barmaid at the Rovers and long-term love interest for Harry Hewitt. The part of chirpy

'Her face lights up when she smiles,' commented Tony Warren when Christine Hargreaves auditioned for the part of Christine Hardman. Brian Rawlinson played her plumber boyfriend, Joe Makinson.

Concepta Riley quickly became Annie Walker's best friend and confidante.

Concepta was given to Dublin-born Doreen Keogh who had a long theatrical career behind her, having worked at the Gate Theatre and with Lord Longford's company. Immediately before joining the cast she was working in the West End. Doreen fondly remembers her time in the programme and recalls an early live episode when things did not go exactly according to plan: 'I was standing outside the pub, talking to Jack [Walker]. And I said to him "I'll have a word with Mrs Walker", and he said "She's inside." I went to open the door into the pub and it had been locked on the inside. And I turned round and said to him "You're as bad as Harry, he's always locking himself out as well. I'll go round the back." So I went round the back and when it was over the director rushed down and embraced me, thanking me for saving the scene.'

Concepta's boyfriend, Harry Hewitt, had an eventful Christmas. His daughter Lucille ran away from the orphanage to be with her father. She had become increasingly hard to cope with since her mother's death in 1958.

EXTENDED RUN

At the end of 1960, the first sixteen episodes had been written by both Tony Warren and H.V. Kershaw. Granada was told that the series was to be continued and new writers were brought in. Warren worried about other writers not understanding the fibre of the individual characters. He started to define the major characters through their speeches: 'I had to lay down foundations, that's why I refer to those as the "foundation episodes". I did a speech for Doris [Speed] which defined her once and once for all – "My idea of Heaven is doing a fox-trot on a French-chalk floor in a big gown, knowing I look right."'

By the end of the year, certain members of the cast were struggling to cope with instant stardom and became overwhelmed by the public recognition. What made matters worse was that they were portraying characters that were so lifelike that Manchester residents felt as if they knew them. Little did the actors know that the next year, when the programme was to be fully networked, would see their popularity soar beyond belief. In May 1961, the Street reached No.1 in the television ratings.

Philip Lowrie considers it an incredible honour to have been in the first episode, and therefore part of television history. He instilled considerable charm into Dennis Tanner and turned him away from a life of crime.

·1961·

'Best years of me life the blackout. Every time I think of it it reminds me of yankee whisky.'

Elsie Tanner

'That Elsie Tanner, she were just the same durin' the war. Skirts up 'ere an' "got any gum chum."'

Ena Sharples

Rovers Jack and Annie Walker • Billy Walker (Jan. - Aug.) • Concepta Riley (Jan. - Oct.) • Nona Willis (Sept. - Oct.)

No. 1 Albert and Valerie Tatlock (Aug. - Oct.)

No. 3 Frank, Kenneth, Ida (Jan. - Sept.) and David (Jan. - July) Barlow • Nancy Leathers (June - Sept.)

No. 5 Esther and Tom (June - July) Hayes

No. 7 Harry, Lucille and Concepta (Oct. Dec.) Hewitt • Alice Burgess (March - May)

No. 9 Ivan, Linda and Paul Cheveski (April - Dec.)

No. 11 Elsie and Dennis Tanner

No. 13 Christine Hardman

shop Florrie Lindley

Shop flat Norman Dobson and Phil Braithwaite (Oct. - Dec.)

No. 16 (Mission) Ena Sharples (Oct. - Dec.)

Non-residents Leonard Swindley • Martha Longhurst • Minnie Caldwell • Emily Nugent • Len Fairclough • Doreen Lostock Sheila Birtles • Dot Greenhalgh

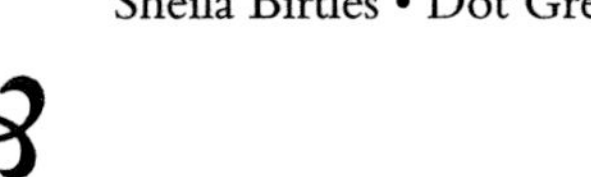

THE STREET'S COMING DOWN!

In early 1961, the news swept through the Street like wildfire. Having survived Hitler's bombs, Coronation Street was to be flattened by Macmillan's slum clearance plan. Frank Barlow and Albert Tatlock organized a petition, while Esther Hayes lobbied the Town Hall. It had all started in March when Ena Sharples had taken a complaint about low gas pressure in the Street to the Town Hall. There, her attention was grabbed by a notice announcing streets to be demolished in the summer. She rushed out without filing her complaint and, back in the Rovers told the regulars that Coronation Street was doomed. Why did the residents kick up such a fuss about the terrace? Most complained about the damp rooms, only the Barlows had an inside toilet and the closeness of the grimy streets helped the spread of diseases. All around Weatherfield high rise blocks were being erected, each flat was spacious and had its

COMINGS AND GOINGS

1961 saw many of the younger residents leave the Street to forge new lives. Within a month of each other, David Barlow and Billy Walker headed south for the bright lights of London. Sadly David had to return shortly afterwards for his mother Ida's funeral. Ida died in September and the same month saw the departure of her mother Nancy Leathers. She was moved to a bungalow on a warden-controlled estate. Esther Hayes' jailbird brother Tom stayed with her in the summer, spongeing off her and trying to interest the residents in juke boxes. When he left she realized how lonely she was. The Rovers lost two resident barmaids – Concepta Riley married Harry Hewitt and moved into No.7 and her replacement, Cockney Nona Willis, only lasted two months. At No.1, pensioner Albert Tatlock was delighted when his niece Valerie moved in, her parents having moved to Glasgow. When she left two months later he was not the only one who was upset; boy-next-door Kenneth Barlow had fallen for Valerie and promised to write to her as she headed north to Scotland. There was a tearful farewell in December, as well, when the Cheveski family sold the family home, No.9, and emigrated to Canada. Shopkeeper Florrie Lindley found an answer to her debt problems by renting out the flat above her shop. The first tenants were two officials from the Town Hall, Norman and Phil. However, they soon decided it was a mistake living across the road from Ena Sharples, who plagued them with complaints about the Council, and sought alternative accommodation.

Fulton McKay was a regular in the Street, cast in 1961 as middle-class Dr Graham. Although he often had to put up with Ena's opinions of the Health Service he was involved in a couple of dramatic stories. In one, he lost a box of pills in the Street; little Lucille Hewitt found them and, thinking they were streets, ate one. Luckily she only slept for four hours, although Dr Graham pointed out that she could have died.

own bathroom. But, however much the Council tried to sell the idea of 'Streets in the sky' to residents they knew that they would miss the community into which they had been born.

The officials at the Planning Department were puzzled by the complaints received from the residents and sent a man to investigate. He was shown Ena's door as the source, and presented the notice she had previously seen and asked her to read it out loud. As she did so, Ena realized she had made a terrible mistake, it was Coronation *Terrace* that was to be pulled down.

The residents shunned Ena and she broke down when Mission supervisor Mr Swindley told her there had been so many complaints about her conduct that she would have to give up her post as caretaker. Ena tried to hang on to her home, at the last minute, when the removal men were attempting to carry out her furniture she fell and twisted her ankle on the outside step. Swindley was quick to bring in Dr Graham who waved aside Ena's home diagnosis of broken bones. She was forced to hobble off to live with her friend Martha Longhurst. However, she returned in triumph a month later, with a rise in salary, as no one else was willing to take on the job in such a rough area.

TA'RA OUR LINDA

In June, the Street's first baby, Paul Cheveski, was born. Anne Cunningham, playing Linda, found herself being filmed in labour: 'All I knew about birth was from old Victorian films where they pulled on ropes and sweated a lot. So I had a lot of sweat and I did a lot of screaming.' At the beginning of the year, the main cast members had been given a six-month contract; after this they were offered a year's contract. Anne Cunningham decided against working the year but agreed to stay six months until Christmas, so the writers were faced with the problem of writing Linda out. Rather than killing her off, it was agreed that the Cheveskis should emigrate to Canada. Ernst Walder, Annie's screen husband, resigning himself to leaving as well. The emigration episode pulled in the highest viewing figures yet, with sixteen million viewers watching Elsie fighting back the tears as she clung to her daughter.

A DEATH ON THE STREET

Like Anne Cunningham, Noel Dyson did not want to stay long in the programme. In the summer of 1961, talks started on what to do with Ida Barlow. Noel was glad when Kershaw assured her that her leaving would not mean the departure of the other family members. She recalls: 'It was a question of if I would have TB. I pointed out that if I'd had TB the public would be expecting me to get better, so it was agreed that I should go under a bus – very discreetly.' Ida's funeral was the first shown on the Street and the script called for the hearse and cars to drive slowly down the cobbles whilst the neighbours stood in the rain watching. Designer Denis Parkin recalls how the feat was achieved: 'The studio was only 60 feet long so it was hard enough getting the whole street in and the houses were only 7' 6" wide. The door to Studio Two only opened one way so we had to grease the floor so that we could spin the hearse round to get it through the door.'

With Ida dead and David playing professional football for a London team, Frank was left in the house with his eldest son Kenneth, who had managed to win a post teaching in a public school in Surrey but turned it down as he did not want Frank to have to cope alone. Instead he spent a couple of months working as a personnel officer at Amalgamated Steel. He left the steel works as he found he cared too much about the workers. Hearing that his son was out of work Frank let rip, telling his son he was nothing but a disappointment to him. Angry, Ken replied: 'When will you stop? When I'm chained to some job I hate the sight of. When you can turn round to your precious pals and say "Oh aye, my lad's doin' very well! 'e's a little cog in a big machine an' 'e wears a white collar an' brings in twenty quid a week!' Ken decided to leave the Street and bought a ticket for London. However, a chance meeting with Christine Hardman at the station made him realize his place was by his father's side. Christine had suffered a domineering parent and was well aware that, like Ken, she had been a big disappointment. But, she pointed out, now her mother was dead she longed for just one day in which to put things right. Ken returned home.

Eileen Derbyshire (Emily)

★ **Eileen Derbyshire** looks back with fond memories of Miss Nugent: 'I think she had been rather squashed by circumstances into being at everybody's beck and call. She was extremely timid and anxious to please.' Miss Derbyshire was born in Urmston, near Manchester. She took a teaching degree in speech and drama but had always wanted to be an actress. One day, whilst taking a ride on a bus, she passed Chorlton Repertory Theatre and acting on an impulse went in and asked for an audition. Eileen was taken on by the company as a student and later as an assistant stage manager. From there she joined a mobile theatre company and toured with the company for two years before becoming a member of the Southport Repertory Company. She joined the Street in Episode 15, transmitted in January 1961.

There was a long tradition of extended families living next door to one another in Coronation Street. A mother would keep an eye on the neighbouring houses and streets, and when a house became vacant, secure the tenancy from the landlord. Having Linda living next door meant Elsie only had to bang on the wall to tell her she had just brewed up.

Poison pen

On 1 October, the residents celebrated the wedding of Harry Hewitt and Concepta Riley. It had been a mixed wedding, he being Protestant and her Catholic. (As such it broke boundaries in British television.) At the

·1961·

'Oh yes, there's another speech you haven't made. You haven't said that she wouldn't like to hear us going on like this. Well, she didn't like it while she was alive but that didn't stop you, did it!'

wedding reception, Elsie Tanner met Bill Gregory, a Chief Petty Officer in the Merchant Navy. They started an affair and Elsie received her first screen kiss in a telephone box, sheltering from the rain. Shortly after this Elsie received an anonymous letter telling her that her affair was putting her divorce proceedings in jeopardy. The letter deeply upset Elsie and she accused her neighbours of writing it: first Annie Walker, who refused to lower herself by bawling in public with her, and then her old enemy Ena Sharples. Mrs Sharples had, since the early episodes, condemned Elsie's morals: 'There's things that go on in that house that decent folk don't talk about. Elsie Tanner's a dirty blackguard and I wouldn't give her houseroom in a decent street.' The climax to the story came in a showdown, filmed as life by director Howard Baker, on the full exterior set, with the whole cast looking on, leaning out of windows or standing about as Ena and Elsie did battle. Elsie had to be physically restrained from hitting the pensioner but soon realized Ena was not the writer, as Ena pointed out: 'I know plenty about you, Elsie Tanner. I know so much I could write a book. But if I did write that letter it would have Ena Sharples at the bottom of it in big black letters and well you know it!'

The identity of the letter-writer remained a mystery for a couple of weeks until Elsie received another letter. This time the writer was her estranged husband Arnold, apologizing for the letter written by his girl friend Norah. Norah had feared that the divorce would be slowed down by Elsie's relationship with Bill.

Strike

In June 1961, twelve of the cast signed long-term contracts, saying that they would continue in the programme another year. Other actors were on weekly or monthly contracts. The long-term contracts turned out to be a blessing when, in November, Equity, the

actor's union, called a strike against the independent television companies. H.V. Kershaw remembered the strike in his autobiography: 'Under the terms of those contracts they were allowed to work throughout the strike and saved the programme from what could have been a death blow.' Whilst other popular programmes simply disappeared from the screens, replaced by reruns of old films, *Coronation Street* landed the top two positions in the ratings. The producers had realized a strike was imminent and quickly placed Peter Adamson under long-term contract because his character Len Fairclough was proving to be the most successful working man in the show. So it was that thirteen actors entered the strike, unaware that it would last seven months, during which time they would all

Rehearsing and recording the showdown scene. Whilst Violet Carson hides her coiffured hair in a hairnet, Pat Phoenix merely changes her blouse to create Elsie. Shoes were seldom seen in the programme; this is probably why all four actresses kept their own on for comfort.

·1961·

Trade was down at the Rovers during the Equity strike, the barmaids were strikebound and there were only eleven regular customers for seven months! Two characters who disappeared over night were Jed Stone and girlfriend Jean Stark. Jed was Dennis Tanner's sidekick and Jean, escaping her surpressive parents, had lodged at No.13 with Christine Hardman. Jed and Jean first appeared in the same episode and the casting director had no idea that Kenneth Cope and Rennie Lister had just married. They literally spent their honeymoon on the Street.

Kenneth Cope (Jed Stone Sunny Jim).

appear in nearly every episode made. During that time, there were no extras in the Rovers, no extra customers in the shop, no factory workers and, one by one, the semi-regulars disappeared. Esther Hayes from No.5 was not seen for six months, nor was Christine Hardman. Factory girls Doreen Lostock and Sheila Birtles faded from the screen, just like Valerie Tatlock and Miss Nugent. Even Mr Swindley was absent. Suddenly all the storylines revolved around Ena, Elsie, Kenneth and co. Sixteen-year-old Jennifer Moss was strikebound, so Lucille Hewitt was always 'upstairs' or 'playing out'. Other younger children were available for work, and experiments were made with the tall ones – dressed as milkmen and postmen. However, Equity soon complained.

Unable to use children, the writers turned to animals, taking advantage of Dennis Tanner's theatrical leaning. He took a job in a talent agency and suddenly the programme was flooded with snakes, sealions, pigeons, dogs and a chimp called Cheetah. The sealions did not actually appear until early 1962. Philip Lowrie remembers them with horror: 'They were meant to be seals. When we came to film it, Derek Granger [the producer] said there had been a mistake, they were sealions, and they were about three times as big! And the man had not fed them for two days so that they'd be active.' They were after any form of food, and at one stage got hold of Bill Roach's clothes and pulled him off.

The Public Reaction

·1961·

In January 1961, a Television Audience Measurement (TAM) survey reflected the popularity of the month-old programme by indicating an increase in viewers of 23 percent during the first week of transmission. On Monday 6 March, *Coronation Street* was transmitted over the whole network. Less than six months later, another TAM survey showed that 75 per cent of viewers tuned into the Street, an average of fifteen million viewers per episode; at the time, the second most popular show was *Emergency Ward 10*, with seven million viewers.

The Street was given a publicity manager, Norman Frisby. His job was to arrange press interviews for the cast, look after their public images and arrange the occasional charity event. Philip Lowrie still remembers the first charity event the entire cast attended, in January 1961: 'Most of us went into this pub to collect money, to raise money for this lady's house which had been burnt down in Salford. And we were completely mobbed. The police had to be brought in, and that was when they knew they'd got something phenomenal on their hands.'

Anne Cunningham remembers another incident when she, Philip, Ernst Walder and Pat Phoenix opened a Granada Rentals shop in Stockport: 'We were trapped inside the car and people were pushing onto us, bending the side of the car. The police didn't know what to do, there were two of them and all these people crushing the car.' Lowrie stopped doing public appearances after a few months as he found them too frightening. One he remembers with terror was the opening of a dress shop with Pat Phoenix: 'The plate glass windows were buckling and all the people had pushed their children to the front to see us. We just got into the shop and the chief of police said we had to go into the basement because the crowd was pressing forward and they had to bring mounted police out to get us out.'

Jennifer Moss found it difficult to cope with the public reaction. She was sixteen in 1961 but she was playing an eleven-year-old girl. As a fashion-conscious teenager she was still treated as a child by the public: 'I was opening a garden fête and this large lady came up to me and whacked me straight across the face, knocked me to the ground and said "That's for being cheeky to your dad".' Her real father made Jenny face the public when she tried to shy away from them. She recalls one occasion when she left Granada by the back door to avoid the autograph hunters: 'He said, "Don't let me ever, ever hear of you doing that again. Those people pay your wages, you walk out the front, if you're ten minutes late, so what. You sign every damned autograph!"' Jenny was not the only cast member to be slapped or even punched in public. In her autobiography Pat Phoenix recalls a personal appearance at a cinema: 'I was "all got up" in a floor-length gown, sequins blazing, and Dennis wore a smoothly expensive dinner suit. We could not have looked less like the Tanner family if we had tried. Crowds were lining

'Violet Carson To Switch On Lights – She wants to be herself, not Ena Sharples'

Blackpool Evening Gazette,
2 August 1961

Standing on a dress shop roof, waiting for mounted police to clear a way, Patricia Phoenix and Philip Lowrie were completely stunned by the crowds.

the entrance and, as Philip and I stepped from the car, a woman ducked under a policeman's arm and fetched Philip a walloping backhander. He reeled back and she shouted: "That's for being so bloody cheeky to your mother." She disappeared back into the crowd and poor Philip spent the whole evening with an angry weal across his face.'

Despite the public recognition, William Roache feels the cast did not turn into celebrities overnight: 'It was a gradual process, we were only shown in the north to begin with, and you got the recognition in the north. That did not have a big effect because we were all together, we sort of moved up into the celebrity status together.' For Roache, it was an exciting and frightening experience when the public became a mob: 'I remember a day in Leeds, quite early on. I was doing an autograph signing session behind a loose table. Suddenly the crowd surged forward all towards me and that was the first time I witnessed that sort of mobbing.'

Like Roache, Noel Dyson found the recognition just too much. 'People used to come down to my cottage and lean over the gate, and I felt like something in the zoo.' The more extrovert Street actors, however, soaked up the public's love and attention. Many journalists commented on Pat Phoenix's image and the way she turned up for appearances in furs and diamonds and the way the viewers loved her for it. To the people of the north, the Street actors were the closest they had to

Hollywood stars and they seemed to expect them to dress accordingly. However, not all the public were so accepting of Pat's newfound image. In her autobiography, she recalls being stopped by a small boy as, dresssed in mink, she entered a chauffeur-driven car:

'"It's all wrong you know," he said.

'"What's all wrong?"

'"You're supposed to be poor," he said. "Living in a street like Coronation Street, and look at that coat. And what about this posh car."

'I had to do some quick thinking. I answered as sincerely as I could. "Now just a minute," I said. "I've been standing in that doorway in the freezing cold waiting for this car that's going to take me somewhere important. I've got to be there in half an hour and I won't get there on the bus, will I? And if I stood in a doorway signing your rotten autographs without a coat like this I'd catch my death of cold and couldn't go on *Coronation Street*, could I? Eh?'

'He looked at me with understanding beyond his years, tapped his finger to his head and said briskly: "Point taken, Mrs Tanner."'

On the evening of 8 September 1961, the cast travelled to Blackpool where Violet Carson, a resident of Blackpool, had been given the honour of turning on the famous illuminations. The Mayor of Blackpool, Alderman Clifford Cross, issued a press statement: 'Violet Carson is one of our best-loved residents, and we have decided to pay this tribute to her long public service in the fields of radio and TV entertainment, and at the same time compliment the country's most popular and successful TV programme.' Although it fell to Miss Carson to pull the switch, the entire cast were invited to attend the ceremony.

The date for the switch on was an awkward one, as the character Ida Barlow was due to die that night. A fill-in episode was written, leaving Ida's fate unknown. Noel Dyson had, as Ida, already played her last scene when she was asked to rejoin the cast for the Blackpool trip: 'You couldn't have public mourning and public rejoicing in the same week. All you saw was my scarf in the road, and it was a sort of cliffhanger. Naturally, the public would have smelt a rat if I hadn't been with the family in Blackpool.'

Noone had anticipated the welcome the cast were to receive as they travelled along the main street in an open-topped bus decorated with red bricks to look like the Street. Eileen Derbyshire remembers sitting on the top deck, surrounded by a moonlit night and thousands upon thousands of cheering people: 'It was a magical night because . . . it was very natural, terrifically fresh, and there was such affection and a tremendously happy bonding in the company. I remember Anne Cunningham squeezed my arm and said, "We'll never forget this, will we, we'll remember this for the rest of our lives". It was just a lovely, lovely, happy, happy night.'

The bus dropped everyone outside the Mayor's Parlour for a lavish reception. Daphne Oxenford recalls seeing the crowds outside the town hall: 'Doris [Speed] said to me "come over to the window

·1961·

The Mayor of Blackpool, Clifford Cross chats to Doris Speed and Daphne Oxenford at the civic reception in Blackpool. During the reception Jack Howarth (Albert Tatlock) expressed a desire to visit Yates' Wine Lodge. He was put off the idea when the police informed him they would have to escort him through the crowds on horses.

'Our Violet' switches on the 1961 Blackpool lights. The first display was a photographic montage of the cast of Coronation Street.

and look" and as far as you could see it was people. Just looking. Because they knew we were all in there.'

After the reception the cast were seated together by the main switch and Violet Carson was invited to turn on the lights. The crowds were surprised to see Miss Carson dressed as herself, not Ena, a fact she referred to in her speech: 'I left "Queen Boss" behind me today. She decided to stay at home "Nay, we can't all go off gallivanting to Blackpool. Somebody has to have a sense of responsibility."' Daphne Oxenford clearly remembers watching the fun: 'Vi came on looking an absolute dream in silver lamé, silver hair and switched on the lights. Behind her there was a board like a huge crossword puzzle, and there was a retort, a bang. With each bang a square of the crossword lit up and there were the Barlow family, the Walkers, Christine and Esther . . . all the characters.' Whilst the crowds gasped at the lights surrounding each illuminated Street picture, Violet Carson brought out a hairnet, pulled an old mac on over her dress and there was Ena Sharples. The cheer rose up as the rest of the Blackpool illuminations lit up.

Summing up the attitude of the people he lives and works among, Barlow described them as 'lazy-minded, politically ignorant, starved of a real culture and stubbornly prejudiced against any advance in human insight, and scientific progress.'

Ken Barlow's 1962 magazine article on the Street upset the residents.

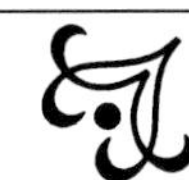

Rovers Jack, Annie and Billy (May) Walker Phillipa Scopes (May) • Sam Leach (Aug. - Sept.)

No. 1 Albert (Feb. - Dec.) and Valerie (July - Aug.) Tatlock

No. 3 Frank and Kenneth (Jan. - Aug.) Barlow

No. 5 Esther Hayes (Jan. - May) • Minnie Caldwell (Aug. - Dec.) • Jed Stone (Nov. - Dec.)

No. 7 Harry, Concepta, Lucille and Christopher (Aug. - Dec.) Hewitt

No. 9 Ken and Val Barlow (Aug. - Dec.)

No. 11 Elsie and Dennis (Jan. - March) Tanner • Christine Appleby (Oct. - Dec.)

No. 13 Christine Hardman (Jan. - June)

Shop Florrie Lindley

Shop flat Doreen Lostock and Sheila Birtles (June - Dec.)

No. 16 (Mission) Albert Tatlock (Jan. - Feb.) • Ena Sharples (Feb. - Dec.)

Non-residents Leonard Swindley • Martha Longhurst • Emily Nugent • Len Fairclough Dot Greenhalgh • Jerry Booth

COMINGS AND GOINGS

In March Dennis Tanner left the Street for London to run a theatrical agency. His neighbour Christine Hardman eloped with salesman Colin Appleby in June, but returned four months later after he was killed in a car crash. Elsie Tanner took her in as a lodger. Esther Hayes also bid farewell to the Street. Her house, No.5, became home to Minnie Caldwell and her cat Bobby. Minnie was moved in by local Good Samaritan Sam Leach who worked as resident pot man at the Rovers. Sam disappeared when the police turned up looking for him for deserting his wife. He left his nephew, Jerry Booth, in the area. Valerie Tatlock returned to lodge with Uncle Albert at No.1 before marrying Kenneth Barlow and settling into No.9. Len Fairclough converted the front room into a hair salon for her and 'Valerie's' opened in August. The Street had to be dug up to install telephone cables as the salon needed a phone, the first in the Street.

·1962·

DENNIS'S TROUPE

The Equity strike started the year and ran until Easter. Dennis left the Street to find work in London. Philip Lowrie had wanted to leave at the end of 1961 but had agreed to stay on as Anne Cunningham was leaving – the writers did not want all of Elsie Tanner's children to desert her at the same time. Luckily the strike ended just as he walked out of the Street and into the job market: 'I was lucky the strike just ended before I left so I was able to go up for jobs.' He still did not get a job for a year – casting directors did not want someone so easily recognizable in their programmes. This was to become the pattern when any long-term actor left the Street; after years of training and becoming established as actors, the Street seemed to take away their own identities.

ENTER MR PAPAGOPOLOUS

Two other characters who returned to the Street after the strike were Mr Swindley and Miss Nugent. By now, as well as running the Mission together, they were working in a haberdasher's, Gamma Garments, part of a chain of stores owned by Greek tycoon Mr Papagopolous. Mr P. never appeared in Coronation Street, but the mere mention of his name sent Swindley and Nugent scurrying around the shop, desperate to please. They were joined by assistant Doreen Lostock and suddenly a successful format was created – pompous Swindley, nervous Nugent and cheeky Lostock. Eileen Derbyshire (Nugent) looks back to the Gamma days as being some of her most favourite in the thirty-four years she has spent

Another hard day at Gamma. Angela Crow played Miss Lostock (on counter): 'Every moment was a joy because we had the same kind of sense of humour. We three had a great rapport and became friends.'

in the show: 'It was huge fun. I loved all the props – wonderful rolls of old curtain tassling and glorious things to play around with. And so much fun with Angela and Arthur.'

Gamma Garments was seldom the scene of long-running stories. Instead, the three characters were used for comic input, chasing orders, holding sales, darting around avoiding Ena Sharples, and, in one glorious scene, holding a fire drill. As Swindley shouted 'fire, fire, don't panic', Nugent collected the ledgers and walked as calmly as possible to the door. Lostock, fed up with all Swindley's planning, strolled out of the shop: 'Mr Swindley, according to the fire manual, all junior members are supposed to do is just to proceed to a place of safety. So can I just go for me lunch like usual?', closely followed by Swindley who slammed the door shop and triumphantly looked at his watch 'Well under the allotted time, good, good'. His self-congratulations quickly faded when he realized Nugent had locked the door and he did not have his key with him.

MA AND SUNNY JIM

Liverpool-born Kenneth Cope turned tough conman Jed Stone into a loveable rogue with just four words. The character was meant to be hard-hitting, but in a scene with Violet Carson Ken changed his whole personality: 'They were doing close-ups of her and close-ups of me and, at the very end, she really got her face up to mine, so I said "give us a kiss", an ad lib, and it was kept in. And then instead of having a toughie, they had a funny character.' Ken Cope feels that Jed was a product of the time – a typical Liverpool humour of the day, laughing in the face of adversity. When the character returned to the programme after the strike he was taken in by Minnie Caldwell at No.5.

Kenneth Cope looks back with affection on his time working with Margot Bryant: 'I think Margot liked Jed because it gave her a good storyline. If she had a lodger she suddenly wasn't one of a trio, she had a background which was not necessarily involved with the three of them in the Snug. I found playing with her smashing because I could rabbit on quickly and she'd bring me back with the slowness of it all.'

HAPPINESS AT LAST FOR MISS HARDMAN

'I was born round 'ere, I live round 'ere, and I suppose I'll die round 'ere.' Christine Hardman was thoroughly depressed in June 1962. It had been building up since the death of her mother and now she could see no escape from the dull existence of working in a noisy machine-room making raincoats and spending evenings in the smoky public bar of the Rovers. Without really knowing what she was doing she climbed onto the raincoat factory roof and for the first time in years smelled clean air. This episode was one of the first to use exteriors filmed outside Granada's Studio 2. Opposite the studios stood an old school-house (it now houses the Granada canteen) and it was on this roof that Christine Hargreaves found herself standing to be filmed by a camera man on the roof of Granada. Bill Roache as Ken Barlow had to talk Christine down, but at least he was able to climb down and go to lunch. At 1pm the crew packed up and went to the canteen leaving Christine Hargreaves stuck on the tiny roof, held secure by a harness. After this, things moved quickly for Christine. A week later an old boyfriend, Colin Appleby, turned up and proposed marriage. Two weeks later she eloped to London.

The cap became Jed Stone's trademark and Kenneth Cope fought hard to keep it. In one scene, Jed was to appear in bed and the director wanted it played minus the cap: 'I said no, this is my character's cap and I never take it off, and she was arguing that you'd take it off in bed. It went up to production level and they came back and said, let him keep his hat on.'

Eileen Mayers

Angela Crow

★Originally Doreen and her friend Sheila had no names. They were just referred to in the scripts as 'the barm cake girls' – factory workers who bought balm cakes (large sandwiches) from the Corner Shop. By early 1961, they had developed names and a friendship, as Eileen Mayers explains: 'They were mates. In the north, if you were a working girl like that you wouldn't go to dances or anywhere else without your mate. They borrowed each other's clothes and hairstyles.'

Angela Crow took the part of Doreen at the end of 1960. She started her acting career young, playing truant from school to appear in *Jane Eyre* by a touring company. She won the Gilbert award for Comedy, the Tree Award for Drama and the Emile Littler award for outstanding talent during her years at RADA. When she joined the Street she had appeared as lead in many theatre productions, including Lily Smalls in the original stage production of *Under Milk Wood*. Her television credits included *The Laughing Woman*, playing opposite Peter O'Toole and *The Dance Dress* for Douglas Fairbanks Jnr.

The part of Sheila Birtles was given to **Eileen Mayers** who had started acting at the age of fifteen. The first person she acted with was Joan Heath, then leading lady at Oldham. She studied her art in a repertory company and first appeared in television in 1955 in a series called *I'm Not Bothered* with Arthur Askey and Betty Marsden. After appearing in the Granada shows, *Knight Errant* and *Sky Port*, she was asked to audition for the Street by Jose Scott. She played Linda Cheveski in a dry run before landing the part of Sheila.

THE NEW MRS BARLOW

On 4 August 1962, Valerie Tatlock married Kenneth Barlow at St Mary's Church. Producer H. V. Kershaw had anticipated the viewer reaction to the joining together of the popular couple. The evening duty officer at Granada was put on stand-by to receive calls of congratulations, but noone phoned at all. However, the *Daily Herald* reported that twenty million people had tuned in. Anne Reid was thrilled to be brought back after the strike and to have her character married within a month: 'It was wonderful, I was just thrilled to pieces. It was security and a lovely part and Bill and I got on terribly well.' Whilst sharing her enthusiasm for working together, at the time Bill Roache feared his character would change too much by marrying: 'I was a sort of young semi-heartthrob in those days, and thought getting married was going to finish all

1962 saw Martha and Minnie breaking away from Ena for their own storylines. Minnie took in Jed Stone whilst Martha took a job cleaning the Rovers Return.

Bill Roache puts the success of the Barlows down to the working relationship between Anne Reid and himself: 'Basically it's how you get on. On screen you can get on with somebody very well but it doesn't mean that you'll get on off screen. And visa versa. You've got to have a certain rapport and we did; it was a good mix.'

★As a child **Anne Reid's** chosen career was not acting. At eight she attended ballet school, but she soon realized she would have to give up her dreams of dancing as she grew too tall. She turned to acting and trained at RADA where she was presented with a medal for her acting by the Queen Mother. She acted in repertory in Bromley before landing a part in *Twelfth Night* with the Regent's Park Company and toured with the company in the Lebanon. Her television credits included *The Tony Hancock Show, Robin Hood* and *No Hiding Place.* When she joined the Street cast in the summer of 1961, she was delighted to find she was playing against Bill Roache: 'Bill and I had been at brother and sister schools in North Wales. He was older than me but I heard about this dishy guy up at the boys' school. We had so much common ground it was really funny.'

that. But then the Street is basically about family life and Anne was a very, very good actress and nice to work with.'

Kidnap

A week after the Barlow wedding Concepta Hewitt gave birth to a baby boy, Christopher. Doreen Keogh quite enjoyed playing pregnant Concepta. The infant was seldom seen on screen but was played by Victoria Baker, the daughter of Street director Howard Baker. The writers created the most dramatic storyline to date when they made the decision that baby Christopher was to be kidnapped from outside Gamma Garments. A record 21 million viewers followed the story as the police started the hunt for the missing baby. Viewers phoned into the studios, fearing that the baby had been snatched in real life. At first Lucille was suspected of snatching the child out of jealousy, but was cleared of suspicion by her genuine upset. The story ran for two weeks, until Elsie Tanner discovered Christopher alive and well in the care of Joan Akers. Joan was played by Anna Cropper, Bill Roache's wife at the time, and her landlady Mrs Webb was played by Jean Alexander, two years before she appeared first as Hilda Ogden.

Concepta suffered a breakdown over baby Christopher's disappearance, wandering the streets searching for him. The ordinariness of the Hewitts made their tragedy all the more poignant. As Ivan Beavis says, 'Harry was a something and nothing character and because of that everyone liked him and I found I had mates all over the country.'

·1962·

Lucille Hewitt was suspected of having something to do with the disappearance as she had been jealous of her baby brother. She ran away and was found by Ena Sharples under the viaduct where they sang 'Sealed With A Kiss' together.

Peter Adamson (Len Fairclough)

Graham Haberfield

★In the Spring of 1962, Len Fairclough took on an apprentice, Jerry Booth. Twenty-year-old **Graham Haberfield** was given the role just after he left Bristol Old Vic Drama School. The Street was his first professional acting role and at the time he told a *TV Times* reporter: 'I couldn't believe my luck when I heard I had got the part. I didn't sleep for several nights after hearing the news.' **Peter Adamson** had started his professional life as a qualified engraver but in his spare time worked with amateur drama companies. He eventually secured a place at the London Academy of Music and Dramatic Art and, in 1954, formed his own company. When ITV began to broadcast he took a job as a comedy host on a TV record show and was soon employed at Granada in shows such as *Knight Errant* and *Sky Port*. These roles led to a dry run as insurance man Harry Bailey (eventually cut from Episode 1) and finally Len Fairclough.

·1963·

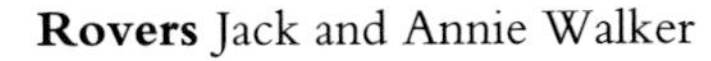

Rovers Jack and Annie Walker

No. 1 Albert Tatlock

No. 3 Frank Barlow

No. 5 Minnie Caldwell • Jed Stone (Jan. - April)

No. 7 Harry, Concepta, Lucille and Christopher Hewitt

No. 9 Ken and Val Barlow • Dave Robbins (Dec.)

No. 11 Elsie and Dennis (April - Dec.) Tanner • Christine Appleby (Jan. - March) Walter Potts (Aug. - Dec.)

No. 13 Jerry and Myra Booth (Oct. - Dec.)

Shop Florrie Lindley

Shop flat Doreen Lostock (Jan. - Sept.) Sheila Birtles (Jan. - Oct.)

No. 16 (Mission) Ena Sharples

Non-residents Leonard Swindley • Martha Longhurst • Emily Nugent • Len Fairclough Dot Greenhalgh • Esther Hayes

'She lit the gas stove and the whole pan went up – this is on live television – and I jumped up on a chair, on to a table and on to the gas stove, putting it out with my feet. Pat looked quite wide-eyed and sort of went "Thank you, Walter".'

Chris Sandford

COMINGS AND GOINGS

Minnie Caldwell lost her lodger, Jed Stone, in April when he 'borrowed' Harry Hewitt's car and drove off to Liverpool. The same month saw the return of his old pal Dennis Tanner. Dennis moved into his old room at No.11, recently vacated by Christine Appleby. She left to share a flat with ex-resident Esther Hayes. Newly-weds Jerry and Myra Booth bought No.13 from landlord Wormold, and next door, in the flat above the shop, Doreen Lostock and Sheila Birtles set about having a wild time. Newcomers in the Street were Dave Robbins, a teaching colleague of Ken's who moved in with the Barlows, and singing windowcleaner Walter Potts who slept on the Tanners' sofa from August.

MR SHOWBUSINESS

Dennis Tanner returned from London in April to find the Street in uproar. His mother Elsie had fallen behind with the rent and the bailiffs had been sent in for her furniture. Elsie refused to pay the arrears or the 10% increase levied on the Street. In true Tanner fashion, Dennis thought the bailiffs seemed a nice bunch and, in Elsie's absence, opened the door and let them in. Outside in the Street, Elsie hung on to chairs and tables while the residents looked on in embarrassment. One who was not embarrassed was Ena Sharples: 'They can't take 'er bed or the tools of her trade, and as far Elsie Tanner's concerned that's one and the same thing!' Elsie finally caved in and agreed to pay the increase. For actor Philip Lowrie it was a return to the programme after a year's break: 'I spent a whole year out of work. So I returned and Jack [Rosenthal] says that when he wrote "ENTER DENNIS" he cried.' Many felt the same way towards Dennis as Street writer Jack Rosenthal, having missed the deep pond of comic material between Elsie and Dennis. The character of Elsie, over the last year, had hardened; with Dennis back she became involved in his lighter, funnier, storylines.

TWIST AND SHOUT

Liverpool-born Walter Potts was smuggled into No.11 by Dennis behind Elsie Tanner's back. When she found out, as of course she did, Elsie agreed to let Walter stay but regretted this when she discovered what a huge appetite the lad had. Chris Sandford, the London-born actor who played Walter remembers his scenes with Pat Phoenix with fondness, especially the scene when Elsie was cooking him some sausages: the pan caught fire when the stove was lit and Chris jumped onto the gas stove to stamp out the flames.

Walter soon became one of the most popular characters, particularly amongst the younger

Christopher Sandford hits the big time. Here, his backing group are the Beatles.

generation. Dennis changed Walter's name to Brett Falcon and launched his pop career. More teenagers than ever before tuned in after his single "Not Too Little, Not Too Much' was played over the end credits. It was timed to coincide with the single being launched in the real world and there it soon reached No.17 in the charts, when the Beatles were No.1 with 'I Want To Hold Your Hand'. Publicity photographs were taken of Chris playing guitar with the Beatles at Granada and suddenly Chris was hot property. He recalls one time when he had to be smuggled out of the television studio: 'Granada was surrounded with screaming girls. I would say at least twenty girls deep right the way round the studios . . . . Pat beckoned me to come out and the noise – I remember it now, it's giving me goose bumps just to think of it – the noise of those girls screaming. I suddenly realized the power of the character!'

A FAMILY AT WAR

Having survived the death of Ida and the departure of David, the Barlow family was nearly wrenched apart completely in the spring of 1963. Father Frank stunned Kenneth and Valerie by announcing his plan to marry widow Christine Appleby. Kenneth made sure Frank knew his feelings: 'Little Christine Hardman! It's only two or three years since you clouted 'er one for breakin' our parlour window! We were in the same class at school! We used to play tig together! I think you've gone simple.' The young Barlows disowned Frank, refusing to listen to his tales of loneliness, but the date was set for 24 May. At the time Christine was living at No.11 with Elsie Tanner and she had a lot to say on the subject! A week before the ceremony,

·1963·

Christine broke the news to Frank that, try as she might, she could not love him and would not marry him: 'I trap myself. I run into traps. I should stand still. But I run on roofs, away from men, towards men. Away from myself, mainly. Why do people never hit me for what I do to 'em? They should hit me more.' Shortly after this outburst, and the ending of the engagement, Christine Hargreaves, the actress who had played Christine since Episode 2, left the programme.

'SHEILA IS SAVED FROM TV SUICIDE'

Margaret Morris, the original casting director on the Street, became the programme's first female producer in the summer of 1963. She was faced with finding a suitable exit for shop assistant Doreen Lostock as actress Angela Crow wanted to leave. Doreen had spent the previous year sharing the Corner Shop flat with Sheila Birtles; with Doreen gone, Sheila needed a new storyline. The writers had attempted to pair her with Jerry Booth but drew back from the idea of marrying the couple. Instead, under Morris' charge the character was given a breath of new life, embarking on a relationship with a married man which would eventually lead to her attempting to take her own life.

While dating Jerry, and allowing him to fall in love with her, Sheila was courted by Gamma Garments manager Neil Crossley. Crossley was a con artist, borrowing money left, right and centre and flirting with all the female residents of the Street, married or not. Sheila, unaware of this, gave him her virginity. When Jerry found out he brawled with Crossley in the Street, knocking him unconscious. Elsie Tanner tried to make Sheila see Crossley was using her, but Sheila was blinded by love: 'I'm not

Living in the L-shaped room at the top of Florrie Lindley's flat, Doreen and Sheila spent many scenes staring out of the window, dreaming of Mr Right. By 1963, Angela Crow (Doreen) had had enough: 'I wanted to do Ibsen and Chekhov. I'd had to turn down two meaty parts in the new wave films. After "Look Back in Anger" at the Royal Court theatre it was an exciting time of change in the theatre and I wanted to get out there and see the world (like Doreen did).'

·1963·

goin' to rot in Coronation Street – I'm not goin' to stay here like the rest o' you. I'm 'avin' somethin' different, an' nobody's goin' to stop me neither. So get out. Go on, get out, you silly old cow!'

Sacked by Miss Nugent for stealing from the petty cash, Crossley left the area without saying goodbye to Sheila. She eventually tracked him down only to be told that he had no feelings for her and already had a wife. Life in the flat alone became very miserable for depressed Sheila. She lost her job at Ellistons through neglect and decided that the only escape would be to take her own life. Scenes were recorded showing Sheila locking herself in the flat, swallowing tablets, turning on the gas, vomiting into a wastebin, taking more tablets and collapsing onto her bed. The news was then leaked to the press that a character was to be shown committing suicide. Granada was inundated with complaints and the Deputy Manchester City Coroner, Mr Roderick Davies, was reported as saying: 'A suicide would be a disgraceful thing to show. I fear that the screening of a suicide might remove the stigma from it, which would be very bad.'

What the public actually saw – Sheila Birtles takes just two aspirins. As the Daily Express (on 12 September 1963) put it: 'Lovesick Sheila calls off suicide bid.'

H.V. Kershaw backed Morris; in fact he watched from the studio floor as actress Eileen Mayers gave a wonderful performance as heartbroken Sheila. He later wrote: 'I can say now that it was the most deterrent piece of television I had seen at the time. Maybe it was too harrowing for many viewers but this would have been a matter for the Archbishop of Canterbury and not for a member of a Coroner's office who should have been glad that we were showing suicide to be such a messy business.

Eileen Mayers remembers the filming of the scene vividly: 'The weeks coming up to the suicide had been quite emotional, because with television you can't just use technique, you have to really feel it. I really had to feel as if I was going to commit suicide. Off screen I was handed a cup of vegetable soup and that was what I sicked up, quite horrid. . . . So it was a bit flat to suddenly feel after all that work it wasn't even shown.' The scene was not shown because the Bernsteins viewed it and took the decision that the end would have to be changed. Eileen Mayers was subjected to a terrifying ordeal: 'The garden was full of Press. They shouted through my letterbox, they climbed, they hammered on the windows . . . my little girl was upstairs crying.'

The studios were opened at the weekend and the scene was recorded again, this time with Sheila swallowing only one aspirin. For Eileen Mayers it was a bitter disappointment: 'I really hated the [ending] that went out. Chris MacMaster [the director] said "Now, I've been talking to a doctor and he says you become catatonic. You just sit there, if something really horrible happens to you, and you just go completely in on yourself, and that's what I want you to do." So that's what I did.' The next episode carried on as scripted, with Sheila being saved by Dennis Tanner and leaving the Street to live with her parents. A week later Doreen left, joining the army as she wanted to travel.

·1963·

The happy couple, Jerry and Myra clashed on the choice of best man: Jerry wanted cycling pal Vincent but Myra announced that Dennis Tanner was ideal for the job, and he duly got it. Vincent was played by Old Vic actor Geoff Hinsliff.

MARRY IN HASTE . . .

With Sheila Birtles living in Rawtenstall, Jerry Booth resigned himself to a lonely future. A shy lad of twenty-three, Sheila had been his first girlfriend. However, his friends took him to Walter Potts' first official engagement, where he met typist Myra Dickenson, the girl whom two months later he would marry. Susan Jameson did not know that her character would marry when she started as Myra: 'She was very young, and I think she thought that there should be more to life than what she had really. I think she had high expectations, and quite a high opinion of herself.' Slow, bashful Jerry suddenly found himself in the middle of a courtship controlled by Myra. She decided that he was her Mr Right and just when he was feeling comfortable in the relationship, she announced they should marry. The white wedding was the first one shown on the Street. Viewers saw bride, groom and guests arrive at the church but did not see the service. The couple bought No.13 Coronation Street, and for a while all was moonlight and roses.

Susan Jameson.
(Myra Booth)

★When **Susan Jameson** joined the Street cast in late 1963 she had just left rep in Canterbury. She was given an audition, alongside Jenny Hesslewood: 'It was between her and me, and she was quite big and blonde, very different; they were obviously trying to decide whether to go for a little dark bird or a big blonde bird.' After a screen test Susan Jameson was given the role. It was only her second role in television, her first being in *Dixon of Dock Green*. She soon befriended Graham Haberfield, who played Jerry, and was helped by Peter Adamson with whom she had been in rep, but she made an early mistake during rehearsals by sitting in Pat Phoenix's chair: 'I sat in the chair and she just came and stood over me until I moved.'

'Coronation Street! You should use houses like these like boxes of matches, use them and chuck them away.'

Ken Barlow

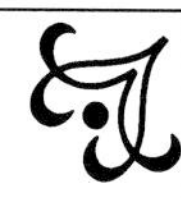

Rovers Jack and Annie Walker • Lucille Hewitt (June - Dec.)

No. 1 Albert Tatlock

No. 3 Frank Barlow (Jan. - May)

No. 5 Minnie Caldwell • Charlie Moffitt (June - Dec.) • Tickler Murphy (Sept. - Oct.)

No. 7 Harry, Concepta, Lucille and Christopher Hewitt (Jan. - May)

No. 9 Ken and Val Barlow • Dave Robbins (Jan.)

No. 11 Elsie and Dennis Tanner • Walter Potts (Jan.)

No. 13 Jerry and Myra Booth (Jan. - May) Stan, Hilda, Irma and Trevor Ogden (June - Dec.)

Shop Florrie Lindley

Shop flat Empty

No. 16 (Mission) Ena Sharples

Non-residents Leonard Swindley • Martha Longhurst • Emily Nugent • Len Fairclough Laurie Frazer

COMINGS AND GOINGS

In 1964 there were many changes in the houses in the Street. Lucille Hewitt moved to the Rovers as the Walkers' ward when the rest of her family moved to Ireland to help Concepta's father run a garage. Minnie Caldwell took in two lodgers – comic Charlie Moffitt and, for a couple of months, Irish Tickler Murphy. Tickler moved out when his girlfriend Florrie Lindley mentioned marriage. Frank Barlow sold up and left No.3 in May after he had a stroke of luck and won £5,000 on the Premium Bonds. He went to live in Bramhall. The Barlows lost their lodger, Dave Robbins, in January when he moved into the flat above Frank's shop. The same month saw Walter Potts leave No.11 to embark on a European tour. No.13 changed owners in May when the Booths, looking forward to the birth of a baby, sold the house for £573 to Stan Ogden who moved in with his noisy and boisterous family. The Booths moved in with Myra's father, who paid off their debts.

·1964·

AN ENGAGING COUPLE

Leonard Swindley suffered a great deal throughout 1964. Early in the year Laurie Frazer, Elsie Tanner's theatrical boyfriend, announced his plans to open a night club and gambling den in the basement of Elliston's Factory. Swindley was horrified by this attack on the moral tone of the area and forged an unlikely alliance with Ena Sharples. Ena went straight for the jugular: 'Look here, Mr Frazer. I've lived on this street for over half a century and there's decent people live here. We're not having it turned into a Sunset Strip by Johnny-come-latelys like you.' Swindley was horrified when his assistant Emily Nugent sold the club owner 100 metres of velvet curtains. Emily had expected Swindley to accept the inevitable but she was wrong: 'It shall not stand! I will not betray my principles! I personally will cancel the order!' Gamma Garments' boss Papagopolous was furious when such a larger order was cancelled and demanded that Swindley reordered. However, Frazer had already placed the order elsewhere. Emily looked on in concern as Swindley swiftly drifted into confusion, upset and anguish. He disappeared from home and was found wandering the streets in tears. A doctor diagnosed a nervous breakdown and he was sent away to recuperate.

Three months later Leonard Swindley reappeared as if nothing had happened. Emily Nugent was delighted and, taking advantage of leap year, lost no time in proposing: 'We share so much . . . I wonder that we don't share it all. Share our lives. Why don't we join our interests in nuptial agreement?' The lay preacher's first response was to bolt from the room, but the next day he reconsidered and agreed to marry Emily.

On the day of the wedding, 22 July 1964, Swindley and best man Len Fairclough waited at the Mission Hall along with all the residents. In fact everyone was there apart from the bride. Emily calmly announced to Jack Walker that there would be no wedding: 'He doesn't want to get married, Mr Walker. Not to me, anyway. Not to anybody, I don't suppose. It was all *me*. He probably wouldn't admit it . . . but we both know. There has to be affection, you see. If there isn't. . . .' Swindley seemed very understanding, almost relieved, when the news was broken. He bore no malice and within a month was again standing with Emily behind Gamma's counter.

Money Problems

Jerry and Myra Booth had lived at No.13 for less than six months before they had money problems. Jerry had a good job with Len Fairclough but Myra had no experience of running a house and filled her home with furniture bought on HP. Jerry was horrified when he discovered they owed £85, were two months behind on the mortgage, the electricity was cut off, and Myra was pregnant. Everything built up to a horrendous row which lasted seven minutes and was recorded as live. It remains the second longest two-hander in the history of the Street (topped only

The jeweller offered friend Swindley some aid in picking an engagement ring for Emily: 'Shall I tell 'er it's £10 more and then knock it off? It generally impresses 'em.'

by a Len/Elsie fifteen minutes in 1968).

Susan Jameson found it relatively easy 'because we both had time to really get going. No, it wasn't difficult . . . the difficult things are stress things and it's quite easy as long as you are secure within your character and the relationship. To get going and give it a bit of a wellie is easier than some other things we had to do.'

The outcome of all the rows and tears was that Myra's father stepped in to pay the debts on the understanding that the Booths left the Street to live with him. The house was sold to lorry driver Stan Ogden who moved in with nattering wife Hilda and children Irma and Trevor.

As Susan Jameson recalls: 'I went on holiday to France and there were some English people who followed me around, saying things like "How could you be so awful?" I mean, quite bizarre. I think everyone thought I was totally vile . . . the public hated me.'

'It's a travesty of the marriage service. Leonard Swindley has never loved, honoured or obeyed anybody in 'is life apart from 'imself.'

Ena Sharples

'Oh, Myra, you think t' world owes you a living. You're like a kid of three.'

Jerry Booth

END OF THE TRIO

One May evening, when the residents were celebrating Frank Barlow's Premium Bond win, Martha Longhurst suffered a fatal heart attack at the table in the Snug. She was the first character to be written out in a purge by new producer Tim Aspinall (see pages 54-55) and the actors involved in the death scene still remember the incident with bitterness.

As Eileen Derbyshire says: 'Ena, Minnie and Martha were the classic trio, like the Greek chorus, and we thought they'd go on forever. Even at the filming everybody still had that outside hope that there would be a reprieve.'

Pat Phoenix was very fond of Lynne Carol, who played Martha (she had lived in Lynne's house in her struggling rep days), and hated taking part in the death scene: 'Peter [Adamson], whose job it was to pronounce her gone, refused to say the line at rehearsals. When the scene was actually recorded he hesitated, so that his words could be easily cut. For a few deliberate seconds he waited, then said: "She's dead."'

·1964·

Lynne Carol gave an interview the night of her 'death' in which she expressed her regret in being axed from the show: 'I was so sad that I cried after saying my last lines at the thought of leaving all my friends. We always thought that while there was a Street there would always be the trio of Ena, Minnie and me.'

Martha's funeral was filmed at Manchester General Cemetery in Harpurhey on Tuesday 12 May. It was to be the first graveside scene for any Street character and attracted a very high audience when it was shown. It also attracted a high audience at the filming.

One national newspaper, the *Daily Mail* reported on the funeral: 'There were six wreaths on the coffin. Only one had an inscription. It read: "To Martha – from the Props Room".'

Trapped in a Loveless Marriage

Valerie Barlow found herself tied to the kitchen sink. As Anne Reid recalls, her character was very serious: 'The temptation to jazz it up was quite strong but I'm glad I didn't. I don't think I had a laugh line. I had about one I think, in eight and a half years.' Valerie became flattered by the attention showed her by Ken's colleague Dave Robbins. Things reached a head in January when one of Dave's pupils, Susan Schofield, was killed by a lorry as she crossed Rosamund Street. Dave withdrew into himself, while Ken threw himself into a campaign to have a children's crossing on the Street. He was annoyed that Val filled her thoughts with housework rather than pamper his

★**Barbara Knox** made her first appearance as Rita in November 1964. She only appeared in one episode, as a friend of Dennis Tanner's, an exotic dancer who spent the night in Elsie's bed in her absence. Barbara had always been interested in acting and trained at Oldham Rep. When she started in the Street she told a reporter: 'In my dreams I saw myself in the world's most glamorous profession. The reality? It's not glamorous, it's tough, and it's overcrowded – but I still love it.'

A few months before Barbara appeared, the new family, the Ogdens, arrived on the scene. Daughter Irma had been in the show for some time and a family was created for her. Manchester-born actress **Sandra Gough** began her acting career in radio at the age of twelve, after she had written to the BBC to ask for a part. At fourteen she went to drama school in London and later, at sixteen, to Oldham Rep for a year. As well as acting she modelled, posing for the *Daily Mirror*'s 'Daughter of Jane' and for romantic comics. Before joining Granada, as a bit part player in *People and Places* and *Coronation Street* Sandra had worked in shops, and this experience helped when she landed the role of Irma – Florrie Lindley's assistant at the shop.

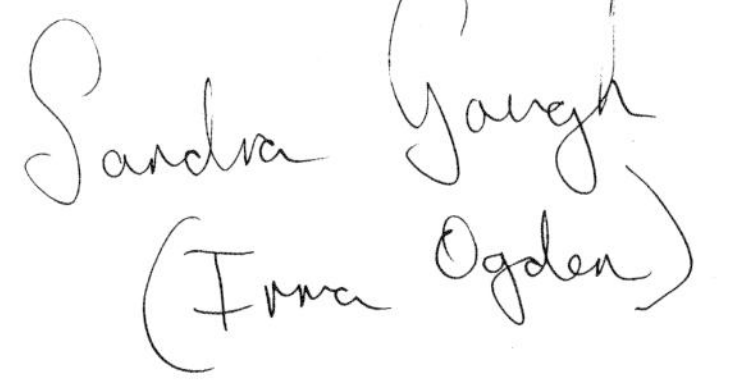

ego and support his cause. Ken marched off to get drunk in the Rovers whilst Val packed a suitcase and told a startled Dave that she had left Ken for him. She was staggered when Dave explained he did not want her, and listened in silence as Dave and Ken debated what was to be done with her. It was decided that Val would return home – which she did, meekly on the surface but burning with humiliation and anger underneath.

★Ex-librarian **Jean Alexander** left her native Liverpool to join a touring theatre company based in Macclesfield. She spent years touring in various reps, not without incident: 'I once tripped over a bit of scenery as I came on stage, came a cropper and broke three ribs. That was at the dress rehearsal, but I still had to do the evening performance because you don't have understudies in rep.' Jean first appeared in the Street in 1962 as Mrs Webb, landlady to Joan Akers, the woman who kidnapped Christopher Hewitt. Hilda Ogden was the complete opposite to quiet, intellectual Jean but 'as a character she's interesting to play, and I like her because she's the opposite of me. She lets fly at people in a way I'd like to myself and never do. When I'm being Hilda, I can get it all out of my system.'

Stan Ogden was played by Hove-born **Bernard Youens**. Like Jean and Sandra, he started his theatrical career in rep, breaking for six years during the war to serve with the First Battalion Loyals, serving in North Africa, Anzio and Egypt. After the war he went back to rep for four years before acting in shows such as *Shadow Squad* and *Knight Errant*. In 1960, he auditioned for the part of Jack Walker but lost out to Arthur Leslie. Instead, Bernard was taken on as a continuity announcer until 1964 when he was given the part of lorry-driver Stan.

Jean Alexander (Hilda Ogden) Bernard Youens 'Stan Ogden'

Valerie Barlow was never unfaithful to Ken during their eight-year marriage, despite her relationship with Dave Robbins. Ken on the other hand was unfaithful in 1966. And in 1964 he had attempted to lure exotic dancer Pip Mistral into bed although she was after his mind rather than his body.

None of the Street cast enjoyed filming Martha Longhurst's funeral. Their thoughts with their now unemployed friend Lynne Carol, and they were all too aware that nine other names were on the list to be axed. Frank Pemberton (left) was next to leave, but Elsie and the Walkers were spared.

Jennifer Moss feels that moving Lucille in with the Walkers was the making of the character: 'I think it broadened her, opened her up to new situations.'

Local talent

The opening of the Viaduct Sporting Club in the Street brought a small ray of showbusiness glamour to the area. Elsie Tanner operated the country's largest roulette wheel for one night (before Laurie Frazer's wife had her sacked) and Dennis worked as Frazer's assistant before Norman Phillips took over. He employed Charlie Moffitt (now lodging with Minnie at No.5) as club comic and compere for the glamorous 'talent contest'. Annie Walker practised her operatic repartee for days before settling on 'We'll Gather Lilacs'. Jack suffered as his wife swanned around the bar, preparing herself for the occasion, and the £10 first prize: 'Oh, Jack, you know what Mr Nuttall used to say. I was the most promising soubrette he'd ever handled.'

On the evening, Annie survived the jeers of the crowd but was extremely put out when her new ward, Lucille Hewitt, walked off with first prize for her rendition of 'My Guy'.

·1964· Four Were Reprieved

'A Chill Wind in Ena's Street'

***Daily Mirror*, 8 April 1964**

After three years of security, the actors of *Coronation Street* were thrown into turmoil by the purge brought about by the arrival of Tim Aspinall, at the age of twenty-eight the Street's youngest producer. The press announced that ten characters were to leave the show within weeks. The *Daily Mail* (7 April 1964) wrote: 'This will leave largely only the show's most colourful characters to carry on the storyline of a programme that has topped the ratings longer than any other TV show in history.'

Jerry and Myra Booth's departure had already been planned as the actors wished to leave. Actress Susan Jameson understood Tim Aspinall's motives: 'I knew what he was trying to do, I think he just wanted to shake everything up. Several other soaps were beginning to start up then and I think he felt something needed to be done as it was all a bit complacent.' Jennifer Moss has different memories: 'I remember Tim Aspinall walked into the Green Room and said "When a growth gets cancerous, it must be cut out." He then announced that the Hewitts would go – the whole family.' Eventually, Harry and Concepta Hewitt did leave the show, but Lucille remained. A few years later Jennifer was told what had happened: 'Mr Cecil [Bernstein] intervened to keep me. I was told that he had said it was ridiculous to have a street with no children.'

Lynne Carol's popular Martha was the first to go.

Out of the ten to go Martha Longhurst was probably the most popular and the press had a field day, reporting on the events between the announcement on 7 April and her screen funeral on 20 May. Actress Lynne Carol seemed resigned to her fate, telling a reporter: 'They've been three wonderful years, and I am sorry to be leaving so many good friends behind me.' Violet Carson was furious that the trio was to be torn apart and rowed with the bosses, threatening to resign. It was Lynne Carol who talked her out of leaving the show. H.V. Kershaw, now producing a police drama called *The Villains*, was unsure that the killing of Martha was what was needed to win the ratings war against the BBC's new comedy show *Steptoe and Son*: 'By killing an established character he [Aspinall] doubtlessly gave us a few episodes of high drama and created a talking-point in the factories and laundrettes which boosted our viewing figures for a period, but when the dust settled we were simply left with a *Coronation Street* without Martha Longhurst. The trio had been reduced to a rather sad duet, and there is little doubt that by that one action many future stories were denied us.'

The Booths left a week after Martha's death, and one week later Frank Barlow made his exit after winning £5,000 on the Premium Bonds. Frank was

Betty Alberge and Frank Pemberton were axed in the purge. Frank joined up with Doreen and Ivan (below) for a Coronation Street *stage play.*

not the only Barlow meant to leave, as Bill Roache recalls: 'Frank Pemberton, Anne Reid and myself were put on the short list and then we were given six months or something. It was all done in front of everybody, no decency or privacy. So it was awful, and morale, all that working together, well, that was the day it all changed.' Ken and Valerie Barlow were put down on paper as emigrating to Australia but were saved when in the autumn of 1964, Aspinall left and was replaced by H.V. Kershaw. Albert Tatlock was also saved, but it was too late for Florrie Lindley (she went to live in Canada) and the Hewitts (they were sent to Ireland).

At the end of 1964 the Hewitts were reunited with some of their fellow residents when Doreen Keogh, Ivan Beavis, Lynne Carol, Frank Pemberton and Ruth Holden toured in a comedy especially written for them by Vince Powell and John Finch. However, the play wasn't exactly what the actors had agreed to – it was a farce called *Coronation Street on the Road*. When Susan Jameson found this out, she walked out of the rehearsals and did not appear in the production. The play was not a success.

'I'm fed up wi' bowin' and scrapin' an' bein'polite to folk with no manners. Some people walk in a shop an' think they own it – treat you as though you wer muck.'

Florrie Lindley

Rovers Jack and Annie Walker Lucille Hewitt

No. 1 Albert Tatlock • David Barlow (April - Dec.) • Ted Bates (Aug. - Sept.)

No. 3 *Empty*

No. 5 Minnie Caldwell • Charlie Moffitt (Jan. - Dec.)

No. 7 *Empty, collapsed*

No. 9 Ken, Val, Peter and Susan (April - Dec.) Barlow

No. 11 Elsie and Dennis Tanner

No. 13 Stan, Irma (Jan. - Dec.) and Hilda Ogden

Shop Florrie Lindley (Jan. - June) • Lionel Petty (June - Dec.)

Shop flat Jerry Booth (Feb. - March) Sandra Petty (June - Dec.)

No. 16 (Mission) Ena Sharples

Non-residents Leonard Swindley • Emily Nugent • Len Fairclough • Clara Midgeley

COMINGS AND GOINGS

David Barlow returned following a leg injury which meant he could not play professional football again. He married Irma Ogden and they rented a stylish flat. Albert Tatlock was pleased to put up an old friend Ted Bates but was upset when Ted's daughter forced him to return to the old folks' home. Albert himself had a narrow escape when Clara Midgeley proposed to him, but he turned her down flat. Minnie Caldwell lost her lodger, Charlie Moffit, who gave up his job as an insurance salesman to return to his first love, the stage. Florrie Lindley was reconciled with her estranged husband Norman and they started a new life together in Canada. The shop was sold to ex-Sgt Major Lionel Petty and his daughter Sandra. Jerry Booth returned, without Myra, to lodge in the flat above the shop before moving in with Len Fairclough. His marriage had ended following the birth of his still-born daughter. Valerie Barlow gave birth to twins – Peter and Susan – in April and the Street bade farewell to Mr Swindley who was promoted to Gamma head office (and a Granada spin-off called Pardon the Expression).

·1965·

FAREWELL FLORRIE

Betty Alberge had appeared in the very first scene in *Coronation Street*, back in 1960, when her character Florrie Lindley had bought the Corner Shop. As a shopkeeper she was regarded by the regulars as 'one of them' and had never fitted into the community. Florrie was the last victim of the 1964 axings. After five years of playing Florrie as a widow, the writers suddenly created a long-lost husband, Norman, who had been working as an engineer in India. He returned to the Street to sort out a divorce and started an affair with Elsie Tanner. Meanwhile, Florrie decided that she was sick of being lonely and, more to the point, sick of the shop counter, so she told a startled Norman that she wanted to give their marriage another chance. The Lindleys emigrated in June and the shop was sold to Welshman Lionel Petty, a retired Sgt Major. He had been talked into buying the shop by his daughter Sandra who had fallen for Dennis Tanner, now a hair stylist. Unfortunately for them, Dennis was not enamoured with Sandra and Lionel was snubbed as he treated his customers as if they were live conscripts. It was up to Miss Nugent to point out customers wanted more than just being served: 'That's why people still come to little shops; a cash register at the supermarket turnstile isn't going to ask about Grandma's lumbago, is it?'

VALERIE'S SURPRISE DELIVERY

On 15 April 1965, Valerie Barlow gave birth to twins, Peter and Susan. Anne Reid recalls how she disliked the boy's name: 'They were going to call them Jeffrey and

Susan and I didn't like that. Peter was my favourite name so I asked if I could call the baby Peter and they said yes.'

Val Barlow closed down her hair salon and became a housewife. There followed occasional scenes showing harassed Valerie dealing with the babies as they grew into toddlers. They were not shown too often on screen, but when they did appear it was a nightmare recording their scenes. Anne Reid recalls: 'I think very few directors know how to handle children and they will try and rehearse them, instead of just rehearsing the grown-ups and then bundling the kids in so they always do something interesting immediately, because the surroundings are new. If you don't get it then, you've had it, because they get bored and start crying.'

The set of No.9 Coronation Street was transformed into a mess of nappies, pram and baby clothes with Valerie in the middle, mopping a brow whilst babies cried off-screen. The nappies were written into one dramatic episode when, later in the year, Valerie started an evening course. She left the twins with Ken and nervously went to the first session. Ken grew bored of babysitting and, leaving

Minnie Caldwell attempts to catch up on her reading. When Ena criticised her Minnie retorted that she was in fact reading to her cat Bobby.

Edward Evans (LIONEL PETTY)

★**Edward Evans** had spent three years in the family series *The Groves* and was a minor celebrity when he was offered the part of Lionel Petty. What surprised him most of all about the show was his first scene in the Rovers Return: 'Everybody walked on and took positions around the bar as though they'd been told about them before, and they hadn't.'

The part of lovestruck Sandra was given to **Heather Moore** who had started at Granada working as an extra. In 1965 Heather was given bit small parts; and the character of Sandra Petty, a quiet, well-spoken girl, eager to please, emerged from that. Heather recalls how the mask slipped one day out of the studio: 'I was sitting in a car and people were hammering on the window and I remember just winding the window down and saying 'F . . . off!' At the end of the year, Heather Moore left the Street to get married and move to North Africa; in the programme, Sandra gave up her job and told a surprised Dennis Tanner she was moving on.

Bill Roache enjoyed his scenes with the twins as they were filmed before the rest of the episodes: 'We were still doing the whole show right through but the children scenes had to be done separately because of noises off.'

the twins asleep upstairs, went to the Rovers. In his absence, a piece of coal fell from the fire onto a nappy and started a fire. Valerie returned early to find the living room full of smoke. She rescued the babies and managed to put out the fire, but accused Ken of attempted murder.

No.7 Collapses

Since the Hewitts had emigrated in 1964, No.7 Coronation Street had remained vacant. Occasionally, Lucille had spent a sad half-hour sitting on the stairs reminiscing about the past. In early 1965, the Street sets were moved from Studio Two to the larger Studio Six and designer Denis Parkin was given the task of staging the collapse of the empty house. In the weeks leading up to the collapse the neighbouring houses had suffered earth tremors caused by movement in disused mining shafts underground. One August morning, No.7 collapsed with a mighty roar. Next door, at No.9, Valerie grabbed the twins and ran outside, fearing the whole terrace was coming down. Annie Walker took the Barlows in as Len Fairclough sorted through the rubble to find out what had caused the collapse. Fairclough calmed fears for other houses by finding that the main window beam had snapped. He gave landlord Wormold an estimate of £300 to make good, but Wormold decided it was not worth it and the house was demolished.

The Uniting of Two Great Houses

'You're the same as the Ogdens underneath and you know it. You were born 'ere – Coronation Street – a two up an' two down terraced, with a backyard an' an outside lavatory. Our Dad was a postman an'

·1965·

Following the collapse of No. 7, the council put a park bench in the gap, where it remained for seventeen years.

'I'm goin' ter be swappin' rude jokes wi' Elsie Tanner an' slagin' Mrs Sharples an' battin' me eyelashes at the fellows till they carry me out in me box. Cos I'm common as muck, me, and bloody proud o' it!'

our Mam was a cleaner in a hotel. Not much to be proud about in that is there?' David Barlow was furious at the way his older brother Ken objected to the news that he was to marry Irma Ogden. Ken, always campaigning for the underdog and social equality for all was horrified at the thought of being related to Stan and Hilda Ogden.

David and Irma had begun their relationship in late December. She had been the only resident to stand by him when he had been suspended from football for apparently taking a bribe. His name cleared but his professional career over, David had decided to return to his roots and soon proposed to Irma. He was fascinated by her wit and her talent for mimicry as well as her looks and personality. Sandra Gough describes Irma in a few words: 'Very bubbly, cheeky, down to earth.' Many of the residents thought the relationship would not last as Irma was seen as too flighty and common for David. Everyone was stunned when they eloped in December.

·1966·

'One magistrate, one doctor and a statement from any one of us and we could have Jed Stone committed.'

Annie Walker

Rovers Jack and Annie Walker • Lucille Hewitt • Brenda Riley (March - April)

No. 1 Albert Tatlock

No. 3 *Empty*

No. 5 Minnie Caldwell • Jed Stone (Jan. - Sept.)

No. 9 Ken, Val, Peter and Susan Barlow

No. 11 Elsie, Dennis and Wally (April - July) Tanner • Linda and Paul Cheveski (Oct. - Nov.) • Sheila Birtles (June - Dec.)

No. 13 Stan and Hilda Ogden • Jim Mount (Jan. - April)

Shop Lionel Petty (Jan.) • David and Irma Barlow (Jan. - Dec.)

Shop flat Empty

No. 16 (Mission) Ena Sharples • Vera Lomax (Dec.)

Non-residents Emily Nugent • Len Fairclough • Clara Midgeley • Jerry Booth Ray Langton • Ruth Winter • Bet Lynch

COMINGS AND GOINGS

Irish Brenda Riley took over the Rovers as relief manager whilst the Walkers holidayed in Ireland with the Hewitts in the spring. She caused a sensation, with her lowcut blouses, short skirts and charming ways. Elsie's father-in-law Wally arrived at No.11. The Cheveskis returned from Canada and moved in on Linda's mam for a couple of months. Later in the year, Sheila Birtles moved in as lodger. January saw Lionel Petty leaving the shop, Jed Stone returning to Minnie at No.5, and telephone engineer Jim Mount moving into No.13 as the Ogden's lodger. He left in April, along with the lovely Brenda.

SUNNY JIM IS BACK IN TOWN

The New Year started with Peter Eckersley taking over as producer of *Coronation Street*. The first thing he did was to invite Kenneth Cope to return to the programme as Minnie's popular lodger Jed Stone. He even came up with a unique way to herald Jed's arrival, as Ken Cope remembers: 'Jed's cap was pushed through Minnie's letterbox, so they saved the performance fee for that episode.' The cap had become a very important part of Jed's character, just like Bet's earrings and Phyllis's blue rinse would be to them in later years.

Jed wasted no time in roping Dennis Tanner into his get-rich quick schemes. He acquired a job lot of old waxwork models and set to work remodelling them, turning Chaplin and Gandhi into Lennon and McCartney, but somehow this did not work. Stone and Tanner Enterprises then rented a unit under the Viaduct and opened an auction room, but this was closed down as they did not have Town Hall approval. It was then that Jed opened a boarding kennels in the unit: 'It's the Taj Mahal of the doghouse world. Jed Stone, the best friend a dog ever had – apart from a corporation lamppost. And me assistant, Mr Dennis Tanner – better known in the trade as Fox Terrier Tanner.' The kennels stayed open for a week, until they managed to lose a couple of hounds.

In September, Jed was warned that the police were after him for possession of some stolen blankets. Jed planned to run away but the police's arrival coincided with the one event that he could not bring himself to miss – Minnie's birthday – and he was caught. Minnie cried to Jack in the Snug: 'I know 'e's a tearaway an' sometimes a bit cheeky. But never wi' me, Mr Walker. 'e's more than a Roger the Lodger to me . . . he's more like a son.' Kenneth Cope remembers Margot Bryant with affection: 'I found playing with her smashing because I could rabbit on quickly and she'd bring me back.' When she died, in 1988 at the age of 90, Ken donned the cap again to introduce a special half-hour show *Minnie Caldwell Remembered* as a tribute to the great actress.

Takeover at the Shop

Lionel Petty's decision to return to Wales came as no surprise to the Street's residents; he had never really fitted in and had upset many customers with his bossy ways. As David Barlow's football career was over for good, he agreed with Irma's plan to buy the shop (£1,750 for the shop, £200 for stock) and his first act was to close down the sub-post office which had never been very profitable. Working behind the shop counter suited actress Sandra Gough, as it cut down on the number of kitchen table scenes: 'I think they're boring on the telly. I want to see reality, I want to see a lot of problems, but I really don't just want to see an ordinary man and wife arguing and the nappy-changing.'

The best of pals – Jed interests Dennis in his latest money-making scheme.

Always game for a laugh, Irma posed as 'Avril' and allowed Ron Jenkins to chat her up, but things turned sour when he pestered her for a date. Ben Kingsley appeared as Jenkins over a span of two years.

★ Born in Heywood, Lancashire, **Julie Goodyear** always planned to enter show business, but as a singer rather than an actress. One night, at a club, she jumped on stage, grabbed the microphone and started to sing 'Blue Moon'. Minutes into the song a meat pie was thrown at her by a member of the audience. Julie picked it up, took a bite out of it, and received a terrific round of applause: 'There and then I decided that, if I wasn't appreciated as a singer, I'd change course and try to make it as an actress.' After various jobs, including selling brushes door-to-door, Julie started work at an aircraft factory, marrying a work mate and giving birth to a son, Gary. The marriage did not last long and Julie turned to modelling to support herself and her baby. It was through modelling that she got her first jobs in the background of Granada shows such as *Scene at 6.30*. Julie landed the part of machinist Bet Lynch in May 1966. During her six weeks in the programme she was befriended by Pat Phoenix, who took her to Oldham Rep. She was taken on, starting as an assistant stage manager.

ENTER BET

Across the street from the houses, Ellistons' raincoat factory was closed down, reopening as a PVC welding factory, making modern raincoats. Eckersley sent a document to all the writers regarding the new project: 'We hope this will give us rather more interesting pictures than in the days when it was working with cloth. The girls will be working with large rolls and sheets of PVC and other plastics.' Lucille Hewitt joined the staff, as did Irma Barlow, convincing David that the money would come in handy. Both women were attracted by the salary – £11 a week. Bet Lynch managed to reign supreme at the factory by sleeping with the foreman, but she resented Lucille's speed at welding and gave her a black eye.

VOTE, VOTE, VOTE FOR ANNIE WALKER

The local elections in May caused a stir in Coronation Street as the residents split into two camps backing two independent candidates – Len Fairclough and Annie Walker. Annie agreed to stand on behalf of the Federation of Women's Association and thought the election would be a walkover until Len announced his decision to stand against her. In their election speeches, at a joint rallying meeting, Len pledged to fence off all the canal while Annie concentrated on more domestic issues: 'If elected I will harangue the Council on the urgent need for rubber lids on dustbins.' She grew determined to beat Len and make a stand for women in politics.

Len made Elsie Tanner's parlour his campaign headquarters but startled her with one of his election issues – classing the Street as slum housing, he wanted to see it demolished or radically improved by the landlord. For a month Annie and Len attempted to score points off each other but on the eve of the elections made their peace: 'There's been a few angry words tossed aroun' but I reckon that's how it

·1966·

Annie could count on all the local ladies' votes – except, of course, for Elsie Tanner's.

Leaving Val at home with the babies, Ken enjoyed a short-lived but passionate affair with Jackie Marsh.

should be. Otherwise it wouldn't be an election, would it? Let's let the voters decide. When the votes were counted Len and Annie had equal votes. A recount followed, but the result was the same. In the end, the future councillor was decided with the toss of a coin. Len was victorious and Annie retired to bed with a migraine.

UNFAITHFUL KEN

January 1966 found Ken Barlow falling into another woman's arms while his wife Valerie struggled at home with nine-month-old twins. The other woman was Jackie Marsh, a reporter on a local newspaper who was writing a piece on David's footballing career. Viewers were horrified to see Ken playing around with Jackie in her flat and, although the couple only went as far as kissing on screen, the writers left no one in any doubt the fact that they were lovers. Actress Pamela Craig (years before she joined *The*

·1966·

Archers) played Jackie and received some rather nasty letters. During the recording of the romance, Pamela had no idea what the outcome would be: 'It was quite clear [the writers] wouldn't tell us. They said they didn't know, but I think they must have. My guess was that it was not going to be anything that came to anything.'

Three weeks into the affair, just as the pair were planning to spend the weekend together, they were spotted kissing by Elsie Tanner. She confronted Ken who told her it was none of her business. However, his conscience was pricked and he told Jackie the weekend – and the affair – was off, he had too much to lose. Ken thought he had managed the affair well and was stunned when, in March, Valerie packed her bags and left with the twins after telling him she knew all about Jackie and had waited for him to confess: 'You've vanished from me. I don't know who you are. . . .' It was left to Ken to prove his love, which he did . . . eventually.

Committed Christians clashed over God's plans for the Mission Hall. Ruth Winter's evangelical crusade affronted Ena Sharples.

ENA'S WORST HOUR

One May afternoon, Ena and Minnie took a trip out to the Summit Supermarket on what should have been a half-hour shopping expedition. It turned into three terrible hours for Ena. Ena's daughter Vera Lomax had been deserted by her violent husband and needed money to feed her son, so Ena had given her all her savings, leaving nothing in her purse for the week. So Ena succumbed to temptation and pocketed two tins of pink salmon. She was caught and the following week found herself standing before a magistrate who did not take kindly to her obstructive manner. The magistrate fined her forty shillings, telling her: 'This is stealing, make no mistake. It is a particularly despicable offence in view of your occupation. There has been confided in you the task of taking care of a Mission, a place of religion, a place where the virtue of honesty is emphasized constantly. You have done more than commit a crime.'

Ena was still reeling from shock when the Mission secretary informed her that the Mission was to be converted into a community centre, run by a warden, Ruth Winter. The decision had been made by Eckersley, who wanted to update the Mission set, which was seldom used, most of the action taking place in Ena's vestry. He talked to Rev. J. Keir Murren, a Unitarian minister from Liverpool whose chapel had been converted: 'Murren says, "Unitarian history of recent years makes the point that each and every Domestic Mission which has attempted to restrict its work to Church members, which has not found a job to do for its neighbourhood, has closed or may soon do so. In 1915 and 1925 there were 16 Domestic Missions. Today few survive."' Ena was horrified as Ruth took over, starting an under-fives play group (for Valerie and the twins), OAP sessions (for Albert and Minnie), and evening sessions for the community (Ken's nature films, Emily's poetry circle). What amazed Ena most was the new policy that the subject of religion was not to be brought up at all unless requested by those using the Centre. Things backfired a bit for Ruth when, in June, she held a youth party which got out of hand; Ena caught two lads who had cornered Lucille in the Vestry, and were threatening to rape her. When Ena tried to stop them one produced a knife and told her he'd 'carve her up'. Ruth Winter walked in on the scene as Ena, fighting her fears, tried to protect the petrified Lucille. The youths were not prepared for Ruth's assault on them and she punched them and threw them into the Street where Len Fairclough finished the job. Ena started to thaw towards Ruth.

LEN FINDS LOVE

Ena was not the only one to be affected by the arrival of social worker Ruth Winter. Councillor Fairclough fell for her and even started to attend the Mission to be near her. She was the first educated woman he had asked out and he was amazed when she agreed to date him. The courtship lasted for six weeks and Len had decided to propose when Ruth broke the news that the Mission community centre was closing and she was going to live in Rome with her boyfriend, a film stuntman.

PAUL CHEVESKI BATTLES FOR LIFE

After five years living in Canada, Linda Cheveski returned home to mother Elsie Tanner with the news that her marriage was over; she had fallen for another man and wanted to divorce Ivan. While Ivan found work in Birmingham and waited patiently for Linda to come to her senses, Linda settled down to live in the Street with her son Paul. Tragedy struck when Paul was dragged from the canal unconscious. He was rushed to hospital where he was put in an oxygen tent, his body racked with pneumonia. Linda refused to leave his side and felt inadequate when the nurses tried to assure her everything would be fine.

Elsie was stunned to discover that Len had rejected a plan to fence in the canal at a council meeting. She went for him claws at the ready: 'ow many more kids 'ave got to drown while the great Len Fairclough plays at bein' God?' Len maintained he was doing what he was elected to do. He managed to talk Elsie round but Paul's father Ivan was not so ready to listen. He cornered Len in the builder's yard and, armed with a plank of wood, went for him. Ernst Walder recalls: 'I remember the others from the cast standing behind the lights and watching us. I came into the workshop with a stick in my hand and fought him. I broke Peter's rib. He must have had very thin ribs.' The next week Peter Adamson suffered, but viewers saw Paul recover and the reconciled Cheveskis leave for Birmingham.

A canal-side scene as Len Fairclough supports Linda Cheveski in the search for missing Paul

SHEILA'S SECRET

The return of Sheila Birtles put a spring into Jerry Booth's step. Elsie provided lodings for Sheila and she found employment back at Ellistons. Actress Eileen Mayers was thrilled to be asked back to the show: 'I was very

Paul's accident brought his parents together again, but Linda refused to be tied to Ivan for life.

happy to return. I love the north and I loved the Street. I always thought it's not so much a programme, it's more a way of life.' Jerry and Sheila's courtship was slow and carefully planned by the writers. Just when he seemed willing to make a long-term commitment, she dropped her bombshell, taking him to meet a little boy, Danny, her love child. The child was played by Billy Haberfield, Eileen Mayers' godson and the son of 'Jerry' himself, Graham Haberfield. Eileen Mayers remembers: 'His little face looked up and it was supposed to be Neil Crossley's and he looked the image of Jerry Booth, it was really quite hilarious.' Poor Jerry did not find it funny and he spent so long mulling over whether or not to stand by Sheila and become an instant father that Sheila decided to leave the area and married Neil Crossley. Jerry was left, once again, on the shelf. Refusing Len Fairclough's advice, he spent a night on the town in a seedy Manchester club, pouring out his heart and all his savings to a seemingly nice girl who lost interest in Jerry as soon as his wallet was empty.

Moira Maxwell turns the tables on victim Elsie.

TROUBLED TIMES FOR ELSIE TANNER

It was a disturbing time for No.11 throughout 1966. Elsie received very abusive phone calls from a mystery woman who plagued her night and day. The caller turned out to be Moira Maxwell, the wife of Robert, who had died the previous year when with Elsie. Mrs Maxwell revealed herself to Elsie when everyone else was out, threatening her with a knife, 'In the old days they knew what to do to women like you. They used to take adulteresses and stone them to death.' The two women struggled but Len burst into the room and held Moira until the police arrived. Dennis, who couldn't pay back £94 he had stolen from a casino, returned home one evening to find two thugs menacing Elsie. He tried to fend them off with a poker whilst the men folk in the Rovers debated what to do. As Jack Walker prepared to join in, Len strolled in and threw £94 in notes on the table.

Jack, Annie and Elsie Drop In

·1966·

In early 1966, an invitation arrived at Granada from three Australian television stations – TCN 9 Sydney, GRV 9 Melbourne and NSW 9 Adelaide – for a party from *Coronation Street* to visit the fans in Australia. The Channel 9 stations had first taken the programme in 1963 and by 1966 it was more popular in Australia than in the UK. H.V. Kershaw thought that the reason for this was the average Australian's high views on standards and moral values: 'And *Coronation Street* had itself avoided the mainstream of permissiveness.'

The party was to consist of five people – Kershaw himself, Norman Frisby from the Press Office and three members of cast. In his report on the tour, Frisby comments on the selection process for the cast: 'It was essential that the chosen three should have been with *Coronation Street* since its early days, should still be with the programme and should figure largely in the stories currently playing in Australia.' This narrowed the field down to nine and eventually it was agreed that Arthur Leslie, Doris Speed and Pat Phoenix should represent the cast.

The tour started on Saturday 12 March when Frisby flew to Sydney to pave the way. The following Monday, Kershaw and the cast travelled to London where they were received at Downing Street by Prime Minister Harold Wilson. Pat Phoenix recorded that the PM was amazed by the reception the party received from the staff at No.10: 'We've had everybody in this place but no one has aroused as much curiosity and comment among the staff as you have.' This visit to No.10 was more than a way of seeing the party off in style. The Labour Government was struggling to keep its slim majority and a General Election had been called for 31 March. On the steps outside No.10 the party posed for the press photographers with Mr Wilson and Chancellor Jim Callaghan. Callaghan draped an arm around Pat's shoulder and said: 'I think she's the sexiest thing on television.' A couple of years ago, when asked to pay tribute to Miss Phoenix, Mr Callaghan told a Granada researcher he had never seen her on the television and only made the comment to please the reporters.

On Thursday 17 March, the main party flew to Australia. It was Arthur Leslie's first time out of Britain and he could not believe what was happening, as Kershaw recalls: 'Arthur surveyed the glass of bubbly and tray of canapés. "If anybody had told me ten years ago", he said, "that I'd be sitting here drinking champagne and eating caviare 42,000 feet over Bali, I'd have said he was bloody barmy!"' While in Sydney the cast met the NSW Premier, Robert Askin, and the Lord Mayor. One evening they were invited to visit a famous striptease club. Arthur Leslie declined, but Pat and Doris were keen to see all the sights. The next day the party flew on to Melbourne where hundreds of fans lined the airport balconies. In the week that followed the party toured the city's five Coronation Streets, presented television awards, visited an animal sanctuary and the children's hospital, and appeared on countless chat shows. On *In Melbourne Tonight*

'By now the word will have reached Buckingham Palace. Never send the Queen Mother to tour a country at the same time as stars from Coronation Street.'

***Melbourne Truth*, 2 April 1966**

Postcard to Ena Sharples – wish you were here.

the actors performed a sketch specially written by Kershaw. At 9pm on the night of Thursday 24 March, Pat Phoenix appeared live on television, introducing that night's episode of *Coronation Street.*

On Tuesday 29 March, the group flew into Adelaide airport to be greeted by thousands of banner-waving, cheering fans. The day before the Queen Mother had visited the city and the reception had been nothing like the crowd waiting for Jack, Annie and Elsie. People lined the route from the airport to the Hotel Australia and the cast was escorted by police patrolmen. The traffic lights were switched off to give them the right of way. That afternoon the party visited a new city, Elizabeth, where a staggering 20,000 people waited, sitting on the lawns of the shopping precinct.

The following day thousands of people lined the streets of Adelaide, in places ten deep, waiting to catch a glimpse of their heroes. For the first time in the history of the city, the crowd surged over the Blue Line – a line painted down the side of the road until then honoured as a barrier. As the cast drove

Oh dear! It seems Jack has bought identical hats – from In Melbourne Tonight.

·1966·

along in open topped cars, all other traffic was stopped. Flowers and gifts and messages were flung into the cars. Tickertape flickered down the fronts of the office blocks. Afterwards, the actors had to be treated in hospital, their backs sore from welcoming pats and hands aching from being shaken so much.

The four days spent in Adelaide sped by, with exhausting tours, receptions and television appearances and the cast were moved by the crowds' love wherever they went. Driving to the airport, Doris and Pat wept as 50,000 people waved farewell. The next day a letter was printed from a reader in the *Adelaide News*: 'After seeing the amazing display given by older and supposedly more level-headed citizens in greeting the *Coronation Street* stars, I consider they can have no cause in future to criticize the antics of teenagers in welcoming their idols. I was staggered to see mature citizens carrying on like the hysterical teenagers. . . . It makes you wonder what our older generation is coming to.'

The Street party spent a couple of days in San Francisco, sightseeing and resting, before returning to England and Granada. After all the attention of the previous weeks from members of the public, it was blissful for the cast to stay in a city where they were not recognized.

Fifty-thousand farewells.

A couple of days after Vera's death, Ruth Holden had a disturbing encounter:

'It was very foggy. The middle of winter. And suddenly, out of the fog loomed the local undertaker, and he said to me, "Ruth, I hope you'll let me have the job, I've known you a few years." I just screamed!'

Rovers Jack and Annie Walker
Lucille Hewitt

No. 1 Albert Tatlock

No. 3 *Empty*

No. 5 Minnie Caldwell

No. 9 Ken, Val, Peter and Susan Barlow

No. 11 Elsie (Jan. Sept.) and Dennis Tanner
Karen Olsen (Aug.) • the Cooks
(Sept. - Oct.) • the Hippies (Dec.)

No. 13 Stan and Hilda Ogden

Shop David and Irma Barlow • Jill Morris (Dec.)

Shop flat Emily Nugent (Jan. - Dec.)

No. 16 (Mission) Ena Sharples • Vera Lomax (Jan.)

Non-residents Len Fairclough • Jerry Booth • Steve Tanner • Dot Greenhalgh
Dave Smith • Harry Hewitt
Concepta Hewitt

COMINGS AND GOINGS

The big shake-up of 1967 occurred in No.11. Following her marriage to Steve Tanner in September, Elsie moved to a luxury flat in Altrincham, Cheshire. For a while she continued to visit her friends in Weatherfield, but on Christmas Day, the Tanners left the country to start a new life in America. Left with an empty house, Dennis took in his Swedish girlfriend, Karen Olsen. He 'borrowed' the Barlow twins and tried to pass them off as his own, claiming that Karen was his au pair. However, the plan failed and Immigration sent Karen back home. Dennis then decided to turn the house into a theatrical boarding house, taking in nine members of a girl's pipe band, followed by a family of acrobats, the Cooks. At the end of the year, Dennis found a group of hippies had started a commune in the livingroom and showed no signs of moving on. Emily Nugent moved into the flat above the Barlows' shop. The old Gamma set was transformed into a swinging his-and-hers boutique, with Lucille running the 'dolls' section and Dennis the 'guys'. At Christmas, David and Irma fostered a little girl, Jill Morris, following Irma's miscarriage. Ena spent a lonely year at the Mission: her daughter Vera died in January and in December she received the news that the building was to be demolished.

·1967·

A SAD YEAR FOR ENA

Ena Sharples' year started off with the terrible knowledge that her daughter Vera Lomax only had days to live. Vera had moved into her mother's Vestry just before Christmas, complaining of headaches and the doctor had told a doubting Ena that Vera had a tumour on her brain which would prove fatal. The first actress Ruth Holden heard of her character's demise was when she picked up her scripts for the week: 'I was sorry about it, but then if you thought about it, there was not a lot you could do with the character. I just accepted it, but I was very sorry to go.' On screen Vera realized something was seriously wrong when her mother stopped bullying her. Ena turned to old friend Jack Walker for advice: 'It's got an 'old of 'er, an' accordin' to .doctor there's nowt yer can do about it. She left it too late, goin'. So what do I do, Jack? Do I tell 'er she's dyin' or what? It's fair crucified me this last few weeks I can tell yer.'

Ena decided, with Jack's help, not to tell Vera and tried to make her last days as happy as possible, but for Ruth Holden, the scenes were anything but happy: 'It made me feel ill. I became very depressed.'

Three months after burying her daughter, Ena herself was buried – alive. On the evening of 10 May 1967, viewers were stunned to see the Street set covered in rubble and dust, whilst Jerry Booth shouted, 'Help, everybody. Come quickly . . . a train's fallen off viaduct!' The exterior scenes were, at this point, still being recorded in studio and it was a tremendous feat to build this scene. Five goods train carriages were wrecked and pulled off the viaduct, its bricks built up into a towering mass with iron girders sticking out. Under all this was placed a squashed Mini from which PC Conway was dragged alive. Nearby, under the rubble, a tiny corridor of bricks and stones was made, protected by wooden rafters, and in this hole Violet Carson, as Ena, had to lie completely still. In the script, the train had ploughed off the viaduct onto the Street and Ena, Jack, Elsie and Lucille were missing. In fact only Ena had been caught under the viaduct. In the middle of the drama, small scenes were played out showing how the residents reacted to the disaster. Hilda Ogden's character suddenly became very vulnerable and her relationship with Stan was put under the spotlight: 'I know I talk too much, but I can't seem to do owt about it. We can't be other than what we are, Stan. An' yer know what we are to them round 'ere? Just a couple o' comedians, that's what we are, Stan.' One by one the missing residents turned up and at the end of the second disaster episode, David Barlow crawled from under the wreckage to report he had found Ena alive. The director of the disaster scenes, Michael Apted, later became an internationally renowned film director.

Minnie attended Vera's funeral, commenting on Ena's plaque, 'What Is Home Without a Mother.' She herself never had children.

HARD UP MINNIE

The plight of sixty-seven-year-old Minnie Caldwell was used by the Government, in conjunction with Granada, to highlight to pensioners the benefits available to them. Producer H.V. Kershaw agreed to assist the campaign: 'We are constantly being asked by government departments to be helpful during a campaign. We do it after the campaign is actually under way and has entered into everyone's life. We do not inaugurate it on the programme, because that wouldn't look natural.' The beginning of the year found Minnie telling Ena that times were hard and she had applied for her supplementary pension: 'They're very nice at the Post Office. You just send this form off and a man comes round to see you at your own home. . . . I'm entitled to four pounds ten a week and they give you your rent as well.' Ena's character was used to put the view of the people the Government were trying to win over: 'I am not going on National Assistance. I am not having Alice Mazey looking over my shoulder when I draw my pension and seeing I'm on the parish.' Ena was eventually won round after a visit from a friendly government official. 'There have been three-quarters of a million people like you who've been entitled to more pension than they've been getting. We want to find them and give it them.' A week after this episode was transmitted the Ministry of Social Security had been contacted by many pensioners entitled to more money, thanks to the power of *Coronation Street*.

★ Canadian-born actor **Paul Maxwell** was cast as Steve Tanner. He had served as a Survey Officer in the Royal Canadian Artillery and was appointed Entertainment Administration Officer. Towards the end of the Second World War he made his first visit to the UK and fell in love with the country and a young Scottish actress called Mary Lindsay, whom he eventually married. After demob, he joined Yale University's Drama School, graduating with a Master of Fine Arts, to become a teacher. In 1956, he gave up teaching and moved to Hollywood, appearing in films *Follow the Boys, City of Fear* and *We Joined the Navy*, and in television shows such as *Highway Patrol* and *Bronco*. Wanting to work in Europe he returned to the UK in 1961 and was soon seen in programmes like *Danger Man* and *The Saint*. He was also the voice behind fearless Steve Zodiac in *Fireball XL5*. When he joined *Coronation Street*, he was not prepared for the public reaction. 'People even stop me in the street and say: "Aren't you Elsie's boyfriend?"' His wife Mary took it more in her stride: 'I see this as just another part. After all, I have seen Paul in the arms of so many attractive women in films and on TV.'

THE YANKS ARE HERE

Elsie Tanner was sent into a spin when the Americans returned to the old air base at Burtonwood. Her pal Dot Greenhalgh reported that Elsie's old flame Steve Tanner was back in town. At first Elsie didn't want to meet Steve, but curiosity got the better of her. Steve was keen to see more of Elsie, promising her the years had been kind, but at first she was reluctant, where could it possibly lead? It led, four months later, to their wedding in a Warrington Methodist Church.

To celebrate Elsie and Steve's forthcoming wedding, producer Jack Rosenthal decided to give the cast a well-earned treat: 'I went to see Cecil Bernstein and said "For years and years, these people have been coming into the studio every Monday morning and working until Friday night. I think it's a treadmill and we need to break it."' Rosenthal proposed that instead of recording two episodes in studio all the cast should be taken into the countryside, put up in a plush hotel, and an episode filmed there, the excuse being Elsie's hen party and Steve's stag party outings. This would mean only one episode being made that week but it would cost the same as two. He was amazed when Bernstein agreed and gleefully went off to tell the cast. He was not prepared for their reaction, what he had mistakenly thought of as a boring treadmill they all cherished as a precious routine. 'When they got out into the country they hated it. One of them hated walking on grass because there were worms in it, another one couldn't act in the open air because of the butterflies, and they drove me crazy for the whole week. I went mad and I regretted it.'

KEN'S PRINCIPLES

The two Barlow brothers' marriages were placed under a lot of strain in 1967. In March Ken spent seven days in prison, and in November David's wife Irma miscarried their longed-for child. Ken had taken part on a banned student demonstration. He tried to explain his actions to Valerie: 'Val, the right to free speech is basic. If we let it be challenged without making any kind of protest, where are we going to finish up?' but she could not understand how he could put his principles before his family: 'Now look, Ken, you've got two kids up those stairs . . . Your duty's to them, not a bunch of larking students who've hardly got their nappies off!' Valerie had one basic concern, the well-being and care of her family, while Ken thought his own intelligence and principles came higher up on life's scale. Valerie was stunned when rather than paying a £5 fine in court he decided to go to prison for seven days.

It was David who felt out in the cold when Irma miscarried. Valerie and Irma's mother Hilda closed ranks around distraught Irma and David was left on the sidelines. Actress Sandra Gough received many letters from women who had lost babies: 'They said we're glad that you did it sensitively – that wasn't me, that was the writers, of course – but the way it was portrayed and everything was nice and they understood and it was very real.'

Returning to Die

Since leaving *Coronation Street* in 1964, actor Ivan Beavis had found television producers were not interested in him because his face was still linked with the Street. In the summer of 1967 he was offered a week's work. His girlfriend Doreen Keogh – who played Concepta Hewitt – had minutes before been asked for two weeks. 'I said bloody hell, they're going to kill me off and you're staying for the funeral!' In the script Harry and Concepta returned to the Street for Elsie Tanner's wedding. After the wedding, Harry was to go with Len Fairclough to see a mate. On the way the van would break down, be jacked up on bricks and these would slip, crushing Harry underneath. The scene seemed fine on paper but the stunt man had not been told that he was going to have to lie under a van jacked up on bricks, so he refused to do the scene. The van was then jacked up out of vision, with a strong jack and the bricks, but when Ivan was placed under the van, he noticed that someone had forgotten to put the real jack in position and the van really was only held up by bricks. The camera had started to roll: 'I thought it's not worth stopping now, so we did it. I wasn't under there for very long. Then I came out and they put the dummy under.' Ivan was watching with the director and the cameraman was getting ready to film the dummy: 'And this van just went bang, and split the dummy's head in two as fast as that. And all I could think was "That could have been me".'

Ken's spell in prison cracked the Barlows' marriage. Valerie was furious that he thought more of his principles than his family.

The news of Harry's death was broken to his daughter Lucille by Jack Walker. The scenes that followed were full of grief and anger, Jennifer could not understand why Harry had to die. 'I didn't see why he couldn't come back for good. To bring him back to finish him off was just a reminder of what had gone on in 1964.' This feeling was shared by many members of the public. In the *Evening News* (14 September 1967) a viewer wrote "Surely if future episodes excluded the appearance of Hewitt it would have been better to let him live happily ever after in Ireland. This would have saved the pain and

·1967·

tears of Concepta and Lucille, the bitter self-reproaches of Len Fairclough and the overall atmosphere of sadness.' A reporter in the *Daily Record* (14 September) agreed, but pointed out it was 'Compulsive viewing, of course. I've cancelled all my Monday and Wednesday engagements for the next couple of years.'

OBJECT OF DESIRE

1967 brought a succession of boyfriends for Emily Nugent, manageress of the Gamma boutique. In January, she returned to the Street after a six-month break nursing her father (Eileen Derbyshire had actually been giving birth to a son, Oliver) and establishing herself in the Corner Shop flat. Miss Nugent was given a new, youthful 'with it' look and the old Gamma set was transformed into a swinging his-and-hers boutique, with Lucille running the 'dolls' section and Dennis the 'guys'. As Eileen remembers: 'They decided Emily must be sort of glamorized and she was fixed up with a blind date, and all that sort of thing.' The blind date was Brian Thomas, a nervous character who had first appeared the previous year with his friend Ron Jenkins (played by Ben Kingsley). Brian fell heavily for Emily, alarming her as he was ten years younger than her. She got rid of him in a gentle way, by encouraging him to take out a girl his own age. Shortly afterwards, she joined a dating agency and had her first screen kiss with farmer Frank Starkey. He planned to propose but she discovered she was allergic to his cows. Hotelier Douglas Preston followed and he *did* propose marriage, but only to escape his domineering sister. At the end of the year, Emily was no closer to marriage than at the beginning.

Brian Thomas's declaration of love startled Miss Nugent.

THE END OF AN ERA

Viewing figures had risen during the Tanner wedding episodes but, by the end of the year, they were down to six million again. Not even a special Christmas edition, showing the Tanners leaving for a new life in America, helped. A National Opinion Poll, aimed at finding out what people liked and disliked on television, was conducted on 11 August. 1,998 people throughout the country were polled and nineteen percent of them said that *Coronation Street* was their favourite programme, making it the most popular TV programme. The programme was more popular in the south; sixteen percent of those polled in the north said it was their least favourite programme. *Coronation Street* director Richard Everitt was approached by Cecil Bernstein to take over the show as producer. Everitt agreed, on condition that he could radically alter the structure of the show. In a memo dated 11 October 1967, Everitt states: 'My intention is to make *Coronation Street* into a vehicle which will be able to reflect contemporary attitudes in a modern community.' The memo went on to lay down plans that would change the programme, the Street itself and its characters for good.

Street Wedding OF THE CENTURY

·1967·

The wedding of Elsie Tanner to Stephen Edward Tanner, US Army Master Sgt, stands as a milestone in the history of *Coronation Street*. Never before had a fictitious television wedding had such an impact on a programme, its viewers and the nation's press. The whole wedding process had been set in motion on screen in July 1967 when Steve proposed to Elsie, his war-time sweetheart. When Elsie accepted Steve's proposal, hundreds of viewers reached for their pens to write to actress Pat Phoenix to wish her all the luck in the world; for seven years they had followed her heartbreaks and felt sure that this time Elsie had met her Prince Charming.

Almost immediately after Steve gave Elsie a diamond engagement ring, writer Jack Rosenthal took over as the programme's producer, H.V. Kershaw having moved on. Rosenthal for one was not happy with the prospect of marrying off the Street's sex symbol. 'I never liked the story, I never liked the idea of the romance with the American. Those days had been and gone with Elsie Tanner, before the programme ever began. Twenty years before.' The producer wasn't alone in his concern; In her autobiography, Pat Phoenix recalled one furious viewer writing threatening letters to her, Rosenthal and the actor playing Steve, Paul Maxwell. The police had to be called in to caution him when he threatened to knife the three as they left the studios.

As soon as the wedding date, 4 September was announced on screen, the action off-screen began to hot up. In the *Daily Mirror* 12 August 1967, Jack Rosenthal reported that he was receiving letters from viewers asking for the date to be changed as they would be on holiday and unable to see it. Pat Phoenix refused to let Granada's wardrobe department have anything to do with Elsie's wedding dress and persuaded the studio to commission her own dressmaker, Patti Burgoine, to design and make the outfit. Phoenix told *TV Post*'s Kate Donnelly (30 August 1967): 'The dress won't be a terribly ostentatious affair. It will, sensibly enough, be within the not very substantial budget of Elsie Tanner. But *I* think it will cause a stir.' *TV Times* produced a special thirty-two page souvenir of the wedding, which sold over one million copies. A series of pages were devoted to the dress; a 'scoop-necked, fitted sheath style in champagne-coffee ribbon lace lined with matching duchesse satin'. The day before the wedding, national newspapers reported that the bride would be carrying a spray of pale green orchids and lemon roses – details noone could pick up as the episodes were transmitted in black and white.

Back at the *Coronation Street* offices, secretaries collated all the telegrams and cards and the 546 wedding presents received were stored for the happy couple to open after their 'honeymoon'. Pat Phoenix insisted on seeing each present and promised to write back to everyone who had written to her. Jack Rosenthal began to worry that Phoenix was taking the wedding a little *too* seriously when a gentleman from H. Samuels, the jewellers, visited him: 'This man came up and he had a jewellery box of rings, an array of rings on red velvet, and I said

'With the possible exception of the Elizabeth-Philip show, Elsie Tanner's wedding has been the biggest thing of its kind ever to be presented on television.'

***Daily Record*, 7 September 1967**

·1967·

well, what's this? He said it's for Elsie's wedding, choose a ring. He said Miss Phoenix contacted us and wondered if we'd come along so you could choose. I said, we get our rings from props, they're not worth anything and they don't cost anything, they're made of paste!'

On the night of the screening of the wedding, photographs of the happy couple and guides to 'Who's Who at the Wedding' appeared in every national and local paper, and the next day the same papers reported back on the upset caused by the episode. The wedding took place over two episodes, the first one ending as Elsie arrived at the church. Viewers were left waiting to find out if she would actually marry her Yank. As Kenneth Oddy reported in the *Telegraph and Argus*: 'Could there still be a hitch? Will Len Fairclough decide at the last moment not to "hold his peace"?'

Viewers never got to see Elsie and Steve fly away.

On Wednesday 6 September the second instalment of the wedding was screened, with Elsie and Steve exchanging vows. In *TV World* romantic novelist Barbara Cartland wrote a two-page open letter to Elsie, advising her on how to keep her husband happy: 'If love dies, it will be your fault. . . . So many women forget that love is like a plant – it grows or dies – and if you don't tend it, then, inevitably, it withers.'

9.45 million homes had tuned into the Monday's episode, 9.20 to Wednesday's, making them the most watched programmes that week. (In third place was *The Bruce Forsyth Show*, and fourth was *World in Action*). Despite this, the network was flooded with requests for the wedding to be screened again. For many viewers, Ena Sharples had stolen the show from the bride when, waiting in the church, she commented to Minnie Caldwell: 'The organ wants to play *March of the Gladiators* when she comes in and *March of Time* when she goes out.' On Wednesday 20 September it was repeated at 9pm.

James Pettigrew in the *Sunday Mirror*, 10 September posed the question: 'Elsie's wedding: Are we all going mad? . . . I'm even getting letters from readers wanting to know if the wedding is real or just "something on telly".' In *The Sunday Times*, Ruth Hall argued against those who said that all the pageantry and pomp was too alien to the Street's working-class roots: 'The trouble is that the characters are only too real. They are small, narrow and boring. They shout endlessly about trivia and mean nauseatingly well under their harsh exteriors. Now that the first impact on romantic southern intellectuals of documentary drama about the industrial north has worn off, such characters no longer command intelligent interest.'

One person who had become totally confused by the reality of the situation was Pat Phoenix. On the day the episodes were filmed, a huge church set dominated the studio and the cast were assembled in

their characters' best clothes and hats. The time came for the bride to appear, but Jack Rosenthal received word from the studio floor that Pat Phoenix was refusing to leave her dressing-room. Rosenthal went down and knocked on the door: 'She said, "I'm not coming out." I said "You've got to come out, we're all waiting to shoot, you've got to come out, it's the wedding scene." She said, "That's why". And that's precisely what it was and this mood had been prevalent and increased during the run up.' Eventually, Pat let him in: 'I sat and held her hand and she said, "Don't you understand, it's my wedding day." . . . . I held her hand and I did what you do with a bride, with your daughter, and I said "You're beautiful and you're radiant and it's going to be the most wonderful wedding. Come on now, I want you to go out there." I couldn't believe it was happening, but it did happen, and she came out and walked down the aisle.'

The Street held two receptions for Elsie and Steve, one as part of the programme, and an earlier one where the residents posed for the TV Times *supplement. Steve never kissed Ena on screen*

'Nowadays, you almost have to have an inspection at the door of the studio, take their fur coats away from them and put the dirt *back* under their fingernails.'

Michael Cox, *Street* producer 1967-68

Rovers Jack and Annie Walker • Lucille Hewitt • Emily Nugent (April - Dec.)

No. 1 Albert Tatlock (Jan. - June)

No. 3 Dickie and Audrey Fleming (June - Dec.)

No. 5 Minnie Caldwell • Jenny Sutton (April - May) • Ena Sharples (May - June)

No. 9 Ken, Val, Peter and Susan Barlow (Jan. - June) • Len Fairclough (June - Dec.) Ray Langton (July - Dec.)

No. 11 Elsie (Feb. - Dec.) Dennis (Jan. - June) and Jenny (May - June) Tanner • Hippies (Jan.) • Ray Langton (July) • Dot Greenhalgh (Aug. - Sept.)

No. 13 Stan and Hilda Ogden

Shop David and Irma Barlow (Jan. - April) • Jill Morris (Jan.) • Les (April - June) and Maggie (April - Dec.) Clegg

Shop flat Emily Nugent (Jan. - April) Gordon Clegg (April - Dec.)

No. 16 (Mission) Ena Sharples (Jan.)

Maisonettes No. 4 Effie Spicer (June - Dec.) **No. 6** Ena Sharples (June - Dec.) **No. 14** Ken, Val, Peter and Susan Barlow (June - Dec.)

Non-residents Miklos Zadic Dave Smith • Myra Booth

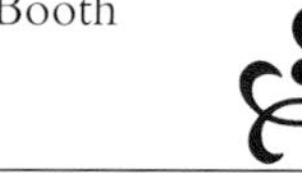

·1968·

FURS FOR THE CAST AND A FACE-LIFT FOR THE STREET

In April 1968, the producers of *Coronation Street* invited a journalist to spend a week watching how the programme was made. Ann Leslie of the *Sunday Mirror* was given the unheard-of licence to roam the rehearsal rooms, taking photographs and interviewing the cast. The three-week series that followed reported faithfully on the cast's attitudes to fame and money, and the producers' concerns that the Street, once praised for its social realism, had become far too cosy. After years of rep and touring companies, the cast revelled in the security the Street had brought them, as Pat Phoenix told Ann Leslie: "What furs have I got? Let's see. Two minks, a Persian lamb, a sable coat, three mink stoles, sable tie, a pony skin coat, black fox fur and an antelope coat trimmed with mink.'

Criticisms were levelled at the programme by critics who thought the Street had lost its sharp edge.

COMINGS AND GOINGS

1968 saw many changes of residence in the Street, with residents coming and going throughout the year. Dennis Tanner married and moved away to Bristol in May. At his wedding reception, Jerry Booth announced he had had enough of the area and he also moved on. In April, the Corner Shop was sold because David and Irma Barlow were emigrating to Australia where David had been offered a career as a professional footballer. Emily Nugent lost her home in the flat above when the Corner Shop was sold, and was taken in by the Walkers as a paying guest at the Rovers. The Cleggs, Les, Maggie and Gordon, moved into the shop, but two months later Les left to live in a hospital in a bid to cure his alcoholism. After four years of standing vacant, No.3 was finally sold – to teenagers Dickie and Audrey Fleming. Ena Sharples was made homeless in January when the Mission Hall, her home for thirty years, was demolished. She moved in with Minnie at No.5 for a while before moving into one of the new maisonettes built on the site of the Mission. Her neighbours were pensioner Effie Spicer and the Barlow family from No.9. They had sold their house for £1,000 to Len Fairclough. He took Ray Langton in as a lodger after Ray had upset landlady Elsie Tanner by making a pass at her. Elsie returned from America to No.11 in March, having separated from Steve. Towards the end of the year Albert Tatlock left the Street to live as resident caretaker at a museum in Bury.

Michael Cox produced the Street from November 1967 to February 1968. He told Ann Leslie that he was in agreement with the critics, and going a step further said he felt the cast's prosperity had taken over the characters. In an article he wrote at the time, Cox attempted to explain why the writers and production team refused to use the programme to tackle issues: 'There is a growing drug problem in this country, which has as much of a hold in Manchester as anywhere, and one doesn't want to ignore it, but any portrayal of an addict would probably encourage imitation rather than understanding. . . . The dilemma is obvious and acute; the popularity and "reality" of the show impose their own restrictions. It isn't that one is afraid of offending people so much as misinforming or even terrifying them.'

Richard Everitt took over from Michael Cox as producer of the Street early in and decided the time had come to drastically change the appearance of the programme. Everitt had been involved with the programme since the dry runs, for which he worked as Floor Manager before becoming a director. When he was invited to be producer, Everitt agreed on the condition that he could change the physical environment: 'The cardboard façade of the Street in the studio in 1968 was ridiculous. The lighting was quite appalling and you could only shoot really close up to it, and that was awful. I wanted to build it outside. Although it was a story about a backstreet community, it was not coming up to date, because in real life most of those streets were being demolished.'

When Tony Warren and Denis Parkin had roamed Salford back in November 1960 looking for real streets on which to base the design of *Coronation Street*, they selected Archie Street as the model. The opening titles were filmed in Archie Street, and over the years the residents' lives had been monitored by the press. Archie Street had another claim to fame – Eddie Colman, the Manchester United player killed in the Munich air crash had been born there. In 1968, the authorities began to move families out of Archie Street (although it would not be demolished until 1971) in accordance with Council planning. In the *News of the World*, John Jarrett reported: 'In 1963, Manchester and Salford planned to have the very last terraced house down in eight years. There wouldn't be any Coronation Streets left anywhere in Manchester or nearby. And the men behind Coronation Street knew it.'

Everitt dismissed the idea of flattening the whole Street: 'I suggested that half the street, which was the raincoat factory and Mission, should be redeveloped by the local council, into flats. Then we could bring in new people.' In a memo to Granada executives, Everitt explained why new flats would be an asset: 'Dramatically, it is a device to bring the old into

'Elsie's a sparrow in a dirty street. She wouldn't survive in an aviary with birds of paradise. She tried it once – and they nearly pecked her to death.'

The building of the maisonettes became a long-running story, with Stan Ogden working as a labourer. He was sacked for scalding the foreman's foot with boiling water.

conflict with the new, to change the street, but at the same time to retain some of its time-worn flavour.' The executives agreed the plans and an old railway yard 200 yards away from the studios was acquired. Denis Parkin was asked back to oversee the building of the Street, costed at £3,400. Parkin had the studio set moved to the railway yard and a brick frontage built in front of the old set: 'I found a couple of bricklayers that lived near me and they came and did it. Joiners transferred the windows from the old plywood street to the bricks, built half a roof and then started shooting on it. I think it was probably about eighteen months after that Harry Kershaw found some more money and I built the backs in the back yard.'

By April 1968, the outside set was completed and seven maisonettes had been built on the site of the factory. The original idea had been to fill them up with new characters but in the end only three were occupied and only one of those was by a new character. The majority of the new characters were moved into the terrace.

Takeover at the Shop

Alan Rothwell decided he wanted to leave the show early in 1968: 'I had never wanted to be in the same thing for ever and eventually in the Street I became unhappy. . . . I couldn't continue to play the same part.' The writers decided to bring a new family in to run the shop and considered the character of

George Greenwood. Greenwood had been seen early in the year as a friend of Hilda Ogden. He was played by Arthur Pentelow (later Mr Wilkes in *Emmerdale Farm*). Everitt felt that Greenwood would not quite fit in behind the counter and the Clegg family were created.

The family had a dark secret – father Les was an alcoholic – and over the first few months their painful story was told. Les struggled to keep sober, while wife Maggie and son Gordon lived in fear of the day when he would succumb. When he did, it led to high drama in the shop as Les hit Maggie around the head whereupon Gordon knocked his father unconscious in order to save her. Les was moved to a hospital to dry out and he never returned to the family home.

Dennis Tanner grows up

Shortly after the Barlows emigrated, viewers saw the final appearance of one of the original cast, the immensely popular Dennis Tanner. For years he had provided light relief at No.11, but Philip Lowrie had had enough: 'I did get very tired of him being Peter Pan. I always looked younger than I was and I didn't mind playing down a bit, but I just wanted him to grow up as an adult. When I left I was thirty-two, and he was still about twenty-two. They wouldn't let him grow up.'

Dennis fell in love. For the first time he was allowed to enter a serious, grown-up relationship which led eventually to marriage and a new life in

·1968·

Looking ahead to a new future together, the Barlows plan to start afresh in Australia. Before they go they reveal that Irma is pregnant with a longed-for child.

Bristol. The bride was Cockney Jenny Sutton and the courtship was played out under the watchful eye of Elsie Tanner. Elsie disliked Jenny as she reminded her too much of herself and refused to allow the couple to share a bed. Suddenly, towards the end of the Swinging Sixties, sex had reared its head in the Street.

SEX IN THE STREET

Elsie moved Jenny out of No.11 and into No.5 where she lodged with Mrs Caldwell. Dennis was amazed by Elsie's hypocrisy when it came to family morals: 'By what right do you account yerself a Guardian of Public Morals?' Elsie explained to Len Fairclough why she would not have Jenny in the house: 'I got the measure of 'er in one. Female version of our Dennis. An' you know what they say about the female of the species bein' deadlier than the male?' As she packed Jenny off for the night Elsie apologized for Dennis's clumsiness in matters of the heart: 'It's my fault, love, I never taught 'im the facts of life.' 'That's all right,

Irene Sutcliffe (Maggie Clegg)

★ **Irene Sutcliffe** had been trained at LAMDA and had travelled widely with the Old Vic Theatre Company all over Europe, America and the Middle East. She had worked with Laurence Olivier's company and had been in Olivier's film version of *Richard the Third*. She had vast experience of acting on the West End stage, including a year in *The Mousetrap*. Despite all this she was petrified of making her first entrance as Maggie: 'I remember my heart thumping, waiting for my first entrance outside the shop, and Pat {Phoenix} saying "Oh, you'll be all right chuck."'

★ **Bill Kenwright's** story of how he came to be employed by Granada sounds like a plot for a Hollywood Stage Door classic – eighteen-year-old boy calls on television company as he is passing, bluffs his way into the building, knocks on casting director's door, is given a script to read and lands part starting straightaway, earning 65 guineas. 'I phoned my mum from the phonebox outside the lift and said, "Eh Mum, I'm an actor, and they're paying me 65 guineas. Bill's first part at Granada was in the series *The Villains* and this led to many roles in series and plays there. When he was offered the Street, Bill was not keen as he had ambitions to play Shakespeare in London and did not want to commit himself to a long-running role. However, Granada persisted, knowing he was just right for Gordon Clegg. Finally, he told his mother: 'She took hold of my hand and she pulled me to the phone. She phoned my Gran, my Auntie Beth, my Auntie Marie, my Uncle George and said, "Just tell him, all I want in life is to walk through our town with my son on my arm and for them to say there's that lad with his mother." The next morning I went in and said, "Can I sign for just a year" and that was that.'

love, I did!' said Jenny, slamming the door in Elsie's face.

A couple of doors down the Street, Emily Nugent was falling in love with Hungarian Miklos Zadic. They danced barefoot together and she allowed him to unpin her hair. When he went to work in Newcastle, the residents were stunned when their resident Miss Prim grabbed her chance for love and went to visit him for a long weekend. On her return, she told Valerie Barlow that she had given herself to him and had no regrets.

Someone who did have regrets was Jerry Booth. Early in the year his estranged wife Myra turned up hoping for a reconciliation. The seduction scenes were quite risqué for the Street, and no-one was surprised when the executives began to panic as rehearsals started. Susan Jameson recalls: 'He was allowed to look as though he had no clothes on but I wasn't. I was setting out to get him into bed and I had to wear winceyette pyjamas. I was furious.'

·1968·

Philip Lowrie's decision to leave the Street caused a rift between him and the actress who had played his mother for eight years. Lowrie was consulted in the casting of Jenny Sutton: "I chose Mitzi Rogers because I thought she was strong and she could stand up to Pat. By this time Pat and I weren't speaking at all; Pat didn't speak to me from the moment she found out that I was leaving.'

Emily Nugent lost her heart – and virginity – to Hungarian Miklos Zadic.

Myra Booth returned to seduce estranged husband Jerry. An opinion poll at the time showed that the majority of viewers thought Myra should win Jerry back, but Graham Haberfield had already decided that six years of playing Jerry was enough. He resigned and then left the programme in May.

Another actress who was furious was Jennifer Moss. Her character Lucille was now in her late teens and as virginal as she had been at the age of eleven. Whilst the world was experiencing the Pill, Free Love and Flower Power, Lucille, the only teenager in the programme, was protected from the outside world by the writers. Jennifer Moss remembers asking H.V. Kershaw if Lucille could possibly have a coloured boyfriend, but he told her it was out of the question. In her articles, Ann Leslie raised the Lucille question: 'Fear of being accused of provoking anti-social or immoral behaviour has continually hampered producers. Should they allow nineteen-year-old Lucille to lose her virginity before marriage? Or will that make thousands of parents think that the programme is telling their children. If Lucille can do it so can you"?'

VALERIE THE HOSTAGE

When the maisonettes were completed they were soon occupied. Ena moved into an OAP ground-floor flat, as did newcomer Mrs Effie Spicer. Above these ladies' flats was a two-storey maisonette which was rented by the Barlow family after they had sold No.9 to Len Fairclough.

Towards the end of 1968, the writers created one of the most dramatic storylines to date. Ken was working on a school play and the children asleep in their beds when an escaped convict forced his way into the maisonette and held Valerie captive. To make matters worse he was a convicted rapist. Valerie told him that she was alone, praying that the children would not wake up. She had agreed with Mrs Sharples to bang on the water pipes when in trouble; making an excuse about a faulty tap, she banged away with a hammer only to wake up one of the twins. Riley used the twins as a threat, telling Val that unless she complied to his wishes he would harm them.

The story was spread over two episodes. In the second, Riley knew the police were outside. He told Valerie that he might as well have some fun whilst he was there. As he grabbed her she screamed, and the police burst through the window. For Anne Reid it was the most thrilling storyline: 'I was used to doing light sort of comedy scenes with Bill [Roache] and suddenly I had this drama. It was so exciting.' Viewed now, over twenty years later, the episodes are still as terrifying as when they were first shown.

The story did not end with Riley's capture because Ken refused to believe Valerie when she said she had not been raped. The incident drove a wedge between them. She realized he would have preferred it if she had been raped so that he could be the injured party: 'I'm just a thing now; a thing you've got. And all you're interested in is keeping it polished. And if anything happened to me you wouldn't lift a finger to help me. Because you don't love me. You love yourself.'

Valerie's ordeal at the hands of Riley marked a turning-point in the Barlow marriage. She shied away from him physically and emotionally.

★ Three new young faces arrived on the screens in 1968. One of them had appeared in the programme in 1966, **Neville Buswell**, who had played borstal boy Ray Langton who tried to lure Lucille Hewitt into bed. Ray now returned and set his sights on Elsie Tanner! After fighting him off, Len took Langton in at No.9 and made him a partner in his firm. Neville Buswell always knew he wanted to act: 'My parents were publicans and there is no history of the theatre in my family, but even as a boy, at boarding school, I wanted to be an actor.' After training at RADA he took a role in *Emergency Ward 10*. The Street casting director saw him and offered him the part of Ray.

The other youngsters, eighteen-year-old Dickie Fleming and his sixteen-year-old bride Audrey, bought No.5 for £400 and settled into premature middle-age. Nineteen-year-old **Gillian McCann** was cast as Audrey. She came from Birkenhead and left school to work in an office at a print's work before training at the Guildhall School of Music and Drama. She never finished the course because she landed the part of Audrey in the middle of her second year, 'I just couldn't believe it. A part in *Coronation Street* for my first professional job!' she told a reporter. Her screen partner was played by seventeen-year-old **Nigel Humphreys**. He had worked at the National Youth Theatre and came from Bognor Regis. He hid his southern accent to land the part after two months on the dole. 'The audition took about an hour and a half. I was worried in case they didn't take to my fake northern accent.'

'It's a long hard road to matrimonial harmony. No wonder there's so many falls by the wayside.'

Ena Sharples commenting on the struggling Flemings at No.3.

Rovers Jack and Annie Walker • Lucille Hewitt (Jan. - Aug.) • Emily Nugent

No. 1 Albert Tatlock (July - Dec.) • Effie Spicer (Jan. - May) • Alice Pickens (April - May/July - Sept.)

No. 3 Dickie and Audrey Fleming • Ray Langton (July-Aug./Nov. - Dec.)

No. 5 Minnie Caldwell • Alice Pickens (April) • Ray Langton (Sept. - Oct.)

No. 9 Len Fairclough • Ray Langton (Jan. - July) • Janice Langton (Feb. - March)

No. 11 Elsie Tanner • Emily Nugent (Jan. - Feb.) • Bernard and Sandra Butler (Nov. - Dec.)

No. 13 Stan and Hilda Ogden • Irma Barlow (Dec.)

Shop Maggie Clegg

shop flat Gordon Clegg (Jan. - March) Cyril and Betty Turpin (June - Dec.)

Maisonettes No. 4 Effie Spicer (Jan.)
No. 6 Ena Sharples (Jan. - June)
No. 14 Ken, Val, Peter and Susan Barlow

Non-residents Dot Greenhalgh • Dave Smith • Ernie Bishop • Alan Howard

COMINGS AND GOINGS

While living away in Bury, Albert Tatlock sub-let his house to Effie Spicer. She took Alice Pickens in for a while, before leaving the area. Albert threw Alice out when he returned, having given up working at the museum. Lodgers became fashionable in 1969 – Minnie took in Alice, and then Ray Langton. For a while Ray's sister Janice had lodged at No.9 before making off in Dave Smith's Jag with £500 in cash. Elsie Tanner's nephew and niece, accident-prone Bernard and man-mad Sandra Butler, descended upon her, and Maggie Clegg was not too pleased when her bossy sister Betty Turpin moved into the shop flat to 'keep an eye on her'. Gordon took a job as an accountant in London whilst his one-time fiancée Lucille Hewitt left in August to live in Ireland. Ena Sharples had never felt comfortable in her modern maisonette and moved out in June. She took the flat over Ernie Bishop's camera shop on Rosamund Street.

·1969·

ANNIE WALKER, THE BIGOT

Early in 1969, Billy Walker returned to the Street after a long absence, showing off his girlfriend, Jasmine Choong. He had plans to make her Mrs Walker and was somewhat puzzled by the violent way in which Annie opposed the plan. Emily Nugent, the Walkers' paying guest, was happy to have Jasmine sharing her room but was disgusted with Annie's behaviour – although pleasant to her face she made bitter, bitchy comments about her behind her back. Annie had decided that her son must not marry a Chinese girl and feigned a nervous breakdown, making herself an invalid to play on his sympathy and to try and scare her off. Kenneth Farrington enjoyed his part but has one complaint about the way he was always written in with beautiful women: 'I found that I would be coming back and doing all the acting, but because they looked so great the camera would be on them all the time. They would have wonderful close-ups because they were so pretty and lovely, and I was always a voice off.'

The writers allowed Annie to drop her mask of social politeness to Jasmine when Jasmine broke the news that Billy had proposed. Annie pulled herself up in bed and shrieked at the girl: 'No! No! He's not marrying you! I didn't bring him up for this! You are *not* marrying my Billy. I will not *allow* it!!!' Jasmine was quick to retort: 'I don't think it matters, Mrs Walker, because when I describe you to my mother and father *they* will not allow it either.' Billy was furious when Jasmine turned down his proposal, explaining she could not bear to be related to someone so obviously bigoted. The relationship finished and Billy swore he would never talk to Annie again.

Annie's bigotry was not the first racial story in the Street. In 1963, Len Fairclough had lost a coloured bus conductor his job when he falsely said he had paid a fare and the conductor must have pocketed it. The man lost his job without an enquiry as he was black.

Lucille Hewitt had grown up on the Street and many viewers longed to witness her church wedding to Gordon. They, and Lucille, were to be disappointed.

ALWAYS A BRIDESMAID, NEVER A BRIDE

Towards the end of 1968, teenagers Lucille Hewitt and Gordon Clegg had run off together, planning to elope to Gretna Green and return as man and wife. Both Annie Walker, Lucille's guardian, and Maggie Clegg had opposed the courtship, feeling the pair were too young to throw away their lives. A delayed train at Preston station led to the couple returning home unmarried, but they were now encouraged to pursue a more conventional engagement. A white wedding was planned for Easter and Lucille chose a full-length grown and veil. Whilst the writers were busy penning the service Bill Kenwright dropped a bombshell. He reminded producer H.V. Kershaw that he had only signed up for a year and had no intention of staying longer: 'I just wanted to act. That was all I wanted to do. I said I'm really thrilled and grateful and all of that, but I don't want to stay after my year. They were really upset and the story had to be changed really quickly.'

·1969·

The writers chose to let Gordon have a change of heart and jilt Lucille as she tried on her wedding dress. Jennifer Moss feels the story worked better with Lucille being jilted but would have liked to have seen her become a married woman: 'I thought they should have married her off, but not to Gordon. I don't think that would have been the right marriage. I think marriage to Ray Langton would have had the fire in it. It wouldn't have lasted but there could have been a lot of mileage in it.' While Annie Walker smarted about her jilted ward and threatened to sue Gordon for breach of promise, Maggie was delighted at her son's commonsense. However, Gordon was very ashamed of his actions and left the Street to work in London, leaving Maggie alone at the shop.

★**Betty Driver** was born in Leicester but, by her own admission, never had a childhood; her stage-struck mother pushed her into performing and she had turned professional by the time she was eleven. At fourteen she made her first London stage appearance in a variety show at the Prince of Wales Theatre. She received a standing ovation. There followed a leading role in the revue, *Mr Tower of London*. In the 1930s and 1940s, Betty was a major recording artist, becoming famous for songs such as 'Jubilee Baby' and 'Sailor with the Navy Blue Eyes'. For seven and a half years she worked with legendary bandleader Henry Hall and his BBC Dance Orchestra and appeared in films like *Penny Paradise* and *Let's Be Famous*. Betty's first contact with the Street came in 1964 when she had auditioned for the part of Hilda Ogden: 'I'm glad I didn't get it; I couldn't have lived my life with curlers in!' and the following year she starred in the Street spin-off *Pardon the Expression* with Arthur Lowe.

BETTY TURPIN – A BREATH OF FRESH AIR

Maggie Clegg was just beginning to adjust to living alone when her elder sister Betty bustled in with husband Cyril. Betty said she wanted to help, but Maggie feared she would take over – and she did. The scripts called for the sisters to be completely different and director Howard Baker thought he knew the ideal Betty. He had directed a stage play, *The Love Birds*, in which Betty Driver had appeared. He told Kershaw that Betty would be perfect for the role and she was tracked down to where she was running the pub with her sister, Freda, having decided to give up show business. Betty recalls how Kershaw approached her. 'He came round to see me and said "Instead of just pulling pints here why don't you come and do it at the Rovers?"' Before she began, Betty had a throat operation and was not allowed to talk for six weeks. She discovered she had lost her confidence and could barely whisper. 'So I came in on the Monday and Arthur Leslie, God love his face, said "Don't worry, Betty, I will always be with you in the bar. I shall always be there and every time you're going to say a line, you'll know I''m there because you'll feel my foot on your foot or I'll put my hand on the middle of your back, you'll know I'm there." And do you know, I got through, it was wonderful – he never left me. It was through Arthur that I really got my confidence back.'

Betty Turpin – dark-haired, bossy, loud and big-boned – visually dominated her sister Maggie – blonde, quiet, gentle and slim – and it did not take long for Maggie to become depressed as Betty took over the shop, rearranged everything and tried to organize Maggie's personal life. When Annie Walker went on holiday for a couple of weeks

Maggie sold Jack the idea of employing Betty as jovial barmaid. he did and she has remained there for over twenty-five years.

Albert Meets His Match

Lucille and Gordon were not the only couple planning a wedding in 1969. Just after the teenagers split up two pensioners celebrated an engagement. Albert Tatlock was seventy-four years old when he was forced into proposing to sixty-nine-year-old Alice Pickens – 'forced' because he had taken a fall, broken his arm, and needed someone to look after him around the clock. As soon as Alice had accepted Albert started to plan the service and hymns, and Valerie Barlow agreed to be Matron of Honour – thrilled as she was with the prospect of someone taking on her grumpy uncle. Unfortunately, Alice never became Mrs Tatlock. Both she and Albert turned up at the church, but the vicar's car broke down and he was an hour late. By the time he turned up Alice and Albert decided they were fated never to wed and had parted company. Doris Hare remembers her time as Alice as being fun and light-hearted: 'It was a very comic character and I've always thought comedy is so important. It's the hardest thing of the whole lot, and the most exhausting.'

Colour

The year 1969 stands out as the turning-point in how *Coronation Street* was made. Throughout the 1960s, every episode was recorded as live and actors carried on regardless of mistakes, wrong camera movements or fluffed lines. In 1969 that all changed. *Coronation Street* was forced to embrace bright, stunning colour. All the cameras had to be realigned and the technicians struggled to balance the colours. Scenes had to be stopped halfway through as colours flared, and for the first time the cast faced re-takes and pick-ups. These quickly became the norm with the material moving on to tape rather than film. Once the Street was recorded on tape it could be easily edited and studio days stopped being so terrifying for all involved. Not many people wanted the programme to become colour, as Bill Roache explains: 'Everyone said it's a black-and-white show, that colour would not assist it. There was always a sort of reluctance to change. We thought colour would not be good for it although it obviously enhanced it and had to happen.' Irene Sutcliffe was directly affected by the change to colour as her set, the Corner Shop, boasted row upon row of tins and packets which were a nightmare to balance. The designer had to paint them all with a dull grey wash to tone down the colours.

In 1970, journalist James Towler of *The Stage and Tevevision Today* attempted to explain why the Street did not look so good in colour: 'For some reason or other, colour hasn't improved the Street. People in whom one believed seemed to lose a touch of their authenticity. . . . Perhaps it is because, as in the cinema, there will always be some subjects that come

Nine years after turning down the part of Ena Sharples, Doris Hare MBE joined the cast as chirpy Alice Pickens, and set her beret at Albert Tatlock.

What the viewers should have seen – glamorous Elsie amidst the beauty of the Lakes.

over more effectively in black and white. *Coronation Street* has always reflected, in dramatic terms, the drabness, greyness and solidarity of the industrial north. This has been a major factor in its appeal.

COACH TRIP ENDS IN DISASTER

The first colour episode was to be transmitted on 29 October 1969. To mark the historic event, H.V. Kershaw storylined a street outing to the Lake District, showing off the beautiful colour of the north. The filming would take two days and the majority of the cast would be involved. Unfortunately, the technicians were not quite ready for colour and when it came to filming Kershaw only had black-and-white stock, but he was assured that the episode following the outing would be in glorious colour. This was no compensation as the next episode was played in hospital because the coach was to crash and all the residents injured. The first glimpse of colour was not Elsie Tanner walking in the glorious countryside but a bloodied Hilda Ogden searching hospital corridors for missing Stan. To make matters worse, some of the film sequences were to be used in the hospital episode as establishing shots. Viewed today the hospital episode is very strange as it starts with black and white titles, goes into colour studio scenes and has black and white filmed sequences scattered about in it.

The outing episode is very memorable, and includes many classic scenes between the characters, for example Annie's imperial speech to Jack, standing in the gardens at Brockhole: 'Doesn't it make you long for a more gracious age. For crinolines, yes crinolines. And scented cachous and lavender bags and China tea on the terrace.' The Ogdens, on the other hand, decided to go boating, a scene that Jean Alexander remembers with glee: 'We did the boat scene after lunch, when we'd had a couple of drinks. They took us to this little jetty, to a little rowing-boat, with the water lapping against it and we were there for about half an hour before we

Director Howard Baker turns the camera on Eileen Derbyshire for a crash reaction shot.

started to do anything. Bunny [Bernard Youens] sudenly said to me "I'm dying for a pee" and I said "Me too!" but it was a long way back to the hotel and we couldn't stop filming as the light would go. When we finally got into the boat there were these ducks floating about nearby and as soon as we started the dialogue they went QUACK, QUACK, QUACK, QUACK. So we had to start again. We did this about six times and Bunny suddenly said "I'll strangle those bloody ducks!" When we finally got it in the can we had this long walk back to the hotel, we daren't run of course. It was agonising.'

The filming of the coach crash was very time-consuming. There were shots of the residents' horrified faces as the coach veered off the roadside. The coach was then positioned, smashed into a tree with its windscreen shattered.

Filming the boat sequence. The Ogdens spent so long getting into the craft that they never actually took to water. 'Oh well,' said Hilda, 'at least we got a feel of it.'

★ The Casting Department at Granada took a gamble employing **Alan Browning** as Alan Howard. For nearly three years he had played Ellis Cooper in the BBC programme *The Newcomers*, but he refused to believe that viewers would not accept him in the Street: 'The immediate identification is of no importance. The public accepts actors as actors. Years before joining the Street, Alan Browning had worked as a journalist in his native Newcastle. Alan eventually left newspapers to follow the passion for acting he had nurtured in amateur dramatics. In 1968, he starred in a Granada series, *The War of Darkie Pilbeam*, written by Tony Warren and directed by Richard Everitt.

A NEW MAN FOR ELSIE

Elsie Tanner had had a rough couple of years since her return from America in 1969. Husband Steve had been murdered and Elsie was a prime suspect, then towards the end of 1969 she lost her job after appearing in court on a shop-lifting charge. As the year drew to a close she discovered she was falling in love. She tried her best to fight her feelings but as she confided in Valerie Barlow: 'Every time I look at him my knees give way.' *Him* was hairdresser Alan Howard who employed Elsie as receptionist at his Rosamund Street salon. For weeks, viewers urged Elsie on but they had to wait until New Year's Eve for handsome Alan to take Elsie in his arms and give her the kiss for which they had been waiting. As the 1960s ended the Street's sweetheart was heading towards her biggest romance yet.

The SEVENTIES

'I'm frightened. It's just that it's like a curse...Ken's family, like the Kennedys. Violence and sudden death. They don't grow old. I'm frightened of it. It's more than coincidence.'

Valerie Barlow

Rovers Jack (Jan. - June), Annie and Billy (Aug. Dec.) Walker • Lucille Hewitt (Feb. - Dec.) • Emily Nugent

No. 1 Albert Tatlock

No. 3 Dickie and Audrey Fleming (Jan. - June) • Ray Langton (Jan. - June)

No. 5 Minnie Caldwell • Joe Donnelli (Nov. Dec.)

No. 9 Len Fairclough • Ray Langton (June - Dec.)

No. 11 Elsie, Alan (June - Dec.) and Mark (Oct. - Nov.) Howard • Bernard (Jan. - May) and Sandra (Jan. - Aug.) Butler

No. 13 Stan and Hilda Ogden • Irma Barlow (April - July)

Shop Maggie Clegg

Shop flat Cyril and Betty Turpin (Jan. - July), Irma Barlow (July - Dec.) • Bet Lynch (July - Oct.)

Maisonettes No. 14 Ken, Val, Peter and Susan Barlow

Non-residents Dave Smith • Frank Bradley Ernie Bishop

COMINGS AND GOINGS

Billy Walker and Irma Barlow both returned home in 1970. Billy helped to run the Rovers following the death of his father Jack. Irma took a job running the shop following her husband David's death. Lucille Hewitt also returned to the Rovers, after living in Ireland for nearly a year. The Flemings left the Street in June following the break-up of their marriage and their lodger Ray Langton moved down the Street to No.9. Elsie Tanner married again; she became Mrs Alan Howard in June. Her new husband moved into No.11, and the Butlers moved out. For a month, Alan's son Mark lived with the couple and did his utmost to split them up. The Turpins vacated the shop flat to move into a semi in Hillside Crescent. Irma moved into the flat with her old friend Bet Lynch. In November Minnie Caldwell took American Joe Donnelli in as a lodger, completely unaware that he was a murderer. By the end of the year, he had held Irma captive in her flat before pulling a gun on Minnie.

·1970·

EVERYONE LOVES RAY LANGTON

The new decade started with a new producer, June Howson. June had directed the Street and had experience of drama, with *Family at War*, and comedy *Nearest and Dearest*. She was thrilled to be given the chance of running the Street, but discovered in her first week that she had to inform a handful of actors that their contracts would not be renewed. She recalls now that it was the worst thing she has ever had to do. The programme lost four of its young people – the Butlers and the Flemings. The writers decided to take advantage of the established relationships to ensure they left with a big dramatic story.

For over a year, Audrey Fleming and Ray Langton had enjoyed a mild flirtation which had climaxed on the coach outing. Dickie had fought Ray when Ray had enticed Audrey away. Later, when the coach crashed, Ray was thrown through the windscreen and came to in hospital, paralysed from the waist down. Encouraged by a concerned Audrey, Dickie took Ray in as lodger at No.3, and Audrey devoted herself to looking after 'her men' who, forgetting the past, formed a matey alliance. Domestic matters were complicated when Ray proposed marriage to hairdresser Sandra Butler. Faced with the possibility of losing Ray's attentions, Audrey did all she could to split them up, telling Sandra that Ray was only interested in her because he was stuck in a wheelchair and needed someone to look after him.

In the spring of 1970, Ray suddenly regained the use of his legs and made it clear to Audrey he was still interested in her. The pace picked up with the return of Ray's old flame Lucille Hewitt, who decided that

Fed up with society, Albert Tatlock decided to drop out and locked himself into Number One. Minnie Caldwell got Sgt Turpin to break his door down.

The Ray/Audrey/Dickie emotional triangle brought advice for the teenagers from all parties. Here, Ena Sharples gives Audrey a dressing-down.

if anyone was going to have Ray it was her.

The residents took an interest in the goings on at No.3, the women understood Audrey's attraction to the masculine, roguish Ray when compared to the sensitive, awkward Dickie. Ena Sharples warned Lucille not to interfere but Lucille felt they were all on a downward slope without her help: 'Like I said, Mrs Sharples. I don't have to cause trouble between them four. There's trouble there already.' Ena herself refused to stand by and watch Audrey wreck her marriage as she openly flirted with Ray: 'Life's still a battleground between good and evil. Your generation won't admit as much, they don't uphold my sort of religion. But they've only to look inside themselves. It's still a battlefield and there's still such a thing as goin' to the bad, goin' over to the devil.'

Dickie Fleming packed his bags in June and left for good – Audrey had finally declared her love for Ray and had even kissed him in public. As he left the

·1970·

Street, Dickie warned Sandra that Audrey and Ray had been having an affair. Sandra turned on Ray and broke their engagement, leaving the field clear for Audrey, and mild-mannered Bernard surprised everyone by thumping Ray. However, Audrey was not prepared for Ray telling her that he had only ever seen her as a bit on the side. 'If you've tears to shed, shed 'em for your husband.' She went to live with her parents in Preston.

TRAGEDY IN AUSTRALIA

Valerie Barlow was distressed in April 1970, when she heard that her brother-in-law David had been killed in a car crash. His eighteen-month-old son Darren died shortly afterwards in Adelaide Hospital. The news affected the whole Street. Hilda Ogden flew out to fetch daughter Irma home but Ken refused to attend David's funeral, saying it would be a waste of money. Ken admitted to Valerie that he felt guilty as he had never allowed himself to become close to David although he had always wanted to. Valerie was horrified when, on Irma's return, Ken was able to transfer his feelings of guilt onto Irma, who admitted she had caused the crash by nagging David as he drove: 'You can only live for yourself, because that's all you're capable of. Believe me, when you got married, I thought you were wrong for Dave. But it goes far deeper than that, now I know. You'd be wrong for anybody! If you have to spend the rest of your life alone, then that's the best way for you, it's the only way you know how! You've got two graves to prove it. That brands you, Irma. That brands you for life!'

Sandra Gough was glad to return to the programme as Irma. Irma went into partnership with Maggie Clegg at the shop and moved into the flat above, with Bet Lynch.

Stan Ogden borrowed money from Dave Smith to buy widowed Irma Barlow a partnership in the Corner Shop. Hilda was delighted until her daughter refused to allow her credit.

THE BIGGEST BLOW TO DATE

Shortly after the fictitious death of David Barlow, the cast heard of the sudden death of Arthur Leslie who, as Jack Walker, had been in the programme since the second episode. June Howson, as producer, was the first to receive the news on the morning of Tuesday 30 June: 'I immediately phoned Harry [Kershaw]. Harry came with me, and we got the rest of the cast together and broke the news. They were distraught, all terribly upset.' Jennifer Moss remembers being late in to work that day and missing the meeting: 'I came in and everybody was very quiet. They said June Howson wanted me in the office and I thought, oh I've been sacked and everybody knows except me. June told me to sit down in her office and gave me a glass of brandy, so I thought, well, I've definitely been sacked! And then she said that Arthur had died.'

Scripts were quickly rewritten so that Jack died off screen, holidaying with his daughter in Derby. Out of respect for Mr Leslie's family there were no scenes of grief. Annie and Lucille were written out for a couple of weeks and, when they returned, it was obvious the grieving had already taken place. Annie was quickly made licensee of the pub and Kenneth Farrington as Billy was rushed in to help.

Over 3,000 people lined the streets of Blackpool

to say goodbye to Arthur Leslie when he was buried. One reporter, Weston Taylor, wrote in the *News of the World*: 'I remember best the actor's own words the last time we met. "Everybody has turned me into a celebrity since I joined *Coronation Street*, but all I really want is to be remembered as an actor," he said. "Maybe as a good un, too."'

THE THIRD MR ELSIE TANNER

When Alan Browning joined the cast at the end of 1969 he did not know that he had been hand-picked by Pat Phoenix. Phoenix did not want her character Elsie Tanner to become involved with another man, but Kershaw won her over by saying she would pick the actor herself. After being told she could not have Peter Falk, whom she admired in *Columbo*, she settled for Browning: 'It was, I promise, a purely professional decision on my part although I must confess it idly crossed my mind that he was an attractive man whenever I watched him on television. . . . But selecting him for my screen boyfriend was not a romantic affair. It was simply that I admired the man's acting tremendously.'

At the beginning of 1970 Elsie and Alan started a slow courtship. Alan Howard was presented as a man of some wealth, with a house in the country and a string of businesses. A wedding seemed likely and the writers realized they were in danger of losing Elsie unless something drastic was done. On the day Elsie married Alan and went off to Paris on honeymoon the viewers discovered that he was in fact insolvent. On his return, he was declared bankrupt and was forced to settle into No.11 with Elsie. She assured him that she did not care, so long as she had him: 'All I wanted, all I ever wanted, was to be loved . . . I just wanted somebody to look after me. To protect me.' Watching scenes with the Howards fighting for each other and loving each other, viewers knew there was something about the relationship that transcended the programme. It was hardly a surprise when the press announced Browning and Phoenix were an item.

★ One actor who thoroughly enjoyed all his appearances on the Street is **Reginald Marsh**. From 1962 to 1976 he came and went as bookie Dave Smith. For most of the time he courted Elsie Tanner with memorable lines such as 'Stick with me kid, and you'll be buried in a silver casket.' Never for one moment did Elsie think Dave was her Mr Right. In the late 1960s and early 1970s Dave Smith was lord of the manor, buying and selling businesses, employing the residents and using them in his schemes. As a Londoner he was always treated as an outsider.

Marsh began acting in repertory in 1942, but first joined Granada as a contestant finder for quiz shows such as *Criss Cross Quiz*. He was offered the part of Dave Smith without an audition, and the part was only meant to last two episodes. In 1970, Marsh formed a theatrical production company called 'David Gordon' with Bill Kenwright. The company was named after their characters in the Street.

HAPPY ANNIVERSARY

In June 1970, the 1,000th episode of the Street was transmitted. To celebrate the event the *TV Times* brought out a special supplement, priced two shillings. The magazine took all the cast, dressed as the characters, on a trip to Belle Vue Zoo, featuring the photographs in the supplement. John Braine, author of *Room at the Top*, attempted to unlock the secret of the programme's success: 'The most important

Violet Carson was among the mourners burying their fellow Blackpool resident Arthur Leslie.

Elsie Tanner marries Alan Howard.

character in the Street is the Street itself. No matter who comes and goes, the Street remains.' Braine suggested that part of the appeal was that the viewers were invited into the programme, to get to know the characters and their histories: 'Sooner or later, if we follow each episode, we see everyone in the Street from the inside, we're taken into their lives and they cease to be strangers. We lift the roofs of all the houses and have a look at the people inside. In the supplement June Howson shared her thoughts on 'being in charge', likening taking the Street over to marrying into the aristocracy: 'It's sheer presumption for someone to walk in and decide to revolutionize it.'

By 1970, ten countries other than the United Kingdom had shown the Street. In Sierra Leone, the programme was voted the most watched series, although there were only 3,000 television sets in the country. When shown in Hong Kong, the series had Cantonese subtitles, shown vertically. In Holland it was also subtitled, although the broad Lancashire dialogue caused problems for translators – Albert Tatlock's line, 'He can jump in 't cut' was translated as 'He can fly up to heaven'. For four consecutive years the Street was voted best programme in New Zealand. In Singapore, 370,000 sets tuned into the Street. In Greece, it was put on at the same time as *Peyton Place* and beat it hollow. It was also a hit in Gibraltar. In Canada, viewers were invited to phone in questions to a local radio station and twenty lines were jammed. Sadly, Trinidad did not take to the programme and it finished there in 1969 after only sixty episodes.

BET JOINS THE ROVERS

Julie Goodyear had been absent from the Street for four years after her initial appearance as Bet in 1966. During that time, she had worked in rep and, after appearing in *Family at War*, she was amazed when June Howson offered her work on the Street: 'I really didn't take the question seriously because it was my dream and sometimes when dreams come true you find it very hard to believe that it's happening.' Having brought Bet back in May, June Howson realized the ideal arena for Bet's straightfoward vulnerability was the Rovers bar.

Annie Walker was horrified when son Billy employed the then laundrette manageress as a barmaid. Bet was popular with the local menfolk, and had a reputation for sexual generosity. Annie was not the only one to disapprove of Bet. Barmaid Betty Turpin had been used to being the centre of attention behind the bar and her nose was put out of joint. Billy persuaded Annie that Bet would be an asset to the pub, but Annie had to tread carefully, so as not to upset Betty: 'You and Bet Lynch share the same Christian name and that could lead to friction. I was wondering if you'd mind if from now on I called Bet "Bet" and referred to you by your full name of "Elizabeth". There is, after all, a world of difference between a full name and its diminutive.

·1970·

Betty Turpin and Lucille Hewitt were not impressed when Billy Walker introduced the new barmaid, Bet Lynch. They hoped Annie would show her the door, but were to be disappointed.

·1970·

Take your name for instance – Elizabeth. In its full flower, immediately evocative, I always think, of all that is finest in our English heritage. Whereas Bet, don't you think it's just a little common?'

A MURDERER AT LARGE

For two years, the verdict on the death of Steve Tanner had remained open. He had been found at the foot of a flight of stairs in September 1968 but there had been no evidence to condemn anyone of foul play. Then, at Christmas 1970 Joe Donnelli confessed. Joe had been one of Steve's friends, a fellow American serviceman stationed in Burtonwood. Now he returned as a deserter and was taken in as lodger by Minnie Caldwell. Donnelli was a dangerous character, a man who hit women and enjoyed going to war. Locking up Irma Barlow in the shop flat he described to her how he had pushed Steve downstairs over a gambling debt. Threatening her with a pair of scissors, he warned her he would not let her share the secret with anyone else. Shane Rimmer was cast as Donnelli and now recalls how much he enjoyed playing a bad guy: 'I think I prefer playing the villain. A villain is always up to something, he's always threatening someone, and somebody who is usually a favourite of the audience.'

Irma was certainly a favourite with the audience and viewers followed the action, fearing for her, as for over two weeks, he kept her prisoner at the shop. Eventually, the residents, knowing something was wrong, lured them both to the Rovers and the Military Police were called. Joe escaped through the toilet window and sought refuge at No.5, holding a terrified Minnie at gunpoint with his service revolver. Unaware of the gun, Stan Ogden crashed into the house after hearing how his daughter had been threatened by 'a damn Yank'. Joe let Minnie walk free and turned his gun on Stan, forcing him to sing carols. Just as the end credits rolled on Christmas Eve, a single shot ran out from inside No.5 and viewers had to wait until after the festivities to discover that Donnelli had shot himself. Stan Ogden was proclaimed a hero!

Violence came to the Street when Police Sgt Cyril Turpin was forced to resign for attacking a criminal with a lead pipe after he had subjected Betty to a reign of terror.

The writers decided Valerie had to die. But how? The most popular idea was that Joe Donnelli, after holding Irma hostage (December 1970) would break into the maisonette and shoot Valerie before killing himself. However, some of the team thought that was going too far.

Rovers Annie and Billy (Jan. - Aug.) Walker • Lucille Hewitt • Emily Nugent Lorna Shawcross (June)

No. 1 Albert Tatlock

No. 3 Ken Barlow (March - Dec.) • Peter and Susan Barlow (March - May)

No. 5 Minnie Caldwell

No. 9 Len Fairclough and Ray Langton Jerry Booth (Oct. - Dec.)

No. 11 Alan and Elsie Howard

No. 13 Stan and Hilda Ogden

Shop Maggie Clegg

Shop flat Irma Barlow (Jan. - Dec.) • Janet Reid (Aug.)

Maisonettes No. 14 Ken, Val, Peter and Susan Barlow (Jan.)

No. 16 (Centre) Ena Sharples (May - Dec.)

Non-residents Dave Smith • Ernie Bishop Bet Lynch • Alf Roberts • Ivy Tilsley Edna Gee

Comings and Goings

The New Year started with tragedy as Valerie Barlow burnt to death in a fire that gutted the maisonette and led to them all being demolished. Ken rented No.3 from Audrey Fleming and attempted to bring up the children there. He found it impossible and after two months they were sent to live in Scotland with Valerie's parents. Jerry Booth returned to the Street in October after Lucille Hewitt found him at the Labour Exchange. He had been sleeping rough so Len took him in at No.9 and gave him work at the yard. Billy Walker left the Rovers following the break-up of his affair with Lorna Shawcross, a family friend who lodged with the Walkers. Irma Barlow also left; she went to live in Llandudno in December in a bid to escape the Street where everyone knew her history. A warehouse was built on the site of the maisonettes, as well as a Community Centre. Ena was employed to caretake at the Centre, and mail order firm Mark Brittain took over the warehouse employing some residents and bringing in workers such as Edna Gee and Ivy Tilsley.

·1971·

The Barlows Plan a New Life

January found the Barlows busy packing when Ken accepted a teaching post in Jamaica. Valerie was concerned at leaving Uncle Albert to fend for himself, but was won over by the knowledge that the twins would have a better lifestyle away from Weatherfield. They sold their car, visited family members to bid farewell and left the twins with Albert so they could enjoy their last night in England, and a farewell party at the Rovers. While Ken waited with the other residents, Valerie attempted to dry her hair. The drier had a loose-fitting plug which she tried to mend with a vegetable peeler but this did not work. Forcing the top of the plug down, she jammed it into an already crowded adapter and put it in the wall. One gasp was all she made as the electricity shot through her and she collapsed, knocking an electric fire into a packing case. The credits rolled over her limp body as flames lapped around her – at least that was how the episode was meant to end. Anne Reid remembers well the now famous death scene. It was towards the end of studio time, and no one wanted to go into overtime so the final scene was rushed through: 'They put this newspaper round me and they set fire to it. And I lay there and kept thinking keep your eyes closed, keep your eyes closed. Then I got nervous and I got up as I could feel my arm getting hot. It was probably quiet safe but I couldn't lay there with all those flames.' A new ending was therefore devised, with the credits rolling over flames licking at a teddy bear.

Valerie Barlow did burn to death, but that was not the ending intended for the character. Anne Reid had given her notice in late 1970, as June Howson recalls: 'She wanted to go and I did

·1971·

everything possible to persuade her to stay but she said, "No, I want to go and I never want to come back, so I would be grateful if you would get rid of me in some way." I had enormous respect for Anne. I think she's a marvellous actress and always did. I really, really did not want her to go. The Street goes on but it was one of the things I thought was a mistake for the show. But she was determined.'

Bill Roache recalls attempting to save Valerie: 'Asbestos was flying out, it was highly dangerous and I was knocked back at one point as this stuff was exploding. The flames were under control but the asbestos was cracking and banging.' After Valerie's body was recovered, a scene was included where Ken walked around the gutted flat, remembering Val. For Bill Roache it stands out as one of the highlights in thirty-five years of playing Ken: 'Carol Wilks directed it. Usually everything was tightly done and that was the time I said can you just leave me and she agreed and she let me just walk into this room and eventually I picked up Val's contact and sat down and I just cried. I managed to do it because I knew there was time to just naturally feel it. It was nice as I was given the freedom to indulge in it.'

Worried and perplexed, Ernie and Emily had a brief spell of happiness during their engagement before he left to photograph models abroad. Weeks later, news reached Emily that he had been arrested for taking part in an orgy.

TRUE LOVE FOR MISS NUGENT

Emily Nugent led the public rally against the building of the warehouse on the site of the maisonettes. Along with many others she feared it would lead to traffic congestion in the Street and would dominate the area as the old raincoat factory had done. She organized a human barrier across the entrance to the site but a dumper spilt its load of sand all over the protesters. Residents were therefore surprised when Emily was offered, and accepted, a job by the warehouse bosses, to act as a clerk.

Emily was not the only resident employed 'across t' Street'. Elsie Howard was given the plum job of supervizing the checkers, a group of women that included Ivy Tilsley. In the offices, Emily quickly made friends with a nervous woman with whom she had shared interests; her name was Mavis Riley. In August 1971, Emily Nugent agreed to marry her boyfriend of two years, photographer and lay preacher, Ernest Bishop. They threw an engagement party at the Community Centre (both of them being on the committee at the Centre) and invited all their friends, including Mavis who grew bitter over the engagement: 'I really think it's too much of Emily to get herself engaged. I mean she's quite past it, and ought to have more sense. I wouldn't care so much if she didn't flaunt herself. That's what she's doing. Flaunting herself. Like a latter-day Rita Hayworth!'

AN AFFAIR OF THE HEART

Alan and Elsie Howard's year-long marriage hit the rocks in August. He was now running the Canal Garage, in partnershp with Billy Walker, and she was working long hours at the warehouse. Slowly they began to drift apart and he started a flirtation with Corner Shop owner Irma Barlow. The actors worked well together on screen and the writers decided to let them have an affair. Unfortunately, just before recording the start of the affair Sandra Gough fell ill. Rather than scrapping what was potentially a good story, the writers quickly brought Janet Reid (played by Judith Barker) back. Janet had first appeared in 1969 as Len Fairclough's girlfriend. She was able to slide back into the programme with relative ease, helping Maggie Clegg at the shop in Irma's absence. By the second episode she was kissing Alan, and by the second week the characters were spending the night together.

Judith Barker recalls how odd it all felt, being rushed in in an emergency: 'I got an emergency phone call to come back and take over the story line from Sandra, which was a bit odd because it was written for her and she was a completely different character to me – a much more upfront, tarty character than I was. So I remember having problems with some of the dialogue because it was specifically written for her and I was having to adapt it to the way I played the part.'

The affair did not last long because, of course, Elsie found out. She confronted Janet in the shop flat and told her to leave town. The scene lasted for six minutes and Janet tried to explain her actions: 'I just want what everyone else has already got. Someone who cares what happens to me. Not out of pity or some kind of smug sympathy. Someone who cares because he cares. And where's the rule that says a man can only care what happens to one woman?' Janet realized that Alan would never leave his wife for her and agreed to pack her bags. Before she left though Elsie forced her to appear at the Rovers in front of all the regulars, Elsie the proud victor, Janet the humbled wreck.

COMIC CUTS

Two Popular British comedy actors made appearances in the programme in 1971. Mollie Sugden had been associated with the Street since 1965 when she first appeared as landlady Nellie Harvey. In 1971, Nellie was

★ After working as a secretary for some years, **Thelma Barlow** put her name down for a speech and drama course at night school and suddenly a whole new world opened up for her. She joined amateur companies and began to get work on radio. Thelma joined the West of England Theatre Company in Exmouth, gaining experience before marrying designer Graham Barlow. They worked together in repertory companies in Liverpool, Birmingham and Nottingham before moving to Scotland where he took a job. Thelma found it hard to find work in Scotland and was despairing until she was given a part at the Liverpool Playhouse. Someone from Granada saw her performance and she was offered the part of Mavis.

Lynne Perrie's background was cabaret-based. From the 1960s she had operated the cabaret circuit, working with the Beatles and Sacha Distel. She was spotted by Ken Loach who gave her the part of the mother in the film *Kes*. Loach thought Lynne was a natural and so did the critics. It was through Kes that Lynne landed the part of Ivy; director Paul Bernard saw the film and remembered Lynne's performance when he was casting. 'I was "Ivy Tyldesley" when I first came in in 1971. I was married to three different men in three different weeks! I said I must be the most promiscuous woman on the Street. There was a Jack, then a Wilf and finally a Bert!'

·1971·

A passionate storyline was started by Alan and Irma and then finished by Elsie and Janet.

reintroduced, more snobbish than before and anxious for any opportunity to put down Annie Walker: 'Course that's the trouble with houses in working-class districts. There's only money about at weekends.' One episode had her questioning Annie as to her age as she celebrated her birthday. Annie refused to be drawn but hinted she kept up her strength by taking a special treatment: 'It's financed by an admirer. A gentleman. Owing to his most difficult domestic situation, all I can tell you is he's something in the City.'

Bill Owen was given a one-off cameo role in 1971 as Unionist Dickenson. Stan Ogden was working for Fairclough and Langton at their building yard. Feeling put upon by the bosses he decided to set up his own union to fight for better conditions. He called the union the Stanley Ogden District Union before Hilda pointed out that its initials were SODU, so he changed to the Stanley Ogden Labour Organization – SOLO. Charlie

Mrs Nellie Harvey graces Annie with her presence.

Bill Owen made a cameo appearance for only one episode as Charlie Dickenson.

Dickenson delighted in taking on the bosses on Stan's behalf, demanding he had his own key to the outside toilet and being paid £1 over the union rate.

THE STREET IS LEFT CHILDLESS

Following Valerie's death, Ken struggled to bring up the twins. He employed a nanny but she left after a month when Lucille Hewitt identified her as someone who has mistreated her when she lived in an orphanage. The residents helped as much as they could, and Bet considered giving in notice at the Rovers to look after the children. Ken was all for Bet helping out but Edith Tatlock had other ideas. Edith was Valerie's domineering mother and she had a reputation for speaking her mind. She stated she did not want a 'backstreet tart' looking after her grandchildren. For a while the family survived day to

day, with Edith acting as housekeeper, but tension was always present as she and Ken had differing views on how to bring up the twins.

Edith eventually let rip after he had returned drunk from a night out with the lads. Telling him he was not fit to be a father, she announced her plan to fight for custody of the twins. Ken did not want a family war and, a bit relieved, told Edith that her plans for the children were right – they would be better off living with her and her husband in Scotland. As they headed off to Glasgow, Ken began the batchelor life he soon came to enjoy. Bill Roache, however, was upset by the way the twins were cast aside: 'I did not like that. It would have been better if he struggled as a single parent. It was obviously a contractual convenience, which I don't think was well handled. No, I never liked that, I think it would have been good if he'd brought them up himself.'

Ken Barlow gave up the battle for Peter and Susan at an early age, a fact that was to haunt him until Peter told him, in 1986, just how it felt to be abandoned.

The Christmas crib is brought out to the Community Centre by the main Christian characters – Ena and Emily. Right from the start the programme had been based on morality and decency as well as a God-fearing attitude. As Ena once said, 'Me biggest regret regret is that I've never been able to speak in tongues.'

·1972·

'Where are all the poor? They're obviously not poor enough to stick to a job with reasonable hours and pay. Easier collecting Social Security, I suppose.'

Annie despairs of replacing Hilda

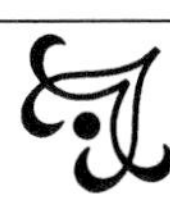

Rovers Annie and Billy (Jan. - Dec.) Walker • Lucille Hewitt • Emily Nugent (Jan. - April)

No. 1 Albert Tatlock • Ken Barlow (April - Dec.)

No. 3 Ken Barlow (April - Dec.) • Ernie and Emily Bishop (April - Dec.)

No. 5 Minnie Caldwell

No. 9 Len Fairclough, Ray Langton and Jerry Booth

No. 11 Alan and Elsie Howard • Ivy Tilsley (April)

No. 13 Stan and Hilda Ogden • Archie Crabtree (May)

Shop Maggie Clegg • Jacko Ford (July - Dec.)

Shop flat Norma Ford (May - Dec.)

No. 16 (Centre) Ena Sharples

Non-residents Betty Turpin • Cyril Turpin Bet Lynch • Alf Roberts • Rita Littlewood Benny Lewis • Terry Bates • Edna Gee

COMINGS AND GOINGS

The year started with the return of Billy Walker. He sold his interest in the Canal Garage to Alan Howard and settled down to run the Rovers with his mother. Emily Nugent left the pub in April when she married Ernest Bishop: 'I'm just very glad I'm marrying somebody who checks three times if they've locked up at night.' The Bishops returned from honeymooning in Edale to move into No.3, buying it from Audrey Fleming. In their absence the residents had redecorated – including a purple ceiling. Ken Barlow made room for the Bishops, moving in with Albert Tatlock at No.1. Maggie Clegg took in assistant Norma Ford in May, and for part of the year, Norma's father Jacko stayed at the shop. The Howards were put upon by Ivy Tilsley, who was suffering from marital problems. Elsie threw her out when Ivy made a play for Alan. Stan Ogden was injured in a motoring accident, so Hilda's brother Archie Crabtree moved into No. 13 to keep her company. He built a porch outside the house without planning permission, but it was stolen by Ray Langton.

CLEANING AND CURLERS

Since she first appeared in 1964, Hilda Ogden had cleaned at the Rovers. She had put up with Annie Walker's snobbish behaviour and Bet Lynch's practical jokes, but in 1972 she delighted in telling Annie where to stick her job. Benny Lewis opened a betting shop and Hilda was given the sought-after post of cleaner, both of the shop and of his luxury apartment above. Jean Alexander enjoyed playing Hilda the char: 'Initially, at the pub, she was a very good cleaner; it was only later she deteriorated into cutting corners and getting up Annie's nose. It was great fun mopping round and brushing and nattering.'

Annie Walker was put out by Hilda's departure but refused to let her see this: 'Thank you, Mrs Ogden, for leaving my employment. It has saved me the distasteful task of dismissing you, a task that was becoming more certain with each day you skimped and fell down on the job.' When Benny Lewis went into partnership with Alan Howard and opened a nightclub, it was Hilda who thought of the name 'Capricorn' and landed the job of head cleaner, but her staff of one – played by Jill Summers – refused to acknowledge her seniority. Back at the Rovers, Annie despaired of ever finding a replacement. She was forced to ask Hilda to return, with a hefty pay increase. By the end of 1972 Hilda had five jobs – cleaning the Rovers, the Club, the bookies', Benny's flat and washing up at the Club.

The sight of turbaned Hilda, mop in one hand, cigarette butt in another, singing gaily was a common and much loved one. Jean Alexander explains: 'I remembered seeing the women working on munitions during the war. All the girls in the factories had to have their heads covered because of

Colour television came to the Street in mid-1972 when the Ogdens hired one as a status symbol. When the TV man came to repossess it because of lack of payments he kindly agreed to take it through the back way so the neighbours would not notice. As he told Stan, 'I did the same for me mother!'

the machinery. They used to wear these scarves, like pudding clothes, tied up and the curlers would be in. . . . I thought Hilda would have worked on munitions and would have her hair tied up. . . . She was always ready to go out – only she never went out. The curlers were always in, just in case she happened to be going out in the evening.'

THE PINK BATHROOM

In the spring of 1972, Elsie Howard has a spot of good fortune. An endowment policy she had taken out on Dennis suddenly matured and she was given £296. Alan encouraged her to spend the money how she wished, so she did. She fulfilled her only remaining ambition and had Len Fairclough refurbish her bathroom with black wallpaper and a pink bathroom suite. Alan was astonished and the gossips had a field day. Ena Sharples was first to view 'And all to keep your knees clean!' Betty Turpin followed: 'Decent women have white baths!' And Hilda Ogden completed the run: 'Only a Jezebel would have a pink bath. That's not a flippin' bath, it's phonographic (sic).'

RUNNING THE SHOP

By 1971, Maggie Clegg had lost her two shop assistants: Valerie Barlow was now dead, and Maggie's partner Irma Barlow had left to live in Llandudno. Betty Turpin tried to buy Irma's share but Maggie refused, saying she would rather die than spend all day with her bossy sister. Borrowing money from Gordon, now a successful accountant, Maggie bought out Irma. Irene Sutcliffe recalls with fondness the seven years she spent as Maggie running the shop. She enjoyed handling all the props and using the bacon slicer. Because of the risk of being seen to endorse products, all the packets and tins in the shop were false, with the brand name 'Key'. If a tin of beans was bought it was 'Key's own brand, as was the bread, soup, and everything else. If any prop was to be handled it couldn't be a dummy tin. It had to be a proper tin because I think you can tell when a suitcase is empty, when a handbag doesn't have anything in it and you can tell when it's an empty tin.'

Maggie took on Norma Ford as a live-in assistant. Norma was popular with the customers but hid a dark secret – her father was in prison. When the truth came out, Maggie invited Jacko Ford to stay at the shop on his release and the Street began a series of stories to show how difficult it was for someone with a conviction to be integrated into the community. Every time there was a local break-in, the police came knocking on Maggie's door. When Jacko was taken on at the Rovers, the rest of the staff did not trust him and he was framed by local villains to take the blame for a big robbery. Diana Davies played Norma and recalls getting letters of support from families of ex-cons. She recalls one vividly; 'This letter said go to the police and tell them that Ray Langton gave the keys to his girlfriend and she gave them to a crook. Tell them it wasn't your father, you're so right to stand by him. '

RITA SINGS THE BLUES

Barbara Knox returned to the Street in 1972 after an absence of eight years. She had appeared in one episode before, back in 1964, as exotic dancer Rita Littlewood. Now, as Rita Bates, she returned and made it obvious she was interested in Ken Barlow. Matters were complicated however as she had a twelve-year-old son, Terry, who was a pupil at Bessie Street School, where Ken had gone back to work in January. Ken's headmaster Wilfred Perkins warned Ken about associating with parents and Ken cooled the relationship. Rita was not that bothered as she had already moved on to a new man, Len Fairclough. Their affair was passionate, but he backed out of it when she admitted she was not married to Bates, and Terry was not really her son. She left the area for a few months only to re-emerge singing in a night club. When Barbara Knox (then Mullaney) saw the scripts for the club scenes she was very alarmed as she had no professional training: 'I had suggested to the writers that she should work in a club. I thought she would be written in as somebody behind a counter in a club either taking the hats or serving drinks. When I actually got the script it said Rita is discovered singing. I nearly died! I honestly thought it was a joke because nobody had ever asked me if I could sing!'

After the Producers' Run she was taken into a committee room and introduced to Derek Hilton

·1972·

Irene Sutcliffe spent most of her time as Maggie stuck behind the Corner Shop counter. She enjoyed this as it varied the people with whom she played scenes. Here Maggie, Lucille and Ken listen in as the Ogdens row next door.

★The character of Councillor Alfred Sydney Roberts had first appeared in Episode 18 and had been a semi-regular ever since, as Len's friend and in the early 1970s would-be boyfriend of Maggie Clegg but 1972 saw Alf Roberts' character grow more with the death of his unseen wife Phyllis. Actor **Bryan Mosley** was highly praised in the Press for the scene in which he broke down and told Jerry Booth that his wife had died. Leeds-born Bryan made his stage debut aged ten, as the back part of a cow in a production of Cinderella. He trained at Bradford after completing his National Service in the RAF. He working in rep all over Yorkshire and did a season in Butlins in Clacton. Bryan developed a passion for stunt work and became a founder member of the Society of British Fights Arrangers, taking parts in films such as *Get Carter, Charlie Bubbles* and *This Sporting Life*, and television programmes such as *The Avengers* and *The Saint* – always as the villain! When he started on the Street, Bryan realized that Alf was certainly not a villain. Director Howard Baker summed up the character very neatly by saying 'he's the sort of bloke who'd be a Sunday School teacher.'

Bryan Mosley
"Alf Roberts"

★Norma was not the first role **Diana Davies** had taken on the Street. She had served as a waitress as Jackson's Chippie and had been a voice on the police radio at the time of the coach crash. The part of Norma was especially written for Diana. By the end of the series she had worked on before, *Family At War*, she was quite a major character. The day it ended was a magical day for Di as she was offered five parts on different shows. One of the offers was a part in the Street and 'of course that was the one I wanted'.

Norma inherited an instant wardrobe. 'They dressed me in all the clobber that Paula Wilcox had worn in *The Lovers*. And then there was a repeat of *The Lovers*, and I was on screen wearing the same gear as Paula – suede mini-skirts and things like that.' The viewers took to Norma instantly; she was straightforward, normal and, as Di Davies puts it, 'common as muck'. Miss Davies recalls that Norma 'was very common, but I liked her.'

Diana Davies
(Norma Ford)

With Derek Hilton behind her on the piano, Barbara Mullaney hits the right notes.

who was to back her on piano. He approved her choice of *It Had To Be You* and struck a chord. Suddenly Barbara found herself singing. She remembers Derek signalling to the Floor Manager who rushed into the Producer's office. 'It was obviously a signal to say, "she *can* sing" and we took it from there. Not being a trained singer or ever having sung in a club I found myself on the actual day having to pick up the middle lines. It's all right if you start singing at the beginning of a song, but in television it didn't work like that because the camera would just pan over to where I was singing. I'd be in the middle of a song and I found that very difficult.'

Luckily, the scripts did not have to be rewritten; in Barbara Mullaney the writers had found the perfect Rita and they balanced her fiery rows with Len Fairclough against her romantic soft voice as she sang ballads over the next year. They also invented a nightclub for her to sing in.

Apple-Blossom Time

Rita Littlewood showed off her singing talents in the Christmas event at the Rovers, a special 1940s show. Albert Tatlock dressed in uniform to give a Rob Wilton monologue, and Alf and Ernie Bishop donned DJs as the Western Brothers. Ray Langton and Jerry Booth tried to keep in step with each other as Flanagan and Allen, and Rita sang as Marlene Dietrich, but Emily Bishop did not make it onto the stage as Carmen Miranda as her bananas kept falling off her head. Highlight of the evening were the Andrew Sisters – Betty, Norma and Bet – singing 'Apple-Blossom Time'. Julie Goodyear who recalls how Bet had to sing a solo in the middle of the song: 'It was so very difficult as the director decided that Bet would not be a good singer and so I had to sing off-key. It was awful . . . just awful!"

·1973·

'I just wish I could think of a way to bring her down a peg or two. Take the wind out of her sails. But then again, she is superior to us, you know.'

Bet Lynch on Annie Walker

Rovers Annie and Billy (Jan. - June) Walker • Lucille Hewitt (Jan./Oct. - Dec.) Glyn Thomas (June - July)

No. 1 Albert Tatlock • Ken and Janet Barlow (Oct. - Dec.)

No. 3 Ernie and Emily Bishop

No. 5 Minnie Caldwell • Ena Sharples (Dec.)

No. 9 Len Fairclough, Ray Langton and Jerry Booth

No. 11 Alan and Elsie Howard (Jan. - Oct.) • Lucille Hewitt (Jan. - Oct.)

No. 13 Stan and Hilda Ogden

Shop Maggie Clegg

Shop flat Norma Ford (Jan. - Dec.)

No. 16 (Centre) Ena Sharples (Jan. - Dec.)

Non-residents Betty Turpin • Bet Lynch Alf Roberts • Rita Littlewood • Mavis Riley Deirdre Hunt

COMINGS AND GOINGS

After nine years of living at the Rovers with Annie Walker, Lucille finally decided at the start of the year that she had had enough of interference in her life. To Annie's annoyance she packed her bags and moved down the Street to lodge with the Howards at No.11. She stayed until October when Elsie and Alan left the area to start their new life in Newcastle. There were quite a few changes in the Rovers this year. Billy left in the summer, having been caught gambling the pub's takings. Ray Langton tried to buy a newsagents and persuaded his girlfriend, Deidre Hunt, to run it for him, but Len Fairclough went over Ray's head and bought the business himself. Annie retired and planned to move to Derby, and the pub was taken over by manager Glyn Thomas who upset the regulars by installing fruit machines and heavy rock groups. Everyone was relieved when Annie was persuaded to come out of retirement. Ena Sharples lost her job at the Community Centre on Christmas Eve, when she was sacked for inefficiency by the Bishops. The same month Norma Ford left; all year she had dreamed of marrying her idol, Ken Barlow, and she was horrified when, in October, he married Janet Reid. Ken and Janet settled into No. 1 until they could find a detached property far from the Street.

MAYOR AND MAYORESS

In 1973, Weatherfield ceased to be part of Lancashire and became integrated into Manchester. As such, it lost its tradition of having a Mayor and the battle for the post of last Mayor of Weatherfield was centred on two Councillors – Len Fairclough and Alf Roberts. Len blew his chances by his choice of Mayoress; nightclub singer Rita Littlewood had a brawl with a drunken woman and ended up on the exiting mayor's lap, cursing. Alf on the other hand, had problems even finding a Mayoress; he assumed Maggie Clegg would be willing to oblige and was taken aback when she turned him down. Bryan Mosley was surprised when he was told Alf was to beat Len and become Mayor – 'Fairclough was the big one in the show at the time' – but he was interested to discover what was in store for the character over the twelve months to come: 'Harry Kershaw said the intention was to show people how Mayors operated, where they got their suits from and all that sort of stuff. But this was deemed not to be part of *Coronation Street*, so it was never actually shown. All we ever saw him do was go off looking posh, but it didn't tell you anything as to how the Mayoralty functioned, which was a missed opportunity, I think.'

Now he was elected, Alf again asked Maggie to be his consort, and again she turned him down. It was then that Annie told him it was obvious he was too embarrassed to ask but *of course* she would be delighted and, opening a hat-box, did he approve of the little creation she had bought for the investiture? Poor Alf accepted, and the Rovers' staff realized that they faced a year of living with Weatherfield's leading lady.

THE KABIN

Len Fairclough bought a run-down café/newsagents shop for £3,000 in the summer of 1973. Rita Littlewood was not impressed, 'It's just a grotty little hole!' but was won round when the upstairs' flat was thrown in as well. Rita wanted to call the shop 'Rita's' but Len decided upon 'The Kabin.' Having refused to run the place single-handed, Rita took on Mavis Riley as her assistant. Barbara Knox remembers falling in love with the Kabin set, almost at first sight: 'I thought it was wonderful. I loved it. I just thought, "This is mine. This is wonderful. I feel happy in here." We had a lending library which I loved as well, because when I was a kid there was a shop like that very near to me so I felt very at home.'

Having promised girlfriend Deirdre Hunt a job at the Kabin, Ray felt obliged to find her employment. Discovering she had secretarial skills, he employed her at the yard working for Jerry, Len and himself. When Jerry Booth started an awkward relationship with Mavis, the three men and three ladies paired off nicely. On New Year's Eve they threw a party at the yard, and Mavis allowed Jerry to kiss her for the first time. Not usually a gambling woman, Rita made a wager with Mavis, betting her £1 that Len would propose in 1974.

THE HOWARDS LEAVE

Patricia Phoenix and Alan Browning married in real life on 23 December 1972, two years after their screen characters Elsie and Alan tied the knot. Although they were still enjoying success in the Street, both were anxious to return to acting on the stage. As Pat Phoenix explains in her autobiography, she decided in October 1973 that if she did not make the break with Elsie Tanner soon, she never would: 'For thirteen years she had loved, lost, laughed and lamented across millions of television screens twice a week, give or take a break or two. Time had wrought changes. She was no longer the blowsy, buxom sexbomb of the early 1960s, satin blouses slashed at the neck, beads and tight black skirts. With posh Alan Howard for a husband and a stainless steel sink installed at No.11 Coronation Street, Elsie had reached respectability. It was time for me to say "tara" to Mrs Tanner.'

'Mayoress? Me? Oh Councillor Roberts, I don't know what to say! What a surprise!'

The press splashed the news of Elsie's departure across all the front pages, forecasting the end of the Street. Pat was widely quoted as wanting to leave slobbish Elsie behind: 'Playing Elsie has been rather like spending thirteen years laced into a corset that was too tight. It was claustrophobic.' Alan Browning told reporters that they hoped to make a film together, as an English version of Spencer Tracy and Katherine Hepburn. Although the film was never made, the couple were launched on stage together, starring in productions such as *Gaslight*. On screen there were no emotional farewells; Elsie went to train for a job in Newcastle and never returned. A couple of weeks later, Alan moved north to be with her, and to give their failing marriage one last go.

·1973·

Married on screen and off – the press commentated as much on the Phoenix/Browning marriage as they did the Taylor/Burton one.

Anne Kirkbride (Deirdre) xx

★ **Anne Kirkbride** got her taste for acting at Oldham Rep's Junior Theatregoers's Club. She joined the Saddleworth Junior players and then the Oldham Youth Theatre. When she left school she took a job at Oldham Rep as a student assistant stage manager, a time she recalled in a 1975 interview in *The Weekly News* 'I got quite a few parts, but it was terribly hectic combining it with buying props, helping to make sets and so on. Then one day, the late director of Oldham Rep, Carl Paulson, took me to one side in the car park, I thought I was going to get the bullet. Instead he told me I would be going over to acting full time and I would get £18 a week. I ran through the streets as if I'd just won the pools.'

KEN HUNTS FOR A WIFE

1973 was a crossroads for Ken Barlow. He spent the summer months trying to impress headmaster's daughter Elaine Perkins. Beautiful, sophisticated Elaine enjoyed Ken's company and was amused to see the change in his appearance as he spent more time with her, as he exchanged collar, tie and jacket for open-necked shirts and loosely tied cravats. However, when he proposed marriage she quickly retreated from the relationship.

Ken felt bitter over the rejection and turned to the one woman he knew wanted to marry him more than anything else in the world – Norma Ford. For over a year, Norma had cooked meals for him, ironed his clothes and generally made herself available, but Ken was not interested. Only after Elaine's rebuff, in fact the same afternoon, did he show any interest in her, kissing her to prove to himself that he was desirable. Norma allowed herself to believe Ken had feelings for her and was devastated when he stood her up the minute a more appealing woman became available. After falling out with Len, Rita Littlewood wanted to hurt him so spent a night with Ken in her flat. The next day Norma surprised Ken by telling him what she thought of him: 'You came to me as you knew I was a sucker for you. I really cared for you but you used me. You think of nothing but yourself, Ken Barlow!'

Diana Davies enjoyed the strong storylines that involved Ken and Norma: 'I do remember at the time that they were very much trying to get Ken married off again because his marriage with Val had worked so well. He'd had a lot of girlfriends and I remember Bill [Roach] saying to me that they were trying to marry him off and he had actually said, "I like working with Di, if you want to marry me off, marry me off to Di". But they had said that Norma was too common for Ken.'

It was after the row with Norma that Ken decided he had been wasting his time searching for a lover, and that what he needed was a mother for the twins.

Joanna Lumley appeared as Elaine Perkins, daughter of headmaster Wilfred. When she finished with Ken he turned to Rita for comfort.

Filming in London – a stunt double dressed as Elsie is hit by a taxi. Quick change then for Pat Phoenix so she lies sprawled on the pavement for the episode's end credits.

He visited the children in Scotland and returned to the Street with a wife. Bill Roache remembers feeling totally confused over the move: 'I was very cross about the whole thing. There was no wedding, she just arrived, no build-up to it. It was just like an idea that was shoved in. I wasn't happy.' The wife was actually Janet Reid, making her third appearance in the Street, after her affairs with Len in 1969 and Alan in 1971. The viewers took against Janet straight away, remembering the way she had tried to break up the Howards. Two months into the marriage, she made plans to send the twins away to boarding-school. Judith Barker enjoyed playing Janet because she was interesting and gusty, and also unpopular: 'We did row a lot and people used to say, "Oh, it's not working, I don't think you're very good to him. I think you should leave him. Why don't you want the twins?"

Ken soon realized that he was in a loveless marriage; that he and Janet were just two lonely people clutching at what seemed a last chance of happiness. Their rows became spectacular – he slapped her and at one stage smashed a bottle on the dining-table. As far as the viewers were concerned, as the Barlows spent a frosty Christmas together, the marriage did not have long to go.

★It took **Judith Barker** many years to lay the ghost of Janet Barlow after she left the Street for good in 1977. Janet's character was too unpleasant and the public disliked her from the start: 'People always imagine that you're like the character you play, especially in something like the Street, that people relate to strongly. I think she was used as a device quite often, certainly in the relationship with Ken . . . people got stuck into hating me in a big way when Janet was married to Ken. I used to go about being terribly nice and pleasant to everybody in the hope that people would like her more.'

Judith Barker was born in Oldham and worked as a GPO telephonist after leaving school. At seventeen, she turned to acting, eventually joining Oldham Rep. Her television credits included *Pardon the Expression, Dixon of Dock Green* and *Inheritance*. Before playing Janet she appeared as 'Babs', a friend of Lucille Hewitt's.

'It was lovely. It's like a family . . . and the atmosphere was very happy.'

Irene Sutcliffe fondly recalls working on the Street

Rovers Annie and Billy (Jan. - Dec.) Walker • Lucille Hewitt (Jan. - July)

No. 1 Albert Tatlock • Ken and Janet Barlow (Jan.)

No. 3 Ernie and Emily Bishop • Vernon and Lucy Foyle (Nov. - Dec.)

No. 5 Minnie Caldwell • Ena Sharples (Jan. - Feb./Dec.) • Eddie Yeats (Dec.)

No. 9 Len Fairclough, Ray Langton and Jerry Booth • Alison and Jon Wright (June)

No. 11 Ken (Jan. - Dec.) and Janet (Jan. - May) Barlow

No. 13 Stan and Hilda Ogden • Michael O'Ryan and Tommy Deakin (May - June)

Shop Maggie Clegg (Jan. - July) • Idris, Vera and Megan Hopkins (July - Dec.)

Shop flat Tricia Hopkins (July - Dec.)

No. 16 (Centre) Gertie Robson (March - Sept.) • Gary Turner (April - May)

Non-residents Betty Turpin • Bet Lynch Alf Roberts • Rita Littlewood • Ivy Tilsley Edna Gee • Mavis Riley • Deirdre Hunt Blanche Hunt • Gail Potter

·1974·

ANNIE'S NIGHTMARE

Annie Walker could not believe her ears when Billy announced his plans to marry Deirdre Hunt. She hoped ignoring the event would make it go away. This attitude infuriated Billy: 'I'm waiting for you to say "Congratulations Billy. You've found yourself a really nice girl at last."' In Annie's opinion, however, Deirdre was not a nice girl at all; nice girls did not work as secretaries for backstreet plumbers and their mothers were not blowsy women who had reputations of being friendly with more than one man at a time: 'They all grow up like their mothers, dear, and Blanche Hunt put me in mind of no one so much as Elsie Tanner!' Eventually Annie was forced to accept Deirdre into the family rather than lose her son for good. However, she was never reconciled to the idea of Blanche as an in-law.

COMINGS AND GOINGS

Ken and Janet Barlow started the new year with a new home; they rented No.11 from Elsie Howard until they could find a property to buy. By May, Janet had had enough of Ken sabotaging her plans to buy a Georgian detached, and she left him. Maggie Clegg also left the Street; after six years of running the shop, she married draughtsman Ron Cooke and emigrated to Zaire, leaving the sale of the shop in Gordon's hands. He rented it to the Hopkin family for six months on the understanding they would eventually buy it. Ena Sharples left the Street in February to live in St Anne's. Her job at the Centre was given to good-natured Gertie Robson. Gertie's nephew Gary Turner lodged with her but left because of pressure from his father to become a professional footballer. Life at No.9 was thrown into chaos by the arrival of Alison Wright and her baby, Jonathan. Everyone assumed Ray Langton was the father but she was only seeking refuge because her wealthy boyfriend did not want to know. Fairclough, Langton and Booth persuaded him to take Alison and the baby back. Billy Walker returned once again to the Rovers and soon became engaged to Deirdre Hunt. Lucille Hewitt left the country in July following the return of Gordon Clegg for his mother's wedding. With Hilda away cleaning on a cruise ship, Stan took in as paying guests rag-and-bone man Tommy Deakin and his nephew Michael O'Ryan. They left owing rent and Stan was reported to the Health Authorities for allowing them to keep their donkey Dolores in the backyard. At Christmas the Bishops became foster parents, taking two coloured children in while their father was in hospital. Minnie Caldwell also had a busy Christmas – Jed Stone's friend Eddie Yeats arrived out on parole just as Ena returned for the festivities.

Pat Cutts created the role of Blanche Hunt, but only for two weeks.

A NEW LIFE FOR MRS CLEGG

Maggie Clegg was due to marry Alf Roberts in late 1974, or at least that was how the writers had plotted the future. However, Alf had to wait a further eight years before he got his hands on the Corner Shop (by marrying Renee Bradshaw) because Irene Sutcliffe announced that she wanted to leave the programme. Reformed alcoholic Ron Cooke entered Maggie's life and proposed marriage at the same time as Alf. Maggie turned Alf down but agreed to marry Ron.

The marriage of Maggie and Ron was seen as an ideal opportunity to bring Gordon Clegg back into the series. Scripts were written in which he would seduce Lucille and then dump her. However the story had to be altered because Jennifer Moss and Granada parted company rather suddenly; Jenny had a drink problem which affected her work and she was written out of scripts while the producers decided what was to be done with her. In the scripts, Annie Walker told customers that Lucille had gone to visit family in Ireland. She never returned.

The writers reworked the Gordon Clegg storyline and he quickly picked up a local girl, took her back to Betty Turpin's house and was caught, by Betty, with his trousers down. Betty laid into him about abusing her home and hospitality but Gordon refused to be belittled: 'Oh, now, come on Auntie

Alf proposed marriage to Maggie but her heart was set on another man and life far away from cobbles and canals.

Betty. People in London aren't all raving perverts, and folk in the north a bunch of saints. London morals and fashions are only a couple of hours away by Inter-City. And vice-versa. There's no north and south anymore!' Betty refused to condone his behaviour: 'Oh, yes there is. I'm north. You're south now. And we couldn't be more different. Did you say you were going back today? Then sling your hook!'

Gordon was left in charge of the shop and, as sales were low, he decided to rent it out on a weekly basis. Megan Hopkins had recently stopped trading at her fish-and-chip shop and viewed the Corner Shop as an ideal proposition. Her son Idris worked nights at the foundry so his wife Vera would help Megan run the shop.

A NEW POSITION FOR KEN

The Barlow marriage dissolved quickly during the spring of 1974. Ken was shattered to learn Janet did not like his children, while she was furious to discover she had married a man with no ambition and drive. She urged him to look for a headmastership: 'You've got the brains and even the commonsense. I just wonder if you've got the guts to use it for yourself once in your life.' But Ken decided he did not want to lose his day-to-day contact with pupils.

When Janet packed and left, Ken made no attempt to stop her. Ironically, that same week he was offered a high-powered job at the warehouse as north-west manager. With Janet gone and no one else to push him, Ken decided to give up teaching and become an executive. Janet was delighted to hear of his good fortune, but Ken was quick to tell her it made no difference – their marriage had been a sham and was now over.

Ken started work in a comfortable office with a secretary, Tricia Hopkins, and a workforce which included shop stewards Ivy Tilsley and Vera Duckworth. He soon discovered that there was nothing for him to actually do.

★ Tragedy struck the programme in September 1974 when Patricia Cutts was found dead in her London flat. At the inquest, the coroner reported that 'she had taken a massive overdose of barbiturate and she had had a considerable amount to drink.' The verdict of the inquest was suicide.

Patricia Cutts had only appeared in two episodes of the Street, playing Deirdre's mother, Blanche. She was reported to be thrilled that her career was picking up. Her death came as a terrible shock to friends and the cast of the Street. It also threw the production office into chaos; Blanche had been written into future scripts and looked as if she might turn into a long-running character. The character could not be cut so had to be recast very quickly. At the original audition, Susi Hush had had to decide between Patricia Cutts and actress **Maggie Jones** to whom the producer now turned: 'I'd been on holiday in Spain and coming back met Hurricane Dolly and we were thrown about the Channel like a little cork . . . I went straight to bed when I got home. After two hours, my agent phoned and said "they want you to be in Corry".' Maggie had previously played a police woman and a drunken shoplifter in the programme. She trained at RADA, appeared in the film *Every Home Should Have One*, and had become a household name as Polly Barraclough in *Sam*.

Maggie Jones (Blanche Hunt.)

★The Hopkins family were created around two existing characters, Tricia and her mother Vera. The part of Tricia was given to **Kathy Jones** who had been a child singer since the age of eight. She had just finished the children's programme *A Handful of Songs* for Granada when she was contacted regarding a long-term contract on the Street: 'They said that they were going to build a family around me. I went to lunch and met the rest of the family. There was Jesse Evans and Richard Davies and Kathy Staff and we all got on very well and it carried on from there.'

Kathy Staff, known for Nora Batty in *Last of the Summer Wine*, appeared as Vera, the down-trodden wife of Idris. She was not down-trodden by him, but by his Welsh mother Megan. Violet Carson had been forced to leave the programme due to ill health, and Kathy hoped Vera Hopkins would take over the Ena role: 'Unfortunately, it was Jesse Evans that they got in to play my mother-in-law. And I was in between her and the rest of the people in the Street trying to keep the peace, because she did some rather nasty things.'

Not long after establishing the character of Vera, Kathy had to ask Susi Hush to write her out for a while so she could go and do *Summer Wine* studio work.' Vera went to look after her dying mother and returned a rich woman.

A WEEK IN THE SUN

In the early spring of 1974, Susi Hush was made producer replacing Eric Prytherch who had run the show since mid-1972. Whereas some Street producers had attempted to reshape the programme and cast, Susi Hush concentrated on the look of the show, feeling that it had become too glamorous and had shifted too far away from its backstreet roots. After upsetting a few members of the cast by insisting on the removal of real jewellery and ensuring hairstyles were toned down, Susi Hush came up with the idea of filming two episodes with all the women in Majorca. In the scripts, Bet won a Spot the Ball contest and eight of the ladies flew out for a week in the sun. Writer Adele Rose went along, in case there were any rewrites needed, and Susi Hush joined the team to make sure all went well. The actresses were not impressed when they were shown to the hotel where they were to stay. Julie Goodyear recalls the incident: 'We were actually in this two-star hotel. . . . the crew were put in a five-star hotel. . . . We were popped in the two-star with genuine holidaymakers who really did not want their holidays disrupted.'

Matters were made worse when the actresses were called at 6am for make-up. Thelma Barlow takes up the tale: 'Two poor girls had to do the make-up in a room that was next to an open sewer. The smell was disgusting.' It is the swimming-pool that Betty Driver remembers most about the week: 'Quentin Lawrence was the director and he used to go down and stand in the pool in his little shorts and his camera, and used to order the other

★ Elizabeth Dawn used to watch the backs of internationally known actresses as she stood, dressed as a warden, throughout countless episodes of Grandada's *Crown Court*. She went on to act in *Play For Today* while working the cabaret circuit in the evenings. In 1974, she was given another minor part, that of troublesome Vera Duckworth at the warehouse. She played the part on and off when required for nine years, then became one of the Street's major characters. She recalls how nervous she felt, starting work with people she had watched for years: 'But when I walked into the Street studios for the first time I was already acting. I felt that from the first moment I had to show them I was capable, and you can't act capable if you behave like a mouse, can you? So I would grit my teeth, switch on my most confident smile and stride into action as though I'd just called in from the Royal Shakespeare Company.'

A rare intimate moment for the Barlows just before he started a new job and she left him.

Fun and frolics by the sea for the Street's ladies.

holidaymakers out of the pool and away from the poolside and, of course, people soon got fed up.'

However, on screen the women had a marvellous time. Deirdre won Annie's approval by shunning the attention of an insistent young man; Bet fell for a property tycoon; and Mavis surprised everyone by having a fling with a Spanish electrician called Pedro.

Back in Manchester the women returned to work only to receive a cold shoulder from their screen partners, as Betty Driver recalls: 'Bernard Youens said to me, "Don't come near me." I said, "Why, what's the matter?" He said, "It's all right for you lot out there having a good time." I said, "Ask any of the girls, they would swap places."'

·1975·

'It was wonderful, like having a playmate. Tricia and Gail became two girls of the Seventies. They'd missed the Swinging Sixties but they'd got the backlash from that, all the good things. They had a Seventies lifestyle but in the confines of the Street.'

Kathy Jones

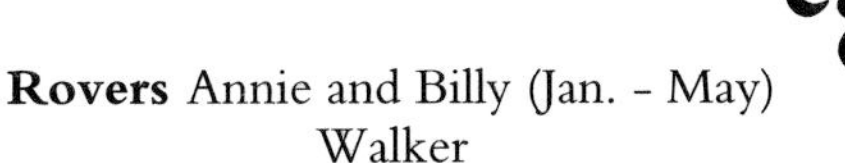

Rovers Annie and Billy (Jan. - May) Walker

No. 1 Albert Tatlock

No. 3 Ernie and Emily Bishop

No. 5 Minnie Caldwell • Eddie Yeats (Jan. - July)

No. 9 Len Fairclough, Ray Langton (Jan. - Sept.) and Jerry Booth (Jan. - Nov.) EddieYeats (July - Sept.)

No. 11 Ken Barlow

No. 13 Stan and Hilda Ogden

Shop Idris, Vera and Megan Hopkins (Jan. - April)

Shop flat Tricia Hopkins • Gail Potter (April - Dec.)

No. 16 (Centre) Ena Sharples (Oct. - Dec.)

Non-residents Betty Turpin • Bet Lynch Alf Roberts • Rita Littlewood • Ivy Tilsley Edna Gee • Mavis Riley • Deirdre Hunt Blanche Hunt

COMINGS AND GOINGS

There was little movement in the Street this year. The Hopkin family left under the cover of night, although Tricia stayed behind to rent the shop flat. Her workmate Gail Potter moved in to keep her company. Billy Walker took a job in Jersey and his his fiancée quickly married Ray Langton. Ray left No.9 and converted the upstairs of Blanche Hunt's house into a flat for Deirdrè and himself. Eddie Yeats lodged at No.9 for a while before being arrested for acting as lookout for a burglary. Jerry Booth's sudden death in November left Len quite alone at the house. There were celebrations in October when Ena Sharples returned from St Anne's to resume her post of caretaker at the Community Centre.

GORDON'S MOTHERS

It was a startling discovery. Megan Hopkins was moving Maggie Clegg's old furniture when she found, stuffed down the back of the sideboard, a birth certificate – Gordon Clegg's. She thought nothing of it until she had a close look at it and found his mother was 'Elizabeth Preston', his father 'unknown'. This had been towards the end of 1974, and Megan spent days investigating the mystery until she uncovered the fact that Betty's maiden name was Preston. Vera made Megan reassure Betty that her secret was safe after Betty explained how she had fallen for a married man during the war and Maggie had adopted the baby – Gordon.

A few months later Megan decided to use the information to blackmail Gordon into lowering the price of the shop, not knowing that Betty and Maggie had told Gordon the truth. He and Betty stormed out of the shop, leaving the Hopkins to fly at Megan in fury. That night they loaded their belongings into a van and left under the cover of dark. Kathy Staff was sad to leave the Street but realized that the family were not popular with the viewers: 'I think it was because they were Welsh and grandma was always making trouble. It was certainly something different, having people in it who weren't Lancashire. Unfortunately it did not work out.'

Bill Kenwright had been shocked by the story line: 'They sent me the scripts, I read them and I cried.'

Betty Driver received obscene mail: 'I had one, the heading was "you dirty cow." It went on, "You've always been so goody-goody and there you are, you've a child long before you were married."'

Irene Sutcliffe was cross about it: 'It was a silly story.'

Kathy Jones had not been told about the future of Tricia, who was now the only teenager on the Street. She had no idea if her contract was to be renewed when the others left: 'I was terrified at one point. I thought, "They've gone, it's me next," but they said, "No, no, we want to keep you on, we've got this other character Gail, coming in."'

·1975·

Gordon Clegg was bitter to find mother Maggie was really auntie Maggie. Irene Sutcliffe still finds the storyline insulting as she feels it demolished all the effort put into making her mother-son relationship so believable.

★ **Helen Worth's** first television role was in *Z Cars* at the age of ten. She had always loved showbusiness, an interest inherited from her grandmother who ran a boarding-house in Bradford where all the stars of the day, such as Vesta Tilley, used to stay. Helen's big break came on her twelfth birthday when she landed a part in *The Sound of Music* in the West End. She remained in the musical for nine months, at the end of that time she concentrated on her school. At fifteen she moved to London and worked with various repertory companies in the South of England. Finally, at the age of twenty-three, Helen landed the part of seventeen-year-old Gail.

TRAGIC BET

Betty Turpin was not the only barmaid with an illegitimate son; at the age of sixteen Bet Lynch had given birth to a boy, Martin, who she had been forced to have adopted when he was just six weeks old. In 1974, Martin tracked her down to the Rovers but left the pub without introducing himself, disgusted by her cheap, tarty image. In early 1975, Bet started a relationship with Len Fairclough and hoped that it would be permanent, but he, like all the other men in her life, just wanted her as a casual one-night stand whenever he was lonely. Bet refused to go along with this.

Bet finished with Len at lunchtime. She went into work late and was met by a young soldier who broke the news, as best he could, that his mate, her son, had been killed in a car crash. He handed her Martin's photograph and left. Annie and Betty tried to comfort her but Bet sought solitude and reached for the bottle of aspirins.

Realizing something was wrong, Eddie Yeats forced his way into her bedsit. She had not taken any of the tablets yet and was perched on her bed, crying. Julie Goodyear had been a regular for five years at this point and these scenes were the strongest and most dramatic she had ever played: 'I am pleased with them. I've looked back on them and thought that my earlier work is better than the work I do now. It's raw talent really. I look at it sometimes and it just takes my breath away.' After finding Bet, Eddie sat and listened as she poured out all her heartbreak and anger over losing the one thing she had always wanted and had never really been her's: 'The one decent thing a man ever gave me was wrenched from me.' Eddie took the tablets away.

Len Fairclough let Bet Lynch down badly at a time when she needed him most.

DEIRDRE MAKES AN HONEST MAN OF RAY

The New Year started well for nineteen-year-old Deirdre; she was engaged to Billy Walker and the big white wedding she had always dreamed of lay just round the corner. The date was set for May, Len

★**Geoffrey Hughes** was born in Liverpool and turned to acting as an eighteen-year-old amateur. He joined the Merseyside Unity Theatre Company and acted in Alun Owen's *Progress To The Park*. Geoff then worked in repertory in Stoke and was given a part in Owen's musical *Maggie May* in the West End. Geoff has appeared in films such as *The Virgin Soldiers* and *Adolf Hitler – My Part In His Downfall*. His television credits before the Street included *The Likely Lads*, *Z Cars* and *Crown Court*. Eddie Yeats was Geoff's second part in the Street. In 1967, he played a thug who roughed up Albert Tatlock. He started work as Eddie late in 1974 and finished recording his initial three episodes in early December: 'Suzie Hush, who was the producer, said "Would you like to stay on for six months?"' Geoff was to stay for another eight years.

Geoffrey Hughes wore a torn old hat as his trademark

Geoff Hughes
Eddie Yeats

Bernard Youens and Jean Alexander as Stan and Hilda Ogden

Fairclough had agreed to be Billy's best man, Deirdre's mother Blanche had made a white full-length flock, and Annie had prepared the Rovers for the couple's new home. At this point Deirdre began to feel she was too young to commit herself: 'What am I doing? I'm popping round corner to get wed. Then we'll pop round next corner, find somewhere to live. Then it'll be round next, taking kids to school.' Billy had no patience with his teenage bride-to-be and called off the wedding. He left the area, taking a job as barman in a Jersey hotel.

The break-up happened so quickly it startled both the characters and the viewers. In fact, the wedding episode had already been written when Kenneth Farrington pointed out that his contract had run out and the deal he had negotiated for a new six-month run had failed to come through: 'I stayed on for a few weeks while they changed the storyline, but I did not do another six months. It was a point of principal – if you're running a business and you agree something then you stand by the agreement.' Farrington left the Street to work in theatre and the writers were left with a problem: the programme was full of unmarried men and women and everyone felt a wedding was needed. Then someone had the idea that Deirdre could still be a bride – after all, for two years she had endured a love-hate relationship with Ray Langton. Anne Kirkbride remembers the courtship: 'There had been a sort of bond between Ray and Deirdre the whole time. There'd been this sort of little undercurrent going on which obviously speeded up considerably when they decided to marry them off. Suddenly they were in each other's arms. This vague sexual current turned into undying love. There were no hearts and flowers involved and it was all very much matter-of-fact really. But it worked.'

Ray and Deirdre were married in a registry office on 7 July 1975. The bride's beautiful white gown stayed on Blanche's tailor's dummy and Deirdre wore a fawn suit she used for work. After the wedding, Ray moved in with the Hunts in Victoria Street.

Warehouse Fire

Vandalism came to the Street in the shape of three truant schoolboys. They stole comics from the magazine, cheeked Mrs Sharples and ran amok in the area. Some residents wanted the police involved, but Ken attempted the social worker's sympathetic route, chatting to the parents. Albert Tatlock, however, was sick of Ken's softy softly approach: 'You're trouble is yer soft. You see life through rose-coloured specs. Or bury yer 'ead in t'sand altogether if there's sumat you don't want to even see.' He reported them to the police. The boys thought Barlow had informed on them and smashed up his house before seeking refuge in the storeroom at the warehouse. When they ran off from the building they left a lighted cigarette behind. The storeroom, full of flammable goods, was soon ablaze.

By mid-morning Edna Gee was desperate for a cigarette so made her way to her usual smoking-hole – the stock room. As she pulled open the door a wave of flames covered her and she screamed out in terror. Lynne Perrie played Edna's best mate Ivy and recalls how upset Mavis Rogerson was over the fate of her character: 'I said something to her during the week and she snapped me head off, "Don't you know what's happening?" I said, "What do you mean what's happening?" "Well," she said, "I'm getting burnt. I'm dying."' Lynne could not believe the special effects: 'It was the first time I'd seen any kind of pyrotechnics. When she went through that door and the fire came up, I thought it was wonderful!' Someone else who remembers the fire well is Kathy Jones. Her character Tricia had to flee the fire from the ladies' toilet next to the storeroom. She had to be covered in smoke and rescued by Ken Barlow: 'I was worried at the time that it wasn't going to look frightening enough, because any sign of special effects they moved you away, they didn't want to get involved with it. They pieced it all

Billy Walker's decision to leave for Jersey left the field open for Ray Langton to make his move on Deirdre. Deirdre's decision to marry Ray left Blanche Hunt wondering if her daughter had lost her sanity.

The Street's residents turned out in force to celebrate Albert Tatlock's seventieth birthday in August.

Larking around between takes – Graham Haberfield is fondly remembered by all who worked with him. As the floor manager counted down to prepare everyone for a recording Graham would wail 'Farewell real world!' and the giggles would start.

Gail Potter comforts Tricia after she is rescued from the warehouse fire.

Happy fifteenth birthday.

together afterwards in editing. But I had to put glycerine in my eyes to make them sting and cry.'

The residents were evacuated because the warehouse contained tanks of liquified petroleum gas. The warehouse was completely gutted and at the end of the day two bodies were found, one of which was identified as Edna Gee. Ivy was left to comfort her distraught husband Fred.

THE DEATH OF A GENTLEMAN

On 18 October 1975 the cast heard that Graham Haberfield had died from heart failure linked with a liver condition. Graham was only thirty-four years old. Bill Roache summed up the cast's feelings when he was stopped by a journalist: 'His death means a great loss to us all personally.' Graham had recorded two episodes before his death and at his widow Valerie's request they were broadcast, as a tribute to him. The writers then wrote Jerry out of the show: in November Len received the news that he had died. The residents attended his funeral less than a month after the cast had attended Graham's.

'Ken is an intellect born from within so his roots grow under the cobbles of the Street and the ghosts of his family are there.'

Bill Roache

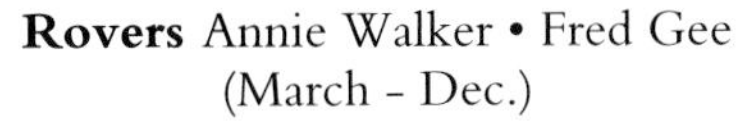

Rovers Annie Walker • Fred Gee (March - Dec.)

No. 1 Albert Tatlock • Ken Barlow (May - Dec.)

No. 3 Ernie and Emily Bishop

No. 5 Minnie Caldwell (Jan. - Oct.) • Mike Baldwin and Bet Lynch (Dec.)

No. 9 Len Fairclough

No. 11 Ken Barlow (Jan. - June) • Wendy Nightingale (May - June) • Elsie Howard and Gail Potter (June - Dec.)

No. 13 Stan and Hilda Ogden

Shop Elsie Howard (April - June) • Renee Bradshaw (May - Dec.)

Shop flat Tricia Hopkins and Gail Potter (Jan. - May) • Terry Bradshaw (June - Dec.)

No. 16 (Centre) Ena Sharples

Non-residents Betty Turpin • Alf Roberts Rita Littlewood • Ivy Tilsley • Mavis Riley Ray Langton • Deirdre Hunt • Blanche Hunt • Eddie Yeats • Derek Wilton Vera Duckworth

·1976·

KEN AND WENDY

It was Hilda Ogden who was first with the news: 'I don't know whether you noticed that Nightingale woman's car outside Ken Barlow's last night? Well, it's still there! And I looked out of our bedroom winder at one o'clock this mornin' and it was there. *And* I looked again at five . . . an' it was still there!' Free love had finally arrived in Coronation Street. Wendy Nightingale, a graduate, had fallen for Community Centre manager Ken Barlow. Separated from Janet for two years now, Ken was keen to enter a new relationship and it only took two home-cooked meals at No.11 to seduce Wendy. It was not long before the news reached the ear of Wendy's husband Roger. Wendy told Ken she had never been unfaithful before but her marriage had become boring. He urged her to leave Roger and to move in

COMINGS AND GOINGS

One winter night Stan and Albert were locked into the Rovers' cellar by accident. Annie Walker was furious to find them in the morning – drunk! After this, for security reasons, Annie Walker was persuaded by the brewery to take on a resident potman. She feared her home would be invaded but widower Fred Gee, in blazer and bow tie, impressed her so much she welcomed him. By the end of the year his true nature – idle, shiftless and coarse – came out but, as Annie told her friend Nellie Harvey, she had trained him in her little ways. Albert Tatlock also took in a permanent guest when Ken Barlow moved from No.11. Ken had a bad year. He moved Wendy Nightingale into No.11 with him, becoming the first couple to live 'over the broom' as Hilda Ogden put it. Wendy was a married woman who had left husband Roger to be with Ken, but she did not fit in on the Street and returned home. Ken gave the house back to Elsie Howard who returned from Newcastle following the break-up of her marriage to Alan. The Shop was sold, in June, to ex-supermarket assistant Renee Bradshaw. She evicted Tricia and Gail from the shop flat so her brother Terry could live with her but still retain his independence. Gail was taken in at No.11 by Elsie, but Tricia left the Street to live on the other side of town with her parents. Minnie Caldwell left the Street in October to keep house for an old friend in Whaley Bridge. Her house, No.5, was completely remodernised by Fairclough and Langton. Londoner Mike Baldwin bought it and installed Bet Lynch in it as his 'housekeeper'. Mike stayed at the house during the week while looking after his new denim factory in the refurbished warehouse. At the weekend he returned to London and his common-law wife. Renee Bradshaw was upset when her brother left for the Army in December after Gail Potter told him she did not love him

Ken expected Wendy's husband to admit their marriage was over but Roger Nightingale was not quite so cooperative.

with him, which she did, but not before Roger had left Ken bleeding and unconscious on the floor.

Whereas Ken had always known the backyards of the Street, barren except for the outside 'cludgy'. Wendy had certainly not. She had been raised in leafy, open Bramhall and could not cope with the clutter, noise, smoke, noisiness and openness of the denizens of the Street. After five weeks, she had had enough and returned to a forgiving Roger.

Ken had reached a crossroads in his life – his bosses had threatened to sack him for living with a married woman and he felt they were no longer trustworthy, he missed his children and lacked stability in his life. 'The Story of My life. Two marriages. Two kids. Several jobs. A variety of dreams and ambitions, some shattered, some just getting a bit tatty round the edges.' He gave in his notice at the Community Centre and made plans to start afresh away from Weatherfield. But Albert Tatlock, Ken's uncle by marriage, changed his mind. Albert had tried his best not to interfere with Ken's life and had struggled on alone at No.1 with his pension. Ken was outraged to discover that Albert could not afford to pay his bills so his electricity had been cut off. Barlow realized that he had to stay in the Street, that he belonged there, helping the community at large and Albert in particular. He moved into No.1 as Albert's paying guest and the lights were put back on.

A NEW BROOM

In the early spring of 1976, Bill Podmore replaced Susi Hush as producer. Bill had worked as a cameraman and director on the show since 1961 and, immediately before producing the Street, had worked on comedy shows such as *Nearest and Dearest* and *My Brother's Keeper*. When he took control, he was determined to resurrect the comedy situations and comic characters of the early days. 'Once behind that desk, I began a detailed survey of the Street, seeking the areas crying out for a facelift or even a face change. I had in mind redecoration rather than demolition, but then I spotted cracks in the Corner Shop which could never be papered over.' The shop had been run by Blanche Hunt until January, when she had left the area with Dave Smith to run a nightclub. Since then Gail and Tricia had been playing shop behind the counter and Bill realized the set had ceased to become the hive of gossip it had been in its heyday: 'Youngsters have always played an important role in the Street's life, but without a more mature shop staff, the nitty gritty of conversation and tittle-tattle were never going to bounce around its walls.' Bill created a feisty, fun new character in the shape of independent Renee Bradshaw who bought the shop and fought Annie Walker in court to obtain a licence to sell alcohol.

ELSIE RETURNS

After nearly three years away, Pat Phoenix returned as Elsie to the delight of millions of fans. Bill Podmore agreed to Elsie's return after Pat wrote explaining that she had had enough of touring in the theatre, although he laid down a few ground-rules: 'If we are to recreate the gritty and earthy character of the Elsie Tanner of old, then there must be some

★**Fred Feast** started in showbusiness after he left the RAF where he worked as a paratroop instructor. On impulse he asked for an audition at the Windmill Theatre and learned his trade as a stand-up comic. There he worked with another comedian, Bruce Forsyth. He later turned to acting, appearing in television programmes such as *Nearest and Dearest, Soldier and Me* and *Another Sunday and Sweet FA*. He also appeared in two films, *The Red Beret* and *All Creatures Great and Small*. Fred first appeared on the Street as Fred in 1975 when his screen wife Edna was killed in the warehouse fire. Fred had been contacted by Bill Podmore. 'Bill said, I want a gritty barman, that'll take Coronation Street by the scruff of the neck. So I did my research in the bars in Salford and came up with Fred Gee. . . . Having grasped the northern humour, I asked Bill if I could just fit bits in and he agreed.'

big changes to the way you used to look.' Pat agreed to a more down-to-earth look for Elsie but on her first day of filming chose to forget the agreement, turning up in a designer raincoat. She later explained to Podmore: 'The way I look and dress gives hope to all those millions of women out there of my age.'

Elsie, separated from Alan, lodged at the Corner Shop until Ken vacated her old house, No.11. She moved in with Gail Potter and together they found employment at the boutique, Sylvia's Separates. With Renee buying the shop and Gail moving out of the flat, it was time for Trica Hopkins to leave the Street and move in with her family somewhere on the darker side of Weatherfield.

Co-respondent Gail

Nineteen-year-old Gail Potter found herself drawn into a messy divorce in the summer of 1976. Despite Elsie's warnings she had fallen for older sales rep, Roy Thornley. Gail believed this was love and gave Roy her virginity in the stockroom at Sylvia's Separates. Elsie discovered Roy had a wife and two children, but Gail refused to believe her: 'I'm not stupid, Elsie. I'm bright enough to know a jealous woman when I see one. Jealous of me. Cos I'm nineteen an' I'm 'aving fun. An' them are two things you said goodbye to a long time ago.'

Elsie cornered Roy and he was forced to admit the truth in front of Gail. Then Mrs Thornley cited Gail as co-respondent in her divorce case. Helen Worth enjoyed playing the story immensely as it put all her acting skills to the test: 'At the time it was quite a risqué story, not like doing it now. At the time, for a young girl to be going out with a married man, to be having an affair, was quite something.' The story reintroduced the caring motherly side of Elsie and Helen especially remembers the thrill of recording episodes as if they were live: 'If Pat was going to dry she used to bang her hand on the table and that was the cue for me to come in. Because Pat used to get carried away with what she was doing, her lines would go out of the window. I always thrived on that. We'd find our way back to the script at some point!' Elsie confronted Mrs Thornley and begged her to leave Gail out of the divorce, but Doreen Thornley refused to believe Gail was the innocent Elsie said she was. Eventually Doreen discovered a new co-respondent – the boutique boss, Sylvia Matthews.

Mavis finds a soulmate

Romance entered Mavis Riley's life in the shape of furniture salesman Derek Bernard Wilton. Mavis confessed to Rita that she enjoyed his hesitant nature and immediately saw beyond this to the passionate

·1976·

Ray Thornley declared his love for Gail and she naively believe him.

★ **Madge Hindle** did not have to audition for the part of Renee: 'I'd been in *Nearest and Dearest*, which Bill had directed. He just rang and said, "How would you like to be on the Street."' It was a few months before Madge managed to sort out Renee's character: 'I think they wanted somebody to be strong and argumentative like Ena Sharples. But unfortunately you can't do that in a shop because people won't come in.'

Madge's first appearance on television was in drama series *On the Margin*, written by her friend Alan Bennett. *Nearest and Dearest* made Madge a household name and numerous television plays and series followed before the Street, including *Porridge, Open All Hours, The Cuckoo Waltz*. But nothing prepared her for work behind the counter of the Corner Shop: 'I couldn't ever work in a shop because I can't add up, could never calculate the correct change or even weigh anything properly.' The biggest problem came in the shape of the till: 'I had to press 20 and it would shoot out, hitting me in the stomach. I tried to anticipate it and step back, but it always caught me unawares even though I knew it was going to happen!'

Madge Hindle - (Renee)

heart beating inside. Just a week into the relationship Derek asked Mavis to go away for the weekend with him. Mavis dithered about, while Rita urged her to throw caution to the wind and enjoy herself: 'You're right about men, Mavis. They're all rotten and you can't trust them. They're totally selfish and deep down every one of them's a rapist. But what beats me is how you *know*. I know how I know. I've known too many of them too well. But how is it you know to pull up the drawbridge minute a feller comes over the horizon?' In the end it was Derek's gentle nature and honesty that persuaded Mavis to put herself entirely in his hands and, when she returned on Monday for work, she told Rita everything had been perfect.

Things did not remain perfect for long after Derek's widowed mother, Amy, inspected his new 'friend' first-hand. Mavis found Mrs Wilton's directness alarming: 'How old are you?' 'Why aren't

Waiting for a cue – Peter Baldwin and Thelma Barlow relax before transforming themselves into Derek and Mavis.

Peter Baldwin

★It was by accident that **Peter Baldwin** landed the part of Derek. Another actor from the same agency was asked to audition, but he was not available so Peter went in his place. He was delighted to learn he would be playing opposite Thelma Barlow; they had worked together in the West of England Theatre Company and at the Bristol Old Vic, at one stage sharing a house with some other actors. After a spell with the BBC Repertory Company he started his television career in *Girls About Town*, created by Street writer Adele Rose. His career has spanned plays and series of all nature, from *Miss Marple* to *Bergerac*, and until he joined the cast permanently in 1988 he was rarely off the stage, and worked all over the country.

·1976·

you married?' 'What do you want from my son?' But Mavis missed the conversation when she was visiting the 'little girl's room': 'She won't do. She's nice to the point of being a walking ice-cream sundae. But that's not what I'm talking about. She's also you in a tweed skirt. You're as alike as two robins. Neither of you could decide what time of day it was in a roomful of clocks.' Derek humbly accepted his mother's opinion and told Mavis they should cool their friendship. It was a path he continued to take well after Amy's death, until he married Mavis twelve years later.

THE 'MURIEL'

When Hilda Ogden wanted her living-room redecorated she asked Eddie Yeats to find wallpaper. He turned up with rolls of a beautiful pattern only to find that four rolls were faded because it was old stock. Eddie wanted to please Hilda as he saw himself lodging in her back bedroom, so he pulled out all the stops. He brought rolls of paper to make up a mural. Hilda was smitten straight away.

Eddie used his best salesman patter to sell the idea 'That's your scenic panorama contrast wall that is. You see, it gives you what they call a muriel. It's your muriel feature scenic panorama contrast wall. Dead trendy. Latest there is.'

In the same episode, Ray Langton threw a birthday party for Deirdre and the recording schedule concentrated on the complex party scenes, with the scenes at No.13 being recorded at the end of the day. All Jean Alexander remembers is the rising panic that the scenes would not be recorded and so dropped from the programme: 'We had about six scenes, with the room in various stages of stripping and repapering. we had fifty minutes of studio time left to do these six scenes. It was so fast! We'd do one scene and then the prop men would come on and strip a bit more wallpaper off. You couldn't enjoy it because nobody dared dry.'

The mural in place with the famous flying ducks. The ducks had originally appeared in No. 11 on Elsie Tanner's living-room wall.

·1977·

'You can't really be a tremendous character in a shop ... They married me to Alf hoping that that would work but it was constant bickering.'

Madge Hindle

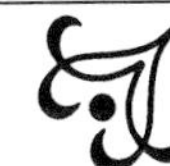

Rovers Annie Walker • Fred Gee

No. 1 Albert Tatlock • Ken Barlow

No. 3 Ernie and Emily Bishop

No. 5 Mike Baldwin and Bet Lynch (Jan. - March) • Ray, Deirdre and Tracy Langton (March - Dec.)

No. 9 Len and Rita (April - Dec.) Fairclough

No. 11 Elsie Howard and Gail Potter Suzie Birchall (Feb. Dec.)

No. 13 Stan and Hilda Ogden

Shop Renee Bradshaw

Shop flat Bet Lynch (March - Dec.)

No. 16 (Centre) Ena Sharples

Non-residents Betty Turpin • Alf Roberts Ivy Tilsley • Mavis Riley • Eddie Yeats Derek Wilton • Vera Duckworth Steve Fisher

COMINGS AND GOINGS

Bet Lynch's cosy lovenest at No.5 was destroyed when Mike Baldwin threw her out and sold the house to Ray and Deirdre Langton, whose daughter Tracy had been born at the start of the year. Rita Littlewood comforted Len Fairclough after Janet committed suicide in his house. She finally moved into the Street when she married Len in April and set up home at No.9. A spring fishing trip brought together Renee Bradshaw and Alf Roberts. Renee Bradshaw took pity on homeless Bet and took her on at the flat shop while Mike secretly subsidized her rent. Elsie Howard was landed with a second lodger in the shape of confident Suzie Birchall who moved into Gail Potter's room at No.11.

THE COCKNEY WIDE BOY

Mike Baldwin took the Street by storm in November 1976 when he first opened his factory, employing local women such as Ivy Tilsley and Vera Duckworth to turn denim into jeans and jackets. He bought up Sylvia's Separates, moving manageress Elsie Howard from the boutique to the factory to be his supervisor and employing Ernest Bishop as his right-hand man. He renamed the boutique 'The Western Front' and took on Suzie Birchall to work under Gail Potter. He had given Bet Lynch the keys to No.5 as a Christmas present but, early in 1977, he ordered her to vacate the house as his wife Anne was coming up from London. Bet had always known he was married and complied with his wishes only to be told by Anne that she was not Mrs Baldwin, just Mike's common-in law wife. Bet was furious that she had been lied to: 'Hope keeps people like me going. You hope that one day there'll be someone who won't cheat or lie or pretend they care about you when all they really want is a willing tart. I've been kicked in the teeth often enough so it doesn't really come as a surprise. But it doesn't stop hurting.' She finished with Mike but refused to leave the house, until he changed the locks and sold it cut-price to new father Ray Langton.

Johnny Briggs enjoyed the scenes at the factory, with Mike at the hub of all the activity: 'I loved it when the character was wheeling and dealing, and had a factory and the fun with the girls. Trying to pull one over on them and them trying to pull one over on him.' When the set was first built, real sewing-machines were installed, but the actresses who had to use them were given no training. For Elizabeth Dawn this was no problem; before acting she had spent years in various factories: 'I can work ten machines in a factory. I can do lapel-pasting, I can do edging, I can make trousers. And I think that helped from what the viewer saw; I used to get on that machine and assert myself; I didn't wait for anyone to tell me what to do.'

Lynne Perrie had not had Liz's training on the

★ Mike Baldwin was the second character to be played by **Johnny Briggs**; he had already appeared as a lorry driver working at the warehouse. He was employed as Mike when Bill Podmore wanted to introduce a cockney who would steal the hearts of the female viewers.

Johnny's career had started when, aged twelve, he won a scholarship to the Italia Conti Stage School. His first professional engagement was at the Cambridge Theatre in 1947 when, as a boy soprano, he sang 'La Bôheme'. At sixteen, his voice broke and he went into rep before doing his National Service. Afterwards, his career really took off. He appeared in television shows such as *The Younger Generation, Z Cars* and *The Avengers,* and as Sgt Russell in the long-running *No Hiding Place*. His film credits include *Office Party* in which he rowed with the director, refusing to take his clothes off for a love scene.

In 1977, Mike Baldwin employed cocky Suzie Birchall at his shop 'The Western Front'. For actress **Cheryl Murray** it was her first big break into television after years of stage work: 'I was doing a tour in *Separate Tables* when I was given a month off. I was asked to play two weeks in *Coronation Street*, which I did.' It was soon clear to Cheryl that the part was open-ended and she had been cast as the new Elsie Tanner. She was persuaded by her agent that she was perfect for the Street and managed to get out of her stage contract.

machines: 'I was concentrating on what I was saying and pressing the foot pedal and I felt something which I thought was the foot pedal. I'm talking away and Pat Phoenix suddenly screamed and I looked down and there was this blood. And I couldn't move me finger because the needle had gone right through it. So they had to undo the machine and take the needle out as it was bent from underneath, and they took me to hospital to have it pulled out.'

JUBILEE BABY

Deirdre Langton gave birth to a bouncing baby girl on 24 January 1977. She was glad the pregnancy was finally over although Anne Kirkbride had hoped it would continue a bit longer: 'I've never been pregnant but I always think pregnant women look really good. I like pregnant women. So that was quite nice.' The writers had decided that the baby, the first to be born on the Street since the Barlow twins in 1965, would feature heavily in scripts and on screen. The Manchester hospitals were put on alert by a casting department who needed a tiny baby who would look newborn on screen. Christabel Finch was born on 21 December and weighed just 5lbs 10oz. She was given the job on the spot.

Deirdre had wanted the baby to be called Lynette and rowed with Ray who planned to call her Tracy. There were so many scenes with everyone rowing over the name that Maggie Jones playing 'granny' Blanche Hunt got completely confused and, instead of saying 'Ta ra then, love' as she exited, turned to Anne Kirkbride and said 'Tara then love', feeling certain that that was what the baby was to be called. Eventually, Ray registered the baby Tracy Lynette behind Deirdre's back.

Shortly afterwards the Langton marriage was put under a strain when Deirdre was molested under the viaduct. She broke down, abandoned Tracy and disappeared, only to be found contemplating suicide on a motorway bridge. Anne Kirkbride recalls how funny she found the whole incident: 'It was great fun, a wonderful night shot. You never saw the guy who molested me, you just saw his feet. I had to slide off under the bridge and my coat was getting all dirty. Then I had to stand on a bridge, only it wasn't a bridge, it was a subway. So they had the cameraman strapped underneath it to get shots of my face looking down. And somebody else was flashing a light on and off, into my face, to make it look as if cars were going underneath. And all the time there were these kids down below shouting "Jump!"' Eventually, a lorry driver broke Deirdre's trance by asking her for directions and she went home.

Another Funeral for Ken

Judith Barker had made occasional appearances as Janet Barlow since the break-up of the Barlow marriage in 1974. In late 1976, she was approached by Granada to make her final appearance. In the middle of a run of *A Taste of Honey* at Manchester's University Theatre, Judith agreed to film Janet's suicide. In the scripts, Janet had been thrown out by her lover and begged Ken to give them another chance, swearing she had changed. He refused but agreed to let her stay the night. Upstairs, alone and frightened, Janet opened a bottle of pills and swallowed the lot before falling into bed. Ken was to find her there in the morning, only what Bill Roache found was a sleeping actress. Judith Barker explains: 'I was so tired, I was rehearsing and playing and somehow time had been found to bring me back to be killed off and I was just exhausted. I remember all this dramatic tracking with the camera and I was discovered snoring! I went absolutely spark out.

Sir Edmund Hillary and his Sherpa attempt the north face of some scaffolding. The Jubilee celebrations found the Street making a float entitled Britain Through the Ages.

With only hours to go to live, Janet Barlow pleads with estranged husband Ken to give their marriage just one last try. His refusal leads to her suicide.

Rita wears her expensive headpiece as she marries Len Fairclough.

Ken was shattered by Janet's death and filled with remorse for not helping her when she needed him most. To make matters worse the police initially suspected him of murdering her. He could not understand why death followed him around – his mother, brother, father and two wives were now dead. It was old flame Rita Littlewood to whom he turned for comfort: 'We've all had our nightmares, Ken. We're all the walkin' wounded, love. It's just that some of us get more wounded than others.'

ANOTHER *TV TIMES* SUPPLEMENT

'20 April will always be remembered as Len and Rita's day, the time when the Street forgot its differences and gathered at St Mary's to wish them long life and happiness. . . .' So reads the *TV Times* supplement celebrating the wedding of Fairclough and Littlewood. The couple had been involved in an on-off relationship since 1972 and now, finally, they were to marry.

·1977·

All the residents gathered for the wedding, including Len's old flame Elsie Howard. They went through the ceremony with the *TV Times* photographer clicking away and then, a few weeks later, went through the whole process again, only this time the event was filmed for the programme. All went well apart from the fact that Pat Phoenix phoned in ill, so Elsie's part was cut from the church sequences. The art directors at *TV Times* then had the arduous task of painting Elsie out of all the group and church shots taken for the magazine.

Barbara Knox enjoyed the spectacular way the wedding was filmed and scripted. Unfortunately, she was in slight pain during the filming as she had been involved in a car accident shortly before, and was still wearing a brace. Many columnists in the press commented on Rita's 'Miss Muffet' style head-dress, now part of the Granada Tours experience. It was chosen by Barbara who insisted that Rita would have matching shoes and handbag. Barbara remembers clearly how cold it was: 'It was bitterly, bitterly cold on the actual filming and it was supposed to be spring and there wasn't a daffodil, and I remember the prop man planting plastic daffodils all outside the church.'

A DAY'S FISHING

Four people set off on a fishing trip in April. Mavis Riley expressed an interest to enthusiast Fred Gee, and he gallantly offered to take her on the river but then asked Alf Roberts to join them. Alf wasn't keen: 'Look, what do you want me for? I'll only be splitting up a nice little twosome if I come.' 'That's why I want you to come,' replied desperate Fred.

Alf reluctantly agreed but cheered up when he discovered shopkeeper Renee Bradshaw was tagging along too. This was to be the start of an awkward courtship which eventually ended in marriage.

The script called for Renee to fall into the river, for Mavis to fall in trying to rescue her and then for Fred to follow. What the writers did not know was that Madge Hindle could not swim: 'Nobody bothered to ask. It was only when we got to the river on a freezing cold March day and were handed wetsuits that I said, "You know I can't swim." I could have done the rescuing bit but it was the actual being confident enough to fall in that I was bothered about.' The director called for a stand in and to Madge's amazement a six-foot man was dressed in a frock with a red wig on his head. He fell into the river beautifully but looked nothing like Renee Bradshaw. Madge expected to have to do the stunt herself and was bewildered when the director seemed happy with the stuntman. Thelma Barlow, waiting to jump into the river after 'Renee', was having problems of her own. She was not looking forward to jumping into the river and can remember the day very clearly: 'A pale, weak sun was filtering through these bare trees, and the river looked very cold and swirly.' On the command she jumped in to save Renee and was thrilled to find how warm she was in her wet suit. Location Manager Gordon McKellar, having no idea that Thelma had already been drinking whisky to keep warm, gave her cups of brandy-laced tea to warm her up afterwards, and she ended the day giggling through every scene.

The intrepid adventurers set off to catch fish.

·1978·

Lynne Carol, who played Martha Longhurst, was stopped by a lady in the London underground:

'Excuse me, but I know you don't I? How long have you been dead now?'

Rovers Annie Walker • Fred Gee

No. 1 Albert Tatlock • Ken Barlow

No. 3 Ernie (Jan.) and Emily Bishop

No. 5 Ray (Jan. - Nov.), Deirdre and Tracy Langton

No. 9 Len and Rita Fairclough

No. 11 Elsie Howard Tanner • Gail Potter Suzie Birchall

No. 13 Stan and Hilda Ogden

Shop Renee and Alf (March - Dec.) Roberts

Shop flat Bet Lynch

No. 16 (Centre) Ena Sharples

Non-residents Betty Turpin • Ivy Tilsley Mavis Riley • Eddie Yeats • Mike Baldwin Vera Duckworth • Steve Fisher Ron Mather

COMINGS AND GOINGS

Ernie Bishop's violent death at the hands of an armed robber in January plunged the Street into mourning and Emily had to adjust to living at No.3 by herself. Two months later Alf Roberts finally moved into the Street, after having been a regular in the Rovers for 18 years. He married Renee Bradshaw and moved into the Corner Shop with her. At the reception Alf thumped Renee's step-father when he commented that Alf had only married her to get his hands on the shop. Deirdre Langton's world was turned upside down when she discovered husband Ray had been unfaithful with a waitress from the Rosamund Street café. She agreed to start afresh with him in Holland but changed her mind. He refused to let her muck him about and emigrated anyway, leaving Deirdre at No.5 with baby Tracy. At the end of the year, Gail Potter falls for Brian Tilsley.

THE DEATH OF A LAY PREACHER

A lot of newspapers have reported and speculated on the killing of Ernest Bishop. There were many untrue reports at the time that the actor Stephen Hancock was sacked because he dared to ask for more money. In fact, Stephen Hancock had told producer Bill Podmore that he would not be signing up for another year as Ernie because he felt the contracts were not fair. Under the system the cast were guaranteed at least fifty-two episodes a year and paid accordingly. However, for some of the older members of cast the contracts differed, as Podmore explains in his autobiography: '. . . there existed a handful of people, including Pat Phoenix, Doris Speed and Peter Adamson, who were guaranteed payment for every one of the year's 104 episodes. It didn't necessarily double their pay packets, but these were obviously fatter and the artists were never, of course, called upon to work the full fifty-two weeks a year.' Over a period of time Podmore attempted to change Hancock's mind but unless the contract system was changed and made the same for all the company Stephen Hancock was adamant that he wanted to leave, and Bill Podmore refused to change the system when he realized that Stephen was speaking for himself alone.

It was John Stevenson who came up with the ideal departure: 'We could not see a believable story where the Bishops split up and were divorced. We couldn't see him going away from the area and not taking her. We eventually came to the conclusion that if Emily Bishop was to stay in the Street, Ernie had to die. It did not seem fair to send her away when she did not want to leave the show. The death of Ernie Bishop was to save Emily Bishop.' Ernie was working as wages clerk at the factory and there Bill and John planned an armed robbery that went wrong: 'There was to be none of the usual television drama of cops and robbers, no car chases leaving skid marks all over Weatherfield. It was decided that in the aftermath of the shooting we would stay in the Street reflecting on the utter futility of Ernie's death and concentrate on portraying the desolation and immense sadness it had caused.' The scripts were written, with armed robbers bursting into Ernie's office at Baldwin's Casuals, demanding the wages. As Ernie handed them over, Mike walked into the office, nudging the gunman who blasted Ernie in the chest. The frightened men ran for it whilst Mike stared in horror at Ernie's lifeless body.' Stephen Hancock recalls the recording: 'The gun wasn't loaded whilst we were filming until the moment of the actual shooting when they loaded the gun with a blank and got me out of the picture. So all you saw was the bloke firing the gun, with me not there and then you cut to me lying on the floor . . . I picked myself off the floor at the end and I suddenly thought this is the last time that I'm going to be seen on Coronation Street.'

In fact it was not the last time Stephen would film on the Street. A few months later, Granada made a special documentary in the *This England* series called 'A Death in the Street'. It came about because of the tremendous public outcry following Ernie's death. In the programme, viewers' reactions were filmed as they watched the death, many openly crying. Stephen talked about how it felt to be killed off, as did Noel Dyson and Lynne Carol, who both recalled stories of how they were still identified by the public as Ida Barlow and Martha Longhurst.

With Ernie dead, Emily was left a widow and Eileen Derbyshire struggled to adjust to scenes without Stephen, whom she had played against for nearly ten years. 'I was genuinely upset that he'd left, and what I found very distressing was the public reaction, which was quite strong. Some of the letters I have never replied to because I didn't know how to. Of course people wrote to me as if I had really been bereaved which gives you a horrible feeling because you feel an absolute fraud.' Stephen Hancock has many happy memories of his time as Ernest and enjoyed his too-short marriage to Emily: 'I think they were genuinely in love. I thought their relationship was awfully nice, very sweet and gentle. A sea of calm in the middle of a rather bustling Street.'

A pause in rehearsals as Stephen Hancock records his last scene as Ernie.

ENA SHARPLES GROWS UP

Coronation Street came of age on 9 December 1978 as the cast and writers celebrated the programme's eighteenth birthday. The press concentrated on how the cast had aged with their characters. In 1974, Violet Carson had left for nine months following an illness and since then had refused to discuss her thoughts on the Street and Ena. She only agreed to be interviewed on condition that her true feelings be reported. She told reporter John Deighton how she had come to despise Ena Sharples: 'Said Vi, "As an actress I have been destroyed. That's the word to use and I use it quite fearlessly. Ena Sharples killed Violet Carson on Day One of *Coronation Street* eighteen years ago."' A few months later she was interviewed by *TV Times*. 'I'm in two minds over this celebration. I realize that *Coronation Street* has made

After eighteen years of playing Ena, Violet Carson admitted that she never wanted the part but knew as soon as she had screen-tested that it was going to be hers.

The Langtons split in November 1978 was upsetting for Anne Kirkbride who was told she had to leave as well.

me, but it has also destroyed me. I've played a marvellous character who has become a household name, but let's face it, it's Ena Sharples who's famous, not Violet Carson. She's taken over. She rules my life. I've begged them to bury the old girl and let me go, but they won't hear of it.'

In the *Reveille* interview, Miss Carson was asked if she felt the Street would survive without her. Violet knew more than anyone that the Street was bigger than any individual: 'Graveyards are full of people who are indispensable. I suppose I shall go on as long as I'm physically capable of playing Ena. I don't think I'll ever retire.'

RAY LEAVES

In the autumn of 1978, Neville Buswell announced his plans to leave the Street. The news shocked the writing team.

1978

However, this time there was no question of his character – Ray Langton – being killed off. The first Anne Kirkbride heard of the news was when Bill Podmore told her that *she* was to be written out: 'They did not know what they were going to do with me, because they'd already got a lot of single women in the Street. And that was the end of it.' However, Neville Buswell pleaded with Podmore to save Deirdre and after a couple of weeks the writers decided that Deirdre the single mother would be a very interesting concept. A delighted Anne Kirkbride was asked to stay.

The news of Neville's departure broke in the Sunday papers and there was wild speculation as to how he would leave. The writers led the viewers down a variety of blind alleys. First of all, Ray had an affair with Janice Stubbs, waitress at the newly opened café on Rosamund Street. The tabloids announced they would run off together. Then, when Deirdre found out, the press decided that she would throw him out. A reconciliation blocked that and, with Janice off the scene, the Langtons planned to emigrate to Holland. Perhaps Anne Kirkbride was being sacked after all? But then, as the regulars handed over the carriage clock at the farewell party, Deirdre broke down and told Ray she could not go. 'Suit yourself,' replied Ray and took the flight himself, realizing his marriage was over. Deirdre was composed and resigned to her fate: 'But I'll never understand Ray. He had *me*. And he went to her.'

Gail Meets Brian

Helen Worth looks back fondly of the days in the late 1970s when her character Gail Potter shared

Suzie and Gail clung to their childlike silliness, wrapped in cotton wool at No. 11 by Elsie 'I've bin there, kid' Howard.

★**Chris Quinten** earned his Equity card by performing acrobatic stunts in a cabaret at a theatre restaurant. He had wanted to act from a young age but only studied at drama school for a year before being persuaded to 'get a proper job'. For two years, he served as an apprentice fitter at a shipyard, but knew it was not right for him. He went to London and soon acquired an agent. Before the Street he appeared in various television shows and had a part in the film *International Velvet*.

Elsie's back room with Suzie Birchall: 'The Street goes through all the years and comes back to the archetypal characters, doesn't it? . . . Suzie and Gail were like the original Doreen and Sheila.' Like Sheila Birtles before her, Gail assumed the role of the more serious friend, but was quick to fall in with her confident friend's plans. Suzie Birchall, like a latter day Doreen Lostock, was cheeky, assertive and fun-loving. Cheryl Murray agrees with Helen that their characters were so successful because they were believable, they were mates: 'Suzie was very worldly and tried to protect Gail. She was very fond of Gail. I remember one line where somebody had said something about Gail Potter, and Suzie had tried to put this girl through a window or something for insulting Gail.'

Suzie and Gail had many memorable storylines. They persuaded Baldwin's driver Steve Fisher to take them to Southport on a delivery with him, and got stuck on the beach and were late delivering the jeans. They attempted to clean Elsie's chimney with a brick, but got the chimney pots mixed up and covered the Ogdens with soot. They ran up enormous phone bills at the Western Front when they rang their French boyfriend.

This all finished when, at the end of 1978, Gail fell for biker Brian Tilsley. Suddenly, Gail embarked on a large-scale love affair and, as Cheryl Murray puts it, Suzie faded into the background: 'Brian became a challenge for Suzie because he seemed as worldly as Suzie was and totally wrong for Gail.' The part of Brian was given to Christopher Quinten who became an instant hit with the female fans as he rode down the Street in tight jeans and t-shirts, showing off his athlete's body. Chris understood Brian: 'Brian for me is how Chris Bell – which is my real name would have ended up if I'd not gone into show business. I used to work at a shipyard, and Brian was very much like me when I was a young kid. And Brian went the way that all my friends have gone.' Brian happily saw in the New Year with Gail, who did not yet know that his mother was, in fact, factory worker Ivy Tilsley with whom she had had more than one run-in.

1979

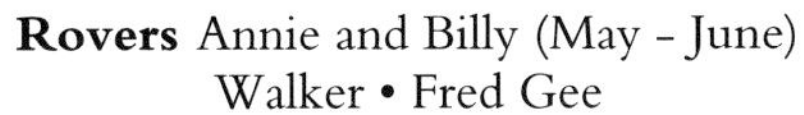

Rovers Annie and Billy (May - June) Walker • Fred Gee

No. 1 Albert Tatlock • Ken Barlow

No. 3 Emily Bishop • Deirdre and Tracy Langton (Feb. - Dec.)

No. 5 Deirdre and Tracy Langton (Jan. - Feb.) • Bert, Ivy and Brian Tilsley (Feb. - Dec.) • Gail Tilsley (Nov. - Dec.)

No. 9 Len and Rita Fairclough

No. 11 Elsie Tanner • Gail Potter (Jan. - Nov.) • Suzie Birchall (Jan. - Dec.)

No. 13 Stan and Hilda Ogden

Shop Alf and Renee Roberts

Shop flat Bet Lynch

No. 16 (Centre) Ena Sharples

Non-residents Betty Turpin • Mavis Riley Eddie Yeats • Mike Baldwin • Vera Duckworth • Steve Fisher • Ron Mather Audrey Potter

'I spent two days shouting "Tracy", stood on a woodpile with smoke being pumped out. It was easy to do because the whole thing was so horrifically real.'

Anne Kirkbride

COMINGS AND GOINGS

There was plenty of activity at No.5 this year. Ray Langton wrote to Deirdre from Holland asking her to sell the house as he needed money. She flung herself and Tracy onto Councillor Roberts' mercy but refused to live in the flat he found for them – on the 7th floor of a tower block. She agreed to sell No.5 to Bert and Ivy Tilsley for £7,000 but backed out when she realized she would be homeless. Emily Bishop at No.3 came up with the solution and moved the Langtons into her back bedroom, leaving No.5 vacant for the Tilsleys. In November, they were joined by Gail Potter after she wed Brian. Suzie Birchall left for pastures new in London in December. Elsie Howard changed her name back to Tanner and saw the new decade in by herself.

POISON IVY MOVES IN

Since 1971, Ivy Tilsley had been a regular at the Rovers as she worked first at the warehouse and then Baldwin's Casuals. The character was popular so the writers decided to move her into a house and create a family. Brian had already appeared at the end of 1978 and husband Bert completed the picture. Lynne Perrie enjoyed playing Ivy because she controlled the family: 'I was always strong. I used to let Bert think he was the boss, but he wasn't. I thought, "This part is good, I can work on this." And I did. I started to love "Poison Ivy" because it meant that people either believed in me or hated me, which is far better than being just a nondescript person.' Ivy set to work straight away, upsetting neighbours. She refused to pay Stan Ogden for cleaning her windows (which caused Hilda to throw a bucket of dirty water over them) and set out to split up Brian and Gail. Ivy found out about Gail's affair with Roy Thornley and told Brian that his girlfriend was not a virgin. The news did not have the desired affect for Ivy; she was attacked by Elsie: 'As a matter of interest, how many fellers did you have before you waltzed your Bert up the alter. And how many did *he* have a right to know about?' Brian packed and left home for a week, and Ivy broke down with relief when he returned with the news that Gail had agreed to marry him.

LORRY CRASH

Anne Kirkbride clearly remembers the two cold February days she spent clawing at timber in 1979. A lorry had crashed into the front of the Rovers, shattering windows and throwing glass and timber into the pub. While bar staff and customers picked themselves off the floor and tried to free each other from the wreckage, Deirdre Langton struggled to move the timber, as only minutes before she had left Tracy in her pushchair in front of the pub. Anne Kirkbride remembers: 'There was this lorry upside-

down with all this wood and a big hole in the front of the Rovers. The wheels were still spinning on the lorry. It really got to me. You knew it wasn't a real place but in your mind somewhere it was and it was as if it was really happening. That was the effect it was supposed to have on people and just for a moment I had a little shiver.'

Inside the pub, Mike Baldwin clutched a broken leg and winced with pain as Bet offered him a glass of water: 'It's me flamin' leg that's injured, not me throat!' Len Fairclough tried to pull his friend Alf Roberts from under a table, wood and glass, but Alf was completely stuck and unconscious. Outside, the police led by Sgt Broady (played by Michael Melia), tried to make sense in all the confusion but Deirdre's screams and the noise of the onlookers hindered all attempts to listen for a baby's cries. He needed help: 'Put Control in the picture. Tell 'em we need more bodies. It's a major incident.'

The thing that sticks in the mind of all the cast

After eight years of playing Ivy, Lynne Perrie was given a family. The writers glossed over the fact that in 1975 her husband had been called Jack and she had, the same year, admitted her own heartache because she had never been blessed with children.

Bill Roache as Ken tries to free Deirdre from the crash.

was not the lorry, the wood or the drama of the situation. As Bill Roache puts it: 'I can just remember walking about on planks and things, but what I can really remember is Anne shouting.' Anne Kirkbride laughs when she remembers the amount of shouting she had to do: 'I remember I lost my voice. I was screaming on this wood pile for about two days. Shouting "Tracy" and they got this smoke all over me and at the end of the two days I just couldn't speak. I'd completely strained my voice and I had to rest it totally. It just came back in time for studio on Friday.'

Deirdre was certain that her daughter was dead and she shrugged off Emily and Ena Sharples' caring words: 'It's my fault. I started it. Families have to stick together. That's what you have a family for. They're like flowers. Take one petal away and before you know it, it's all gone. Tracy's dead. Like me and Ray.' The police arrived with the miraculous news that Tracy was not under the timber and had in fact disappeared. Emily rushed to tell Deirdre only to find that she too had gone. Eventually, Tracy was found – she had been kidnapped just seconds before the crash – and was reunited with Deirdre on a canal bank where Deirdre had been contemplating suicide.

★ Bert Tilsley was the fourth Street character to be played by Manchester-born **Peter Dudley**. The other three were minor parts and Peter was relieved that Bert was to be a more substantial role as it meant he could spend time with all his friends in the cast. Some, such as Barbara Knox and Julie Goodyear, had acted with Peter at Oldham Rep and everyone admired his acting. After a couple of months it seemed as if Bert Tilsley had always been a regular at the Rovers. Peter started his acting career after walking out of his first job as a doffer in a mill (a doffer collected the full bobbins and replaced them with empty ones). Despite a strong desire to act, he undertook a series of jobs as window-dresser, salesman and shop assistant until he had completed his National Service. He was taken on at Oldham Rep, and also worked with the Contact Company and with Manchester's Library Theatre Company.

LITTLE HILDA THE RED HEN

'Eddie was always keen that his next scheme was going to make him a millionaire,' chortled Geoff Hughes as he recalled one of his most enjoyable storylines. Eddie installed six hens in a tiny pen in the Ogdens' backyard and planned on living on eggs and selling the rest to the neighbours. Stan was keen and Hilda was eventually talked round, although she was alarmed to find a hen on her kitchen table. The trio enjoyed eating the eggs but it was not long before the scheme, like all Eddie's plans, started to go wrong. Geoff explains: 'We thought you just put them in a cage and then you sell the eggs and of course in order for Hilda to keep feeding them, they had to produce eggs. So Eddie was having to go out and buy eggs and put them under the hens.'

Geoff Hughes ran a farm so he knew all about keeping hens. What upset him, and Jean Alexander, most of all was the end of the story. The script stated that, to celebrate Stan's birthday, the favourite hen, 'little Hilda', would be killed and cooked. When Stan heard it was Hilda he refused to eat her, as did Hilda and Eddie. The upset occurred when the actors realised that the dead hen was not one bought especially for the scenes but actually *was* little Hilda, the bird they had acted with for nearly a month! Geoff recalls that Jean Alexander was so upset she nearly walked out of the studio.

A Catholic wedding for Brian John Tilsley and Gail Potter.

MIKE BALDWIN GIVES AWAY THE BRIDE

Gail Potter was illegitimate. The man she had referred to as her father had been a boyfriend of mother Audrey's, and Gail had been embarrassed to let her friends and neighbours meet blonde Audrey. Sue Nicholls describes her as being 'loud, very upfront, common and slightly tarty' in those early days. She likens Audrey and Gail's relationship to that of the mother and daughter in *A Taste of Honey*, with the daughter mothering the mother. No one had condemned fatherless Gail, although Ivy had barely stifled a puffing noise, but when the church wedding came closer, Gail had to decide who would give her away. She was counting on Elsie's boyfriend Ron Mather, but he and Elsie went off on holiday to Majorca and missed the wedding. Eventually, it was Gail's ex-employee Mike Baldwin who stepped in to make the long walk with her. Helen Worth was surprised by the way the wedding sorted itself out. She was unsure about Gail's relationship with Audrey (after referring to her 'Dad' for three years it came as a blow to discover Gail did not have one) and the idea of Mike giving Gail away was odd: 'That's the wonderful thing about the Street. It is allowed that anything can happen and you can make anything happen. If you believe it personally, the viewers will believe it. That's the power of the Street, I don't think it could happen anywhere else.'

Brian and Gail married at St Boniface church in a

Roman Catholic ceremony to please Ivy.

As Gail settled into No.5 and adjusted to sharing a kitchen with Ivy, Helen Worth had no idea what lay in store for her in the ten-year marriage that was to follow. She enjoyed playing the changes in Gail's character: 'Gail was desperately in love and all she wanted was a marriage and children. She didn't really have any ambitions beyond being a mother and wife because of her mother Audrey, the upbringing she had. It was only when she got married she realized that perhaps it wasn't all in life. She started diverting her attention and became more ambitious – a stronger woman.'

Fred Gee hoped no one would notice when he donned a wig. The regulars pretended nothing was amiss until Albert Tatlock loudly asked why he had a dead rat stuck on his head.

★The joining of the Tilsley and Potter houses saw the reappearance of Audrey Potter, Gail's giddy mother who had taken the menfolk by storm at the engagement party. Audrey was played by **Sue Nicholls** who was well known for her part as waitress Marilyn Gates in *Crossroads*. She was born in Walsall in the West Midlands, the daughter of Conservative MP Lord Harmar Nicholls and was set to study languages at Oxford, but decided instead that she would like to try her hand at acting. She trained at RADA and then worked in rep. Sue joined *Crossroads* in 1964 and stayed for four years, during which time she brought out a hit single 'Where Will You Be'. The record was so successful that she left the Motel to work on the cabaret circuit. Sadly, her second single flopped and she found herself working in a stripclub in Vienna, her act sandwiched between strippers and Can-Can girls. Television work on shows such as *Dixon of Dock Green* and *The Professionals* led to the role of secretary Joan in *The Rise And Fall Of Reginald Perrin* and eventually the Street. She portrayed Audrey, on and off, from 1979 to 1985 when she was given a long-term contract.

Sue Nicholls [Audrey]

GUINNESS
STAY
COOL
GUINNESS

The EIGHTIES

·1980·

'I introduced Bet to leopard skin. I thought she should be a "leopard lady" and it was proved right.'

Julie Goodyear

Rovers Annie Walker • Fred Gee

No. 1 Albert Tatlock • Ken Barlow

No. 3 Emly Bishop • Deirdre and Tracy Langton (Jan. - Sept.) • Arnold Swain (Sept. - Dec.)

No. 5 Bert and Ivy Tilsley • Brian and Gail Tilsley (Jan. - Aug.)

No. 9 Len and Rita Fairclough

No. 11 Elsie Tanner • Dan Johnson (March) • Martin Cheveski (June - Dec.)

No. 13 Stan and Hilda Ogden • Eddie Yeats (July - Dec.)

Shop Alf and Renee (Jan. - Dec.) Roberts

shop flat Bet Lynch (Jan - April) • Deirdre and Tracy Langton (Sept. - Dec.)

No. 16 (Centre) Ena Sharples

Non-residents Betty Turpin • Mavis Riley Mike Baldwin • Vera Duckworth Audrey Potter

COMINGS AND GOINGS

The decade started with domestic problems at No.1. as Ken Barlow bought a car of German make and Albert had it removed by the police. With Gail and Suzie gone, Elsie was lonely and turned to lorry driver Dan Johnson He moved in to No.11, but after two weeks she threw him out when she caught him kissing Bet Lynch. Bet rented a bedsit in Victoria Street for them but Dan walked out on Bet, telling her she was just one of his tarts. Elsie's life brightened up with the arrival from Birmingham of her sixteen-year-old grandson, Martin, who stayed for six months. Brian and Gail Tilsley moved out of No.5 into a one bedroom mini-house on Buxton Close. On New Year's Eve, Gail gave birth to a son. The Roberts decided to sell up and open a post office in Grange, but Renee was killed in a car crash, so Alf cancelled the sale and stayed on at the shop. Deirdre became his assistant, and she and baby Tracy moved into the shop flat. Emily married pet shop owner Arnold Swain in September, but three months later the marriage ended when she discovered he was a bigamist. Ena Sharples was messed about by the Council over the redecoration of her flat at the Centre. She left in April to stay at St. Anne's with old friend Henry Foster. As Albert Tatlock waved her off, he had no idea she would never return.

THE KILLING OF A SHOPKEEPER

Madge Hindle was shocked to hear through the cast grapevine in April 1980 that she was going to be dropped from the programme: 'I'd just signed a contract in November and I had thought I would sign up for another year. Then, about two days later, Bill Podmore called me up to his office.'

The writers had decided that the Roberts' marriage was not working, something both Madge and Bryan Mosley had felt for a long time, and Madge Hindle decided that Renee's death might be a good turning-point in her career: 'I thought, if I'm going to die I might as well go out in style. Killing me off was very, very good. It meant I would never be tempted to come back for odd episodes.' Years later, Podmore felt the right decision had been made: 'If time proved anything, I think it underlined that the decisions to kill of characters were correct. Alf Roberts emerged into the sunlight from the shadows of a rather humdrum marriage.'

The script called for Renee and Alf to get stuck down a tiny country lane in their car. He had been drinking, so learner Renee took the wheel. When she stalled the car, agitated Alf got out and made her change places, but before she could move a lorry hurtled down the lane and smashed into the front. There were no stuntmen involved in the scenes and Madge really enjoyed herself: 'The first shot is of me going towards the windscreen, and then they cut before I got there. Once they decided that that was okay they reversed the shot; they broke the glass and stuck my head through it and then I came back from the windscreen on to the seat.'

At this point, Bryan Mosley, a trained stuntman in his own right, sprang into action as Alf: 'I found climbing over the car a bit difficult as I'm not built for it. I remember having to climb over the car to get to Renee and not really believing anything was wrong because there was no real blood.' It might have looked as if there was no 'real blood' but Madge was actually caked in artificial blood. Renee was rushed to hospital, and underwent emergency surgery because her spleen had burst, but she died on the operating table.

BET LYNCH – TART WITH A HEART

Binman Eddie Yeats caused trouble in 1980 when he chatted away at the Rovers' bar about the contents of Annie Walker's bins. She was furious: 'What I put into my dustbin is between me and my Maker,' and refused to let Eddie's crew touch her bins. No other crew would touch the bins, and the Rovers' yard was boycotted. Eventually, Annie had to apologise, but not before the local press had photographed Bet sitting on top of a bin.

Julie Goodyear had, in the ten years she had been a main character, turned Bet into a three-dimensional character with the use of earrings, beehive hairdo and leopard skin: 'She was always a plastic beads and earrings person but [the earrings] evolved as the fans, particularly children, began to send them as presents for me to wear. . . little girls and little boys like dressing up and could identify with Bet, and with their pocket money they started to send little gifts with tremendous love and affection and, reciprocating that love and affection, I started to wear them for the little viewers.'

Julie researched the character of Bet on the streets of Salford with Street creator Tony Warren: 'Everytime we went out, we would see a Bet at the bus stop or a Bet at the market shopping, and Tony or I would say "Look at that silver mac/hairdo/ earrings etc." You would see people who looked

It was a sad day for Alf Roberts when he inherited the shop. He had always seen himself as a grocer but the prospect of running a shop alone did nothing for his morale.

'I might be dead but I can still smile!' Madge Hindle kept her sense of humour during the crash scenes.

Worn out, fed up and used by the world, Julie Goodyear based her portryal of Bet on the women she observed in real life.

about twenty-one years old from the back, and when they turned round they could be any age!' When Bet first appeared, her hair was ironed flat and she wore tight black dresses. After observing the Salford characters, Bet instructed make-up to pile her hair up in a beehive and steered the character from black to leopard skin.

The writers also worked hard to make Bet vulnerable in love. Unlike Elsie Tanner, who was feisty and strong, Bet's strong appearance behind the pub bar often dropped when she left that arena. She was lonely and clung to any man hoping he would be Mr Right. In the Spring of 1980 she stole Dan Johnson from Elsie (Elsie never once took another woman's man) and set up home in a grimy back street bedsit for them both. She was annoyed when he thumped a neighbour for talking to her: 'You're as good as saying I've got to lead a life like a nun when you're not here.' She wanted to thrash things out but he wasn't bothered: 'I'm not into explanations, darling. I do things or I don't. But I tell you this. One thing I can do without – aggro in my private life. I get enough of it on the road. If one bird starts causing me trouble, there's always another one waiting and itching round the corner. And they're all birds like you, Bet. You can hardly tell one from the other. So long love. Be lucky.'

THAT NICE MR SWAIN

'I really began to think you know, the dormant creature that this woman is, it almost became funny. I mean, really, can all these things happen to one woman?' Eileen Derbyshire had played Emily for twenty years. She'd jilted one man, had her husband shot, run off with a Hungarian and was now told she was to marry a bigamist. She was delighted to discover George Waring was to play her new husband, Arnold Swain, as they had worked together in theatre. Mr Waring had no idea that Swain would be such a swine: 'I was just told that he was a chap who ran a pet shop and was to start an association with Emily. I played him without the foreknowledge that he was a bit of a dubious devil. Then when the change came the character did alter a lot'

Arnold Swain entered Emily's life when she took on his books to help out with his accounts. She and Deirdre had formed the Coronation Street Secretarial Bureau, and Arnold was one of their first customers. Eileen Derbyshire has fond memories of Deirdre and Tracy vacated the house as Emily's courtship with Arnold hotted up and wedding plans were made. The first inkling for the viewers that all was not well was when Arnold persuaded Emily to marry in a registry office not a church.

After the wedding, Emily was startled to find Arnold making plans to sell up and move to the country. Shortly after this a group of people in Manchester formed the Arnold Swain Haters Association. They celebrated with a pub crawl when Arnold was unmasked as a bigamist. The scene in which Emily confronts Arnold with the evidence of his fraud remains a Street masterpiece. Emily started off as calmly as she could: 'There is another Mrs Swain. And she's not dead. She's still alive. And you were not going to tell me?' He tried to explain, saying his wife Margaret had left him after three weeks and he had told everyone she had died to avoid the humiliation. The more he blabbered on, the more Emily felt he was insane. Arnold broke down completely. He begged Emily to forgive him but she demanded he left. The hardest step for Emily was when she went to the police to report Arnold and have her marriage declared void. The police refused to believe she had married at all, and she was disgusted when they implied she was just a lonely depressed soul who had made up the whole story.

·1980·

Emily Bishop knew something was wrong when husband-to-be Arnold Swain refused to marry her in church, but she had no idea his wife Margaret was still living.

·1981·

'Podmore told me I was going to be married off, so I said "Oh, who to?" He said "Meg Johnson" and I said "terrific, smashing."'

Fred Feast

Rovers Annie Walker • Fred Gee (Jan. - Sept./Dec.) Eunice Gee (May - Sept.)

No. 1 Albert Tatlock • Ken, Deirdre and Tracy (July - Dec.) Barlow

No. 3 Emily Bishop

No. 5 Bert and Ivy Tilsley

No. 9 Len and Rita Fairclough • John Spencer (Aug. - Sept.)

No. 11 Elsie Tanner • Audrey Potter (Sept. - Nov.)

No. 13 Stan and Hilda Ogden • Eddie Yeats

Shop Alf Roberts

Shop flat Deirdre and Tracy Langton (Jan. - July)

No. 16 (Centre) Fred and Eunice Gee (Sept. - Dec.)

Non-residents Betty Turpin • Mavis Riley Mike Baldwin • Brian Tilsley • Gail Tilsley Nicky Tilsley • Vera Duckworth • Jack Duckworth • Alma Sedgewick

COMINGS AND GOINGS

The big event of the year was the July marriage of Ken Barlow and Deirdre Langton, just two days before the Royal Wedding of Charles and Diana. Deirdre moved from the shop flat into No.1 with Tracy. The family had hoped to move away to a semi somewhere with a garden, but the plans were dropped when Deirdre found Albert collapsed on the pavement. He felt he was too old to leave No. 1, explaining that he still looked out of the window and saw the ghosts of all the old friends and residents. The Fairclough became foster parents, taking in twelve-year-old John Spencer for a month when his mother went to hospital. Fred Gee took a wife, Eunice Nuttall, and together they lodged at the Rovers, interfering in Annie's life. When she threw them out, they moved into the Community Centre flat and Eunice was employed as Centre caretaker. The marriage was put under strain towards the end of the year and he eventually left him for another man, and thrown out of the flat, Fred had to rely on Annie's back bedroom again. Gail's mother Audrey Potter moved in No.11 as Elsie's latest lodger following a break-up with a boyfriend. She used her charms to sweet-talk Alf Roberts into buying her car, but promptly left the area when she heard he was contemplating a proposal.

FREDDIE TAKES A WIFE

For years, Fred Gee had wanted a pub of his own. After four years working under Annie Walker, he finally felt he had the experience he needed to branch out on his own. The only problem was that the brewery were only giving pubs to married men, so Fred put his name down for a pub and went looking for a bride. She came in the shape of Eunice Nuttall, a dry-cleaner who had once been a barmaid and was played, to Fred's delight, by Meg Johnson.

After a whirlwind romance, Eunice became Mrs Gee and the following week the couple attended an interview at the brewery. It was then disclosed that Eunice had been sacked from a pub on suspicion of theft and so they were refused a pub. Fred was upset: 'You were me passport. I needed a wife, didn't I? To get a pub. I could a' married any woman in the world.' Meg Johnson strugged to understand Eunice's way of thinking throughout this period. 'It was sad really. People saw her as fairly miserable. I don't know that she was, I just think she was probably a woman who had a lot of disappointments. To have fallen for Freddie, as Eunice called him, she must have seen something there that other people didn't and I think her life was a lot of missed opportunities. She was ambitious and I think she wanted to do better for herself and they would get a pub.'

Annie refused to let the Gees stay at the Rovers as she found Eunice overbearing and bossy and feared they had their eye on her little kingdom. The marriage was doomed from the start, and Eunice decided to leave Fred for Councillor Critchley. Fred was left with a colour portable television, the spoils of his short marriage.

Annie Walker threw the Gees out of the Rovers when they failed to win a pub of their own. Alf Roberts used his contacts to get them into the Community Centre, as he did not want them lodging at the shop flat.

A SUICIDE BID

Arnold Swain made a short re-appearance at the beginning of 1981 when he returned to sort out his marriage to Emily Bishop. 'I had two marvellous episodes of going mad,' recalls George Waring. He decided against doing any research into mental illness and relied on the script: 'They were very well-written scenes. They were a joy to play, so they gave me a good send-off.' In the scenes, Arnold explained to Emily that God had told him to return to her and that they should enter into a suicide pact. Emily had to fight for her life before escaping Swain's clutches. It is an episode which Eileen Derbyshire remembers with affection: 'I'm afraid that I behaved rather disgracefully on that occasion, there was a lot of giggling in it. Next door, the Tilsleys were listening to the radio. . . Scottish music I think. So Arnold was going on about his suicide pact and we would do those terribly torrid scenes, and then through the wall was coming this music and I'm afraid in between takes we went dancing round the room together.'

★ Manchester-born **Meg Johnson** started her career at Oldham Rep, where she worked on and off for fourteen years. In between she worked on radio and in television. In the Street she appeared as a friend of Rita's who ran the Kabin for a couple of weeks, and in 1972 fought Rita at a brawl in a nightclub. Her television credits included *Yanks Go Home, The Good Companions, Empire Road* and *Country Matters*. She was thrilled to be given the part of Eunice as it meant working with so many old friends from Oldham. 'I was asked to come in and it was only going to be three weeks, six episodes. I didn't know where Eunice had come from and where she was going.'

Deirdre removed her glasses to marry Ken in July 1981.

Maggie Jones made her last appearance as Blanche Hunt when Deirdre married Ken. She recalled a conversation in the 70s when she'd admitted to fancying Ken herself!

Wedding Bells for Ken – Yet Again!

Twenty-one million viewers sat dewy-eyed as Deirdre, resplendent in blue and without her glasses, walked down the aisle on Alf Roberts' arm to marry Ken Barlow. They were all there – Annie, Albert, Elsie, the Ogdens. Len was best man, Susan Barlow and Tracy Langton were bridesmaids, and Maggie Jones made a guest appearance as Blanche Hunt. Even Ray Langton sent a congratulations telegram. For Anne Kirkbride, it was one of the highlights of playing Deirdre: 'It was very special, very exciting. There was a lot of excitement in the air generally during that time, because of the Royal Wedding and it was the middle of summer. It was a good time.' Filming in the church did have its drawbacks, however, as Anne and Bill Roache had to kneel through the service. Normally this would take five minutes in a real wedding; because of the filming, they were on

their knees for two hours.

Bill Roache felt very positive about this screen wedding: 'Anne and myself had a chemistry on screen . . . we both knew we could just pick it over and then actually go for it on the take.'

Anne was pleased that Deirdre had a man to look after her again, as well as an aged uncle and Tracy, who was not four years old: 'I've always wanted to be a mum, that was my real ambition in life, to get married and to be Deirdre. And I've never had children but I can wear all that out on Deirdre – I can wear all the pinnies I like and be domesticated and down to earth and as maternal as I want to be. It all gave me a chance to express another side of my nature.'

Troubled teenager John Spencer had his ear pierced whilst being fostered by the Faircloughs.

THE FAIRCLOUGHS UNDER STRAIN

Len Fairclough had never understood women. His wife Rita was no exception. He knew something was wrong when she refused to cook his dinner and spent an afternoon walking around town, but was not prepared for what she had to say when she finally shared what was on her mind: 'I know I've been happy enough to let things carry on as they are. But I couldn't go through life without being a mother.' Len was amused when Rita outlined her plan to adopt a baby or toddler, someone little she could love. She knew he would refuse, but he was forced to take her seriously when she broke down, telling him how desperate she was to be a mother: 'I don't feel old. I don't feel too old to bring up a baby and show it love.'

Len finally agreed to go along with Rita's dream and was as furious as she was when they were turned down by the adoption agency as being too old. Remembering how Emily and Ernie had taken on a couple of children in 1974, the Faircloughs applied to be foster parents and were successful.

Barbara Knox really enjoyed the change in Rita's character as her mothering instinct showed through: 'That was a new thread that came in which I thought was a good idea of these two people who'd married later on in life. It was a good thread. I mean, in the Street, you have good threads, gold threads, happy threads, like in the tapestry of life. And some threads are more interesting, more demanding, funnier, sadder, whatever. A good thread for Len and Rita.'

Being stuck behind a sewing machine in a back-street factory was not how Elsie Tanner thought she would end her days.

'You can insult me as much as you like Stanley, but don't you dare say anything complimentary about Elsie Tanner.'

Hilda Ogden

Rovers Annie Walker • Fred Gee

No. 1 Albert Tatlock • Ken, Deirdre and Tracy Barlow

No. 3 Emily Bishop

No. 5 Bert and Ivy Tilsley

No. 7 Len and Rita Fairclough with Sharon Gaskell (Aug. - Dec.)

No. 9 Len and Rita Fairclough • Sharon Gaskell (March - Aug.) • Chalkie Whitely (Aug. - Dec.) • Craig Whitely (Aug. - Nov.)

No. 11 Elsie Tanner • Marion Willis (April - Dec.)

No. 13 Stan and Hilda Ogden • Eddie Yeats

Shop Alf Roberts

Shop flat Bet Lynch (June-Dec.)

No. 6 (Centre) *Empty*

Non-residents Betty Turpin • Mavis Riley • Mike Baldwin • Brian Tilsley • Gail Tilsley • Nicky Tilsley • Vera Duckworth • Jack Duckworth • Alma Sedgewick • Maggie Dunlop • Phyllis Pearce

COMINGS AND GOINGS

The Faircloughs moved house this year, from No.9 to No.7. Len had bought the land between Nos.3 and 7 and spent all his time rebuilding No.7. He wanted to sell it at a vast profit but Rita schemed with new foster-daughter Sharon Gaskell. Together they persuaded Len to let them move next door whilst selling No.9 to binman Chalkie Whitely. Chalkie moved in with grandson Craig but Craig's widowed father Bob claimed the child and they emigrated to Australia leaving Chalkie alone. Eddie Yeats' latest girlfriend, Marion Willis, moved into the Street as Elsie Tanner's lodger, while her boss Maggie Dunlop became Mike Baldwin's live-in girlfriend. Bet Lynch was made homeless when her flat was demolished and used emotional blackmail to persuade Alf into letting her move into the shop flat.

·1982·

A ROYAL VISITOR

On the afternoon of Wednesday 5 May 1982, the cast of *Coronation Street* put on their characters' best clothes and stood outside their homes to receive a special visitor. For months, designers and builders had been at work building a new Street lot. This new Street had a new house at No.7 and an alleyway running between the Rovers and No.1. The alleyway was built to put an end to letters from people who were concerned that the Rovers' toilets led straight into Albert Tatlock's kitchen. 'Perhaps,' wrote one viewer, 'that is why he's so grumpy all the time.'

The Queen agreed to officially open the new Street, along with the Duke of Edinburgh. They met Tony Warren, H.V. Kershaw, Bill Podmore and Denis Parkin, the original designer. The visitors were led down the Street where they met the residents. The only regular cast member not present was Violet Carson who was too ill to attend. Eileen Derbyshire, standing outside No.3 with Thelma Barlow, invited the Duke of Edinburgh into the house when he enquired about the set's interior. He disappeared inside with the two ladies, hastily followed by a bunch of detectives. Bet Lynch, Julie Goodyear, wore 'Royal' earrings – cut-out pictures of the Prince and Princess of Wales.

VERA MEETS HER JACK

Since he first appeared at Brian and Gail's wedding in 1979, Jack Duckworth had slowly been making his mark on the Street. For years loud-mouthed Vera had been first with all the gossip, and now she had a shifty, idle husband who stole money from her handbag and had a roving eye. Right from the start, Liz Dawn and Bill Tarmey hit it off, literally, as Liz recalls in her autobiography. 'I was freezing, so I stood right up against the heater and my crimplene skirt kept brushing on to it. It caught fire... suddenly Bill grabbed me and threw me on the floor and started slapping my backside. I screamed. I thought. "I'm sure this isn't in the script. He must have flipped." Bill said, "I'm sorry, but you're on fire." And of course we had a great laugh about that. It was a real ice-breaker between us because we both saw the funny side straight away. It was the start of what has been for me a wonderful partnership.'

During 1982 Jack's eye roved on to Bet Lynch, while behind *his* back Vera entertained her own boyfriend. The Street had given Bill Tarmey his first big break in acting and he recalls how terrified he was to have to say chunks of dialogue and act in two-handed scenes with Julie Goodyear. 'I used to be a nervous wreck, and for one scene Julie, bless her, went to the floor manager and said, "Look, do me a favour and do the lad a favour, don't say we're going for a take; he's a nervous wreck." We had this long scene in Bet's flat. In the scene, Julie is passing and takes a pair of knickers and in dialogue throws them over my shoulder. I just looked at them, thought "Well, it's a rehearsal", carried on talking and threw them over my shoulder. And it was actually a take. It was a six, seven page duel-hander and I'd been thrown into it! I still look at that scene with pride.'

Somebody else who is proud of that particular storyline is Elizabeth Dawn, who sees it as a turning-point in the characters of Jack and Vera. 'It was very cleverly written, because Vera knew that Jack had a girlfriend on the side but she didn't know the other woman was Bet. So she chose Bet as someone to confide in, and she really opened her heart. It was quite moving as well as funny and it helped me to establish that Vera was not just a big mouth. There was actually a real human being behind that voice.'

When Vera told Jack she had spent an evening out with Bet, he knew that she was lying as *he* had been out with her. Unable to let this just go by he told Vera that she was a liar. This led to a classic

★Manchester-born **William Tarmey** never had an audition for the part of Jack Duckworth: 'I'd worked on *Coronation Street* for about ten years throwing darts in the background and whilst I was doing that I was also doing little cameo parts, on other programmes. I was either the policeman, or the guy who got shot, or the one with the mad dog. Bill played bit parts in Granada shows such as *Crown Court* and *King Lear* after giving up work in the building trade. He turned to singing, spending his days hanging around Granada, watching actors in the Street and other quality dramas, and his evenings singing in cabaret. When the part of Jack grew bigger and his scenes meatier, Bill found himself working alongside people he had admired for years. He acknowledges that his fellow actors helped him immensely and taught him everything he needed to know: 'I've had so many helping hands through the years from Jean and Liz and Julie and Bill Roache, from all of them.'

The bunting and flags were brought out as the Royal Party strolled down the cobbles.

A case of ideal casting as Bill Tarmey and Liz Dawn slipped into the roles of Jack and Vera Duckworth.

Street showdown in the Rovers where Vera told Bet what she thought of her. 'Yer a brazen article. You've no more morals than a cat's backside,' and Bet, ignoring Annie Walker's furious expression: 'Don't know why you married him. Seeing he doesn't have hairy shoulders. You are a flamin' hypocrite, Vera Duckworth!' Annie had Fred Gee escort Mrs Duckworth from the premises and warned Bet that she would not tolerate such behaviour in her pub. The Duckworths had arrived.

THE DUSTBIN MEN

The sight of a huge grey dustbin lorry was a common sight during the summer of 1982, parked outside No.13 as Eddie and his chums popped into Hilda's for a cuppa. The lorry driver, Chalkie Whitely, needed somewhere to live with grandson Craig and bought No.9 from the Faircloughs. They came complete with Craig's drum-kit and Chalkie's

·1982·

pigeon loft, as well as Craig's maternal grandmother Phyllis Pearce.

Chalkie had not told her their new address in the hope of shaking off the interfering battleaxe, but Phyllis tracked them down. After her first appearance, the press announced that the Street had found a replacement Ena Sharples. While Chalkie settled down to life at No.9, Eddie started a new hobby, buying a CB radio outfit and adopting the 'handle' Slim Jim. Over the air waves he fell for 'Stardust Lil' and an 'eyeball' was arranged. Lil turned out to be florist assistant, Marion Willis, and Eddie fell in love. Geoff Hughes was pleased that his character did not change over night into a serious, responsible citizen now he had the love of a good woman. 'He was always a softy. His villainy had been opportunist nicking or thinking of a good idea and it didn't matter if it was actually legal or not. If somebody had offered him a load of paint and he thought he could earn a shilling, he'd have had it. What happened was that just another facet of the character came along, using Marion as a sort of catalyst to bring out other sides of Eddie Yeats.'

Veronica Doran was thrilled to be cast as Marion: 'I think she could have become the power behind Eddie's throne, so to speak. Encouraging him in his ambitions. . . .'

She also recalls how she was given advice by two other actresses, Jean Alexander and Pat Phoenix: 'Jean encouraged me to play Marion as I saw her and the writers would pick up on that, which is what happened. Pat was very kind to younger actresses. She was terribly helpful technically. She was able to keep one eye on the monitor and the other on what she was doing. I remember sitting at the table with her and she said "Look up at that monitor. Now knock the back legs of the chair back a bit . . . Isn't that better? People can see you now."'

Eddie, Chalkie and new boy Curly Watts brought style and panache to the Street as the local bin team.

·1982·

THE BRUTAL SIDE OF WEATHERFIELD

Following a spate of muggings in the area, the police asked Community Centre boss Ken Barlow to keep his eyes open to see if any young people at the Centre were flashing money around. Deirdre suspected seventeen-year-old Raymond Attwood of being involved and wanted to inform the police, but Ken refused for two reasons – Deirdre was merely neurotic and he needed the kids' trust: 'Look love, with the experience you have, you may be just a little bit prejudiced. It's quite natural. Bound to feel it if you've suffered from some sort of random violence yourself. If those kids find out I've been running to the police, then what confidence would they have in me? What trust?' Deirdre agreed to drop the subject – until the next day when Betty Turpin was followed home. 'They said "You're going to be mugged and you've got to scream",' recalls Betty Driver. 'Since my throat operation I haven't been able to scream.' The task went to the Assistant Stage Manager. 'She had to scream for me, this tiny little girl . . . and me, this hefty piece.'

After visiting Betty in hospital, where she lay in bed with a bruised face and broken arm, Deirdre went to the police. Attwood was questioned and later charged with four muggings. Deirdre was upset when Ken refused to give her any credit.

★**Jill Summers** expected the part of Phyllis Pearce to last only a couple of weeks: 'I loved it and then Phyllis grew on me and grew up as a character. I suppose she was just a lonely lady who wanted company.' Jill was able to call on over fifty years' experience in variety comedy to build up the character of Phyllis. She had appeared on stage as a singer – 'one write-up said I have the panache of Beatrice Lillie and the voice of Gracie Fields.' Her father was a circus tightrope walker and her mother was in revue. During the Second World War she served in ENSA entertaining the troops, but the audiences were not all that keen on singers. Then one day she tripped on stage and came out with a mouthful. The audience roared with laughter and a new career as comedienne was launched. She became a hit in musical revues and was given her own television show *Summer's Here*. Many television roles eventually led to Phyllis.

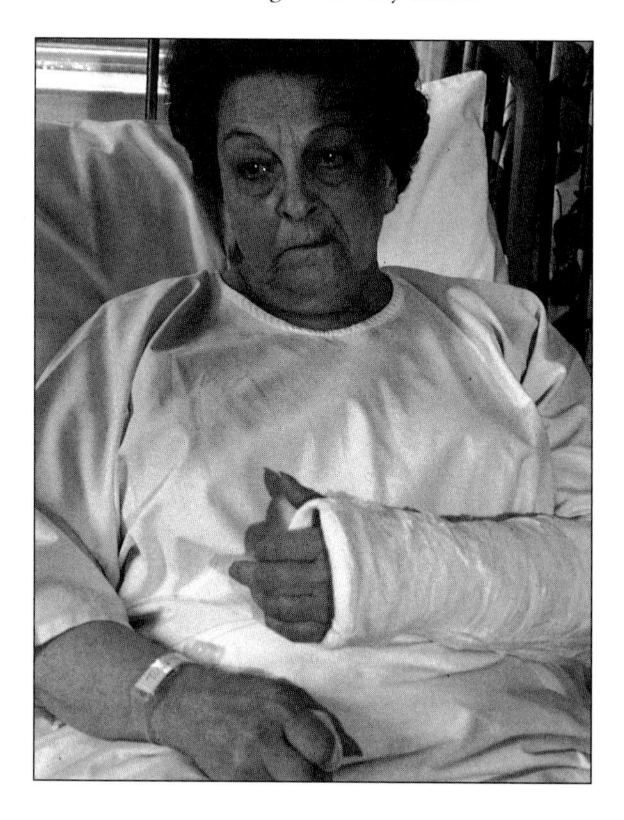

Betty Turpin ended up in hospital after a savage attack by a couple of youths.

'The most explosive, romantic situation in the history of Coronation Street.'

The *Daily Mirror*'s report on Deirdre's affair with Mike.

Rovers Annie Walker • Fred Gee

No. 1 Albert Tatlock • Ken, Deirdre and Tracy Barlow

No. 3 Emily Bishop • Curly Watts (Nov. - Dec.)

No. 5 Bert (Jan. - July) and Ivy Tilsley Brian, Gail and Nicky Tilsley (Oct. - Dec.)

No. 7 Len (Jan. - Dec.) and Rita Fairclough

No. 9 Chalkie Whitely (Jan - July) • Jack, Vera and Terry Duckworth (Sept. - Dec.)

No. 11 Elsie Tanner • Marion (Jan. - Dec.) and Eddie (Oct. - Dec.) Yeats • Suzie Birchall (Jan. - June)

No. 13 Stan and Hilda Ogden • Eddie Yeats (Jan. - Oct.)

Shop Alf Roberts

Shop flat Bet Lynch

No. 16 (Centre) Percy Sugden (Sept. - Dec.)

Non-residents Betty Turpin • Mavis Riley Mike Baldwin • Des Foster • Kevin Webster • Phyllis Pearce

COMINGS AND GOINGS

Suzie Birchall returned to Weatherfield and Elsie's back bedroom, this time sharing with Marion Willis. Suzie was followed by her violent husband who left her battered and bruised and suing for divorce. She then attempted to lure Brian Tilsley into bed. Brian told Gail, Gail told Elsie and Elsie showed Suzie the door. Bert Tilsley suffered a breakdown after being involved in an explosion at Brian's garage. He disappeared and was found wandering the streets in Southport where he was admitted into a psychiatric hospital. The younger Tilsleys sold their house to finance the garage and moved in with Ivy at No.5. Following a win on the horses, Chalkie Whitely sold up and went to live with son Bob in Australia. No.9 was bought for £10,000 by Jack and Vera Duckworth. Up the Street at No.3, Emily Bishop took in binman Curly Watts as a lodger. Eddie Yeats married Marion Willis in October and moved into her bedsit briefly before the couple moved to Bury to nurse her sick mother. The Street was plunged into mourning in December when, while the Ogdens were celebrating their fortieth wedding anniversary, news reached the residents that Len Fairclough had been killed in a car crash.

·1983·

THE TRIANGLE

It was the most explosive storyline to hit Coronation Street or even British television. It had newspapers and viewers arguing for months over the outcome, and the three actors involved received awards for their acting. But how did it all start? To answer that question we have to go right back to the summer of 1982, as the then producer Mervyn Watson recalls: 'It was normal story conference and we looked at the Ken/Deirdre marriage and had the idea of her having an affair with somebody in the Street. It was extremely passionately debated because there were categorical and opposite view points expressed.'

The affair started with Mike taking bored Deirdre for a romantic meal out. Bill Roache was not happy with the idea of Deirdre having an affair, as Mervyn Watson recalls: 'Some actors become very disturbed by the prospect of what their character is about to experience and find it uncomfortable, But then if they sort of bite their bullet, as they have to really, and get on with it, then they turn in probably the best performances of their careers. I think certainly that was the case for Bill.' If Bill Roache had worries concerning the plot, Johnny Briggs loved every moment: 'I thought that was magnificent. I mean the whole of the country was locked in their rooms watching it. I thought it was a fabulous piece of writing to get the trio going.'

Adele Rose, the Street's longest-serving writer, feels that it is storylines such as the Ken/Deirdre/Mike triangle that help to keep the programme fresh and the writer's creative thoughts active. 'You are conscious of how long the Street has been going and how respected it is, and you are conscious and proud of being part of something

The doorstep row between Mike and Ken did not go as rehearsed for Anne Kirkbride.

legendary. And when people say to me, "How can you still want to do it after all these years?" I say "It's because, after all these years, there's always a challenge to be different and keep the comedy and drama going."'

When Deirdre declared her love for Mike and then continued to see him behind Ken's back, the national press took up the story and ran with it. The *Daily Star* asked their readers what Deirdre should do. The result declared that 'Deirdre should go ahead and have her fling.' A London bishop, writing in the *Sunday Mirror* on 30 January, warned Granada, 'Don't be too realistic – it might backfire.' A housewife in Halifax was reported to have had her baby in the ambulance on the way to hospital as she had delayed leaving home because she wanted to see Deirdre kissing Mike.

Devoted Street fan Sir John Betjeman came out on the side of Barlow: 'I think Ken is a nice man and he deserves better,' as did the *Daily Express* columnist Jean Rook, who gave Deirdre some advice, 'Don't wander off into the mire, Deirdre – stick with Ken.' Her rival, Lynda Lee Potter, writing in the *Daily Mail*, urged Deirdre to leave boring Ken for exciting Mike. Stanley Reynolds, the *Manchester Evening News'* TV critic compared the Street with Ibsen, saying, 'I rather think Ibsen comes off second-best.'

After two months, Deirdre finally confessed her affair to Ken. They ranted, raved, blamed each other and sobbed their way through an episode until Mike arrived to find out why Deirdre was so distressed. The script called for Ken to throw Mike out of the house, but Bill Roache refused to believe he would allow him over the threshold. Director Brian Mills was worried that the actors would not be able to control the emotion that had built up over the months. After the first rehearsal, he felt the performances lacked passion but was assured by Bill Roache that, when it came to the take, he and Anne Kirkbride would give him exactly what he wanted. Anne Kirkbride had no idea that Mills was leaving the action up to Bill and was expecting to deliver her lines to Johnny Briggs inside the house, in the way they had rehearsed it. As the cameras recorded and she opened the door to Johnny, Bill Roache sprang into action: 'I let everything rip. Here was a man who I hated and wanted to hit. I got hold of Anne and slammed her against the door, my hand round her throat. The door slammed on Mike Baldwin and she started to cry. One paper accused Ken of wife-bashing and that was a dramatically great moment.' Anne Kirkbride acknowledges it was a great scene but wishes she'd known what was going to happen. 'I wasn't prepared for it. All of a sudden he grabbed me and I was fighting for my life. I couldn't believe it. I thought he'd gone mad. I was literally fighting to get away. I finally managed to free myself and I ran to the other room and I just say there at the table and started to cry. And there was a camera on me the whole time.'

Ken and Deirdre were reconciled in the next episode, which clashed with an important football match at Old Trafford with Manchester United playing Arsenal. The *Daily Mail* hired the electronic scoreboard and, during the match, the 56,000 fans let up an almighty roar as the board flashed up the news 'Deirdre and Ken united again!'

·1983·

A WATERY EXPERIENCE FOR BET AND BETTY

'It was the worst thing that I've ever had to do, and I'm sure Julie will say the same, because we've never been the same since!' This is Betty Driver's initial reaction when asked if she remembers the 'car-in-the-lake' episode. The action took place in Tatton Park, with Fred having talked Bet Lynch into a day out in the country. Wary of being alone with lecherous Fred, Bet talked Betty into tagging along and, despite the cold, they had a few relaxing hours sitting beside a lake. Realizing they were late for work, the three rushed to the car, and Fred threw the picnic gear into the boot as Bet and Betty sat in the car. As the car boot slammed down, the Rover 2000 started to roll down a slope towards the lake, picking up speed as it careered into the lake.

Betty Driver remembers the fateful day as if it were yesterday: 'It was March and it was snowing, hailing, and raining.' Both actresses were relieved to find two stunt women wearing frog suits in the car, which had holes drilled in it to help it sink quickly. The actresses watched with interest as the stuntwomen tested the car for director Gareth Morgan. The car shot into the water, supported by a huge chain at the rear so that it could easily be winched back. 'We were more than happy to see these two very nice ladies in the car' recalls Julie. 'We thought they were our stand-ins but no, they were just there for the testing.'

Betty asked the wardrobe lady for their wet suits: 'She said to me "you'll be all right; I've got a pair of waterproof trousers and some wellington boots".'

Betty at least got the trousers. Julie was horrified when she was given her 'wet suit': 'I had on a pink skirt, a jacket and a very flimsy pink T-shirt and some plastic beads and a pair of white high-heels. and they gave me a brown plastic bin-liner with two holes in it for my legs. I stepped into that and it was tied around my waist. And of course the water went up as soon as we went in and the bag was immediately filled with lake water. The car sank and we were both waist-deep in very, very cold lake water,' 'Now, me wellies were full of water to start with,' says Betty, 'and I said to Julie, "There's a

Stranded in the lake waiting for Fred to provide piggy-backs.

stickleback in the water here, dodging all around me. I hope to God it doesn't go anywhere else!" We were terrified and there was a swan swimming by and every time it passed the window it hissed at us and I thought it was going to attack us.'

The sequences took two days to film, with the actresses sat in the water all the time, having cups of tea brought out to them by the props man while everyone else went to sit in the warm coach for tea. At the end of the day, returning to their warm dressing-rooms, the distressed actresses were greeted by bottles of brandy with notes from Mervyn Watson thanking them for all their hard work. They had, he wrote in personal letters to them, done the impossible.

A WEDDING AND A DEPARTURE

In 1983, Geoffrey Hughes was in the enviable situation of having high-quality drama and comedy written for him every week. He admits he loved Eddie Yeats' antics – 'You'd pick up the script 'cos you were waiting to see what comic situations the Ogdens and Eddie had got into next' – and was thrilled to be part of the country's number one show. Why then, in the autumn, did he suddenly announce he was quitting it all? Since Bernard Youens' health started to deteriorate, Geoff had led the Ogden storylines with Jean Alexander, and he was appearing in the majority of Street scenes as well as learning scripts for the next week's work. Slowly, he found himself spending less and less time at home: 'The character was becoming so popular and he was being used more and more. I just found it harder and harder to do. I was unable to concentrate and I was really tired.'

Faced with Geoffrey Hughes' decision to leave, the writers decided that Eddie's girlfriend Marion Willis did not have a future in her own right. Veronica Doran hoped that her character would continue in the programme and was upset to be told by the press that Marion was to become pregnant, and then leave with Eddie. Geoff Hughes felt the

★ **Nigel Pivaro** was originally auditioned for the part of Curly Watts: 'I was very close to getting the part, going through various stages and then being second choice to Kevin Kennedy, who got the part.' Three weeks after the last audition, Nigel was contacted by Granada to audition for Terry Duckworth and this time was successful. Nigel had been brought up in Salford by his Italian father and English mother. His acting talent was spotted by the school's English teacher and he was accepted at RADA, afer spending two years working in a shop in South Africa. Nigel was a rebel and ended up serving nine months in Strangeways' prison. During his spell behind bars he decided to reform himself and, after his release, was taken on at the Theatre Royal in Stratford, East London.

When **Kevin Kennedy** finished his training at Manchester Polytechnic's School of Theatre, he spent the summer living in Spain with his guitar. On his return, he landed the part of Warren Mitchell's son in the West End production of *Ducking Out*. He was working in a play in Cardiff when he was asked to audition for the part of Curly: 'On the night before my audition I went out to celebrate the last night of the play in Cardiff. I managed to stagger on to the early morning train for Manchester and arrived at Granada looking more dead than alive.' The following week he filmed his first scene as binman Curly.

story was all wrong. 'I don't think he should have married. But if the writers were going to lose a character they may as well get as much burn as they can out of the situation. It was a political decision.'

Returning from their honeymoon, the Yeats received the news that Marion's mother had suffered a stroke and needed nursing. The move to Bury was on the same day that the Ogdens threw a party at the Rovers to celebrate their fortieth wedding anniversary. Jean Alexander had shared many wonderful memorable scenes with Geoff. 'It was all fun. It was all good fun when it was the three of us. One thing that I remember distinctly was when Hilda had left the washing in a black bag, and Stan threw the washing out and kept the rubbish. And Hilda made them go to the tip. It was a wet Monday and we were on the tip in Manchester, climbing round all this filthy rubbish, looking for the washing bag. And there were flies and rain and smells and agh!!! I never spent a more miserable morning, but it was afterwards you can laugh about it, because it really was funny.'

Stan and Hilda Ogden became the longest-married couple in the history of the Street when, in 1983, they celebrated their fortieth wedding anniversary.

The Street's newest married couple – Eddie and Marion Yeats left during the Ogdens' party.

'Somebody stuck a sex symbol label on me which I find very embarrassing. But that was never my intention – I have too many curves which I have been trying to get rid of for years.'

Pat Phoenix

Rovers Annie (Jan - Feb.) and Billy (March - Dec.) Walker • Fred Gee (Jan. - Aug.) • Gordon Lewis (May/Dec.)

No. 1 Albert Tatlock (Jan. - May) • Ken, Deirdre and Tracy Barlow

No. 3 Emily Bishop • Curly Watts

No. 5 Ivy, Brian, Gail and Nicky Tilsley

No. 7 Rita Fairclough

No. 9 Jack, Vera and Terry Duckworth

No. 11 Elsie Tanner (Jan.) • Linda Cheveski (May - July) • Bill, Kevin and Debbie Webster (July - Dec.)

No. 13 Stan (Jan. - Nov.) and Hilda Ogden Terry Duckworth (May - June)

Shop Alf Roberts

Shop flat Bet Lynch

No. 16 (Centre) Percy Sugden

Non-residents Betty Turpin • Mavis Riley Mike Baldwin • Phyllis Pearce • Derek Wilton • Audrey Potter

COMINGS AND GOINGS

Annie Walker, Queen of the Rovers Return, retired from public service in February. Her presence had not been felt at the pub since October 1983, but it was not until February that she decided to give up the pub and go to live with her daughter Joan in Derby. She sent son Billy as her replacement but, until he finally agreed to take on the tenancy in May, there was a succession of temporary managers living in the pub, including Fred Gee and Gordon Lewis. Fred lost his home in August after thumping Billy and found lodgings locally. In December, he was sacked by Mike Baldwin and left the area completely. Elsie Tanner also bade farewell to the Street – she disappeared into the sunset on 4 January with Bill Gregory, the man she had fallen in love with back in 1962. They went off to run a wine bar together in the Algarve. The Street also lost two long-standing residents: Albert Tatlock died at the age of 89 in May, and Stan Ogden died in hospital following a long illness. Linda Cheveski returned to No.11 to look after mother Elsie's affairs but, instead of selling the house, she tried to keep hold of it. Eventually it was sold over her head to Bill Webster, and Linda returned to Birmingham.

·1984·

GOODBYE LADIES. . .

1984 found Bill Roache standing alone as the last of the original cornerstones of the programme – the Street had been struck by a run a bad fortune which left actors ill or dead and saw main cast members departing for pastures new. Doris Speed last appeared as Annie Walker in October 1983 after which she was admitted to hospital suffering from a mystery stomach ailment. At the same time the *Daily Mirror* printed Doris Speed's birth certificate, showing that she was not sixty-nine as she claimed but really eighty-four. The shock of this exposure was too much and she fell ill again. Granada and the press showed their disgust. The *Stage and Television Today* wrote: 'Fleet Street must report on something readers are curious about and papers will compete for news – that's fine. But we reckon their readers – and not a few journalists – would have thought that the *Mirror*'s Diary piece just didn't seem fair, even if it were all absolutely true.'

Shortly after the *Mirror* piece, Doris Speed woke in the night to find intruders in her home. She locked her bedroom door and phoned for the police as she listened to her belongings being wrecked. Everything she cherished had been stolen or destroyed and she felt she could no longer live alone, so she retired from the Street and moved into a nursing home in Bury.

A month later, eighty-five-year-old Violet Carson died. For twenty years, before her retirement in 1980, the actress had delighted millions with her portrayal of Ena Sharples. In an interview after her sister's death, Mrs Nellie Kelly spoke of how frustrated Violet had been after leaving the Street. 'Having led the life she had, she became very depressed. Whenever anyone said to her *Coronation*

Street would die if she ever left it, she used to reply that the only star of the programme was the Street itself.' In February 1984, a memorial service was held to pay tribute to Violet Carson's unique talent and personality. During the service, Bill Roache quoted Violet Carson when she was once asked if Ena controlled her: 'Good Lord, no. I can lock her away in the vestry and walk away from her at any time I like.'

Of the original three immortal female characters, only Elsie Tanner survived in 1984, but everyone knew that the episode transmitted on 4 January would be her last as, in the autumn of 1983, the newspapers had filled their front pages with Pat Phoenix's sudden decision to quit the show. This happened just after the press coverage of Peter Adamson's dismissal from the show, for breaking his contract and selling behind-the-scene stories to a national newspaper. Of the period, producer Mervyn Watson recalls: 'It became a matter of course. Each weekend brought with it another illness, revelation or death.'

The moment Pat Phoenix announced her departure, Fleet Street went to town speculating how Tanner and Fairclough would leave. Most viewers hoped, deep down, that the couple, on-off lovers for twenty years, would either run off together or die in each other's arms. But Len Fairclough died off-screen in a motorway crash, returning home after visiting his mistress. Elsie Tanner was reconciled with ex-boyfriend Bill Gregory, with whom she had had her first screen kiss back in 1961. As she headed off for a new life in the Algarve, Elsie was asked by the taxi driver if she was going for long. 'Ah,' she replied, 'there's a question.'

A NEW MR AND MRS NASTY

With the departure of the old school – Annie, Elsie, Len, Albert and Stan – the writers were quick to create new characters and introduce families as well as to re-establish two of the original characters, Billy Walker and Linda Cheveski. However, they did not retain any of the two characters' charms. Anne Cunningham returned as Linda, having last appeared in 1968: 'It was really alarming to go back. It was a nightmare really because time had rolled on and that feeling of togetherness, with everyone helping everybody, had gone.' Linda returned as a bitter divorcee, desperate to hang on to her mother's house and find herself a new man. She was paired on screen to Bill Webster, the builder who wanted to buy No.11, but it was obvious that the actors were not suited and Ann Cunningham left after a few weeks.

Linda Cheveski, née Tanner, used all her feminine charms in the hope that Bill Webster would invite her to share No.11 with him.

Ken Farrington was another unhappy soul when he returned as the Rovers' heir apparent Billy Walker. 'They'd really changed the character quite drastically, which caused a lot of upset for me because I found it wasn't the same.' Billy had changed from chirpy Jack the Lad to down-and-out Mr Nasty, blackmailing Emily Bishop, sacking and threatening the pub staff and trying to rival Mike's business deals. 'Doris got very upset watching me on screen. She used to phone me up and say, "What on earth are they doing to you?" and I found it all pretty one-dimensional. They tried to do a JR on it, but it became a bit unplayable. Just nasty for the sake of being nasty.' By the autumn, he had had enough and told executive producer Bill Podmore he wanted to

leave. The writers decided to sever all connections between the Walkers and the Brewery, so Billy sold the Empire and headed off down the motorway to start afresh in a new hotel venture in Jersey. He has never been heard of since.

Other characters were introduced to fill the gaps. Kevin Webster, a young mechanic employed by Brian Tilsley was given a family – widowed father Bill (taking over Len Fairclough's yard) and rebellious sister Debbie. Bossy caretaker Percy Sugden was moved into the role of old soldier following Jack Howarth's death and the departure of Albert Tatlock. Percy was linked romantically with Phyllis Pearce who was reintroduced, transferring her attention from Chalkie to gallant Percy. Machinist Shirley Armitage became the first major coloured character as her role, replacing Elsie at Mike's sweat shop, was built up, and Ken Barlow's new job as editor of the *Weatherfield Recorder* brought him into close contact with young secretary Sally

Billy Walker returned to the Rovers as heir to Annie's kingdom. His first act was to bar Mavis Riley for complaining about too much pickle in the sandwiches.

Victor Pendlebury and Derek Wilton threatened to come to blows over the hand of Mavis.

Waterman. Sally confessed her love for Ken in the middle of a passionate affair with Billy Walker.

A JILTING EXPERIENCE

A September wedding promised so much, but left such grief in its wake. For eight years Mavis Riley had been courted, on and off, by hapless salesman Derek Wilton. He had stayed away from her after his mother had ordered him to find a stronger spouse, but fate had brought them colliding back time and time again. Now his mother was dead, and he had his own detached house and a bright future ahead of him, so Derek came a-calling once again with the object of making Mavis his bride. Mavis was charmed by this new image of Derek, dynamic and thrusting. She agreed to marry him, despite Rita and Emily urging her not to get involved, and straight away complications arose. For a while, Mavis had been involved with potter Victor Pendlebury and he was alarmed to hear she had a fiancé. He proposed to Mavis himself, begging her to drop Derek. For a week Mavis was given advice by the tabloid papers as to which beau to pick. 'Dopey Derek' eventually won over 'the Saddleworth Sage' and Mavis showed Victor the door.

Thelma Barlow recalls the fun of this storyline with amusement: 'I think the public reaction was about 30 percent marry Derek, 30 percent marry Victor and 40 percent don't marry either of them! It was fun because Mavis doesn't often hit the big headlines or anything like that. She's just consistently there. I think that's the best way of describing the Street; it's like a sort of tapestry, things woven in and woven out, and it creates a big picture.'

The guests gathered at the church, eager to see Mavis lose her spinsterhood, were to be disappointed. Mavis decided she could not go ahead with the wedding because it was the wrong thing to do and she was not sure of her love for Derek. At the same time, Derek also decided that marriage was not for him and the couple actually jilted each other.

★ **Michael Le Vell** landed the part of mechanic Kevin, Terry and Curly's mate, by complete chance: 'I was at Granada waiting to audition for a programme called *Scully*, and the casting director Judy Hayfield walked past and said, "Am I seeing you tomorrow for *Coronation Street*?" I said, "No" so she said, "Oh, I'll get on to your agent." So I came back the next day and got the part!' He had already appeared in two episodes, back in 1981, as cheeky paperboy Neil Grimshaw. For years he acted at Oldham's Theatre workshop after playing the lead in a school production of *Kes* in which he played the lead. Before landing the part of Kevin he appeared in television shows such as the BBC's *One by One* and *Fame is the Spur*. **Bill Waddington** was another actor to have appeared in more than one part – he played four characters, including Arnold Swain's best man in 1980 – before appearing as Percy Sugden. He did not audition for the role, rather the part was created for him. The writing team were well aware of his experience as a comedian and his unique talent was felt to be perfect for cantankerous Percy. In his autobiography, Bill Waddington expresses how similar he feels he and Percy are: 'There are one or two things I have in common with Percy which arrived as coincidence. The writers didn't know it when they prepared my early scripts. For instance, I volunteered for the forces in 1949, and inside six weeks, like Percy, I became an NCO cook. . . I also live alone now, and understand how he feels. Anyone like that who has been a man of the world, when they retire they want to go on being involved.'

'It has to be sparkling, the glasses *have* to be clean, pumps *have* to work. The living room set is also my responsibility. I don't allow people to sit about in it, I don't want props moved.'

Julie Goodyear recalls her pride in the set of the Rovers Return.

Rovers Bet Lynch (Jan. - Dec.) • Frank Mills (Aug. - Dec.)

No. 1 Ken, Deirdre, Tracy and Susan (Nov. - Dec.) Barlow

No. 3 Emily Bishop • Curly Watts • Kevin Webster (Jan. - May)

No. 5 Ivy Tilsley • Brian, Gail and Nicky Tilsley (Jan. - June)

No. 7 Rita Fairclough

No. 9 Jack, Vera and Terry Duckworth

No. 11 Bill, Kevin and Debbie Webster (Jan.) • Harry, Connie, Andrea and Sue Clayton (Jan. - Aug.)

No. 13 Hilda Ogden • Henry Wakefield (Jan. - Feb.) • Kevin Webster (May - Dec.)

Shop Alf Roberts (Jan. - Sept.) *No longer living accommodation*

Shop flat Bet Lynch (Jan.) • Alf Roberts (Sept. - Dec.) • Audrey Roberts (Dec.)

No. 16 (Centre) Percy Sugden

Non-residents Betty Turpin • Mavis Riley Mike Baldwin • Phyllis Pearce • Wilf Starkey • George Wardle • Gloria Todd Martin Platt • Shirley Armitage

·1985·

BET TAKES ON THE ROVERS

'Being in the Street has given me somewhere to belong, as a person. It's a tremendous responsibility being in charge of the Rovers.' Julie Goodyear takes a great pride in her set, the Rovers Return. On Bet's mantelpiece, in place of honour, stands a framed photograph of Annie Walker. Julie ensured this was put in place when Bet took over as landlady of the Rovers: 'There could *never* be a replacement for Annie Walker. She was an original. When an actress like Doris has done her job to such a standard you can never step into their shoes, you can only stand next to them.'

Supported by the regulars, Bet applied to become Newton and Ridley's first single landlady. She stood against Gordon Lewis who wanted to enlarge the premises and make it a high street pub. The brewery knew this might make commercial sense but would

COMINGS AND GOINGS

Bet Lynch achieved a personal ambition when, in January, she was made landlady of the Rovers Return Inn and moved into it, her first real home. Bill Webster married Percy Sugden's niece Elaine Prior early in the year and they moved to Southampton where Elaine was to open a hair salon. Bill's daughter Debbie went with them, but Kevin refused to leave Weatherfield behind and moved into Emily Bishop's at No.3, sharing Curly Watts' room. This arrangement did not really suit Kevin; Curly and Emily had a set routine and he was horrified when they suggested his weekly task would be polishing the silver. Added to this was the fact that binman Curly had to be up at 4.30am and his alarm clock was very noisy. In May, Kevin moved out and became Hilda's lodger at No.13. Hilda had started the year with another lodger, Henry Wakefield. He worked at Baldwins', but was fired after the machinists refused to work with him as he was a blackleg. Henry felt he could not remain in the Street and moved on. Gail Tilsley walked out on husband Brian, taking Nicky with her, when he refused to consider buying another house for them now the garage business was on its feet. She moved into a bedsit but was finally reconciled with Brian when they agreed to take on a council house, at 33 Hammond Road. Gail's mother, Audrey Potter, returned to the area and, deciding the life of a single girl was not all that swell, manoeuvred Alf Roberts into proposing to her. They married on 23 December and set up home in the flat above the shop. In September, Alf had enlarged the shop and turned it into a self-service mini-market. A new family, the Claytons, moved into No.11, and daughter Andrea fell for Terry Duckworth. They left after Andrea fell pregnant, fearing the interference of the Duckworth clan. Ken was delighted when daughter Susan moved into No.1 but upset by her attraction to Mike Baldwin.

rip the heart out of the community. Bet was given the job and was confident in her own abilities. 'I was pulling pints before I was legally old enough to drink 'em. And I've been doing it ever since. I've given meself body and soul to the public house trade. There's not a lot I don't know about pubs. And even less I don't know about customers.'

A FAMILY PASSES THROUGH

The Claytons – milkman dad Harry, dressmaking mum Connie, and schoolgirls Andrea and Sue – were created by the writers as a stable, normal family. The BBC was just about to launch its new drama serial *EastEnders* and the London press were going overboard to promote it and the cast. The writing team felt that the new occupants of No.11 should reflect one of the programme's strongest points – family unity. Unfortunately, the family did not work well, as Mervyn Watson explains: 'The Claytons seemed to get stuck. It's always quite a complicated, organic thing, planting a whole family. It's down to us to make the right choices. Once we've made the right choice there is an intangible thing which you can't predict which only becomes evident on the screen.' Mervyn is full of respect for the actors concerned, but feels that they were not quite right for *Coronation Street*.

Susan Brown, the actress who played Connie Clayton for seven months, is the first to agree that the family did not work: 'But the really interesting thing is that the four of us got on fantastically well together, we were inseparable. There was a lot of talk about them wanting a very ordinary family but the characters were never defined and I never felt I

'Bet Lynch's place is behind a bar, wearing a pair of daft earrings and very little else.'

Hilda Ogden

·1985·

The Street's Romeo and Juliet. In real life, best pals Nigel Pivaro and Caroline O'Neill shared a flat together.

had a big handle on the character.'

Susan's screen daughter, Caroline O'Neill, playing eighteen-year-old Andrea, agrees that as actors they never knew where to pitch the family. 'They wanted just a normal, ordinary family, but you can't just give that on speck, you have to have specifics. In the end I spent six months moaning about my A Levels, which was terribly boring and uninteresting. I had a couple of scenes just before I left when I was pregnant which were quite nice but they never followed that through either.'

Andrea met unsavoury Terry Duckworth from next door behind her parents' backs. To her horror, she discovered she was pregnant but refused to let Terry be involved. The Claytons closed ranks and a fight broke out in the Rovers when Jack Duckworth asked if they were certain Terry was the father. Nigel Pivaro had some very positive feedback from viewers over his portrayal of Terry at this time: 'So many women wanted to see me with the baby. A lot of people empathized with him wanting to keep the kid and not wanting her to have an abortion.'

When Vera started to voice plans for her grandchild's future, the family packed up overnight and, putting the house on the market, moved out of town. Eventually word reached Terry that his son had been born.

TROUBLE FOR THE TILSLEYS

Following Bert's death in hospital in 1984, the Tilsleys at No.5 had been slowly pulling apart. When Nicky came down with chickenpox Brian expected Gail to stay away from Jim's Café, which she managed, to look after him. Gail asked Brian to find them a house of their own and he refused, so she walked out. The conflict in the Tilsley household stemmed from the ordinariness of the characters, although unlike the Claytons, who had been grafted on to the programme en masse, the audience had seen Gail grow up and were familiar with the family. Helen

Worth feels Gail's normalness is her strength. 'I think she's quite a real character and I think people do associate with her.'

Ivy threw Brian out and he pleaded with Gail to take him back. The episode after the reconciliation started with the first ever Street bed scene. Bill Podmore recalls how the cast reacted when the press billed it as the sexiest scene in the history of British soap: 'It was *Coronation Street*'s first sexy bedroom scene in its twenty-odd year history, and Chris managed to reduce the first take to the level of a Whitehall farce. Helen was waiting in bed, respectably covered in her Marks & Spencer's nightie and looking fairly nervous, when Chris made his entrance. He stopped at the foot of the bed and threw open his dressing gown like some demented subway flasher. He was sporting the hugest pair of blue cotton underpants anyone had ever seen. Quite where the wardrobe department had found them is anyone's guess. But they came up to his armpits and the sight of him standing there reduced the whole set to tears of laughter.'

★ For **Sean Wilson** it was a case of third time lucky when he landed the part of Martin Platt; he had auditioned as Terry Duckworth and Kevin Webster but was turned down for both parts. Sean had always been interested in the Street and was determined to be part of it. 'When I was a kid, my dad took me to Granada TV to look through the gates and see where *Coronation Street* was made. It felt like fate, coming back.' Sean trained at the Oldham Theatre Workshop, his first television role was in Granada's *Crown Court* and, in one Yorkshire TV dramatisation, he portrayed Mozart.

The 1985 split in the Tilsley marriage started the rot which would result in their separation two years later.

'It was hard running down the cobbles in my slippers; it was like running on hot coals. At the same time I had to appear to be in a panic and it was a very hard move. It was the most uncomfortable moment I've ever had in the Street.'

Bill Waddington on filming the Rovers fire.

Rovers Bet Lynch • Frank Mills (Jan.)

No. 1 Ken, Deirdre, Tracy and Susan (Jan. - May) Barlow

No. 3 Emily Bishop • Curly Watts

No. 5 Ivy and Brian (Aug. - Dec.) Tilsley Ian Latimer

No. 7 Rita Fairclough • Jenny Bradley (Jan. - March/Oct. - Dec.)

No. 9 Jack, Vera and Terry Duckworth

No. 11 Alf and Audrey Roberts (March - Dec.)

No. 13 Hilda Ogden • Kevin and Sally (May- June/Sept. - Dec.) Webster

Shop flat Alf Roberts (Jan. - March) Audrey Roberts (Jan. - March)

No. 16 (Centre) Percy Sugden

Non-residents Betty Turpin • Mavis Riley Mike Baldwin • Gail Tilsley • Nicky Tilsley Phyllis Pearce • Gloria Todd • Martin Platt Shirley Armitage • Alan Bradley

COMINGS AND GOINGS

Bet Lynch's sometime resident boyfriend, Frank Mills, left on 1 January when Bet discovered he had made a violent pass at her barmaid Gloria Todd. Paper girl Jenny Bradley was orphaned when her mother, Pat, was knocked down by a car. Foster mother Rita Fairclough took her in and tried to reconcile her with her father Alan, whom she had not seen for eight years. Eventually Jenny moved into a local flat with Alan, but returned to No.7 in October when he took work abroad. Audrey Roberts tried to push Alf into buying a big detached property and was aghast when instead he bought No.11 for £11,000. Kevin Webster fell for local girl Sally Seddon, and she lodged at No.13 after her parents threw her out. Kevin and Sally married in October and became Hilda's lodgers. Brian's Australian cousin Ian Latimer lodged with Ivy at No.5 while having an affair with Gail. Gail confessed the affair to Brian when she found she was pregnant. Brian left her and returned to No.5, starting divorce proceedings. Susan Barlow had a rough few months during which her relationship with Mike Baldwin blossomed into a May wedding. Ken was horrified.

·1986·

TWO-TIMING ALAN

Looking after Jenny Bradley rekindled all Rita Fairclough's mothering instincts as she was shown struggling with rebellious Jenny. Sally Ann Matthews recalls how she was criticised for being rude to Rita: 'There was a lot of sympathy but there were also a lot of people who wanted to slap Jenny and shake her up a bit. She was never really nasty, although she and Rita had fights, and there was always a lot of love there as well.' Just as they were settling down to some sort of relationship, Jenny's estranged father Alan arrived on the scene. While winning Jenny over, he started to take Rita out and they slowly began an emotional affair; but Rita did not know that Alan was also involved with barmaid Gloria Todd. Mark Eden identified with his character's need to find the ideal woman: 'Gloria had the youth and the glamour and Rita had this lovely calmness and security. Gloria only worked at the pub but Rita had much more. If you could combine the two women. . . that's what Alan felt.' Sue Jenkins, playing Gloria, fought to stop her being played as a dumb blonde. She enjoyed being part of a triangle, even if on-screen Gloria hated it: 'Anyone worth their salt begins to find the various assets of their character. There was naivety about her, but it was not stupidity, so I did my best to make her a fully rounded character although she was naive and a bit silly sometimes about men, which a lot of women are.'

Rita found out about Alan's secret love and gave him an ultimatum. He decided to stick with Gloria but she changed his mind when she told him she could not cope with the situation and they were finished. Alan and Rita eventually settled down to a more peaceful relationship.

Fire at the Rovers

An electrical fault in the Rovers' cellar, one night in June, led to panic and terror as fire spread through the pub while landlady Bet Lynch slept upstairs. Sally Seddon spotted the fire at 5am when she was returning from a concert with boyfriend Kevin Webster. They banged on the doors of the residents and the whole street sprang into action as everyone tried to rescue Bet. For Sally Whittaker it was a totally thrilling experience. 'I'd only been with the Street a few months and there I was involved in this brilliant story. It was just the most exciting thing that had ever happened. This wonderful building that everyone in the country knew was about to burn down.' Not everyone shared her enthusiasm, Julie Goodyear for one was wary of the story and noted that Gareth Morgan was to direct the episodes. It had been Gareth who had directed the

Alf and Audrey Roberts spent £11,000 on No. 11.

Jenny Bradley refused to co-operate with father Alan when he returned to her after an eight-year absence.

·1986·

car-in-the-lake story (see 1983) and Julie jokes that, having failed to drown her, Gareth intended to burn her to death instead.

The idea came from the storyliners Tom Elliott and Paul Abbott (both now writers on the Street), as Tom explains: 'We were asked if we could write some episodes without the Rovers, to give the designer the chance to update the interior. Both Paul and I felt it would be difficult to write episodes without the Rovers Return because that was where everyone met. However, the flats were in a bad state of repair and something drastic had to be done. We took the problem to the story conference with the idea that the pub could be damaged by fire, this would mean it would have to close and could be refurbished.' The story worked well on paper, with Bet waking and crawling through smoke-filled rooms to the stairs, and she was scream as she saw the flames lapping up the stairwell. Unfortunately, when it came to filming the scene, Julie Goodyear arrived at the stairs to find them completely burnt out. Gareth Morgan is full of admiration for her bravery: 'The intensity of it really worried me and I knew she was frightened too, but she was adamant that she should do it. And it made the scene so much better, because she is such a well-known figure to the public that we couldn't really disguise somebody else.'

Having seen the stairs consumed by flames, everyone knew how dangerous the situation was. The pyrotechnic experts watched as the fire was lit for the second time. Julie recalls her feelings at the time: 'It was real fear the second time; I'd seen what fire could do. The fire brigade gave me oxygen every four minutes because the smoke was real.' Floor manager John Friend Newman gave Julie the cue and she staggered to the stairs, saw the flames and screamed. John shouted 'Cut!' rushed forward and picked Julie up and threw her on to the floor, beating the flames off her feet: 'Gareth was working so intently on getting the shot he wanted that he didn't notice the nightdress catch fire. I can assure you that the scream at the top of the staircase was authentic.'

Bet was eventually rescued from the fire by Kevin Webster and taken to hospital in an ambulance. She recovered but the Rovers was completely gutted. Bet was shattered when she viewed the wreckage the following day with Rita: 'When I come here to the Rovers, it was the first time in my life that I'd found a place where I finally belonged. Jobs came and went, fellas came and went. But at this old dump I felt that I'd found somewhere I could hang on to.

★ **Mark Eden** was thrilled when Sue Jenkins was given a job on the Street. 'We'd worked together in *Educating Rita* and I thought she was a brilliant actress.' Mark had been a British matinee idol, appearing in films such as *Seance on a Wet Afternoon, The L-Shaped Room, Night of the Iguana* and *Heaven's Above*. He acted at the Royal Court and with the Royal Shakespeare Company. In 1981, he had appeared in the Street as Wally Randle, on whom Elsie Tanner had a crush.

Sue Jenkins joined the programme after making children's programme *How We Used to Live*. She was only meant to appear in a few episodes but the writers enjoyed her performance: 'The part on the page really wasn't very much at all, but Betty Driver was off for two episodes because of illness and it meant that two more episodes were written for me. And those particular episodes meant that I met Bet Lynch and there was a clash between Bet and Gloria and there was a spark of something or other.' Gloria returned and stayed for three years.

Not just a job, but a place where Bet Lynch finally amounted to summat. I suppose what it give me was some self-respect.' The brewery decided to renovate the old ruin and a few months later the pub was reopened, the most startling difference being that the Select, Public and Snug rooms had been knocked into one bar.

KEN'S DILEMMA

'He'd do anything to get one over on Barlow,' says Johnny Briggs about his character Mike Baldwin. 'I think he detests him you know, because of his snobby attitude and the way he managed to hang on to Deirdre.' The year of 1986 found the Barlow/Baldwin situation reaching new heights as Susan Barlow declared her intention to marry Mike. Johnny Briggs was not happy with the idea of Mike being tied down by a woman and was not convinced the characters suited each other: 'I didn't like it because I thought that she was a bit too young for Mike. I was told by Bill Podmore that it wasn't going to last anyway so I did not really worry at the time. But really it was just a means of getting back – having a go at Barlow.'

Three years after the Mike/Deirdre affair, Ken finally got to thump Mike, much to the delight of the press and the viewers. However, it was not so pleasing for Bill Roache: 'It wasn't satisfying at all because I couldn't really hit him. It was staged; I did the hit. Stop. Then the reaction.' On screen Ken ranted and raved at Susan and blamed Deirdre for starting the whole mess: 'It seems to me that all

The residents worked together to free Bet from the inferno at the Rovers. At a given cue they all had to run from the pub as the glass shattered on to the Street and flames burst out. Bill Roache had to hold on to a terrified Anne Kirkbride to stop her running too soon.

Ken Barlow thumped Mike in the factory. Johnny Briggs had to wait a further four years before he had the chance to thump Ken in the Rovers.

Two women who loved Mike Baldwin - Deirdre and Susan Barlow.

Baldwin has to do is snap his fingers and the women of this household behave like idiotic, infatuated adolescents. I don't understand it. A little weasel like that!' Ken refused to give Susan his blessing and was stung when she went ahead with her plans. He stubbornly refused to get involved until, on the actual day of the wedding, his son Peter laid into him with the anger and frustration pent up over years of hurt. Peter accused Ken of packing off the twins because he could not cope with the responsibility, and said he should grasp the one chance he has to be a proper father to Susan. Ken raced to the church in time to give away the bride.

KEVIN FALLS IN LOVE

While Kevin enjoyed Hilda Ogden's fry-ups and put up with the constant interference in his life, Michael Le Vell was constantly amazed that he was working with one of his heroines: 'When I found out I was going to move into the Ogdens it was fantastic. I couldn't believe I was going to move in with Hilda Ogden, who was a living institution. I was completely carried away and excited by that. Jean Alexander is a genius.' Kevin was driving the works van one January morning when he drove through a puddle, splashing Sally Seddon and ruining her stockings, just as she was going for a job interview. She flew at him and he took her back to No.13 to dry off. Romance blossomed and Hilda was horrified to discover a Seddon in her house – the family had a reputation for being common, rough and criminal. Sally Whittaker admits her character has changed a lot over the years, from street-wise Sally to comfortable, secure Mrs Webster: 'Then, she was quite feisty and strong and tough, and quite hard. I think because of her family background she was just a little fighter really – a street urchin.'

When she was thrown out by her parents, Sally sought refuge at No.13 and Hilda agreed when she witnessed Sally handing her dole money over to a nervous Mrs Seddon. 'It's obvious what goes on in that house. It's him, the husband. She's frightened to death o' 'im. I don't want Sally to have to go back there and be scared out of 'er wits. But you behave yourselves whilst yer under my roof. You know what I mean. I don't have to draw no diagrams.' Hilda was determined to keep the youngsters apart at night and laid a trap on the stairs involving a mop and metal pail. Unfortunately, she forgot it was there and tripped over it, spraining her ankle. No-one was prouder than Hilda, though, when in October the couple married. She stayed the night with Bet at the Rovers so the Websters could have the run of No.13 on their wedding night.

PATRICIA PHOENIX

On 17 September 1986, Patricia Phoenix died of lung cancer, aged sixty-two. Since her departure from the Street in 1984 she had taken a variety of television, stage and chat show roles, although she always acknowledged: 'I'll never shake off Elsie and I don't want to. Everything I've got I owe to *Coronation Street*.' In late August 1986, she was admitted to the Alexandra Hospital in Cheadle, and on 7 September made her last public appearance, surrounded by flowers and teddy bears. It was obvious to all the reporters who saw her that she was in terrible pain and all commented on her bravery. Jean Rook summed up the reaction of her fans in her *Daily Express* column: 'Like millions praying for her recovery, I trust Pat Phoenix's words won't be her last in public. But those words were truly famous. Unforgettable. "Thank you very must, luvs. . . and ta-ra,". . . How very typical of this huge-hearted lady to thank us. When we desperately want to thank her for the twenty-two years of joy and fun she gave us. For her generous spirit. Her honesty. Her refusal to tell a whitening lie about the tragi-comic, hectic life she shared with us.' A week later, Pat Phoenix, married actor Anthony Booth and received the last rites on the same day. Television cameras showed the fans weeping outside the hospital and laying flowers in the grounds. The news of her death, although expected, sent millions into mourning. Obituaries in the national newspapers paid tribute to her great talent: '. . . Elsie Tanner, the wayward but warm-hearted stalwart of *Coronation Street*. As Elsie Tanner she was a variation on the clichéd good-bad girl who loves well but not too wisely and is generally agreed to be no better than she should be. The actress took this stereotype and softened and rounded it, creating a potent character who breathed life through the screen,' (*Guardian*). 'Red-haired, resilient and remarkably stylish "Elsie" epitomized northern warmth,' (*Daily Telegraph*). 'Only when Miss Phoenix left the series. . . did the BBC dare launch its rival series EastEnders,' (*The Times*).

★ **Sally Whittaker** auditioned for two parts before landing the role of Sally Seddon. She was turned down for Andrea Clayton and Michelle Robinson (Kevin Webster's posh girlfriend in 1985). Sally originally wanted to be a ballet dancer but changed her mind when she realized she could not cope with the discipline. She turned to acting, her first television role being that of a heroin addict in *Juliet Bravo*.

'I absolutely adored waddling around and I did walk behind women in supermarkets and copied their waddle.'

Helen Worth remembers Gail's pregnancy.

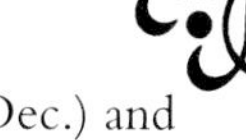

Rovers Bet (Jan. - May/Aug. - Dec.) and Alec (May - Dec.) Gilroy

No. 1 Ken, Deirdre and Tracy Barlow

No. 3 Emily Bishop • Curly Watts

No. 5 Ivy and Brian (Jan. - March) Tilsley

No. 7 Rita Fairclough • Alan (Feb. - Dec.) and Jenny Bradley

No. 9 Jack, Vera and Terry (Jan. - June) Duckworth • Amy Burton (Nov. - Dec.)

No. 11 Alf and Audrey Roberts

No. 13 Hilda Ogden (Jan. - Dec.) • Kevin and Sally Webster (Jan. - May)

Shop flat Kevin and Sally Webster (May - Dec.)

No. 16 (Centre) Percy Sugden

Non-residents Betty Turpin • Mavis Riley Mike Baldwin • Susan Baldwin • Gail Tilsley Nicky Tilsley • Sarah Louise Tilsley Phyllis Pearce • Gloria Todd • Martin Platt Shirley Armitage • Derek Wilton • Don Brennan

COMINGS AND GOINGS

Bet Lynch borrowed money from Theatrical Agent Alec Gilroy to buy the tenancy of the Rovers. However, she soon ran into problems and she disappeared completely. Alec persuaded Newton & Ridley to let him take on the pub and he eventually tracked Bet to Spain. She returned to the Rovers as his financée and they were married in September. Brian was reconciled with Gail following the birth of their daughter Sarah Louise and moved back in with the family. Alan Bradley returned from the Middle East and proposed to Rita. She refused to marry him but invited him to share her house letting all the neighbours know that they were living together. Terry Duckworth ran off to Scotland with Linda Jackson, the wife of an old friend. His bedroom did not stay empty long as Vera moved in her mother, Amy Burton, much to Jack's horror. The Websters left No.13 when they moved into the Corner Shop flat after Sally was taken on as Alf's assistant. Hilda Ogden left the Street at the end of the year. All the residents gathered at the Rovers on Christmas Day to bid farewell to Hilda Ogden when she moved to Hartington to housekeep for Dr Lowther after his wife died.

·1987·

THE AUSTRALIAN CONNECTION

'Of all my storylines, the one I remember most is the Australian one, I think that was one of the best.' Helen Worth is rightly proud to recall the work she put into Gail during her 1986-87 split with Brian. Gail had had a brief affair with Ian Latimer, Brian's Australian cousin, and refused to drop him when her mother Audrey begged her to see sense. 'I'm sick of being made a drudge, which is what this marriage has made me. No one can live their life, year in year out, for other people.' When Gail discovered she was pregnant (after Ian had left the country), she told Brian that it might not be his child. Brian started proceedings and in early 1987 they were granted a divorce. However, by that time little Sarah Louise had been born and Ian had taken a blood test which proved he was not the father. Sarah had been a month premature after Gail was rushed to hospital. She had stopped Brian thumping Ian, and the Tilsley clan battled it out in the hospital waiting-room while she gave birth. Although he accepted the fact that Ian was not Sarah Louise's father, Brian's ego prevented him from accepting the baby as his own. It was only months later, after he kidnapped Nicky and tried to leave the country with him, that Brian realized he wanted Gail and Sarah in his life. The family were reconciled.

LOVE BLOSSOMS FOR BET

Since the burning down of the Rovers, Bet Lynch had been aware of the presence of Alec Gilroy. He had run the Graffiti Club where the locals gathered while the Rovers was being renovated. A sly weasel

Gail Tilsley had risked everything during her affair with Ian Latimer. He returned and proposed marriage, but she wanted to bring up her baby alone.

of a man, he tried to fleece as much money off the regulars as possible. When Bet reopened the Rovers he tried to sell her the idea of hiring his cabaret turns. Rita Fairclough, who in her singing days had been represented by Gilroy, warned Bet not to have anything to do with him. However, Bet ignored the advice of her friends and slowly formed an alliance with him, borrowing money off him to buy the pub. Then real life took over and Julie Goodyear was written out of the show for three months when she nursed her mother who was suffering from cancer. To explain the landlady's absence, the writers had her running off and Alec, concerned about his investment, being given the licence to run the pub. Bet returned and within a couple of months had married Alec. It was not a marriage welcomed by either Julie Goodyear or Roy Barraclough. Julie remembers how startled she was when arriving at the church for filming she was greeted by crowds of fans chanting 'Don't Do It!' Roy found it difficult to believe that Alec would enter into a marriage with

Sally Ann Matthews x
(Jenny)

★ **Sally Ann Matthews** was still a schoolgirl when she made her television debut as Jenny Bradley in 1986. She had learnt her craft at Oldham Theatre workshop, and auditioned for Jenny without knowing what the part was. 'They gave me a script to read,' she says, 'and I looked through it and saw I was in a scene with Mavis Riley and I nearly fell through the floor. I cried!'

Alec Gilroy was wary of introducing the barmaid to the vicar.

someone like Bet: 'They were a most unlikely couple. I think that Julie and I both thought that. I wasn't very enamoured with the idea because I thought that the marriage, however unlikely it was, would of necessity mellow the characters down and I thought there was more fun to be had with the sharp banter that they had before.'

Much attention was given on the day to Bet's wedding gown. It had hundreds of petals and leaves hand-sown on to it and was, according to Julie, a joy to wear. However, while all the wardrobe department rushed around Julie making sure the dress looked perfect, Roy Barraclough's outstanding memory of the day is the way his costume was completely neglected: 'These seamstresses had toiled for weeks, creating this Emmanuel-style wedding dress. I mean, if she fell off the Forth Bridge, she could have quite happily parachuted to safety. Yet there was no one available to hem up my trousers for the wedding suit. They were like concertinas, round the shoes, and in desperation the floor manager rushed forward and turned them up with sellotape. There I stood, with a crowd of what must have been 300 members of the public, who'd gathered outside the church to watch this very special wedding being filmed with these awful trousers.'

·1987·

Terry Leaves Under a Cloud

Vera Duckworth was devastated when Curly Watts broke the news to her that her son Terry had run off with a married woman. The woman in question, Linda Jackson, had entered Terry's life at the beginning of the year. She was married to Pete, with whom Terry had been in the Paras, and it was obvious to the viewers that there was a sexual chemistry between the two as soon as they appeared in the same scene together. Terry and Linda fought against their emotions for a month before their first kiss led to a passionate affair. It was a scenario which was so real: man falling for best mate's wife, or girlfriend, as Nigel Pivaro explains: 'He was a passionate person, she was a passionate person, they couldn't help themselves. They were blinded by this passion, it was so intense and so strong that they thought it would last forever.' Terry decided he could not bear to see Linda with Pete so, buying himself out of business partnership with Curly Watts, he headed off into the sunset, calling at the Jacksons first of all to collect Linda.

Councillor Barlow

Alf Roberts had been an Independent councillor since 1968, with no serious opposition. However, he met his match in May 1987 when his shop assistant Deirdre Barlow became Councillor Barlow. She had been spurred on by husband Ken who hoped she and Alf would split the Independent vote between them and Labour would win. At first, Anne Kirkbride was not happy with the idea of Deirdre becoming a councillor: 'It was a complete departure which was crazy. I remember Tom Elliott telling me about it one day. I said, "You're kidding." But it was amazing, in a very short time it suddenly felt right and natural. It was just that I had to get my head round a complete departure like that.'

Ken was surprised by the change in Deirdre's character, as she took on issues and fought for them passionately. Anne Kirkbride was pleased with this change as it got Deirdre out from behind the bacon slicer and into the main arena: 'It broadened her whole life and outlook. And I think it changed her relationship with Ken, because suddenly he couldn't see her as a dim little wife and she was doing something. She became worthy of respect.'

Alf was shattered by his defeat and suffered a heart

★**Roy Barraclough** served as an apprentice draughtsman. During the eight years he spent in a Preston engineering factory he spent his spare time acting in local amateur dramatics groups, at one time being a member of five different groups. He decided to become a holiday camp entertainer on the Isle of Wight, and eventually joined Huddersfield Rep which he used as a springboard to the prestigious Victoria Theatre in Stoke. He moved on to Oldham where he worked with Barbara Knox and Eileen Derbyshire. His first television appearance was in the soap *Castlehaven*, playing Kathy Staff's husband. During the run of that programme he first met comedian Les Dawson and they started working together. One of their more famous collaborations was the creation of Cissie and Ada, the grumbling Northern ladies of mature years who suffered from endless ailments.

·1987·

attack, for which Deirdre blamed herself. However, he recovered and resumed his place behind the shop counter with Sally as his new assistant. Alf was now living at No.11 with Audrey, a match which no one expected to last, but Sue Nicholls for one feels they work well as a comic couple: 'I suppose one does know of couples that are totally opposite in probably character and physique too, as I am kind of thin and Alf's rather roly-poly.' Bryan agrees, 'And it works very well, it's amazing how popular the marriage it. I'm always getting letters saying how good they are together.'

Locking the world outside, Hilda stayed in No. 13 with her cat Rommel.

TA-RA CHUCK

'Don't Go Hilda!' That's the message loud and clear from the great British public this week. News that Hilda Ogden was hanging up her *Coronation Street* curlers has caused as much uproar as anything happening in Court No.13 of the High Court or even at the Irangate hearings! Radio stations throughout the country have been inundated with calls pleading with Hilda to change her mind. Some have even started their own "Hilda Must Stay" campaigns,' (*The People*).

For twenty-three years, Jean Alexander had played the viewer's favourite, Hilda Ogden. In 1982, she was voted the fourth most popular woman in Britain, after the Queen, the Queen Mother and the Princess of Wales; and in 1979 Michael Parkinson, Russell Harty and Sir John Betjeman formed the British League for Hilda Ogden.

Over the years, Jean Alexander had found that, with the departure of stalwarts such as Pat Phoenix and Peter Adamson, she had been given more and more lines. She decided, in June 1987, that enough was enough: 'I went in to see Bill Podmore and said, "I've decided I want to leave at the end of my contract – Christmas." "Oh," he said, "I've been dreading the day when you'd come in and say that."' Podmore was among many people who urged Jean to change her mind, but she stuck by her decision: 'It was nice and it was a secure job and all that, but suddenly I thought, I don't want to be here for the rest of my life. I'd like to do some of the things I was doing before I ever came into this show. I would like to play other parts before I fall off me perch.'

The writing team decided to see Hilda off in style. After she was attacked in a violent robbery, which left her employer Mrs Lowther dead, Hilda became withdrawn. When Dr Lowther retired to the country she jumped at the chance to be his house-keeper. Her last appearance, on Christmas Day, broke all *Coronation Street* viewing figures, with 26.65 million people tuning in to see Hilda off as she sang 'Wish me luck as you wave me goodbye.'

'Perhaps he's over-helpful: he washes up, peels the potatoes, makes the food and gets on her nerves!'

Bill Waddington suggests how Percy annoys Emily.

Rovers Alec and Bet Gilroy

No. 1 Ken, Deirdre and Tracy Barlow

No. 3 Emily Bishop • Curly Watts (Jan. - April) • Percy sugden (May - Dec.)

No. 5 Ivy and Don (June - Dec.) Brennan

No. 7 Rita Fairclough • Alan and Jenny Bradley

No. 9 Jack, Vera and Terry (Sept. - Dec.) Duckworth • Amy Burton (Jan. - March)

No. 11 Alf and Audrey Roberts • Malcolm Reid (July - Aug.)

No. 13 Kevin and Sally Webster (Feb. - Dec.) • Gina Seddon (March - April/Oct. - Dec.)

Shop flat Kevin and Sally Webster (Jan. - Feb.) • Curly Watts and Shirley Armitage (April - Dec.)

No. 16 (Centre) Percy Sugden (Jan. - May)

Non-residents Betty Turpin • Mavis Wilton • Derek Wilton • Mike Baldwin Brian Tilsley • Gail Tilsley • Nicky Tilsley Sarah Louise Tilsley • Phyllis Pearce • Gloria Todd • Martin Platt • Sandra Stubbs

COMINGS AND GOINGS

Curly Watts bade farewell to his cosy back room at Emily's to set up home above the Corner Shop with machinist Shirley Armitage. His room did not stay empty for long because Percy Sugden moved in, assuring Mrs Bishop it was only temporary, when he lost his job as caretaker of the Centre. Ivy Tilsley married cabbie Don Brennan in June and he moved in to No.5 with her. The Websters bought No.13 at a cut-down price from Mrs Ogden, and Sally's sister Gina lodged with them for a while. The Roberts' marriage was put under strain by the arrival of Canadian Malcolm Reid, who urged Audrey to run off with him. She resisted and Alf threw him out. Amy Burton left the Street rather quickly when Vera discovered she was shoplifting locally. Terry returned to No.9 briefly, working for Mike and using his Jag to impress women. Vera hoped he was back for good, but Mike sacked him when he discovered his car graffitied with the message: 'Stay Away from My Life.'

·1988·

RACISM IN THE STREET

'Why can't people see beyond the colour of me skin, I'm just a northern working girl, you know.' Shirley Armitage had had enough of living in her overcrowded family home and had asked Alf Roberts if she could rent to shop flat. He turned it down, saying he was keeping it as a storeroom and then the next day told Curly Watts it was his if he wanted it. What Alf did not realize was that Curly and Shirley were going out together and one brief conversation made them realize that Mr Roberts was not playing fair. Emily Bishop, whilst upset at the prospect of losing Curly as a lodger, was infuriated at Alf's behaviour and called him a bigot in the middle of his shop. Alf backed down and offered it to Shirley. By this time she had decided that her future lay with Curly and so it was that the pair moved into the flat together and Curly lost his virginity. Lisa Lewis, the actress, who played Shirley for four years, was thrilled at this, her first big storyline. 'I thought it was wonderful that they were living together. It's caused a big effect, because Curly is white and I'm black, and that brought its own little problems for both of the characters in terms of families not accepting the other.'

PUT UPON EMILY

The departure of Curly from No.3 left a vacant bed at Emily Bishop's. Any plans she might have had of enjoying a peaceful life were shattered in May when ex-Sergeant Sugden of the Catering Corps moved himself and his budgie Randy into her house. Percy had been forced to leave his cosy flat at the Centre

Shirley Armitage came up against predjudice from Curly's parents.

because he had reached the council's retirement age. Emily agreed to house him whilst his new flat was being prepared for him, only Percy had no intention of moving once he got his feet under the table. Bill Waddington was determined to make the most of his time working with Eileen Derbyshire, little knowing they would be sharing scenes for a further eight years.

While Emily was quick to complain to friends that Mr Sugden was driving her completely up the wall, Bill was amazed by the amount of letters he received praising interfering Percy: 'A lot of people say how lucky she is to have a man in the house like me who is not looking for anything, he just wants to be nice to her.' After a week of Percy's company, Emily begged Councillor Deirdre to get him out of her house: 'He suffocates me. I can't go anywhere, talk to anybody.' Deirdre managed to move Percy

Have budgie, will travel. Percy moved Randy across the Street in May 1988.

into his new flat, but Emily made the fateful mistake of visiting him. Once she saw how unhappy he was, away from all his friends, she moved him back to No.13. 'I know,' she told Deirdre, 'I'm my own worst enemy.'

A NEW LOVE FOR IVY

After Bert Tilsley's death in 1984, Ivy busied herself with work at the factory and with family business. Then, in September 1987, she met cab driver Don Brennan. Like Ivy he was Catholic, and had also lost a spouse. They were ordinary working-class people who drifted into an ordinary courtship and then, in June 1988, they married. Lynne Perrie had always been pleased that her character had kept her normalness: 'Bill Podmore once said to me, "Look love, you might not always hit the headlines with dramatic storylines like some characters, but you'll be the backbone of the show and the scriptwriters know that we can throw anything at you."' She was not keen on Ivy marrying Don, as she thought the character of Ivy worked much better when she was single, submerging herself in the Church and work, and Gail and Brian's family.

Geoff Hinsliff found it very difficult to create a believable character for Don. At the original script-reading Bill Podmore told his that Don was Irish and Geoff pointed out a fake accent would backfire. That was not the only problem: 'One of the basic issues was that the part had to be tailored to Lynne's

Ivy Tilsley met Don Brennan when he dropped her and Vera off at a night club. She later admitted that she fancied the back of his head.

Mavis stammered over the word 'husband' when she said her vows.

Ivy, because that was what the part was designed to do. I think Bill Podmore, from way back, was determined to marry Ivy off.' Both Lynne and Geoff were surprised by the quickness of the courtship and the lack of any apparent warmth between the two characters on screen. As Geoff explains: 'Lynne was for a very romantic relationship. She was for screen lovers and frankly I thought they were far too old for screen lovers. . .. I saw them as Darby and Joan, a relationship based on companionship, not sex.'

MAVIS GETS HER MAN

It is a scene that will always remain a Street classic – Derek Wilton on his hands and knees proposing to Mavis Riley though the Kabin letterbox. In fact, a couple of years later, the actors acted out the same scene on the *Des O'Connor Show*, only they did it in pigeon Russian, in the bid to increase international sales! Since they jilted each other at the church in 1984, Mavis and Derek's lives had intertwined over the years. She had been shocked when he told her he had married his boss's daughter, Angela Hawthorne, and he had turned to her for consolation after suffering Angela's cutting tongue. He once assured Mavis that she was the only woman in his life. Angela divorced Derek (at one point citing Mavis as corespondent) and he managed to persuade Mavis that theirs was a match made in heaven. Peter Baldwin enjoys thinking of the proposal scene: 'I think it set the tone for their relationship, nothing they ever do is ordinary. They manage to turn it all into a drama of some kind.'

TROUBLE AT THE CAFÉ

Gail Tilsley had worked at Jim's café since Jim Sedgewick opened it in 1980. She was made manageress in 1985 and ran it with the help of Phyllis Pearce and Martin Platt. Late in 1988, Jim's ex-wife Alma turned up out of the blue and announced that the café was now legally hers and she was going to move into the flat above and take it over.

Amanda Barrie had first appeared as Alma in 1981 and had come and gone over the years. Her character was vain and idle, always rushing off and leaving Gail to cope alone. But now she needed Gail's friendship as she set about establishing herself as a single girl again. Amanda Barrie describes her character as: 'A frivolous, heartless, work-shy person who wasn't interested in anything except herself.' Working in the café set had its hazards. Amanda recalls director Brian Mills wanting to shoot eggs frying in a pan: 'You can't do that unless you get the oil to sizzle and I had to lean over into it . . . and the fat was hitting me and I had burn marks all over my neck and my face.'

★ Leeds-born **Geoff Hinsliff** headed south as a young man and won a scholarship to the Royal Academy of Dramatic Art. He left RADA to join the Old Vic Theatre Company and then moved to the Royal Shakespeare Company. Around this time he made his first appearance in the Street as Jerry Booth's cycling pal. It was whilst playing George Fairfield in Granada's northern comedy *Brass* that Geoff was approached by that programme's producer, Bill Podmore, and was asked to move from one Granada studio to another, to become a member of the *Coronation Street* cast.

★ **Amanda Barrie** left home at the age of fourteen and drifted to London in search of fame and fortune. She has done everything in showbusiness, from Shakespeare to circus. Her name has been lit up on West End theatre hoardings, her television work extends from children's series *Hickory House* to *Time of my Life*, and she was one of the first Lionel Blair Dancers. She worked with Hughie Green on *Double your Money* and joined the Carry On team for *Carry-on Cabbie* and *Carry-on Cleo*. As a dancer, she worked on the live TV show *Running Wild* which starred Morecambe and Wise. She also got involved in comedy sketches – Spike Milligan threw things at her and Peter Sellers sat her on his knee as a ventriloquist's dummy.

'They were using a proper tram driver ... he kept putting the brakes on and the tram would stop because he couldn't bring himself to knock the stuntman over ... the Floor Manager had to lie underneath the driver with his hand on the brake and hold the driver's foot off the pedal.'

Mark Eden remembers filming Alan Bradley's death.

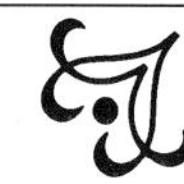

Rovers Alec and Bet Gilroy • Charlie Bracewell (Jan.)

No. 1 Ken, Deirdre and Tracy Barlow

No. 3 Emily Bishop • Percy Sugden

No. 5 Ivy and Don Brennan

No. 7 Rita Fairclough • Alan (Jan. - March) and Jenny (Jan - March) Bradley

No. 9 Jack and Vera Duckworth • Curly Watts (May - Dec.)

No. 11 Alf and Audrey Roberts (Jan - Dec.) Jim, Liz, Steve and Andy McDonald (Dec.)

No. 13 Kevin and Sally Webster • Gina Seddon (Jan.)

Shop flat Curly Watts and Shirley Armitage (Jan. - May) • Alf and Audrey Roberts (Dec.)

No. 16 (Centre) *demolished*

Non-residents Betty Turpin • Mavis Wilton Derek Wilton • Mike Baldwin • Brian Tilsley • Gail Tilsley • Nicky Tilsley • Sarah Louise Tilsley • Phyllis Pearce • Martin Platt Sandra Stubbs • Tina Fowler • Alma Sedgewick • Mark Casey • Wendy Crozier

COMINGS AND GOINGS

Alec Gilroy employed retired ventriloquist Charlie Bracewell as barman at the Rovers but Bet managed to palm him off to Stella Rigby at the White Swan after he interfered with Betty Turpin. Curly Watts suffered a blow in May when his resident girlfriend packed and left. Vera Duckworth took pity on him and moved him into No.9 as lodger. Rita Fairclough discovered her resident lover Alan Bradley had mortgaged her house. When she confronted him he tried to kill her and went on the run. He returned to stalk her and disappeared, suffering a breakdown. He tracked her down to Blackpool where he died, hit by a tram. Jenny Bradley took against Rita over the incident and moved out of No.7. The Roberts sold No.11 to the McDonald family in December but a mix up in a housing chain left them homeless so they had to move into the old shop flat. The biggest change to the Street was the demolition of Baldwin's factory and the Community Centre by property developer Maurice Jones.

·1989·

NEW BROOMS SWEEPING CLEAN

The end of 1988 saw the departure of Bill Podmore as the Street's producer. After twelve years he felt he needed a break and retired from Granada. David Liddiment, the Head of Light Entertainment, was given the role of executive producer and Mervyn Watson returned to the programme as producer. David was adamant that he was going to bring about changes to the Street: 'The machine of producing two [episodes] a week was going on and on and on, much as it had done for many years. And it was kind of caught, gathering up and not going anywhere. The show wasn't evolving, it had stood still, and an enormous amount of hidden creativity had been held back.'

Liddiment thought that the Street was depending upon comic storylines too much and had moved away from the progressive, socially relevant storylines of the 1960s. 'At the same time,' he says, 'a lot of technical changes had been made in the television industry, but the way *Coronation Street* was made had not changed at all. The schedule was substantially the same as it had been from the time when the Street stopped being broadcast live. It was a five-day-a-week routine and the show's producer was entirely constrained by that routine.'

For year, writers had been restricted to using only one or two location scenes per episode. This was because the scenes would have to be shot on expensive film rather than cheaper studio tape. By the late 1980s, however, lightweight equipment that used tape rather than film made location filming more economic. The cast suddenly found they had to learn a new technical term 'PSC' (Portable Single Camera), and adjust to working at weekends, as Bill Roach explains: 'We'd never worked weekends under usual circumstances and all our leisure activities went straight out of the window. Normally filming would be a couple of lines walking up the Street and now suddenly we were getting big scenes, and with no rehearsals, because you just got on and did them.' David Liddiment walked around Salford when he took over the show and noticed there were pockets of modern houses being developed alongside old terraced blocks. He decided that if the factory and Centre were to be flattened, the Street itself could be made to look more visually exciting. By building shops and houses on the site, established characters living off the Street could be moved on, as well as new characters introduced. 'It gave us all the advantages of bringing more characters on to the Street itself, made the Street a more vital, living place. Because we then increased the episodes from two to three, and increased the volume of location shooting, both on and off the Street, the whole texture of the show changed.' The Granada bosses wanted to ensure the programme would remain a success. Research was carried out which showed that the viewers were not happy with the big gap between the Wednesday and Monday episodes. Liddiment led the fight for a third episode, adamant that the creative demands would not be compromised. In October 1989, the first third episode was transmitted on a Friday.

THE MURDER OF BRIAN TILSLEY

The last act Bill Podmore made as producer was to kill off Brian Tilsley, a character he had introduced ten years earlier. Christopher Quinten had married American television personality Leeza Gibbons and had moved to the States. He thought Brian would work abroad or something similar, and was horrified to discover that Brian was to die. Bill Podmore explains his decision: 'There seemed little point in bringing him back just to live with his mum. Whichever way we assembled the pieces the jigsaw wouldn't fit, and after a lot of soul-searching and heartache we came to the inevitable conclusion that

The knocking down of the factory and Centre brought a whole new Street to the residents' doorsteps.

Brian Tilsley died outside a night club leaving his widow Gail to fall for Martin, who had worked by her side for four years at the cafe.

Waiting for the cue to run across the Prom, Barbara Knox and Mark Eden in their last scene together.

Brian would have to die.' Chris Quinten had no option but to go with the scripts, which called for a split in the Tilsley marriage (they had remarried in February 1988) and for Gail to ask for another divorce: 'I married too young. Grew up afterwards. What was so wrong with me having an identity of my own? You couldn't cope with that. You're like sommat from the dark ages. Women should stay in their place, they're all right in the kitchen, in the bedroom and that's about it!' This led to Brian going out to clubs and casinos at night, and picking up women for the night. After one session at a nightclub, he tried to fight off a gang of youths who started to molest one of his girlfriends. One of the thugs produced a knife and stabbed Brian in the stomach. Gail was left trying to explain to nine-year-old Nicky what had happened to his dad. A few months later, Martin Platt, only twelve years older than Nicky, took him under his wing. Nicky blossomed under Martin's care, as did Gail. When she broke down under the strain of it all Martin comforted her with kisses and they ended up in bed together. Sean Wilson realized that this was his big chance to make an impression on the writers: 'I was glad they'd given me the chance of doing some decent work, instead of just hanging around. I took that with both hands and just went for it. That was what I'd been looking for for years.'

THE BRADLEY AFFAIR

February found Alan Bradley stealing the deeds to the house. He called himself Len Fairclough and mortgaged the house for £15,000. He used the money to open his own security firm and took on Dawn Prescott as his receptionist. Things started to go wrong for Alan when he tried to rape Dawn. During rehearsals, Mark Eden, playing Alan, held back: 'I thought I'm not going to do anything near to what I'm going to do when we do it on tape, because she'd be prepared for it . . . So on the actual take I grabbed hold of her and she couldn't get away from me and I started to pull her skirt up. She was fighting for her life to get away, I mean she wasn't kidding. We were knocking things over and she shoved me off and I grabbed her as she was running out of the door . . . afterwards, she was shaking and white-faced but it worked.' Like Louise Harrison, playing Dawn, Barbara Knox was also frightened by the intensity of Mark's acting as he recalls: 'She'd be shaking afterwards . . . she used to say "You frightened the life out of me."'

Dawn told Rita about Alan's attack and the letters he received in the name of Len Fairclough. Rita did her own investigations and uncovered the truth. She confronted him when Jenny was out of the house at her eighteenth birthday party.

Barbara Knox enjoyed every moment of the story and received letters from viewers urging her to see what Alan was up to. She is pleased the story was so convincing: 'I thought it was a marvellous, well-constructed story and beautifully done. As it would be in real life, Rita was virtually the last to know that he was a crook, after her money and had another woman. All the things that in real life the lady, the wife, is the last to know. So I found it brilliant to play.'

Confronted by Rita, Alan admitted he had been crafty but was pleased with himself for making a successful business. He was furious when she told him that she had told the building society about his fraud and she wanted to see him ruined. He pounced on her, hitting her around the room before trying to suffocate her with a cushion. Jenny rushed in just at the right time to stop Alan from killing Rita, and he was captured by the police a couple of weeks later. The first Friday episode was Alan Bradley's trial, at the end of which he walked free. He took a job at the building site opposite No.7 and made sure that Rita knew where he was all the time. When she disappeared, the police suspected him of murder and the building site was dug up in the search for her body. She was found by the Gilroys, singing in Blackpool, under the name of Littlewood. Alan found out and tried to drag her home. Finally, she ran away from him across a street, he followed and was hit and killed by a tram. Shortly after the episode was transmitted, someone put a plaque by the railings where Alan died. The plaque read: 'Alan Bradley the sham got knocked over by a tram.'

New kids on the block

Research in the late 1980s showed that many teenagers preferred the youthful serials from Australia. The writers made an effort to introduce new young people to the show. However the most successful introduction was that of the McDonald twins, played by Simon Gregory (he had to change his name to Gregson after a month in the show) and Nicholas Cochrane. They were picked by Mervyn Watson and casting director James Bain from their school in south Manchester as Simon reveals: 'The English teacher at school asked if anyone was interested in being on the Street. . . . I went along and they took my picture and then a week later we had to do improvizations.' Beverly Callard had to sit in on them with Charles Lawson, having just been cast as Liz and Jim McDonald: 'I was really nervous; as an actor you don't like to be at the other side of it really. There were about thirty boys in all and at the end of the session we all had to write down on a piece of paper which two we'd liked best and we all chose the same two.'

★ **Beverly Callard** started her acting career by becoming a member of the Leeds Proscenium Players. Before joining the Street cast in 1989, she had made a brief appearance as June Dewhurst, a friend of the Tilsleys, in May 1984. She had also appeared in *Emmerdale Farm, The Practice* and *Lucifer.*

Charles Lawson was encouraged to enter the profession by a teacher who recognized his talent. After leaving drama school, he appeared in the film version of *Wilt* and did television work in programmes such as *Bread* and *Harry's Game.*

Simon Gregson and **Nicholas Cochrane** came to Granada to play the McDonald boys straight from school. They were cast after auditions at their South Manchester school and given the roles even though Nicholas was in fact a full year older than Simon.

SALON
BEAUTY TREATMENTS
Denise's

The NINETIES

'I don't care whose bed you sleep in, but it isn't mine.'

Deirdre Barlow ends her marriage to Ken.

Rovers Alec and Bet Gilroy

No. 1 Ken (Jan.), Deirdre and Tracy Barlow

No. 3 Emily Bishop • Percy Sugden

No. 4 Derek and Mavis Wilton (March - Dec.)

No. 5 Ivy and Don Brennan

No. 6 Des and Steph Barnes (Feb. - Dec.)

No. 7 Rita Fairclough (Jan. - April) • Jenny Bradley (April - Dec.) • Klick (April - Aug.) and Joanne (July - Aug.) Khan • Angie Freeman (Sept. - Dec.)

N0. 9 Jack and Vera Duckworth • Curly Watts

No. 10a Rita Fairclough (April - Dec.)

No. 11 Jim, Liz, Steve and Andy Mcdonald

No. 13 Kevin and Sally Webster

Shop flat Alf and Audrey Roberts (Jan - March) • Reg Holdsworth (May - July) • Ken Barlow (Aug. - Dec.)

Non-residents Betty Turpin • Mike Baldwin • Gail Tilsley • Nicky Tilsley Sarah Louise Tilsley • Phyllis Pearce Martin Platt • Tina Fowler • Alma Sedgewick • Mark Casey • Wendy Crozier Kimberley Taylor • Jackie Ingram

COMINGS AND GOINGS

Just after the stroke of midnight, only minutes into the new decade, Deirdre Barlow threw her husband Ken out of the house. On Christmas Eve she had discovered that he had a mistress. Ken moved off the Street for the first time in his life, living first with Wendy Crozier, and then in a bedsit, before renting the flat above the Corner Shop so he could be close to Deirdre in the hope of a reconciliation. Three new houses, one flat, two factory units and two shops with flats above were built on the Street. The Wiltons bought No.4 and set about cultivating their little back garden. Next door to them, at No.6, were Des and Steph Barnes. Rita Fairclough moved out of No.7 and moved into the flat above the shop unit opposite the Corner Shop. No.7 became a student house. The Roberts bought a large semi-detached house in Grasmere Drive, near the golf course, and Reg Holdsworth, manager of the Bettabuy supermarket, moved into the flat while briefly estranged from his wife Veronica.

·1990·

THE BREAK-UP OF THE HOUSE OF BARLOW

Since October 1989, Ken Barlow had been seeing his secretary Wendy Crozier. He calculated that if Deirdre did discover his infidelity he could always point out that she was no better as she had had an affair with Mike Baldwin (see 1983). However, what came as a complete surprise to him was the news that Deirdre did not feel their nine-year marriage was worth fighting for. She accepted his affair and used it to get him out of her life, starting divorce proceedings and forcing him to sell his newspaper, the *Recorder*, to buy off the mortgage on No.1. While Deirdre did her best to remain calm over the whole business, Anne Kirkbride was upset by the change in the family: 'We were both upset. We just loved working together. When you've worked all that length of time it's so easy. I mean it just makes life so easy and you've got a routine for running lines and it was a pleasure to do it. Suddenly it was as if they'd taken away my security. It was very disconcerting.' Bill Roache found himself struggling to understand why Ken had been unfaithful in the first place: 'All I ever ask from my job is that I can believe and understand what Ken has to do. I had a job understanding why he was being unfaithful. When Deirdre had her affair they had made Ken become sort of boring.'

Ken's relationship with Wendy did not work out and he pinned his hopes on winning Deirdre back. He moved back into the Street and took a job teaching at Weatherfield Comprehensive. Deirdre, however, turned to plumber Dave Barton for comfort. He had saved Tracy from a chip pan fire at No.1 which left the whole kitchen gutted.

Deirdre would not commit herself to Dave

Deirdre Barlow face to face with Town Hall mole Wendy Crozier, her husband's mistress.

Barton so they stopped seeing each other. She then started a relationship with conman Phil Jennings, and went off to see 1991 in with him in Paris. Ken was horrified as he had hoped to break down Deirdre's defences during the festive period. He let himself into No.1, opened a bottle of pills and attempted suicide on New Year's Eve. After only three tablets he was stopped by Bet Gilroy.

RUNAWAY STEVE

When she was given the part of Liz McDonald, Beverly Callard did her own research to find out what sort of woman became an army wife and how she ran her home. One of the things she found out was these women had to run their homes in military fashion and had their houses inspected by officers on a regular basis. She felt that the original characterization of Liz in the first scripts made her too weak and submissive: 'I always imagine Liz and Jim to have passionate rows but passionately make the peace again. I did not believe that Jim McDonald would be happy with a wimp.'

The first occasion when the McDonalds came to blows was in the summer of 1990 when Steve ran off to the Lake District with Jim's motorbike and young Joanne Khan from No.7. Writer Paul Abbott had come up with the idea, feeling that younger viewers would be very interested in Steve and his adventure. On screen the story might have appeared exciting, but in reality Simon Gregson hated it: 'It was freezing and I'd nothing on but a pair of jeans and a T-shirt. I had to push this bike up and down a hill

The Lake District was the ideal setting for disillusioned teenage love.

for ages and ages.'

Liz tracked Steve down to a hotel in the Lakes where he was employed washing up. She brought him home where Jim was waiting to clout him. Liz put herself bodily between the two and shouted at Jim: 'You touch one hair of his head and I walk, and you won't see any of us ever again!'

ENTER THE YUPPIES

Mervyn Watson led the decision: 'We opened up a new row of opportunities, in the sense of the new houses and shops. We basically had another Coronation Street to create over the road. The fact that they were new houses meant that there was a possibility of attracting a different kind of character. We decided to bring in a young couple and we wanted something different. We wanted something that would catch the eye of the audience. A couple with loads of money and values that had grown out of the Thatcher years. We wanted them to make an immediate impact as soon as they arrived and we talked up this couple – young, flashy, exciting, lively characters.'

The Barnes moved into No.6 on their wedding day, the house sold at cost price to them by Steph's father, Maurice Jones. The press called them 'yuppies,' but the couple were just ordinary working people with enough cash in their pockets for ski-ing holidays, ice-cream makers and sunbeds. Their personalities were established as being flirtatious and mischievous, as Amelia Bullmore, the actress cast as Steph, elaborates: 'To start with, they definitely

·1990·

came in as a sort of assembly of opposites to other people. They came in behaving badly, on the new side of the Street, brash house, brash people, not following the Weatherfield code.' The first thing Steph did was to lure Kevin Webster into her bathroom and shave off his moustache.

Amelia Bullmore was not prepared for the reaction she received from viewers, although she could understand why the viewers were so protective of Kevin: 'At that point, nobody had any reason to like me. I came in an impostor, taking up time from other characters. Nobody had any loyalty to Steph because she'd only been in the programme five minutes, and then she defaces one of its institutions. I became a marked woman, I got a terrible response.' Philip Middlemiss agrees that at first both he and Amelia were hated: 'We were terrible disruptive influences. We had interfered with Kevin and Sally and that was a huge step towards disaster.' Then, after six months, it all turned round, and the viewers took to us.'

A NEW COMIC LOCATION

One of the new locations established at the end of 1989 was Bettabuy supermarket. Curly Watts had finished his business studies course and was taken on as assistant manager (trainee), under Reg Holdsworth. The original idea had been that Curly would quickly

The Bettabuy bus was the first venture organised by Curly at the supermarket. He angered Alf Roberts by planning its route down Coronation Street.

·1990·

rise to manager and Holdsworth would be moved on, leaving Curly in charge of a load of women who would include Vera and Ivy. This formula had worked very well in the days of Baldwin and his factory and the writing team hoped for a similar success, but they had no idea at that stage who would be cast as Reg. Ken Morley based Holdsworth on someone he had observed: 'It was based on a supermarket manager that I'd seen in London where I lived. There was a great guy in there who had all these neurotic twitches and this stance as he walked around the store, ordering people about and twitching and rocking his head. He was just the sort of middle management idiot needed.' Holdsworth became an overnight sensation and Morley soon had a huge following. The writers saw potential in the character and fed him pompous, huge speeches. Morley inserted the twitches, gestures and props and a great comic character was born. Kevin Kennedy's character shifted from being straight down the middle to part of a comedy double act. Kevin Kennedy applauds the writers' talent in creating believable comic situations in an established drama serial: 'The balance has got to be right. It's all got to be good drama and very good comedy. The thing that Ken and myself created got a little bit out of hand, because we were isolated to a certain extent, we did most of our work on a Sunday (when the real supermarket was closed) and the powers that be were still in bed. So we created a bit of a Frankenstein, which we really enjoyed at the time but it was a roller-coaster ride, and once you got on it you couldn't get off.'

A BIG CELEBRATION

For thirty years the actors had squashed themselves into shared dressing-rooms and rehearsed in pretend sets, using books as telephones and miming doors opening and shutting. To celebrate the programme's unique achievement of a thirty-year uninterrupted run, Granada gave the company its show case studio, Stage One. Now it was refurbished to include a green room, make-up complex, wardrobe room with washing machines, a huge studio area where some sets, such as the Rovers, the Kabin and the Corner Shop, could stay in place permanently, and individual dressing-rooms for the thirty actors on long-term contracts. Bill Roache was given dressing-room No.1 and the rest of the cast fell into place, right up to Philip Middlemiss in No.30. The actors now had the added luxury of rehearsing in the proper sets, with their own props.

★ **Philip Middlemiss** trained at the London Academy of Music and Dramatic Art and worked at the National Theatre, appearing as a semi-naked satyr in *Trackers*. Before he joined the Street, his television appearances included *Waterfront Beat, Inspector Morse* (he was found dead in a public lavatory), *Closing Ranks* and *Christobel*.

Amelia Bullmore did not have the same television experience when she joined the programme. While a student at Manchester University, she helped form Red Stockings, a radical all-girl comedy troupe. Before being cast as Steph, she had worked mostly in community theatre with the Contact Theatre Group in Manchester.

Philip Middlemiss (DES)

Amelia Bullmore (STEPH BARNES)

·1990·

David Plowright hands over the keys of Stage One to the cast.

★ Lancashire-born **Ken Morley** studied Drama and English as a mature student at Manchester University. When he first appeared as Reg he was still working at a school in London where he taught English, maths and science. He was also seen as General Von Flockenstoffen in the BBC comedy, *'Allo, 'Allo*. He was given the part of Reg after appearing in the Granada show *Watching*.

'On my first day of recording, Ken Morley asked me to lie down in my swimming costume; he then jumped on top of me.'

Sarah Lancashire recalls Raquel's appearance as a beauty queen.

Rovers Alec and Bet Gilroy • Vicky Arden (July - Dec.) • Mike Baldwin (Oct. - Nov.)

No. 1 Deirdre and Tracy Barlow

No. 3 Emily Bishop • Percy Sugden

No. 4 Derek and Mavis Wilton

No. 5 Ivy and Don Brennan

No. 6 Des and Steph (Jan. - Aug.) Barnes

No. 7 Jenny Bradley (Jan. - March) • Angie Freeman • Curly Watts (March - Dec.)

No. 8 Martin, Gail, Nicky, Sarah and David Platt (Dec.)

No. 9 Jack and Vera Duckworth • Curly Watts (Jan. - March) • Joss Shackleton (Feb. - March)

No. 10a Rita Fairclough

No. 11 Jim, Liz, Steve and Andy Mcdonald

No. 12 Reg Holdsworth (Sept. - Dec.)

No. 13 Kevin, Sally and Rosie (Jan. - Dec.) Webster

Shop flat Ken Barlow

Non-residents Betty Turpin • Mike Baldwin • Alf Roberts • Audrey Roberts • Phyllis Pearce • Alma Sedgewick • Mark Casey • Kimberley Taylor • Jackie Ingram • Raquel Wolstenhulme

·1991·

EVERYONE LOVES CURLY

The New Year found Bettabuy assistant Kimberley Taylor breaking off her engagement to assistant manager, Curly Watts. She told him it was because he was always trying to get her into bed and she wished to save herself for their wedding night. This little titbit interested Kimberley's workmate Raquel Wolstenhulme who thought it would be worth giving herself to Mr Watts if it improved her career prospects. Sarah Lancashire remembers being slightly self-conscious when she first appeared as Raquel in a swimming contest, as the store's beauty queen.

Curly's fling with Raquel was short-lived because he was preoccupied with Kimberley who had started a sexual relationship with her cousin Adrian. She asked for, and was given, a transfer after he shouted 'Jezebel' at her in front of customers.

After moving in with Angie at No.7, Curly slowly realized that here was the girl of his dreams – independent, witty, and a best friend. They enjoyed a brother/sister relationship until one fateful night

COMINGS AND GOINGS

At her mother Amy's funeral, Vera Duckworth was introduced to Joss Shackleton who told her that he was her father. Vera moved Joss into No.9, but he soon returned to his flat in Rusholme when Jack made him feel unwelcome. Curly had given Joss his room and moved into with design student Angie Freeman at No.7, Rita's house. He moved into Jenny Bradley's old room, Jenny having left to live with a married dentist. Alec Gilroy lost his daughter Sandra Arden when she and husband Tim were killed in a car crash. Their daughter Victoria became Alec's ward and was forced to live at the Rovers during her school holidays. The Websters brought home their daughter Rosie, born on Christmas Eve 1990, and across the Street, Martin Platt bought three-bedroomed No.8 for the knock-down price of £38,000. He moved in with his new wife Gail, her two children Nicky and Sarah Louise, and their son (born the day after Rosie Webster), David. Next door, at No.6, Des Barnes suffered anguish as wife Steph ran off with another man. The flat next to the Kabin, No.12, was bought by Reg Holdsworth, much to Rita Fairclough's horror (Holdsworth had been attempting to court her for months). The Rovers took in Mike Baldwin as a paying guest for a couple of months after the breakup of his marriage to factory boss Jackie Ingram.

when they drank too much red wine and ended up in bed together. Deborah McAndrew worked out the relationship between Angie and Curly in her head to help her understand why Angie rejected the idea of a long-term relationship: 'She really liked Curly but she was living with him. And if she went into a sexual relationship then it would be very settled and very domestic, instantly, because they were sharing a house. I think if Curly had been living in the next street she might have gone out with him. It was just that it would have made everything too cosy and too domestic and normal for Angie.'

TROUBLE AT NO.6

After playing Stephanie Barnes for a year, Amelia Bullmore told producer Mervyn Watson that she wished to leave to concentrate on her theatre work. She agreed to stay on until the August so the writers could decide if she should leave alone, with Des or with another Street resident. Des had recently bought a boat which had caused problems – first by crashing into the Wiltons' garden and then by being taken away by a crane, with Derek on board. The writers decided to use the boat as a symbol of the Barnes' failing marriage. Steph was seen to grow tired of Des's childlike pleasure in his new toy and used the occasion of a day's boating to tell him that she had taken a lover and was leaving with him. The man in question was architect Simon Beatty. Amelia was pleased by the way the situation was handled as she had feared Steph would ride roughshod over Des's feelings.

Des panicked Steph in to thinking he had killed himself when he blew the boat up. She found him watching the flames on the river bank: 'There goes our marriage, Steph. . .didn't it go with a bang!' When the episode went out, Philip Middlemiss was amazed by the tremendous public response, which has never really died down. 'I suppose I've really got to have more faith in the writers,' says Middlemiss. 'The boat incident seemed to me a bit over the top, simply because I wouldn't do that sort of thing. But people have done sillier things. You've got to go with it I think and if you go with it you've got to go with it 100 percent.'

Des slashed Steph's suitcases in a bid to stop her leaving and begged her to stay, swearing he loved her. It was all too much for Steph and she ran out of the house to start a new life with Simon, leaving housekeeper Phyllis Pearce to pick up the pieces with a shattered Des.

'There goes our marriage my love, didn't it go with a bang.'

·1991·

BALDWIN'S WOMEN

Another marriage doomed to failure was that of Mike Baldwin and Jackie Ingram, although theirs lasted for only a week. After selling his factory and losing all his money in a Spanish land deal to Dawn Prescott's scheming brother Robert, Mike was forced to take a salesman's job working for textile tycoon Peter Ingram. When Ingram dropped dead of a heart attack, Mike quickly moved in to comfort grieving Jackie, advizing her on how to run the business, and was soon given the job of running the whole plant. At the time Mike was sharing a luxury dockland flat with Alma Sedgewick and she feared Mike would fall for the younger, wealthier Jackie. Amanda Barrie recalls she receiving mail from viewers warning her about Mike's ways: 'I get a lot of mail. But then a lot of people liked us together, thought we made a good couple. A lot of letters said I deserved better, which was rather sweet.' And at the same time Shirin Taylor, the actress playing Jackie, was also receiving letters, warning her that Mike was only after her money.

Slowly, Mike made his move on Jackie and manoeuvred her into bed. Alma realised exactly what was going on but turned a blind eye in the hope the affair would end quickly. Johnny Briggs felt confident at the time that Mike had finally found his ideal partner in Jackie: 'I thought that he would have stuck with someone like Jackie if he was going to stick to anyone as she was so intelligent and rich.' Mike moved in with Jackie and Alma moved back to the flat above the café. However, she wasn't lonely for long. As Mike and Jackie planned their wedding, Alma started a relationship with Mike's enemy, Ken

Alma spent months turning a blind eye to Mike's affair with Jackie before being confronted with the truth. In an act of revenge she attacked their bedclothes with a pair of scissors.

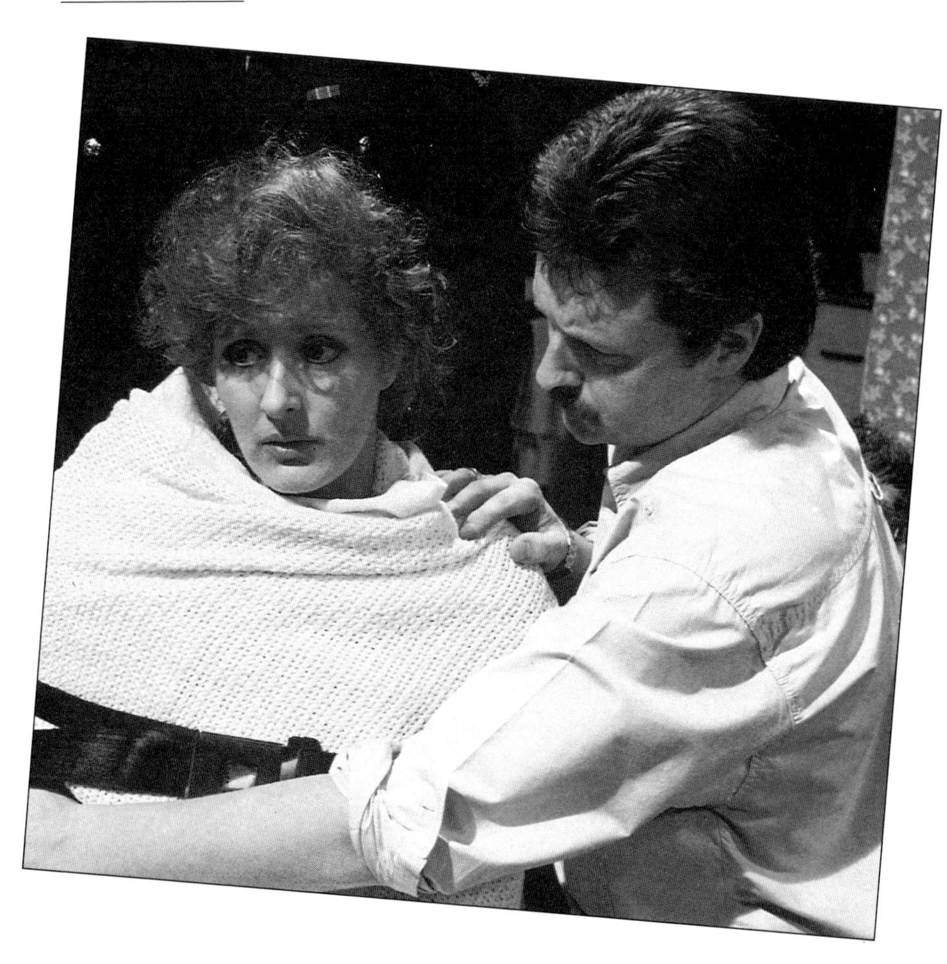

Barlow. The mail Amanda Barrie received showed that this relationship was more popular with viewers than that with Mike. After the marriage, Mike received the stunning news that Jackie had decided to sell the business so they could spend more time together. A run through the accounts revealed the fact that Mike had used company money to buy the lease of Alma's café, and Jackie learnt about Mike's marriage to Susan, his affair with Deirdre and all his shady deals. Throwing her wedding ring at him she reached for her shotgun and ordered him out of her life. 'I enjoyed that scene,' says Johnny Briggs. Shirin Taylor also found the scene good to play: 'The fun of it was that it was such a good script and such a good storyline. Jackie was a strong modern woman who had a momentary lapse and weakness after her husband died and then after she felt betrayed by Mike Baldwin she used all her strength to get herself back together again. She wasn't going to have him play around.' Jackie immediately filed for divorce and gave Mike a £10,000 payoff. He used part of the money to open a garage, MVB Motors, in one of the units in the Street, employing Kevin Webster as mechanic.

On Christmas Day, two special episodes of *Coronation Street* were transmitted. The first was unique because, halfway through the show, Alf Roberts turned on the television and the Queen's Speech was played. Then, in the evening, the next episode picked up where the afternoon's had left off, with Mike luring Alma into bed. He had got Ken out of the way by getting Tracy to persuade Deirdre to have Ken for the day in the hope they would get back together. Alma fell for Mike's charms and went to bed with him, only to become disgusted when he told her how he had out-manoeuvred Ken. On New Year's Eve, in a high class hotel, Alma broke the news to Ken. He walked out on her.

POOR LITTLE RICH GIRL

The character of Victoria Arden was established in 1990 when Alec Gilroy made contact with his estranged daughter Sandra and discovered he had a granddaughter. At the time she was a red-head played by Helen Warburton. When the character was reintroduced a year later the part was recast and blonde Chloë Newsome was introduced. The script had Vicky being left an orphan when her parents were killed in a car crash. Chloë was very frightened on her first day at work and things were not made easier by Julie Goodyear and Roy Barraclough's first words to her when they were introduced: 'They walked up to me and started saying, "She's an impostor, she's not Vicky," and I felt really awful.'

Vicky refused to stay with the Gilroys in the smoky pub with its boisterous clientele, so different from life at Codrington School in Shropshire. However, no one else was willing to put Vicky up so she was forced to stay with her overbearing grandad. Both Vicky and Bet were horrified to discover that Alec was charging her estate £50 a week for her board and lodgings. Vicky became a very rich young lady when her parents died – as well as her horse Saracen, she had assets worth £250,000.

Liz lost her daughter after a mercy dash to the hospital. The flood of letters Beverley Callard received afterwards took her months to read through. Often she'd need comfort from Charles Lawson as she read of someone like Liz who had lost a longed-for baby.

★ *Coronation Street* was the first television work **Deborah McAndrew** had ever done. She was picked for the part of Guinness-drinking design student Angie straight from Manchester University, where she was studying drama. 'I was scared,' she says. 'I didn't sleep for about a week. Although I probably was less scared than I would have been if I had had lots of theatre experience.'

Unlike Deborah, **Sarah Lancashire** had lots of experience. She had been brought up with the Street because her father, Geoffrey Lancashire, wrote for the programme for seven years, penning seventy-four episodes in the 1960s. It was writing that first attracted Sarah's attention when she was growing up in Oldham, Lancashire. However, the acting bug eventually hit her and she trained at the Guildhall School of Drama. After that she sang with a dance band for six years and lectured in theatre studies between acting roles. In 1987 she appeared in one episode of the Street as nurse Wendy Farmer who applied to be the Duckworth lodger; Jack was keen but Vera moved her mother in instead. When she was given the part of Raquel, Sarah was given a thumbnail sketch of the character: 'They said that they wanted a combination of certain other characters, two of whom were Vera and Bet, but they were leaning more towards the young Vera than the young Bet. She was very, very working class, very northern and very brassy, and not terribly bright. And I thought "I've been type cast again!"'

Tragedy at No.11.

'The public did not take to the character at all in the first year. Jim did not work, there's no doubt about that, and then things started to improve with the loss of the baby. I think this was because you saw another side of him.' Charles Lawson really did not have much chance to show Jim McDonald in a favourable light during his first twelve months on the programme; all Jim was ever called on to do was shout and thump the table. And then along came the story that melted the hearts of all the viewers as the McDonalds struggled to come to terms with the loss of their baby.

Baby Katie was born on 1 January 1992 and died the following day, but the story was planned in 1991. At first Jim thought Liz had been diagnosed as having cancer when she broke the news that she had 'something to tell him'. Beverly Callard was alarmed to read in the script that Liz was having a baby: 'My instant thought was, "Oh no, I have to work with an Irish man, twins and a baby!" But then I asked Mervyn Watson about it and was told she was not going to have it.'

Liz nearly went to full term with the baby but went into labour brought on by stress – Steve had got into trouble with a gang of youths who had beaten up Andy as a warning to his twin. Steve went on the run and Liz feared he had been killed.

Following the death of little Katie, Beverley Callard received hundreds of letters of congratulations from viewers on the way the issue had been handled and telling of similar experiences. Bev agrees with Charlie that it was this storyline that secured the family's place in the Street: 'I was very aware that the four of us had to succeed and I think they took to Liz more than they did to Jim because of the shouting scenes. But I don't think the viewers felt the death of the baby brought them closer together. I think everybody thought they were real from the very beginning. But that storyline showed that Jim was sensitive and strong. Of course Liz had always known that but the viewers hadn't.'

★**Chloë Newsome** started her career at the age of eleven when she joined Sheffield's Crucible Youth Theatre. She then landed a part in Granada's *Children's Ward*, whose creator suggested Chloë for the part of Vicky. In her first episode, the Gilroys broke the news of her parents' death: 'Julie Goodyear was all dressed up with her wig and cleavage and heels and she just seemed so big and frightening. She had to cuddle me on the settee and I was shaking in the corner.'

'The millions who watch Coronation Street – and who will continue to do so despite Lord Rees-Mogg – know real life when they see it.'

The Times

Rovers Alec (Jan. - Sept.) and Bet Gilroy Vicky Arden • Raquel Wolstenhulme (May - Dec.)

No. 1 Deirdre and Tracy Barlow

No. 2 Dnise Osbourne (Dec.)

No. 3 Emily Bishop • Percy Sugden

No. 4 Derek and Mavis Wilton

No. 5 Ivy and don (Jan. - July/Oct. - Dec.) Brennan

No. 6 Des and Steph (May) Barnes Raquel Wolstenhulme (Jan. - May)

No. 7 Angie Freeman and Curly Watts

No. 8 Martin, Gail, Nicky, Sarah and David Platt • Carmel Finnan (Oct. - Dec.)

No. 9 Jack, Vera, Lisa (May - Nov.) and Tom (Sept. - Nov.) Duckworth

No. 10a Rita and Ted (June - Sept.) Sullivan

No. 11 Jim, Liz, Steve and Andy McDonald

No. 12 Reg Holdsworth

No. 13 Kevin, Sally and Rosie Webster

Shop flat Ken Barlow

Non-residents Betty Turpin • Mike Baldwin • Alma Sedgewick • Alf Roberts Audrey Roberts • Terry Duckworth Phyllis Pearce • Kimberley Taylor • Doug Murray • Maggie Redman • Mark Redman

·1992·

THREE WEDDINGS, A BIRTH AND A FUNERAL

The year started with a new producer, Carolyn Reynolds, the first woman to take the helm since Susi Hush in 1976. She inherited stories which were midway through, and three of these were romances: 'Within several months of myself being made producer of *Coronation Street,* we had a run of weddings on the programme. I'm sure there were viewers who thought a producer had come in and waved a finger at everybody saying "I want weddings, I want frocks", whereas the truth is that the time was right on those particular stories to move forward. It's true everyone likes a wedding and there were very good audience figures but most importantly they were right for the characters at the time.'

Carolyn and the writing team planned not just one big wedding, but three and all in the space of three weeks. The first to tie the knot were Terry Duckworth and his pregnant girlfriend Lisa Horten. He was allowed out of prison for the day, accompanied by two prison wardens. Vera

COMINGS AND GOINGS

Homeless Raquel Wolstenhulme was taken in by Des Barnes at No.6, moving into his bed a week later. In May, Steph Barnes returned, and Raquel realized Des still loved her. Des hoped Steph had returned for good but she only used No.6 as a safe haven before moving on to her next man. Don Brennan had an affair with barmaid Julie Dewhurst which ended with him trying to kill himself and losing a foot in the process. Terry Duckworth returned to the Street with girlfriend Lisa Horten. She moved into No.9 when he was sent to Strangeways for GBH. He was released for their wedding and, in September, their son Tommy was born. Lisa found Vera too imposing and went to live in Blackpool with her parents after Vera tried to break up her friendship with Des Barnes. On the day Tommy was born, Rita lost a second husband. She had married Ted Sullivan in June and they only had three months together at the at the flat above the Kabin before he died of a brain tumour. Alec Gilroy was offered the job of planning entertainment on cruise ships stationed in Southampton. Bet refused to leave the Rovers, so he ended their marriage by going alone. Curly Watts became a householder when he bought No.7 from Rita on her wedding day.

persuaded them to take the cuffs off for a wedding photograph and, taking his opportunity, Terry ran off. Nigel Pivaro received lots of mail afterwards, telling him how amusing people had thought the scene was: 'Most of the letters came from young men. Running away from prison officers, it's a kind of dream really. People fell about seeing him run away from his own wedding.' But Lisa did not have much fun as she was left wondering if he had only married her to escape. When Terry was caught in Bettabuy's car park, he assured her that he really did love her.

A week after this wedding, the residents gathered at the registry office to watch Rita Fairclough become Mrs Ted Sullivan. Only Audrey Roberts knew of the pain behind the couple's smiles. Rita had broken down at her hen party and told Audrey that she was marrying Ted although he could die at any moment from a brain tumour. She just wanted to make his last days happy.

The final wedding was the long-awaited joining of Baldwin and Sedgewick. Alma had accepted Mike's proposal after he had told her how he'd battled to get Jackie to drop her name from their divorce. Alma then discovered, from Jackie, that it had been Mike's idea all along to have her cited. Mike was forced to sweat on his wedding day as Alma did not make up her mind until the last minute that she would marry him: 'The only sin I've committed, Mike, is knowing you. And I'll be regretting that for the rest of my life.' He was grateful when she arrived and took him as her husband, warning him that he would never be able to lie to her again.

Alma makes an honest man of Mike Baldwin.

Vera went into hospital with Lisa and Tommy was born by caesarean. Bill Tarmey was delighted to work with little Daryl Edwards who played Tommy, and both he and Liz Dawn are Daryl's real life godparents. The birth scene was played against another dramatic scene as the residents gathered at the bowls club to watch Percy Sugden fight to regain his championship title. Rita found Ted asleep on a bench and realized straight away that he was in fact dead. Again Barbara Knox was applauded for her performance as Rita, refusing to grieve for a man she loved and felt privileged to have known: 'You know, people will stop you and say I enjoyed the Alan Bradley saga, or Len's death or even the Ted relationship. It's very strange because you would think that having had three losses, it might have been the end of Rita, but it hasn't. It's been very, very good. Very good threads that people have identified with because people in real life have gone through that sort of thing.'

Don agreed to move back in with Ivy to keep her off the bottle but regained his independence by keeping out of her bedroom.

ALEC SETS SAIL

'I saw a slow and painful death. Visions of hospital bed and a lots of grips, casualty. . .' Roy Barraclough made the decision to leave *Coronation Street* in 1992 because he wanted to return to the stage and concentrate on his theatrical career: 'Initially when I decided to leave I asked the writers to kill Alec off because I thought that would have made a good story.' The writers however resisted taking that route and instead decided to send Alec off on his travels, leaving the Gilroy marriage open. This way Alec could be written back in sometime and Bet had to live with the idea that she was neither married nor single.

Alec was offered a job in Southampton, organizing entertainment on cruise ships. He realized it was too good an opportunity to miss, but he could not convince her that their future lay in Southampton and persuaded the brewery to let her take the pub on as manager: 'It was your home. Was! And it was my home as well. And there's no reason why we shouldn't both have fond memories of it. But we're going forward, Bet. We're leaving all this and we're going to a new life.'

'I'm not.' said Bet and watched Alec drive off down Viaduct Street.

DON'S INDISCRETION

Barmaid Julie Dewhurst was everything Ivy Brennan was not – young, understanding and peaceful. Don fell for barmaid Julie and they started an affair, but he could not cope with the guilt of running two lives and decided to make the break with nagging, critical Ivy. He told Julie that he wanted to start a new life with her but Julie told him she did not want a permanent relationship with him. She pointed out he would never be able to leave Ivy completely and would carry her about with him forever. He was devastated when she told him she wanted him out of her life and that if his life was wrecked then he had wrecked it, not Ivy, her or God. Don jumped into his car, drove at 70mph down a country lane and, intent on killing himself, crashed the car.

He did not die, but his lower right leg needed to be amputated. Ivy was shattered when Don told her he never wanted to see her again. 'Bert, Brian, now Don. . ..Poor Ivy, they say? Shouldn't feel sorry for me though, should they? It's me that brought it on 'em. . . .I'm bad luck.' The car crash was filmed on a disused air field so traffic would not interfere with the filming. Geoff Hinsliff was quite excited about the filming: 'I should know better at my age but I vaguely expected something sensational in the filming of it. There was a stunt man, a very experienced man, and he had his girlfriend with him. After finishing my shots I decided to stay and see the actual crash. The script said the car was to plough off the road, turn over in the air, hit the ground upside down and slide the 200 yards needed. What I ended up doing was pacifying and calming the girlfriend as she was very nervous and worried about what was going to happen to her boyfriend. . ..When the director shouted "action", the car sort of trundled five yards, hit a sort of ramp that pushed it up sideways and plopped down.'

Geoff was not keen on playing Don without one foot: 'It's a great story if it were one part in a one-and-a-half-hour film. I would think it terrific and indeed I did, filming it and the hospital sequences and the way it was written. The fear and dislike of it was that I've got it permanently. I now have to live rest of my life in *Coronation Street* with a limp.'

Following a tradition

Towards the end of 1992, a new character moved into the Street. Denise Osbourne followed on the footsteps of Valerie Barlow, Sandra Butler and Audrey Roberts. Thirty years before this Valerie had opened her salon at No.9 and in the mid-1980s Audrey had turned the front room at No.11 into a salon. Now, a more serious operation was started with Denise setting up a beauty salon in the back room and taking on Fiona Middleton as her assistant. Denise was a woman with a past – her first marriage had ended in divorce and she was separated from her second husband, Neil Mitchell, who was having an affair with Angie Freeman. 'I was very thrown when they offered me the job,' says Denise Black. 'I thought there was going to be far more resistance, I was going to have to fight. I was thrilled. It was like a dream.'

Denise was quite nervous when she was asked to actually cut some of Geoff Hinsliff's hair during a scene: 'I could do it, although they stole him away from me just as I was getting into it!' One actress who will not be letting Denise anywhere near her hair is Liz Dawn as she always makes sure Vera wears a wig: 'When I started as Vera I wanted to look different, I wanted to stand out and not look like everybody else. I thought I couldn't be red as Pat and Barbara were redheads and I noticed that nobody had curly hair. And that's how I came to use the curly wig.'

A shock for Mike

Jill Kerman first appeared as Maggie Redman in 1982, when the character's surname was Dunlop. Maggie was a florist who fell in love with Mike Baldwin and gave birth to his son Mark in 1983. In 1992, the date of Mark's birth was altered, the writers using dramatic

·1992·

Fiona Middleton was employed by Denise Osbourne at the Salon. The Platts' lodger Carmel Finnan was the one of their first customers.

·1992·

licence to make the son two years older. The reason for this was that the writing team wanted to bring Mark to Ken's school where he would meet, and fall for, widowed Maggie. This was the next chapter in the Baldwin/Barlow story. Mike had had an affair with Deirdre, married Susan and had won Alma back from Ken. Now it was the his turn to become distressed as he discovered, on Christmas Day, that his only son was spending the day with his mother's new lover, Ken Barlow.

When Chris Cook was given the role of Mark he had no idea about the character's history: 'I thought he was just Nicky's friend. I did not find out that I was Mike's son till I got the scripts.' Jill Kerman enjoyed her times in the Street: 'I think a lot of the characters are like old friends. It is like a family, and everyone is made to feel welcome, it's quite interesting because I have another life apart from the Street, and so many of them don't because they're so busy all the time.' She was pleased that after all the hassle with Mike, Maggie was to have a good relationship with someone at last: 'Maggie had just lost somebody close to her and people are extraordinarily vulnerable at that time and often it just needs a sympathetic person to unleash the lock. She found Ken, I don't think it was surprising and it all worked.'

★ Portsmouth-born **Denise Black** read psychology at London University and on graduating decided to travel. She found herself in Gilbraltar with not enough money to get to the West Indies. 'In a flash I decided I wanted to be an actress, found fifty quid in my rucksack, came home and found a job.' In 1980, Denise got her Equity card and joined the Actors Touring Company on a year-long tour of South America, Israel, Greece and Yugoslavia. More theatre work followed and she formed a jazz group with Josie Lawrence, calling themselves Denise Black and the Kray Sisters. Before joining *Coronation Street* Denise appeared in television shows including *Casualty, The Bill, Between the Lines* and *Sherlock Holmes*.

Denise Black (Denise!)

·1992·

It was Maggie Redman who broke the news to Tracy Barlow about Deirdre's 1983 affair with Mike. Maggie was cross because Tracy had told her son Mark that Mike was his real father.

Ken could not handle the thought that the new woman in his life was the mother of Baldwin's son and they split, much to Mike's delight.

IS THE STREET BEHIND THE TIMES?

In October 1992, Lord Rees-Mogg, chairman of the Broadcasting Standards Council accused *Coronation Street* of portraying the 'cosy familiarity' of a bygone era. He compared it with programmes such as *EastEnders* and *Brookside*, which had more black and Asian characters: 'The newer soap operas tend to have a wider ethnic mix than the older ones. The older ones are beginning to recognize that they should portray the society that exists now rather than the one that used to exist.'

The reaction from the public and press came immediately. The public pointed to the 1991 census which showed that Salford (the nearest town to fictional Weatherfield) was 97.8% white. The national press ran headlines such as 'Coronation Street "shuts out blacks"' (*The Times*) and 'Put colour in t' Street' (*Daily Mirror*). *The Times* reporter wrote about Lord Rees-Mogg: 'He might do himself a favour by watching *Coronation Street* regularly for a couple of months and discovering that it mirrors life in those mean streets now as accurately as it did three decades ago. The millions who watch *Coronation Street* – and will continue to do so despite Lord Rees-Mogg – know real life when they see it, even if it is heightened and sometimes lightened in the most confident and accomplished soap opera television has ever seen."

Every national newspaper stood firm with the Street and grew indignant about the comments. *Today* wrote: 'Eighteen million people watch the Street because the characters are outstanding and the scripts are the best of any drama on television', the *Daily Mail* warned Rees-Mogg 'Leave the Street alone!' while the *Daily Express* said 'Rees-Mogg attacks it at his peril. If he's not careful we will be forced to get in touch with his own scriptwriters and prevail upon them to write him out.'

'I had to climb under the duvet and up the bed under the duvet, and the bed was literally shaking because we were hysterical. I did not get too wet as I was bouncing up and down on the bed but Ken had to paddle in it.'

Sherrie Hewson on acting in a waterbed.

Rovers Bet Gilroy • Vicky Arden Raquel Wolstenhulme

No. 1 Deirdre and Tracy (Jan. - Sept./Nov. Dec.) Barlow • Craig Lee (Nov. - Dec.)

No. 2 Denise Osbourne

No. 3 Emily Bishop • Percy Sugden

No 4 Derek and Mavis Wilton

No. 5 Ivy and Don Brennan

No. 6 Des and Colin (July - Aug.) Barnes Lisa and Tom Duckworth (Jan. - Feb.)

No. 7 Angie Freeman (Jan. - March) Curly Watts • Any McDonald (Nov. - Dec.)

No. 8 Martin, Gail, Nicky, Sarah and David Platt

No. 9 Jack, Vera, Tom (Jan. - Dec.) and Terry (Dec.) Duckworth

No. 10a Rita Sullivan • Jenny Bradley (Sept. - Oct.)

No. 11 Jim, Liz (Jan. - May), Steve and Andy (Jan. - Oct.) McDonald

No. 12 Reg Holdsworth

No. 13 Kevin, Sally and Rosie Webster

Shop flat Ken Barlow

Non-residents Betty Turpin • Mike Baldwin • Alma Baldwin • Alf Roberts Audrey Roberts • Phyllis Pearce • Doug Murray • Mark Redman • Maureen Naylor Maud Grimes • Tanya Pooley Brendan Scott

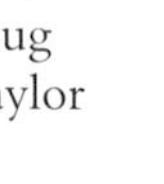

'THE NANNY FROM HELL'

At the end of 1992, Martin Platt was trying to cope with the knowledge that lodger Carmel Finnan was in love with him and wanted to wreck his marriage. Gail remained oblivious to this until New Year's Day 1993 when Martin threw Carmel out after she had tried to get him into bed. Carmel had nothing to hide and told Gail she loved Martin: 'Face facts, Gail, you're no good for him. He doesn't love you, he loves me.' Gail believed Martin when he swore he had never touched Carmel and even stood by him when Carmel annouced she was pregnant with his baby. Then Gail found out that Martin had spent the night with the lodger while drunk (he thought she was Gail).

When she first appeared in the show, Catherine Cusack jumped to the same conclusion as the press – that she and Martin were to have an affair: 'It wasn't until I'd been around for a month that Julian Roach mentioned the word "erotomaniac" in relation to Carmel and I thought "Oh my God! What is that?". The quite soon afterwards I was given a case study to look at about a woman who suffered from this. I'd heard of people with obsessions, and stalkers, but I'd

COMINGS AND GOINGS

Lisa and Tommy Duckworth returned to the Street, but Lisa moved into No.6 as Des Barnes' lover. Their plans to move away were shattered when Lisa was knocked down by a car in the Street. She died three days later. Vera took in Tommy and left work to care for him until Terry could look after him. On his release, Terry sold the boy to Lisa's parents. Jenny Bradley turned up at the Kabin having left her boyfriend. Rita was sympathetic until Jenny tried to fleece her of money. Rita gave her £1,000 and told her to stay out of her life. Liz McDonald left her husband Jim to run her own pub, the Queens. They started divorce proceedings and she had an affair with Colin Barnes who lodged with his brother at No.6. The Corner Shop was taken over by Brendan Scott when Alf Roberts retired, but he dropped dead of a heart attack and Alf bought it back. Tracy Barlow left home at sixteen and moved in with Craig Lee, a twenty-one year old delivery boy.

never heard of the actual mental state before.'

After Carmel spent the night with Martin, Catherine began to receive letters warning her off. At first, viewers had written saying they enjoyed the way the storylines had been stirred up by her arrival. Catherine says she had not time to stop and look at the character, to form any judgements on her behaviour: It was such a fast way of working that I did not really have time. I just tried to underatand the character. 'I tried to remember what her problems were and what it all stemmed from. I never thought she was wicked, I just thought she was sick. And I tried to think of where it came of – need for love, no matter how awfully it went wrong.' Sean Wilson agreed that the pace was so great that he never had a chance to think too hard on Martin and Carmel's states of mind: 'It was nice to have been given the opportunity but you only get an outline of the story. I just took it each week as it came, because I was so busy with the storyline and filming. Eventually it all took over and I did not have time to think about it.'

The story came to a dramatic climax after Carmel tried to kidnap David Platt. Gail took matters into her own hands and warned Carmel off, there was a struggle and Carmel fell downstairs. In hospital, the Platts were told Carmel was not, and never had been, pregnant. Helen Worth is full of praise for Catherine's handling of the whole scenario: 'It would have been so easy for any actress, young or old, to have just screamed and shouted her way through it and she was so subtle. She just held back every time and it was so hard for her to do that but I think that's what made it work.'

Gail's trust in Martin was put to the test during the Carmel incident. Years later, when Martin was unfaithful with a fellow nurse, she would wonder if anything really did happen between him and Carmel.

Milton John tried to make Brendan Scott's stay in the shop as real as possible: 'Brendan thoroughly believes in everything he does. It may be ridiculous to the viewer but as long as the character believes in what he's doing there is a reality created.'

A TIDAL WAVE HITS THE STREET

When Maureen Naylor was taken on as an assistant at Bettabuy she had no idea that her one-time boyfriend Reg Holdsworth was manager. When they met in the cereal aisle, they fell in love all over again. They had split up in the 1960s because her mother Maud Grimes disliked him and had worked to break up their relationship. They had both had disastrous marriages and were keen to finally be together, but the original problem still existed in the shape of Maud, now confined to a wheelchair.

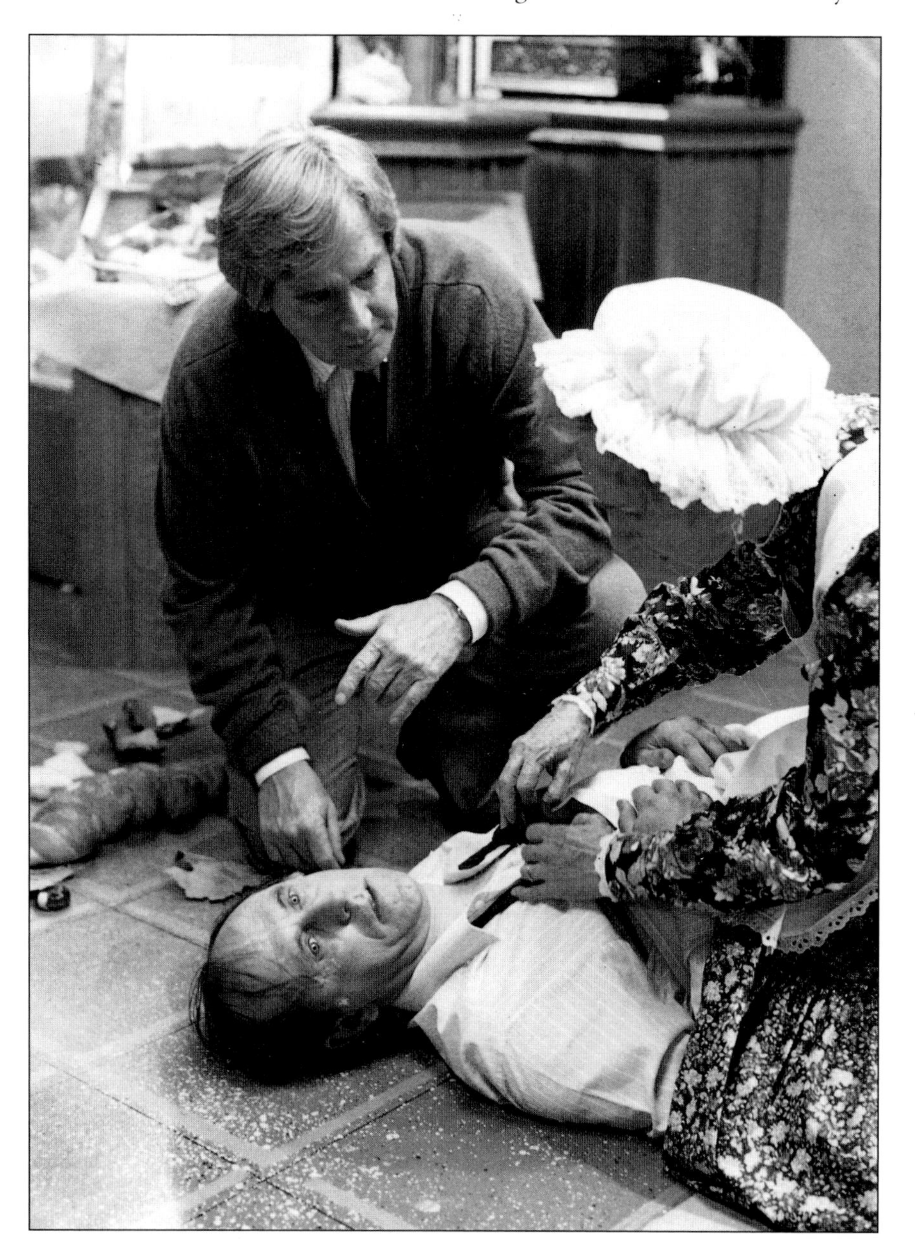

Desperate to consummate his love for Maureen, Reg dragged her from work back to his flat at No.12 Coronation Street, where he planned to seduce her on his waterbed. However, under his flat, in the Kabin's storeroom, Derek Wilton used a huge drill to remount a light fitting on the ceiling. He was horrified when water started pouring into the shop from the hole. The Wiltons rushed upstairs and Maureen screamed as she realized the bed was sinking. Wearing only a towel, Reg attempted to sort out the mess and was quick to turn on Derek as the culprit. The episode went down in history as one of the funniest ever screened. Sherrie Hewson found herself in the position of having only just joined the company and having to act with hardly any clothes on: 'The bed was in a little tank as we couldn't get water on the studio floor and the director just shouted at us both, that they could have one take, which frightened me to death. So we just went for it and fortunately the water burst and it worked perfectly. But underneath it all we were both hysterical. I couldn't stop laughing.' Ken Morley still has people shouting, 'How's your water bed?' at him in the street: 'The paranoia in everybody's mind who owns a water bed, is that it'll burst whilst your having sex. But the idea of somebody else drilling through the ceiling below to fix a light fitting and drilling through the bed is ludicrous and brilliant at the same time.'

A NEW LANDLADY

In the summer of 1993, a new pub was introduced to the residents and viewers. There was press speculation at the time that the Queens was to replace the Rovers as the central meeting-point, but as Carolyn Reynolds points out, that never was the intention: 'The strength of it really was that it was a McDonald story about the marriage, rather than about pubs. For once in Liz's life she was doing something for herself, and when she had to choose she chose the pub rather than Jim. Once we opted for a pub we then said "Let's make the Queens very different to the Rovers." We wanted to get the feeling that the Rovers was some little backstreet pub, whereas with the Queens it had a better clientele, it was much more city life. It was modern, there was a lot more money being spent on it and in it. Maybe not as friendly, quite cold. . . .The Rovers was always going to be the main meeting-point and we spent more time in the back room of the Queens that we did behind the bar.'

Liz had been trained up by Bet at the Rovers and stood in for Bet whilst she was on holiday. This story coincided with a turning-point in Jim McDonald's life. He was working as a security guard and had to stand by and watch his son Andy being attacked by a gunman during an armed hold-up at Bettabuy. Nicholas Cochrane enjoyed filming this scene: 'The guys playing the robbers were the choreographers. They set up the scene with the director Brian Mills and I thought they made it look excellent. Andy's always being beaten up – I think it's eight times now, so I'm getting used to it.' On screen, Andy laid into Jim over his attitude to the whole family after Jim refused to let him drop out from Sheffield University: 'It's not me you're proud of. Your proud of some idea you've got about me. You'd get respect in the world if I stayed at Sheffield. And what you can't take is I'm like you – you're a failed bike mechanic and I'm a failed student. Only difference is I'm not going to end up like some crypto-fascist in a uniform.'

Jim gave up the security job after he found himself beating up a fifteen-year-old who tried to break into a shed. When Liz was offered her own pub to manage, Jim saw it as a way of escaping the downward thread his life was taking. He hoped they could run a pub together but as soon as they moved into the Queens he accused her of making up to the brewery boss, Willmore. He asked her to give the pub up, but she refused. Jim thumped Willmore to force Liz to choose between him and the pub, but she chose the pub and their marriage collapsed. For months, agonizing scenes were played as both

★ The *Daily Express* billed her a 'Miserable Maud, the battleaxe who has finally stolen the crown worn by Ena Sharples', but in real life, actress **Elizabeth Bradley** is softly spoken and genteel. She had ambitions to act at an early age but put them on hold to work as a nurse during the Second World War. She then gave up acting for motherhood and home-making. When her husband died, she returned to the stage. She was nominated for an Olivier Award for her part in *Billy Liar* at the National Theatre.

Sherrie Hewson was born in Nottingham and started performing at the age of six, tap-dancing and singing 'You've Gotta Have Heart'. She went on to become an all-rounder, appearing in the original stage production of *Stepping Out*, and featuring in the film *The Slipper and the Rose*. She has appeared in TV series such as *Z Cars, In Loving Memory, Home to Roost, Never the Twain* and *Russ Abbot's Madhouse*.

Sherrie Hewson (Maureen) xx.
Elizabeth Bradley (Maud Grimes)

Colin Barnes was a welcome diversion for Liz during her separation from Jim.

characters stumbled over their feelings. The writers worked hard to ensure that the couple changed in a way that made them more compatible. On New Year's Eve, Curly Watts threw a party and Jim walked Liz back to the Queens. She invited him in to stay the night and they were reconciled.

THE TEMPTING OF MRS WEBSTER

Registered child-minder Sally Webster took on toddler Jonathan Broughton in the spring of 1994. His father, tax inspector Joe, was separated from his wife Hazel and struggling to bring up the child. He was impressed at the calming influence Sally had on him and slowly fell in love with her. The Websters were happy when Joe arranged for them to holiday at a cottage in the Lake District and it was there that Joe declared his feelings for Sally. Actor John Wheatley found the declaration scene easy to do, what he struggled with was the scene the next day when Joe told Sally why he loved her: 'I felt awkward. If you're in love with somebody that much you are driven by it. You're quite mad, insane and I think being in love can be quite mad; you're stomach is in a knot, you can't sleep, you sweat, you lose weight. He was obsessionally in love with this woman.'

Sally was shocked by Joe's feelings but couldn't help being drawn towards him. Although they never had any physical contact, Sally was tempted by this wealthy young man at a time when Kevin's financial difficulties were highlighted. The press picked up on this story, with agony aunts giving Sally advice one way or the other.

The storyline lasted throughout 1994 with Sally being drawn deeper and deeper into Joe's intrigue. His wife Hazel arrived and told Kevin that Joe and Sally were lovers, so he started his own investigations.

Sally Whittaker admits to becoming totally confused towards the end of the story: 'Towards the end, Sally was stupid. I'm sure the writers didn't know which way to go and it made it really difficult. It was very confusing because she was seeing this man over and over again, who wasn't particularly very nice to her – he was saying awful things about her husband and he put her in terrible situations, yet she kept seeing him and I just couldn't understand why. I wish the ending had been more defined one way or the other, because people are still saying to me now "What happened?" And I don't know.'

Sally's dream holiday in the Lakes was turned into a nightmare as Joe's intentions were made clear. Back in Weatherfield, Kevin dealt with the matter in his own way.

·1993·

THE SELLING OF LITTLE TOMMY

Vera and Jack Duckworth were seen to struggle throughout the year, making ends meet on Jack's salary as they brought up their precious grandson Tommy. In December, Vera counted the days to the date of Terry's release from prison. She had visions of them all living and coping together, as one big happy family. What she did not know was that Terry was negotiating with Lisa's parents over them giving him money in return for Tommy. Nigel Pivaro is adamant that Terry only had Tommy's best interest at heart: 'I definitely argue that he was well into his child only he'd been estranged from him and the child had been tainted by Des Barnes. He wanted to get all the reminders of Lisa out of the way, and that included the child.'

The scripts called for Tommy to be handed over on Christmas Eve. When Terry returned home with Jeff Horten but without Tommy, Vera realized straight away what had happened and rushed to the car where she saw the empty car seat. She became hysterical and a loud cheer arose from every living-room in the country as Jack did what all the viewers had wanted his to do for years – he hit Terry in the face. Bill Tarmey put himself in Jack's position at this point, and as a grandfather knew exactly how Jack felt: 'When I first saw the script I was very sad because I did not think I'd see Nigel for quite some time and I like working with him. I worked out the punch with Nigel and I missed him by a whisker. Since then I've had letters saying "Well done for cracking him one" from little old ladies, young women, kids, guys off the building sites.'

The selling of Tommy Duckworth caused Jack and Vera to disown Terry once and for all.

·1994·

Rovers Bet Gilroy • Vicky Arden • Raquel Wolstenhulme (March - July) • Charlie Whelan (July - Oct.)

No. 1 Deirdre and Samir (Aug. - Dec.) Rachid

No. 2 Denise Osbourne

No. 3 Emily Bishop and Percy Sugden

No 4 Derek and Mavis Wilton • Norris Cole (March)

No. 5 Ivy (Jan. - June) and Don Brennan Nick Platt (Aug. - Dec.)

No. 6 Des Barnes • Raquel Wolstenhulme Steve McDonald

No. 7 Curly Watts • Andy (Jan. - Sept.) and Steve (June - July) McDonald

No. 8 Martin, Gail, Nicky (Jan. - Aug./Dec.), Sarah Louise and David Platt

No. 9 Jack, Vera, and Clifford (Dec.) Duckworth

No. 10a Rita Sullivan

No. 11 Jim, Liz (Jan. - Dec.), Steve (Jan. - June) and Andy (Sept. - Dec.) McDonald

No. 12 Reg Holdsworth (Jan.) • Ken Barlow (July - Dec.)

No. 13 Kevin, Sally, Rosie and Sophie (Nov. - Dec.) Webster

Shop flat Ken Barlow (Jan. - July)

Non-residents Betty Turpin • Alf Roberts Mark Redman • Tanya Pooley • Jon Welch • Mike Baldwin • Audrey Roberts Maureen Holdsworth • Sean Skinner • Alma Baldwin • Phyllis Pearce • Maud Grimes Fiona Middleton

DES STEPS INTO THE FLAME

Every now and again the writers of *Coronation Street* come up with a storyline that grabs the emotions of the viewers and the imagination of the national press. One such story was Des Barnes's affair with Tanya Pooley while he was living with her workmate Raquel Wolstenholme. Raquel moved in with Des when he realized he had strong feelings for her. For Raquel it was a dream come true; a man to love, a position in the community, a home to care for and a future to look forward to. 'Can I hear weddings bells?' asked Bet. 'Well, maybe a little tinkle,' replied Raquel with a grin. Working behind the bar with Raquel was Tanya whose love life could never be in the open as Raquel's was: she was the mistress of Alex Christie, Des's betting shop boss. Eva Pope, the actress who created the character, felt Tanya had made herself tough in order to survive: 'She was lonely. She didn't have anybody. She did not seem to have any friends and was not having a proper relationship.'

When Raquel worked on a modelling assignment overnight, Tanya flirted with Des and invited him

'No amount of fisticuffs between mere men can distract from the fact that it's the women who control the Street.'

***Daily Express*, 30 June 1994**

COMINGS AND GOINGS

Ivy Brennan left the Street to take up permanent residence at a religious retreat. Don took Nicky Platt in after he fell out with stepfather Martin but, to his mother's relief, he eventually returned home in December. There was much to-ing and fro-ing at No.11 with Liz returning home to estranged husband Jim, and Andy moving in with his Bettabuy boss Curly at No.7 before returning home when he returned from University. Steve moved out after a violent row with Jim over his gambling. He slept on Curly's sofa before becoming Des Barnes's lodger at No.6. In July, he splashed out and rented a flat in Weatherfield Quays, next door to the Baldwins. Fiona Middleton moved in with Steve as resident girlfriend. Bet Gilroy had romance trouble with trucker Charlie Whelan. He moved into the Rovers in an attempt to settle down with Bet, but left for Hamburg in October with barmaid Tanya Pooley. Tanya had already broken Raquel's heart by having an affair with her boyfriend Des Barnes. Bet and Raquel were left to console each other. Ken Barlow moved across the Street to live above the Kabin in Reg's old flat and Jack was shocked in December when his older brother Clifford moved in, saying he did not have long to live.

·1994·

'This was the great love of his life,' says Ken Morley. 'He lost her the first time round and unfortunately the gargoyle is still around. What started off as being humourous has developed into a nasty affair. Getting involved with in-laws can sometimes turn very nasty.' During the wedding, Maud overheard Reg rowing with her other son-in-law over who should look after her.

round to her flat. She knew he found her desirable and invited him to 'walk into the flame'. They spent the night together and realized they enjoyed being in each other's company. Their secret affair lasted three months. Philip Middlemiss understood why Des cheated on Raquel: 'He's got a very short attention span. He needs something to keep that attention span as lengthy as possible, and someone like Tanya could do that because she was intelligent and was a domineering partner which is what he wants really.'

Carolyn Reynolds became the executive producer of the Street at the end of 1993, and Sue Pritchard was given the task of producing the programme. The Des/Raquel/Tanya storyline was the first big storyline she was involved with and she was fascinated by the emotional complexities of the situation: 'One of the reasons the story worked so

Raquel enjoyed the intrigue surrounding Tanya's love life before she discovered Des was her other lover.

·1994·

well was that because the character of Raquel was so naive and innocent, it was totally credible that this affair between Des and Tanya could have been going on under her nose and she wouldn't know.' Sarah Lancashire agrees: 'She was absolutely smitten with Des. She was madly in love with him and she's an idealist and lives her life through dreams, because reality means absolutely nothing to her. And Des coming along was part of her dream taking shape. He was the first step.'

The story came to a violent climax when Des finally snapped and confronted Tanya in her bed when she was with Alex. Raquel arrived on the scene just in time to hear Des ordering Alex out of 'his girl's bed'. While Raquel ran off crying into the night, Alex brawled with Des before sacking him and finishing with Tanya. Then Tanya turned on Des for ruining her relationship with Alex, and then convinced Raquel that Des had been beating her and forcing her to sleep with him.

The press loved every moment of it. In her *Daily Express* column Maureen Paton write: 'There is something deeply disturbed about the sly Tanya, who slaps herself violently and then pretends that Des did it so that she may play the role of victim rather than predator in front of the gullible Raquel. . . . And when the female support-system springs into action on behalf of an injured sister, it's unstoppable.' Jack Tinker, in the *Daily Mail*, agreed: 'The exquisite Raquel is the perfect example of a post-feminist romantic. Like the young Bet Lynch-as-was, Raquel appears born to be abused. But like most subtle characters Sarah Lancashire, besides making her one of the Street's great comic creations of the 1990s, has imbued her with a highly up-to-date and beady instinct for self-preservation.' Tinker went on to praise the scene in which Raquel ran to Bet for comfort and a padded shoulder to sob on: 'It was heartbreaking. Watching her face as the missing pieces of the jigsaw puzzle she had been struggling to solve finally fell into place was a play for today in itself. Naturally it was to Bet, that battered but unbowed fount of all human understanding, that she fled.'

When he first read the scripts, Philip Middlemiss expected to receive hate mail for treating Raquel for badly but to his surprise he received an altogether different reaction: 'I'm getting strange reactions. From a pat on the back from the men who say "Well done", which is typical I suppose, to people calling me a bastard in Sainsbury's. The women are all right. They blame it on Tanya rather than Des. It seems to be that my character has had so much sympathy over the last three years, they know that he's not a bad bloke.'

When Eva Pope decided that she wanted to leave the show to move on to other things, the writers turned her love for unobtainable men into a character trait and had her running off with Bet's boyfriend Charlie Whelan.

PROBLEMS FOR THE WILTONS

Malcolm Hebden made a welcome return to the Street as Norris Cole after having last appeared in 1974 as Spanish waiter Carlos. Norris Cole moved in with the Wiltons at No.4 having decided to turn Derek into his own personal guru. Calling him 'Dirk' he hung on his every word and turned to him to sort out all of life's problems. They became salesmen together, but while Norris' fortunes soared, Derek's crumbled and he had to seek employment with his ex-wife Angela. Peter Baldwin has sympathy with Derek and the way he lurches from one disaster to another: 'I had this line once: "If there were any justice in the world I would have a decent job, a decent salary, decent prospects and a decent car." Well, I think he feels that he is hard done by and that God isn't on his side. In the past he has relied on Mavis but at this time he did not rely on anybody, not even Mavis. She became an obstacle.'

Mavis was horrified when Derek was cited as co-respondent in Angela's divorce case and the matter was complicated when he accused her of having a relationship with Roger Crompton, an artist friend who had painted her portrait. Mavis threw Derek out and he went to stay with Norris while Mavis wept on Rita's shoulder. The whole scenario was ended by the death of the Wilton's budgie, Harry. They became united in grief and were reconciled.

DEIRDRE AND KEN FIND ROMANCE

A kiss recorded for the 1993 Christmas Eve programme was never transmitted. Ken and Deirdre's kiss would have probably heralded a turning-point in their estranged relationship. However, Anne Kirkbride fell ill and had to be written out of the show for six months. It was crisis time for the writers and an emergency story conference was called by Sue Pritchard: 'The creative talents of the Street writing team are continually challenged. When Anne Kirkbride had to leave the show through illness, we had to rethink a major storyline which had already been structured and written. It was decided to develop a relationship between Ken and Denise, a woman in whom he had previously shown little interest. The writers made the relationship work and there was terrific chemistry on screen between the two actors. Denise was very different to the other women in Ken's life – earthy and confident. Their affair even had an effect on his appearance – he dressed as a younger man, his hairstyle softened and he smiled more than he had done for years.'

With Deirdre away nursing mother Blanche, Ken started an unlikely relationship with Denise Osbourne. When Deirdre returned, eager to pick up the pieces with Ken, he had to break the news not only of his new romance but the fact that Denise was pregnant with his baby. Deirdre was furious and reminded Ken of all the times she had begged him to let them start a family. Ken struggled with the hope that he could still keep Deirdre as part of his life but she astounded him by flying off to Morocco and having a holiday romance with a twenty-one-year-old waiter. Further more, she borrowed money from Emily Bishop to pay for him to fly over and suddenly

Rita took Mavis in when life with Derek became too much. Mavis felt they were living Wuthering Heights *: 'I am Linton and Derek is Kathy.'*

Samir Rachid, a Moroccan youth, was living in Ken's Uncle Albert's house.

Deirdre was given a new lease of life and the viewers loved it. Margaret Forwood wished her well in her *Daily Express* column: 'I don't think I can honestly recall the word "lover" being uttered in *Coronation Street* before. Don't they usually call them "fellas"? Or "me boyfriend"? But Anne Kirkbride is

Deirdre refused to keep quiet about Denise's pregnancy and shouted the news to the Rovers' customers.

celebrating her return to health with a crackling storyline, a marvellous performance and a whole new vocabulary. Frantic with anxiety at her Arab boyfriend being held by Immigration Officials at Manchester Airport, Deirdre burst out: "I sent him the money and paid his air fare. We're crazy about each other! He's my lover! Is that all you want to know?" Blimey, Deirdre, it's enough to be going on with.'

Everyone tried to warn Deirdre off Samir, saying he was too young, they hardly knew each other and he was probably after a meal ticket. She ignored them all and surprised them, and herself, by marrying him in a registry office in November. A month later the couple left to start a new life in Morocco just as Ken was coping with Denise telling him that she wanted him to have nothing to do with their son.

IVY'S DEPARTURE

Lynne Perrie made her last appearance as Ivy Brennan in March 1994. The news that she was leaving the programme after twenty-one years on screen caused a sensation in the media with much interest in why she was going. Executive producer Carolyn Reynolds listened to a lot of debate and speculation, but the truth of the matter was not as dramatic as the tabloid press would have had their readers believe: 'Every now and again on *Coronation Street* we hold long-term story conferences. These deal very much with broad strokes of the programme – what's the future of the Rovers Return? Those sort of questions. This gives much more of a feeling to the writers and the producer as to where the show is going. We also address certain things that are wrong; maybe we are missing out on a particular age group and we review things, how they've changed. For quite some time we had had difficulty in storylining Ivy; she seemed to go down very narrow routes in terms of stories. There was a lot of soul-searching and discussion, and eventually it was decided that it was time to move away from that character. When an actress has been working on a show for that length of time it's obviously something that you discuss and debate at great length before making such a move. At the same time, though, the show must go on. So I met with Lynne Perrie and we had a long discussion about it and it was agreed that she should leave *Coronation Street*.' Lynne Perrie left the programme straight away and the writers decided not to kill the character off. Instead they had characters reporting back to each other that Ivy had joined a religious retreat where she was enjoying life, meditating and praying for loved ones.

·1994·

THE DUCHESS DIES

The cast and writers of *Coronation Street* gathered at Manchester's Town Hall on the night of 26 November 1994 where the City of Drama paid tribute to the Street. Sir Anthony Hopkins gave a speech about what he classed as 'the greatest television programme ever'. The evening was tinged with sadness however as Doris Speed, the Street's Annie Walker, had meant to attend. Unfortunately she died, at the age of ninety-five on 17 November at the nursing home where she had lived for over ten years. She fell asleep while reading a novel, with a cigarette burning in an ashtray and never woke up. The press marked her passing with headlines such as 'First Lady of the Rovers Return dies' (*Daily Telegraph*), 'Queen Annie dies' (the *Guardian*), 'She was the last of the great stars' (the *Sun*) and 'The Duchess of Coronation Street' (*Today*). Past Street actors Kenneth Farrington, Irene Sutcliffe, Jennifer Moss, Ivan Beavis, Doreen Keogh, Daphne Oxenford and Jean Alexander joined the current cast to pay their respects to a lady they all held in great esteem. At her thanksgiving service, Tony Warren told how he had created the role of Annie with Doris in mind: 'She had something which was nothing to do with age or body or sex appeal. She made the lights shine a little brighter when nobody had turned them on.'

The *Daily Telegraph* summed up most people's feelings for the actress in their obituary: 'Annie Walker struck a chord in the national psyche, as the embodiment of the genteel social climber, an icon of the proud petit-bourgeois-tidiness which was subject to such virulent cultural attack in the 1960s. If there was a distinctly music-hall aspect to her character – and *Coronation Street* is a televisual descendant of that tradition – Speed managed to bring an embattled dignity to her role, as well as affectionate satire.'

★ London-born **Al Nedjari** landed the part of Samir Rachid just three days after he left drama school. Al had had no ambitions to act, he was more interested in being a footballer. He went to university and became a science teacher and it was soon after that that he realized his vocation. He was encouraged by his Algerian father who is an actor, and he enrolled on a part-time course at the Poor School in London: 'I was teaching science all day then dashing off to school for fours hours a night four days a week and then at weekends. It was absolutely exhausting.' When he was given the part of Samir, Al spent as much time as he could with Moroccans who had settled in England: 'I studied their accents, the way they dress and their mannerisms. It took a little while to get the accent right.'

Al Nedj—

·1995·

What Do the Next 35 YEARS HOLD?

'While other soaps follow their characters across the land, use hand-held cameras and exciting new angles, with script editors liberated from regional constraints, "Corry" is the housebound elderly relative. She may have lost the spring in her step, live in a world of her own, but she knows what matters: family, frugality, neighbourliness, values that posit a communality of interest between anyone born into a time and place and an income bracket,'

The Sunday Times

Coronation Street entered its thirty fifth year with a new birth: Daniel Osbourne was born to Denise on 4 January. His proud father, fifty-five-year-old Ken Barlow beamed as he told the residents about the birth. Eighteen million viewers were able to wonder if he would be able to be a proper father to this child; he had given up his twins Peter and Susan when they were six and walked out of the family home only three years after adopting Tracy Langton and swearing to her that he loved her as his own child. Ken was reminded of this when Tracy called on him in January for her eighteenth birthday present. When he tried to give her a cheque for £50 she told him to 'stuff it' and called him mean.

Tracy is now eighteen and the future lies ahead of her, as long as she can stay clear of drugs. This is the same Tracy who was born to Ray and Deirdre Langton in 1977. Where is Ray now? No-one knows for sure, but one day he may return to the Street. And what of Deirdre? Will she ever find happiness and more to the point, as comedienne Victoria Wood constantly asks her audiences, 'When will she get back together with Ken?'

Ken has bought No.1, Albert Tatlock's old home, to provide a stable home for Daniel to grow up in. But is Denise really the settling down type? Deirdre is now living in Crimea Street, in a block of flats owned by Mike Baldwin. Mike is bitterly jealous that Ken stands a chance of seeing his son grow up while Mike was denied Mark Redman's existence for eleven years. No doubt Mark will be back in four years' time to marry Tracy Barlow – unless, of course, Mike marries her himself.

The Rovers Return remains the centre point in the programme. A lot has changed since it was first seen in Episode 1: the old three-bar system has been transformed into one big, light bar, with fruit machine, real ale and wine by the glass. Julie Goodyear celebrates twenty-five years behind the bar as Bet, while Betty Driver notches up twenty-six years of pint-pulling in June 1994. This year sees Betty's reign as Mayoress end and, although she and Audrey Roberts have not come to blows as yet on screen there is still time. Audrey found herself in the dog-house with daughter Gail for not having told her about Martin's fling with a nurse on Christmas Day 1994. Audrey made light of it in an attempt to make Gail feel better: 'You see, the thing is, they've got one-track minds, they can't control themselves! All this stuff about new men, it's all hooey. If a fellah fancies a bit on the side and thinks he can get away with it, there's nowt'll stop him.'

While Audrey meddles in Gail's life, Don Brennan is finding a new lease of life in his relationship with Josie Clarke. She knows all about his marriage to Ivy and the abusive phone calls he made to Denise, yet she is still willing to take him on. Next door to Don, at No.3, Emily Bishop appears to be reassessing her life, bitter and angry and the way people have used and abused her friendship. It is time for her to make radical changes, as she told Ken, 'Now I know what Mrs Sharples felt like.'

Emily's friend Mavis now has what she always dreamt of – a husband, a home of her own and a little garden, complete with gnomes. How long will this last? How will she cope if Derek retires or if Rita decided that after twenty years of standing behind a counter serving toffee she has had enough? Rita is a woman of means and has taken an interest in the Webster family, giving them money and investing more in the new baby Sophie's name. Will her interest turn to interference?

Curly Watts was devastated early this year when Raquel Wolstenholme returned his engagement ring. Will they ever be happy, apart or together? And what of Des Barnes – Raquel will never forget the hurt over his affair with Tanya and now he has become Curly's enemy: Raquel broke their engagement after Des proposed marriage to her.

Steve McDonald is another young man with enemies, although his are caused by gambling debts rather than affairs of the heart. His relationship with Fiona Middleton has pulled him through a lot but she refused to marry him. Together they moved into

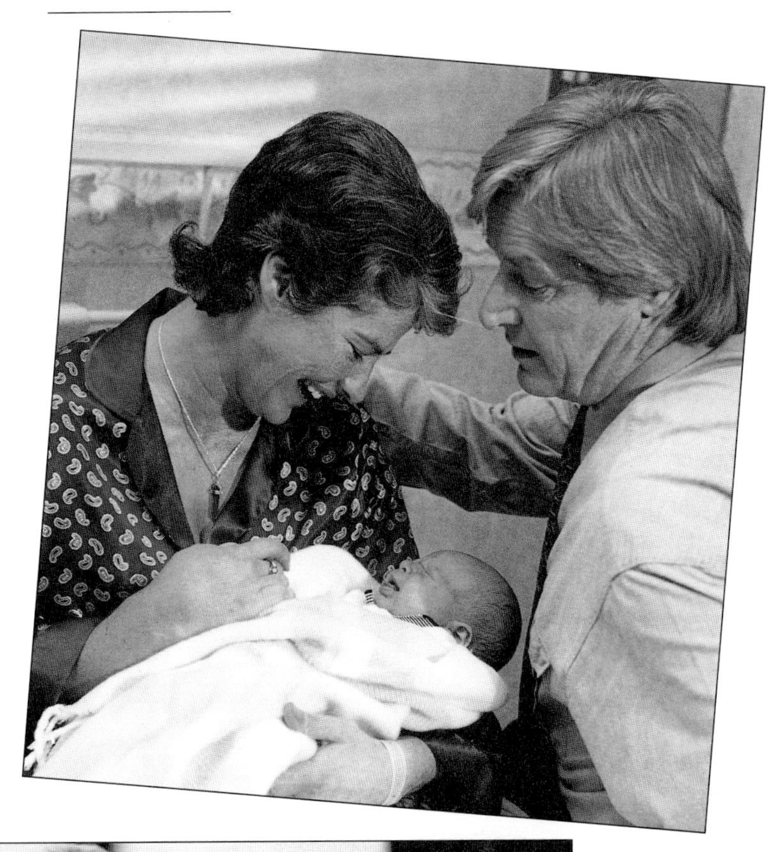

Daniel Osbourne is Ken's chance to prove he can be a good father. Will Denise let him take that chance?

A proud moment for Betty Turpin as she is made Mayoress, wearing the chain Annie Walker had worn twenty years previously.

the flat over Alma's café and he swore he had stopped gambling, but of course he was lying, just as he was when he promised he would not take advantage of Vicky Arden's love for him or the £240,000 she inherited on her eighteenth birthday.

Whatever happens to the present characters of *Coronation Street*, there is nothing to say that it will not run for another thirty-five years. It stands alone in the history of television as being a programme that has consistently remained at the top of the ratings since it was fully networked in May 1960. It was watched all over the world, has a monthly magazine devoted to it, is viewed by royalty and politicians, and remains a faithful chronicle of the times and social attitudes. It is unique.

Des broke Curly and Raquel up once, but will they get back together, and if they do will she ever be able to put Des behind her?

★ **Tracy Brabin** was delighted to see her character Tricia moving into No.1 after she only appeared for a few episodes in 1994: 'I think it's the ultimate compliment to be asked back. The scripts I've read so far are fantastic – there are some lovely moments which remind me of those old kitchen-sink dramas like *Saturday Night and Sunday Morning*.' Tracy trained at Loughborough University and has appeared in television shows such as *Peak Practice, Outside Edge* and *A Bit Of A Do*.

★ 'I feel as if I've been lucky,' says **Angela Griffin**, the young actress who began playing Fiona in 1993. 'I've been gradually introduced into the programme and have had a chance to get used to everything, whereas some actors come into *Coronation Street* and get thrown in at the deep end straight away.' Angela started acting at the age of six when she became a member of Leeds Children's Theatre and her television credits have included *Emmerdale, Under the Bedclothes,* and *Just Us*.

HOW *the Street* IS MADE

Room 600, Granada's executive boardroom, houses a special meeting every third Monday. The meeting is chaired by the producer of Coronation Street and the writers, storyliners, casting director and archivist are present. During this day-long conference, the next nine episodes are planned. Each available character is put under the microscope and their futures discussed. Not all characters will be available for the episodes, because cast members may have booked holidays. As the stories are discussed and agreed upon, the storyliners chart the episodes to ensure balanced content and continuity.

In any one episode it is necessary to have at least three stories running – some can have as many as seven. The writers endeavour to maintain a balance of drama and comedy in each episode, so long as the story content allows this. Those at the story conference draw from their own personal experiences and observations for story subject-matter. Sometimes, a story can stem from a practical problem – the Rovers was burnt down in 1986 because the pub set needed a face-lift, and Liz McDonald became a pub landlady because Julie Goodyear (Bet) needed a holiday.

Coronation Street has always been story-led, rather than issue-led. The writers never try to fit the characters around an issue or situation; the situations stem from the richness of the characters. In the past, the programme has been criticised for not tackling issues such as AIDS or drugs. The producers feel that if the programme became issue-led as it would seem contrived and unbelievable. The issues tackled in Coronation Street tend to be domestic. Will Bert Tilsley find a job after eighteen months on the dole? Will Ivy Brennan stay off the bottle? By keeping such issues the characters remain true to their roots and appeal to a wider audience.

The stories discussed at the conference are about three months in advance of transmission. After the meeting, the storyline writers spend the following two weeks preparing detailed synopses of the nine episodes. The synopses present a scene-by-scene breakdown, listing the characters and sets available or each episode. While they are writing the storylines, they have to keep in mind members of the cast who are not directly involved but will be used in the various common areas of the programme to help colour and progress the stories.

On the Monday morning of the third week, the producer commissions nine writers to write one each of the nine episodes. The writers attend a commissioning conference on the Thursday of that week. By this time they will have read their synopses and come armed with notes and suggestions. Each writer will constructively criticise the way their storyline has been structured, and after discussion and agreement, the storylines will be changed. The writers then go away to work on their episodes. They have two weeks in which to write them.

'Coronation Street is still one of the few shows that has a company feel to it. The cast, writers and crew all have a lot of affection for the Street and its characters. That helps when we are under pressure because there is a real commitment to making the programme as good as possible.'

Sue Pritchard, Producer

A last-minute script query during recording of a 1982 episode.

HOW IT WORKS

The Coronation Street production schedule is geared to a four-week turn round, with four directors. Director 'A' will collect his or her three scripts on the first Monday and begin work. Director 'B' will already be in the second week. Director 'C' will be in the rehearsal and recording week, while Director 'D' will be editing and dubbing recorded episodes.

A director will study the scripts and discuss with the designer any extra requirements like a new character's house. He or she will discuss with the location planner any exterior filming, especially situations which have been written other than on the external Street location, for example, a Street outing to Blackpool. The director will also discuss with the Casting Department and the producer any new character parts that have been written into the scripts. The production assistant (PA) will start arranging for rehearsals and recording.

A camera script is prepared from the rehearsal scripts. This is a detailed visual interpretation as the director sees it. It breaks down into about 400 camera shots distributed among three cameras. When this is competed, the PA will type out the instructions onto the script. Forty three copies are run off and distributed to everyone concerned.

After two weeks of preparation, the director starts the production week, beginning with exterior filming of scenes which are not on the Street. These scenes are recorded on Sunday, and sometimes Saturday too. Scenes on the Street set are recorded on Monday.

During the Tuesday and Wednesday mornings, the director will rehearse each studio scene for the three episodes. This involves where the cast will be sitting, standing, moving to and entering from. These positions are critical and the director will have visualized them when working out the camera script. During rehearsals the artists are asked by the Make-up and Wardrobe Departments what their requirements are.

At 2 pm on the Wednesday of production week, there is a technical run. The cast go through their scenes, in script order, watched by the production team. The Lighting Director will mark on his plan the positions and movement of the artists in each set; from this he draws up a lighting plan; the Sound Supervisor will observe from his point of view and the PA will time each episode. Each episode is scheduled to run for 24 minutes 35 seconds. The producer watches for the artistic interpretation and, after the rehearsal, gives notes to the director. The writer, if available, will also attend.

If the episodes are more than a minute under time then the writer is called upon to introduce a new scene to accommodate that under-run. Over-runs of more than 30 seconds are easier to cope with, as it is much easier to cut dialogue than to write at the last minute.

On the Wednesday night the Lighting Director moves in with his crew to make sure each set and character is correctly lit, and the prop men ensure that all the props are in the appropriate positions in the various areas. On the Thursday morning, at 9am, the cameras, sound, etc. move in and recordings start. Each scene is rehearsed until everyone is happy and it is then recorded onto videotape. This goes on until 6.20pm and is repeated on the Friday until all the scenes have been recorded.

The director and PA move into the editing suite early the following week and have approximately eight and a half hours in which to edit he programmes. The director also collects the next three scripts!

The programmes are transmitted three weeks later, on the Monday, Wednesday and Friday.

Filming on the Street lot is usually restricted to Mondays, the day Granada Tours do not operate.

Who's Who
IN CORONATION STREET

JOAN AKERS

· *Anna Cropper* ·

1962 Disturbed woman who kidnapped baby Christopher Hewitt

CHRISTINE APPLEBY
née Hardman

· *Christine Hargreaves* ·

1960–63 Original occupant of No. 13. Christine was a Cinderella figure, struggling against life in the then grimy street. Following her mother's death, she suffered a nervous breakdown and climbed onto the factory roof. Married Colin Appleby in 1962 who died in a car crash three months later.

SANDRA ARDEN

· *Kathy Jamieson* ·

1990–91 Alec Gilroy's estranged daughter, Vicky's mother. She was embarrassed by the common Gilroys but became reconciled before her death in a car crash.

VICTORIA ARDEN

· *Helen Warburton* ·
and Chloë Newsome ·

1990– After her parents' death she moved in to the Rovers, looked after first by Grandad Alec and later Bet. Privately educated, she has led a sheltered life compared to her streetwise boyfriend Steve McDonald. She inherited £240,000 in 1994 and went into partnership with Steve.

SHIRLEY ARMITAGE

· *Lisa Lewis* ·

1983–89 Factory machinist who moved in with Curly Watts above the Corner Shop flat. She fought his family's racial hatred but left when she realized she could never bridge the intellectual gap between them.

JAMIE ARMSTRONG

· *Joseph Gilgun* ·

1994– Tricia's son, keen on skateboarding, motorbikes and pigeons. Attends Bessie Street Junior School. Caught shoplifting at Bettabuy.

TRICIA ARMSTRONG

· *Tracy Brabin* ·

1994– Separated from violent husband Carl. She moved into the Street in 1995, renting No.1. Cleaner at the Rovers. She went out with Curly Watts and Sean Skinner.

ALMA BALDWIN
prev. Sedgewick

· *Amanda Barrie* ·

1981– After the break-up of her marriage to Jim Sedgewick, Alma took the café as settlement. Mike wooed her for two years before finally winning her off Ken Barlow and marrying her.

FRANKIE BALDWIN

· *Sam Kydd* ·

1980–82 Mike's cockney father, always involved in a dodgy deal or tax fiddle. He once annoyed Mike by showing off his twenty-two-year-old girlfriend Sylvie Hicks.

MIKE BALDWIN

· *Johnny Briggs* ·

1976– London market stall holder, he opened a denim factory and started an affair with Bet Lynch. He has employed many of the residents and has had numerous girlfriends, including Deirdre Barlow, Suzie Birchall and Maggie Dunlop who was the mother of his son, Mark. He married first Susan Barlow, then Jackie Ingram, before settling down with Alma Sedgewick in 1992. He owns the garage on the Street.

SUSAN BALDWIN
née Barlow

· *Wendy Jane Walker* · *Katie Heanneau* · *Susi Patterson* ·

1965–87 Ken Barlow's daughter, twin of Peter. Following her mother Valerie's death in 1971 she was brought up in Glasgow by her grandmother. She returned to the Street in 1985, a postgraduate working in market research, and immediately fell for Mike Baldwin. Despite Ken's attempts to stop her she married Mike in 1986. Always wanting a career instead of motherhood, she aborted their baby and the marriage ended.

DAVID BARLOW

· *Alan Rothwell* ·

1960–68 Ken's footballing brother who left the Street for the celebrity life in London. He returned north to marry Irma Ogden and buy the Corner Shop when a leg injury forced him to leave professional football. He emigrated to Australia in 1968 to relaunch his career and was killed in a car crash two years later.

FRANK BARLOW

· *Frank Pemberton* ·

1960–71 Ken's postman father. Following his wife Ida's death, he enraged Ken by becoming engaged to Christine Appleby, who had been at school with Ken. After Christine broke with him, Frank opened a D-I-Y shop. Following a £5,000 win on the Premium Bonds in 1964 he sold up and moved to Cheshire. He returned to the Street in 1971 for Valerie's funeral, and died at home in 1975.

IDA BARLOW

· *Noel Dyson* ·

1960–61 Frank's wife Ida was a home bird, always anxious about sons Kenneth and David and her elderly mother Nancy. Ida never entered the Rovers and spent all day cleaning – either at work or at home. She was knocked down and killed by a bus in 1961.

IRMA BARLOW
née Ogden

· *Sandra Gough* ·

1964–71 Chirpy Irma was the Street's mimic. As soon as she could she escaped her parents, Stan and Hilda, and married David Barlow. She persuaded him to buy the Corner Shop and her natural jokey nature boosted trade. After she suffered a miscarriage, the couple emigrated to Australia to start afresh. Their son Darren was born in 1968 but both he and David were killed in a car crash. Irma returned to the Street and ran the shop with Maggie Clegg. She left to stay in Wales and eventually settled in Canada.

JANET BARLOW
née Reid

· *Judith Barker* ·

1969–77 Town Hall typist who had affairs with Len Fairclough and Alan Howard before becoming the second Mrs Kenneth Barlow. Ken married her to provide his children with a stable home but she refused to look after them and the marriage ended. Three years later, in 1977, she sought a reconciliation. Rejected, she took an overdose.

KEN BARLOW

· *William Roache* ·

1960– Born and bred in Coronation Street, Ken has outlived all of his family and is still living on the Street. His three marriages – to Valerie, Janet and Deirdre – all ended in tragedy and he has never been lucky in love. Affairs with Rita Littlewood, Alma Sedgewick, Maggie Redman and Wendy Nightingale all ended with Ken being rejected. A University graduate, Ken has been a personnel officer, a lecturer, a taxi driver, a social worker, a business executive, a newspaper editor and is now a schoolteacher. He has four children: Peter and Susan (mother Valerie), Daniel (mother Denise Osbourne) and Tracy, whom he adopted in 1986. He bought No.1 from Mike Baldwin in 1995.

PETER BARLOW

· *John Heanneau* · *Mark Duncan* · *Linus Roach* · *Christopher Dormerr* · *Joseph McKenna* · *David Lonsdale*

1965–86 Ken and Valerie's son. He was brought up in Glasgow with sister Susan but often holidayed in Weatherfield with his father. He now serves in the Navy and has a wife, Jessica.

TRACY BARLOW

· *Dawn Acton* · *Christabel Finch* · *Holly Chamarette* ·

1977– Daughter of Ray and Deirdre Langton of No.5. Ray deserted the family and she was brought up by Ken Barlow who married Deirdre. In 1986, she was legally adopted by Ken. She suffered during the Barlows' divorce. Left home in 1993 to live with boyfriend Craig Lee, but he left her for someone else. Suffered kidney damage after taking Ecstacy at a nightclub.

VALERIE BARLOW
née Tatlock

· Anne Reid ·

1961-71 Albert Tatlock's niece who married Ken Barlow and opened a hair salon at No.9 Coronation Street. The salon was closed after the birth of the twins, Peter and Susan. Valerie always struggled against Ken's lack of faith in her abilities and his intellectual prejudice. After she was held by an escaped convict, Ken refused to believe she had not been raped. Whilst preparing to emigrate with him and the children to Jamaica she was electrocuted by a faulty plug and died in the fire which started afterwards.

COLIN BARNES

· Ian Embleton ·

1993 Des's younger brother who upset the McDonald household by his affair with Liz, his boss at the Queens. He returned to Harlepool when Liz was reconciled with her husband.

DES BARNES

· Philip Middlemiss ·

1990- Des the Bookie who stormed into the Street on his wedding day with new bride Steph. Their passionate arguments at No.6 caused the Street's older residents to gossip. The marriage broke up after Steph had an affair, and Des was consoled by a string of contrasting relationships. He was devastated after the death of lover Lisa Duckworth, but his on-off affair with Raquel Wolstenhulme has entertained the Street.

STEPH BARNES

· Amelia Bullmore ·

1990-92 Fiery Steph established herself by shaving off Kevin Webster's tash for a bet. After marrying Des, she refused to settle down and have children and enjoyed spending her days working as a perfume-seller in a department store. She left Des after falling for Simon Beatty but left him too when he became too possessive.

DAVE BARTON

· David Beckitt ·

1990 Maintenance man Dave who rescued Tracy Barlow from a chip pan fire at No.1. Later he fell for Deirdre and they started an affair after he decorated her house. He broke with Deirdre when she refused to commit herself to him.

PEGGY BARTON

· Lois Daine ·

1974 Union shop steward who had an affair with boss Ken Barlow. He was forced to stop seeing her by his employers at the Mark Brittain warehouse.

TERRY BATES

· Steve Barratt ·

1972-77 Treated by Rita Fairclough as the son she never had, Terry was the son of her common-law husband Harry Bates. After Harry and Rita split, Terry often turned to her for help and support, but Len Fairclough never liked him.

SIMON BEATTY

· Peter Gowen ·

1991 Architect for whom Steph Barnes left Des. They eventually split because of his possessiveness.

SIR JULIUS BERLIN

· Leonard Sachs ·

1974 Owner of the Mark Brittain warehouse on Coronation Street, he employed Ken Barlow.

SUZIE BIRCHALL

· Cheryl Murray ·

1977-83 Gail Potter's one-time best friend and fellow lodger at No.11. Suzie escaped her abusing father to seek a new life with Gail at Elsie Tanner's. She went out with men only if they could show her a good time, like Mike Baldwin. She eventually married for love but her husband, Terry Goodwin, started to hit her after three months. She left him and tried to seduce Brian Tilsley, to prove to Gail that her marriage was not safe either. When her plan failed, Elsie threw her out.

EMILY BISHOP
née Nugent, prev. Swain

· Eileen Derbyshire ·

1961- Timid Emily Nugent was secretary to the Weatherfield Mission Circuit. She jilted Leonard Swindley at the altar in 1964. She had been a shop assistant at Gamma Garments and eventually became manageress. She then worked at Ernest Bishop's camera shop, Dawson's bakery and Mike Baldwin's factory. She married Ernest in 1972, but six years later he was killed. In 1980 she married Arnold Swain who turned out to be a suicidal bigamist. The marriage annulled, she took in lodgers Curly Watts and Kevin Webster before becoming stuck with Percy Sugden. In 1993, the Rev. Bernard Morten proposed marriage but dumped her when he found out she had suffered a mental breakdown. Emily lives at No.3 and is now retired.

ERNEST BISHOP

· *Stephen Hancock* ·

1967-78 Laypreacher Ernest first appeared at Elsie Tanner's wedding, taking photographs under his one time professional name, Gordon Bishop. Ernest married Emily Nugent after taking her on in his photography shop. When the shop closed through Ernie's bankruptcy he took a job as wages clerk at Mike Baldwin's factory and he was gunned down during a wages snatch.

GORDON BLINKHORN

· *Mark Chatterton* ·

1992-93 Raquel Wolstenhulme's cricket-playing boyfriend.

MARIO BONARTI

· *Frank Coda* ·

1961 Italian-born Mario opened a café on Rosamund Street and fell for Christine Hardman, but was too possessive and she finished with him.

JERRY BOOTH

· *Graham Haberfield* ·

1962-75 Bicycle-mad Jerry started work as Len Fairclough's apprentice plumber in 1962, and three years later became his partner. He married domineering Myra Dickenson in 1963 but the marriage ended a year later in debt following the birth of their still-borne daughter. Down-trodden Jerry became the butt of jokes at the Rovers when he moved in as housekeeper at No.9, taking care of Len and Ray Langton. Jerry died suddenly of a heart attack in 1975.

MYRA BOOTH
née Dickenson

· *Susan Jameson* ·

1963-68 Typist Myra, spoilt by an indulgent father, fell for Jerry Booth and pushed him into marrying her. She spent too much on HP and they soon fell into debt. Her father paid off the debts but the marriage broke up.

RODNEY BOSTOCK

· *Colin Prokter* ·

1995 Trombone-playing relief manager who fell for Bet Gilroy's charms.

CHARLIE BRACEWELL

· *Peter Bayliss* ·

1989 Ventriloquist taken on by Alec as resident barman. Bet got rid of him when he goosed Betty Turpin.

ALAN BRADLEY

· *Mark Eden* ·

1986-89 Alan entered the Street following the death of his estranged wife Pat in 1986. He was reintroduced to his daughter Jenny and took an immediate liking to her foster mother Rita Fairclough. He moved in with Rita after she had twice refused to marry him. Tired of her coldness he left for another woman, but returned to Rita as he had no money of his own. Posing as her dead husband he remortgaged her house and started his own security business. When she found out he tried to kill her, haunted her night and day and was finally killed himself, knocked down by a Blackpool tram when he was chasing her after a prom.

FRANK BRADLEY

· *Tommy Boyle* ·

1971-75 Petty villain who had an on-off affair with Bet Lynch. He hit Lucille Hewitt over the head when mugging her in the Street.

JENNY BRADLEY

· *Sally Ann Matthews* ·

1986-93 Following the death of her mother Pat, Jenny moved into No.7 as Rita Fairclough's foster daughter. Reconciled with her father, Alan, the three settled down as a happy family. Jenny's security was wrecked when Alan tried to kill Rita. She studied biology at the Poly but was thrown out of the course for bad attendance. She left the area in 1991 to live with Robert Weston, a married dentist. When he returned to his wife, she arrived back on Rita's doorstep and attempted to fleece her. Rita paid her off and threw her out.

TERRY BRADSHAW

· Bob Mason ·

1976 Renee Robert's younger brother. He worked for Fairclough and Langton, but joined the army after a brief affair with Gail Potter.

DON BRENNAN

· Geoff Hinsliff ·

1987- Taxi-driver Don married Ivy Tilsley in 1988 and soon discovered he had to take on the ghosts of her first husband and son. Her obsession with the dead drove him into an affair with barmaid Julie Dewhurst. When Julie rejected him, he attempted suicide, driving his cab off a road. He survived but lost a leg. Stuck with Ivy he fell for Denise Osbourne and subjected her to a hate campaign when she rejected his advances. When Ivy entered a retreat he started a relationship with Josie Clarke.

C

IVY BRENNAN
prev. Tilsey

· Lynne Perrie ·

1971-94 Catholic Ivy spent most of her working life behind a factory conveyor-belt or sewing-machine. She joined the Mark Brittain warehouse in 1971 and became shop steward and then supervisor at Mike Baldwin's denim factory. In 1979, she moved into No.5 with husband Bert and son Brian. Despite her attempts to stop him, Brian married non-Catholic Gail Potter. Bert and Brian both died and she became obsessed with their memories and the spiritual welfare of Brian's son Nicky. In 1988, she married Don Brennan but their marriage was rocked by his infidelity. After a lifetime of heartbreak and pain, Ivy entered a retreat in 1994 to commit her life to prayer and meditation.

VICKI BRIGHT

· Clare Sutcliffe ·

1972 Audrey Fleming's cousin who oversaw the sale of No.3 to the Bishops. Ray Langton proposed to her even though she was carrying another man's child. She turned him down.

JOE BROUGHTON

· John Wheatley ·

1993-94 Tax inspector who attempted to break up the Websters' marriage by declaring his love for Sally, who was child-minding his son Jonathan.

ALICE BURGESS

· Avis Bunnage ·

1961 Harry Hewitt's widowed sister who kept house for him and daughter Lucille at No.7.

DANNY BURROWS

· Ian Liston ·

1974 Mechanic who left his wife to share a bedsit with Lucille Hewitt. She finished with him when his wife told her how mean he really was.

AMY BURTON

· Fanny Carby ·

1987-88 Vera Duckworth's mother who moved into No.9 and made Jack's life a misery. She charred at the Rovers until Jack caught her stealing the pale ales. Vera threw her out. She died in 1991.

BERNARD BUTLER

· Gorden Kaye ·

1969-70 Elsie Tanner's accident-prone nephew. He and his sister Sandra lodged with Elsie at No.11 and worked together at Alan Howard's hair salon. He returned home to Saddleworth after Irma Barlow rejected his clumsy advances.

SANDRA BUTLER

· Patricia Fuller ·

1969-70 Hairdressing niece of Elsie Tanner. She fell for Ray Langton and the banns were read at St Mary's. However she ditched him after discovering he had wrecked the Flemings' marriage.

MINNIE CALDWELL

· Margot Bryant ·

1960-76 Quiet and timid, Minnie was Ena Sharples' stooge. She moved into No.5 in 1962 with her cat, called Bobby, and she remained there for the next fourteen years. She took in lodgers – Charlie Moffit, Jed Stone, Eddie Yeats, Joe Donnelli – and she spent her evenings in the Rovers' Snug with Ena and Martha Longhurst. In 1969 she was nearly killed in a coach crash, and the following year she was held at gunpoint by Joe Donnelli. In 1973, she became engaged to Albert Tatlock in order to save money on her pension, but eventually she broke off her engagement because of his annoying habits. She left the Street to become housekeeper to her old friend Handel Gartside after his wife died.

Minnie Caldwell, who once said of Ena Sharpes: 'She bullies me. She always has . . . in the name of Christianity.'

MARK CASEY

· Stuart Wolfenden·

1989–90 Mechanic employed at his father Tom's garage to work under Kevin Webster. He ended up being the boss and sacking Kevin.

FIONA CAVANAGH

· Sharon Muircroft ·

1988 Ken Barlow's assistant at the *Recorder*. When the company was seized by the courts she helped Ken smuggle out the templates to publish the paper on time.

YVONNE CHAPPELL

· Alex Marshall ·

1971 Hotel receptionist who fell for Ken Barlow. Ken proposed but she realized he was only after a replacement for Valerie.

IVAN CHEVESKI

· Ernst Walder ·

1960–67 Polish Ivan was Elsie Tanner's son-in-law. He bought No.11 for wife Linda and worked as potman at the Rovers. In 1961, the Cheveskis emigrated to Canada but returned in 1966 when their marriage was wrecked by Linda's affair. He settled in Birmingham.

LINDA CHEVESKI

· Anne Cunningham ·

1960–84 Elsie Tanner's headstrong, moody daughter. She and husband Ivan moved into No.9 in 1961 shortly before the birth of their son, Paul. The family lived in Canada for five years, but returned to England after Linda's affair with a Canadian, Mike. In 1984, Linda started divorce proceedings and returned to the Street to an empty No.11. She attempted to stop the sale of the house but failed.

MARTIN CHEVESKI

· Jonathan Caplan ·

1980 Linda and Ivan's son, born in Canada. He stayed with Granny Elsie at No.11 after leaving school. Len Fairclough employed him as an apprentice but he returned to Birmingham when girlfriend Karen Oldfield refused to marry him.

PAUL CHEVESKI

· Victoria Elton, Marcus Saville
· Nigel Greaves ·

1961–72 Elsie Tanner's grandson, the first on-screen birth in the Street. In 1966, he battled for life after falling into the canal.

JASMINE CHOONG

· Lucille Soong ·

1969 Billy Walker's Chinese girlfriend who stayed at the Rovers. When Billy announced his plans to marry her, his mother Annie collapsed and told Jasmine she would stop the marriage. Annie's blatant racial hatred was too much for Jasmine and she left Billy.

ALEX CHRISTIE

· Gavin Richards ·

1994 Bookie who employed Des Barnes and had an affair with Tanya

Pooley. He sacked Des and finished with Tanya when he discovered they had been having an affair.

JOSIE CLARKE

· *Ellie Haddington* ·

1995 Doctor's receptionist who fell for Don Brennan.

ANDREA CLAYTON

· *Caroline O'Neill* ·

1985 'A' level student who fell for Terry Duckworth when her family lived at No.11. When she became pregnant, she refused to settle down with Terry and the family moved. Her son Paul was subsequently adopted.

CONNIE CLAYTON

· *Susan Brown* ·

1985 Mother of the Clayton family who lived briefly at No.11. A dressmaker by trade she soon fell out with Vera Duckworth over a dress bill.

HARRY CLAYTON

· *Johnny Leeze* ·

1985 Trombone-playing milkman who bought, and sold, No.11.

SUE CLAYTON

· *Jane Hazelgrove* ·

1985 The youngest Clayton girl. She had only just got a job in a bakery when the family moved.

GORDON CLEGG

· *Bill Kenwright* ·

1968-82 Betty Turpin's successful accountant son. When he arrived in the Street he lived at the Corner Shop with Les and Maggie Clegg, who he thought were his parents. Years later, he was told that it was Maggie's sister Betty who was really his mother. He became engaged to Lucille Hewitt but dropped her just a week before the wedding was due to take place. He went to live in London but returned occasionally to visit Maggie and Betty. Now living in Wimbledon, he is married to Caroline with a son, Peter.

LES CLEGG

· *John Sharp* ·

1968 Bought the Corner Shop in a bid to star afresh and escape his drink problem. When drunk, he became abusive and hit wife Maggie. He left after only a few months at the shop and entered a psychiatric hospital. Eventually he and Maggie divorced.

IDA CLOUGH

· *Helene Palmer* ·

1978-88 Militant shop steward at Mike Baldwin's factory. Mother of Muriel and Bernard who also both worked at Baldwin's.

NORRIS COLE

· *Malcolm Hebden* ·

1994 Enviro-Sphere salesman who lodged with the Wiltons after rescuing Derek when he was stranded on a motorway. Whilst Derek's fortunes as a salesman sank, those of Norris rose. In 1995, Norris started a relationship with Derek's former wife, Angela Hawthorne.

JIMMY CONWAY

· *Colin Edwyn* ·

1964-72 Local PC who was eventually promoted to sergeant. His girlfriend Sonia Peters was killed when the train crashed off the viaduct. He was saved by the frame of his car.

MAGGIE COOKE
prev. Clegg

· *Irene Sutcliffe* ·

1968-74 Betty Turpin's younger sister who, with husband Les Clegg, bought the Corner Shop from the Barlows. Her marriage ended due to Les's alcoholism. Len Fairclough dated her but she refused to commit herself. Alf Roberts proposed to her but she turned him down, agreeing instead to marry reformed alcoholic Ron Cooke. After their 1974 wedding, they left for Zaire.

RON COOKE

· *Eric Lander* ·

1972-74 Draughtsman who married Maggie Clegg despite a history of alcoholism.

ARCHIE CRABTREE

· *John Stratten* ·

1971 Hilda Ogden's brother who came to stay with her while Stan was working abroad. he erected a porch for Hilda only to have Ray Langton remove it as he had no planning permission.

ROBERT CROFT

· *Martin Shaw* ·

1967-68 Leader of the hippie commune that took over No.11. Lucille

Hewitt fell for him, much to Annie Walker's horror.

NEIL CROSSLEY

· Geoffrey Matthews ·

1963-66 Unpleasant character who caused a stir in the Street by making Sheila Birtles pregnant. He was sacked from Gamma Garments for stealing from the till. He eventually married Sheila and settled in Scarborough.

SHEILA CROSSLEY
née Birtles

· Eileen Mayers ·

1961-74 Factory girl Sheila lodged at the Corner Shop with friend Doreen Lostock in the early 1960s. She went out with Jerry Booth but ditched him for the more worldly Neil Crossley. She tried to kill herself when Neil left the area, leaving her pregnant. She left herself in 1963 but returned in 1966 to lodge with Elsie Tanner at No.11. She took up with Jerry, but left him again when Neil re-entered her life. She married Neil and set up a home for them and their son, Danny.

WENDY CROZIER

· Roberta Kerr ·

1989-90 Town Hall secretary who leaked Council information to newspaper editor Ken Barlow and eventually had an affair with him.

TONY CUNLIFFE

· Jack Carr ·

1984 Betty Turpin's policeman lodger who had affairs with Bet Lynch and Rita Fairclough.

SUSAN CUNNINGHAM

· Patricia Shakesby·

1960-61 Ken Barlow's university girlfriend. Together they marched against the bomb, but they split after a few weeks.

JOAN DAVIES
née Walker

· June Barry · Dorothy White ·

1961-77 Jack and Annie Walker's daughter who married Gordon Davies in the Street's first wedding.

TOMMY DEAKIN

· Paddy Joyce ·

1968-74 Irish rag and bone man who lodged his donkey, Dolores, in a makeshift stable under the viaduct.

JULIE DEWHURST

· Su Elliott ·

1991-92 Barmaid who had an affair with Don Brennan.

DIRTY DICK

· Talfryn Thomas ·

1972 Tommy Deakin's Welsh brother-in-law and partner.

RALPH DOBSON

· Michael Lees ·

1990-91 Jackie Ingram's trusted friend who brought about the downfall of Mike Baldwin at Ingram's Textiles.

JOE DONNELLI

· Shane Rimmer ·

1967-70 American GI who murdered Steve Tanner over an unpaid debt. He deserted from the Army and went into hiding in No.5 at Minnie Caldwell's. After confessing to Irma Barlow about the violence of his temper he held Stan Ogden at gunpoint before shooting himself dead.

MARTIN DOWNES

· Louis Selwyn ·

1974 Bet Lynch's illitimate son, died in a car crash.

JACK DUCKWORTH

· William Tarmey ·

1979- John Harold Duckworth first appeared at Gail and Brian Tilsley's wedding; his nagging wife Vera had dragged him along. Jack and Vera were seldom faithful to each other, he having affairs with Bet Lynch and Dulcie Froggatt. As 'Vince St Clair', Jack joined a dating agency but was caught out by Vera. In 1983 the couple, with son Terry, moved into the Street and upset the neighbours with their rows. Originally a welder, Jack became a taxi-driver and window-cleaner before landing his dream job – potman at the Rovers.

LISA DUCKWORTH
née Horten

· Caroline Milmoe ·

1992-93 Married Terry Duckworth and then struggled to bring up their son Tommy while Terry was in prison. She moved in with Des Barnes after realizing Terry would always be a villain. They planned a new start but she was knocked down on the Street and died in hospital.

TERRY DUCKWORTH

· *Nigel Pivaro* ·

1983– The bad boy on the Street moved into No.11 after leaving the Paras. He struggled to get along with his rowing parents, but was constantly embarrassed by them. An affair with Andrea Clayton left him a father to a son he never saw, and he left the area in 1987 with Linda, the wife of his pal Pete Jackson. He married Lisa Horten as she was pregnant, but was sent to Strangeways for GBH. After his release and Lisa's death, he sold his son Tommy to the Hortens.

VERA DUCKWORTH

· *Elizabeth Dawn* ·

1974– Loud-mouthed Vera joined the Mark Brittain warehouse as a packer before starting as a machinist at Mike Baldwin's factory. From 1976 to 1989 she made Baldwin's life a misery as she used her trouble-making tongue more than her sewing machine. In 1983, together with Jack and Terry, she moved into No.9, where she was close to her best mate, Ivy Tilsley. Prior to this she had had a brief fling with Fred Gee. She worked at Bettabuys until she gave up work to look after her grandson Tommy. She was heartbroken when he was taken to live with his other grandparents.

EDDIE DUNCAN

· *Del Henney* ·

1971 County footballer who had affairs with Irma Barlow and Bet Lynch before being transferred to Torquay.

Vera Duckworth, of whom Ray Langton said: 'I hear she's anyone's for a gin.'

SHARON DUFFY

· *Susan Littler* ·

1972 Barmaid at the Flying Horse who went out with Ray Langton, thinking he was wealthy.

LEN FAIRCLOUGH

· *Peter Adamson* ·

1961–83 Builder Len Fairclough was a regular at the Rovers for many years before he moved into No.9 in 1968. When his wife Nellie left him he proposed marriage to Elsie Tanner but she turned him down. Len conducted affairs with three women on the Street – Maggie Clegg, Bet Lynch and Anita Reynolds – before settling down with Rita Littlewood, whom he finally married in 1977. In 1962 he started his own business, eventually going into partnership with Jerry Booth and Ray Langton. The three men shared No.9 in the mid-1970s before Len got married to Rita. His son Stanley disowned him following Nellie's death and, with Rita, he fostered Sharon Gaskell. In 1983, he started to have an affair with Marjorie Procter, and it was while travelling back from her house that he was killed in a motorway crash.

STANLEY FAIRCLOUGH

· *Peter Noone, Ronald Cunliffe* ·
Jonathan Coy

1961–77 Len's son who was brought up in Nottingham by stepfather Harry Bailey, following his mother Nellie's death. He resented the way his father had treated Nellie so badly during their marriage, and in an act of vengeance set fire to his building-yard, nearly killing himself.

WAYNE FARRELL

· Ray Polhil ·

1992-93 Vain footballer who had an affair with Raquel Wolstenhulme whilst seeing other women behind her back.

CARMEL FINNAN

· Catherine Cusack ·

1992-93 Student nurse who became infatuated with Martin Platt and attempted to break up his marriage.

STEVE FISHER

· Lawrence Mullin ·

1977-79 Mike Baldwin's sidekick. Gail Potter loved him, but he only had eyes for Suzie Birchall. He left the area to run Mike's London factory.

AUDREY FLEMING
née Bright

· Gillian McCann ·

1968-70 Married Dickie Fleming when she was sixteen and still at school. They bought No.3 and she took a job at a petrol station before becoming Ray Langton's secretary. It was her love for Ray that finished her marriage. When Dickie left her, she went to live with her parents in Preston.

DICKIE FLEMING

· Nigel Humphreys ·

1968-70 Trainee electrician who bought No.3 when he was just eighteen and then married sixteen-year-old Audrey Bright. He struggled with debt and Audrey's on-off love affair with his friend Ray Langton, before leaving in 1970.

GREGG FLINT

· Bill Nagy ·

1967-70 Steve Tanner's best friend from the USA. When in Weatherfield, he romanced Dot Greenhalgh and Maggie Clegg.

JACKO FORD

· Robert Keegan ·

1972-73 Jailbird father of Norma Ford. He moved into the Corner Shop with Norma upon leaving prison, but was never really trusted by the residents. He was framed for the break-in at Benny Lewis flat, but Ken Barlow managed to prove his innocence.

NORMA FORD

· Diana Davies ·

1972-74 Maggie Clegg's assistant at the Corner Shop. She was haunted by her father's prison record, and moved to the Street to escape him but he tracked her down. She was relieved when he was accepted by the residents. She left the Street after realizing Ken Barlow did not love her .

DES FOSTER

· Neil Phillips ·

1983-91 Decorator and councillor who had an affair with Bet Lynch while cheating on his wife and girlfriend. In 1991, Bet tried to use him to make Alec jealous but he beat her up when she refused his advances.

TINA FOWLER

· Michelle Holmes ·

1989-1990 Barmaid at the Rovers who left after an affair with Nigel Ridley. Prior to that she was jilted by Eddie Ramsden on her hen night.

JIMMY FRAZER

· John Barrie ·

1972 Alan Howard's business partner who owned the Capricorn Club.

LAURIE FRAZER

· Stanley Meadows ·

1963-64 Elsie Tanner's married boyfriend who owned the Viaduct Sporting Club.

ANGIE FREEMAN

· Deborah McAndrew ·

1990-93 Fashion student who lodged with Jenny Bradley at No.7. When Jenny moved out, Curly Watts moved in and the couple eventually ended up in bed, although they were full of regrets the next morning. She struggled after graduation, designing for Mike Baldwin. After a painful romance with Neil Mitchell she left for Mexico to study Aztec designs.

DULCIE FROGGATT

· Margi Campi·

1984-87 Lonely housewife who became Jack Duckworth's mistress, but ruined the relationship by sleeping with his son Terry.

HANDEL GARTSIDE

· Harry Markham ·

1970-76 Local who made his fortune in Canada then returned to his roots. Became Minnie Caldwell's friend and part-time lodger. When she left the Street it was to housekeep for him.

SHARON GASKELL

· Tracie Bennett ·

1982-84 The Faircloughs' foster daughter who fell in love with Brian Tilsley and left the Street when he spurned her. She became a kennel maid in Sheffield but returned to comfort Rita after Len's death.

EDNA GEE

· Mavis Rogerson ·

1971-75 Fred Gee's flirtatious first wife and Ivy Tilsley's best friend. With Ivy she worked at the mail order warehouse and it was there that she died in 1975, engulfed in flames by the fire that gutted the building.

EUNICE GEE
prev. Nuttall

· Meg Johnson ·

1981-82 Fred Gee's second wife whom he married in order to gain tenancy of a pub. It all fell through when the brewery discovered Eunice had once been suspected of theft. For a while the Gees ran the Community Centre, but it was not long until Eunice ran off with a councillor. The Gees divorced.

When Rita asked Sharon Gaskell to stop pestering Brian Tilsley, Sharon called her a hypocrite: she'd been with loads of men.

FRED GEE

· Fred Feast ·

1976-84 The Rovers' resident potman, Annie Walker employed him after he had been made redundant as a storeman. As well as keeping the cellar, Fred acted as Annie's chauffeur and manservant. After his wife Edna's death in 1975, Fred turned his eye on the local ladies, dating Vera Duckworth. To impress Audrey Potter he bought a wig, but threw it away when all the residents laughed at him. In a bid to win his own pub, he married Eunice Nuttall in 1981 but she had a bad record at the brewery, and they were refused a pub. After divorcing Eunice he took over the Rovers, temporarily, and was eventually sacked by Billy Walker. He was then employed by Mike Baldwin to drive a delivery van, but again was sacked after he posed as Mike in a crooked deal.

ALEC GILROY

· Roy Barraclough ·

1972-92 One-time theatrical agent, those on his books included Rita Littlewood and Megan Morgan. He ran the Graffiti Club in 1986, before marrying Bet Lynch and taking on the licence of the Rovers Return in 1987. Alec's first wife, Joyce, had run away with a footballer taking their daughter Sandra with her. In 1990, Alec found Sandra again and met his grand daughter Victoria for the first time. A year later Sandra and her husband Tim Arden were killed in a car crash and Vicky became Alec's ward. In 1992, Alec left the Rovers and Bet to take a job organizing entertainment on cruise-liners in Southampton.

BET GILROY
née Lynch

· Julie Goodyear ·

1966- Born and bred in Weatherfield, Bet Lynch became pregnant at sixteen and was forced to have her son, Martin, adopted. He tracked her down nineteen years later, by which time she was working as a barmaid at the Rovers Return. Martin was so upset to see her flirting with the customers he left the pub without introducing himself to her. A year later she received the news that he had been killed in a car crash. After Martin's birth, Bet gained the reputation of being easy and willing. She has been used and then let down by many of the Street's men including Len Fairclough, Mike Baldwin, Eddie Yeats and Jack Duckworth. Bet started work at the Rovers in 1970 after working in various shops, factories and managing a laundrette. After fifteen years of working for Annie Walker, Bet took on the Rovers as manageress. A year later, in June 1986, she nearly lost the pub, as well as her life, when a fire gutted the pub. She married Alec Gilroy in September 1987. Five years later Alec went to live in Southampton. Bet fell for Charlie Whelan but he ran off with Tanya Pooley.

DAVID GRAHAM

· Roger Adamson ·

1964 Disturbed art teacher who fell in love with model Elsie Tanner and threatened to kill her when she tried to break with him.

DR GRAHAM

· Fulton McKay ·

1961 The residents' doctor. He caused a panic when he dropped a box of pills on the Street which were found by Lucille Hewitt who mistook them for sweets.

JIMMY GRAHAM

· Colin George ·

1974 Property developer who had an affair with Rita Littlewood. He promised to leave his wife Muriel for her but, when caught out by Muriel, he passed Rita off as a client. Rita ditched him.

DOT GREENHALGH

· Joan Francis ·

1961-69 Elsie Tanner's best mate and fellow good-time girl. Together they entertained the Yanks during the Second World War and then again when the GIs returned in 1967. Dot's husband Walter threw her out when he discovered her affair with GI Gregg Flint. Elsie took her in at No.11 and together they worked at Miami Modes. Their friendship ended when Dot let Elsie take the blame for some shoplifting she had indulged in.

GEORGE GREENWOOD

· Arthur Pentilow ·

1968-71 Park-keeper with whom Hilda Ogden had platonic relationship. He judged the flower show where Stan tried to win with an orchid. Unfortunately for him, George recognized it as one stolen from the park.

BILL GREGORY

· Jack Watson ·

1961-84 Chief Petty Officer who had an affair with Elsie Tanner. She finished with him when she discovered he was married. He returned when his wife Phyllis had died and proposed to Elsie, but she chose to marry Alan Howard. In 1983 Bill returned to Weatherfield, and was surprised to find Elsie still in the Street. He persuaded her to help him run his wine bar on the Algarve.

MAUD GRIMES

· Elizabeth Bradley ·

1993- Maureen's mother and one-time beau of Percy Sugden's. Percy broke off their engagement when he found out Maureen's father was a GI that Maud had had a fling with whilst her husband Wilfred was fighting in the war. She runs the shop with Maureen and puts up with her son-in-law, Reg Holdsworth.

MAY HARDMAN

· Joan Heath ·

1960 Original occupant of No.13, May was Christine Appleby's mother. In December 1960 she returned home after a spell in a mental hospital following a breakdown. On New Year's Eve she died of a brain tumour.

FRANK HARVEY

· Nick Stringer ·

1984-85 Relief manager who ran the Rovers between Annie Walker and Bet Lynch. He was rejected by Bet but was successful with Gloria Todd.

NELLIE HARVEY

· Mollie Sugden ·

1965-76 Landlady of the Laughing Donkey, and Annie Walker's social rival. Jack Walker was her old dancing partner and he introduced her to Annie. In 1974 she threatened to drag Annie through the courts when her husband Arthur declared his love for Annie and left home.

ESTHER HAYES

· Daphne Oxenford ·

1960–72 Quiet, intellectual spinster Esther rented No.5 before moving to a modern flat in Moor Lane in 1962. In 1963 Esther moved to Scotland but often popped back to the Street for weddings and funerals.

TOM HAYES

· Dudley Foster ·

1961 Esther's conman brother who lived with her for a month following his release from prison. He left the area because no one wanted to invest in his schemes.

HARRY HEWITT

· Ivan Beavis ·

1960–67 Bus inspector Harry lived at No.7 with his wayward daughter Lucille and his whippets. In 1961, he married Concepta Riley and their son Christopher was born the following year. Harry was always found propping up the bar of the Rovers with his drinking pal Len Fairclough. The Hewitts left for Ireland in 1964, leaving Lucille to finish her education. Whilst visiting Lucille in September 1967, Harry was crushed to death under Len's van.

LUCILLE HEWITT

· Jennifer Moss ·

1960–74 Lucille grew up on the Street. Following her mother Elizabeth's death in 1959, Lucille was placed in an orphanage but left there when her father Harry married Concepta Riley. Lucille was heavily influenced by the 1960s pop scene and ran the Brett Falcoln fan club. After leaving grammar school she drifted through various jobs – in factories, a laboratory, shops, a turf accountant's, a fashion boutique and behind the bar of the Rovers Return. Lucille moved into the Rovers as the Walkers' ward when the Hewitts moved to Ireland in 1964. In the 1970s she did all she could to shock her Auntie Annie at the pub, taking a job as a go-go dancer and setting up home with a married man, Danny Burrows. In 1969 she came close to marrying Gordon Clegg, but he jilted her just a week before the ceremony. When Gordon returned to the area in 1974 Lucille was so upset she went to stay with Concepta in Ireland. She never returned.

STUART HODGES

· Vernon Joyner ·

1964 Lay preacher who took over the Mission from Swindley. The local women attended the sermons just to gaze at him.

MAUREEN HOLDSWORTH
prev. Naylor

· Sherrie Hewson ·

1993– In January 1994, Maureen married her sweetheart of twenty-five years, Reg Holdsworth. In 1968 they had been separated by her interfering mother Maud Grimes and Maureen had then married Frank Naylor who treated her badly. Following her divorce from Frank, Maureen met Reg again when she took a job at Bettabuy supermarket where he was manager. After their marriage, she took over the running of their shop on Coronation Street.

REG HOLDSWORTH

· Ken Morley ·

1989– Supermarket boss Reg moved into No.12 Coronation Street, along with his waterbed, in 1991. His wife Veronica threw him out accusing him of an affair with Rita Fairclough, but Rita always spurned his advances. In 1994 Reg married Maureen Naylor after fighting off her mother. The same year, having resigned from Bettabuy, he opened Holdsworths Provisions on Coronation Street but then joined the Firmans Freezer company.

IDRIS HOPKINS

· Richard Davies ·

1974–75 Welsh Idris worked at the local foundry during the night, and attempted to sleep during the day while his wife Vera rowed with his mother Megan.

GRANNY MEGAN HOPKINS

· Jesse Evans ·

1974–75 Idris's domineering mother. She ran a chip show for years following husband Cledwin's death and before renting the Corner Shop with Idris' wife, Vera. Megan wanted to buy the shop so much she tried to blackmail Gordon Clegg into letting her have it cheap. The plan backfired and Gordon saw them off.

TRICIA HOPKINS

· Kathy Jones ·

1973-76 Youngest of the Hopkin clan. She persuaded the family to rent the Corner Shop so she could be near her idol, Ray Langton. Tricia worked at the Mark Britain warehouse along with Gail Potter with whom she rented the shop flat. After the warehouse fire – in which she narrowly escaped death – Tricia ran the shop for Gordon. When Renee Bradshaw bought the shop, she made it clear she did not want Tricia around, so Tricia left.

VERA HOPKINS

· Kathy Staff·

1973-75 Committee member at the Community Centre, Vera was well known in Coronation Street when the Hopkins took over the Corner Shop in 1974. She left the running of the shop of Megan whilst she nursed her sick mother. When her mother died she inherited a tidy sum and Megan welcomed her back with open arms. She was furious when Megan tried to blackmail Gordon Clegg, and they were all forced out.

JEFF HORTEN

· Dicken Ashworth·

1992-93 Lisa Duckworth's father who did all he could to stop her marrying Terry, and then bought their son Tommy from Terry after Lisa's death.

ALAN HOWARD

· Alan Browning ·

1969-74 Businessman Alan arrived in the Street to stay with his war years friend Len Fairclough. Len did the building work for him when he opened up a hair salon on Rosamund Street, employing Elsie Tanner as receptionist. Alan threw his money about and impressed the regulars but, shortly after marrying Elsie, he declared himself bankrupt. He struggled to adjust, taking a mechanic's job while Elsie became the main breadwinner. He upset Elsie by taking money from his ex-wife Laura and by having an affair with Janet Reid. In 1973, the Howards left for his native Newcastle and the marriage split up shortly afterwards.

MARK HOWARD

· Nicholas Jones ·

1970 Alan's son from his first marriage. He disliked Elsie and tried to break up the marriage by telling Alan that Elsie was having an affair with Len Fairclough.

EILEEN HUGHES

· Prunella Scales·

1961 Clippie who had a crush on bus inspector Harry Hewitt.

BLANCHE HUNT

· Maggie Jones ·

1974-81 Deirdre's corset-making mother. She sold her business to run the Corner Shop for Gordon Clegg and nursed Deirdre through her courtships with Billy Walker and Ray Langton. She never approved of Ray as a son-in-law, and was delighted when Deirdre married Ken Barlow. In 1976, she left the area to run a club for her old flame Dave Smith.

JACKIE INGRAM

· Shirin Taylor·

1990-92 Peter Ingram's widow who fell for Mike Baldwin's charms and became his second wife. The marriage lasted a week before Jackie discovered he had been only after her money and had used some of it to help out his girlfriend. She threatened Mike with her shotgun before leaving him.

PETER INGRAM

· Tony Osoba·

1990 Textile king who employed Mike Baldwin rather than have him as opposition. He threatened to make Mike's life a misery at his factory, but died of a heart attack.

LINDA JACKSON

· Kazia Pelker·

1987 Wife of Pete Jackson. She had an affair with his friend Terry Duckworth and left Weatherfield to live with him in Scotland.

PETE JACKSON

· Ian Mercer ·

1987 Terry Duckworth's old army pal. Terry employed him at Cheap and Cheerful, and Peter was happy before discovering that Terry and his wife Linda were lovers. He was shocked when they ran off together.

REV. JAMES

· Eric Dobson·

1968-69 Vicar of St Mary's Parish Church. He befriended the residents and tried, in vain, to get them to church.

RON JENKINS

· *Ben Kingsley* ·

1966–67 Likely lad who tried to court Irma Barlow before discovering she was married.

PHIL JENNINGS

· *Tommy Boyle* ·

1990–91 Born Phil Smith, Phil changed his name after a spell in prison. He met Deirdre Barlow when she campaigned against his amusement arcades. He charmed her into bed and made her his secretary. His businesses failed and he was beaten up by his debtors before leaving the country with his wife.

DAN JOHNSON

· *Richard Shaw* ·

1980 Lorry driver who two-timed Elsie Tanner with Bet Lynch. When Elsie threw him out Bet took him in, but he left for pastures new.

JUD JOHNSON

· *Neil Kennedy* ·

1970 Frank Bradley's sidekick from Borstal. He eventually run off with Sandra Butler.

LYNNE JOHNSON

· *Ann Kennedy* ·

1975 Battered wife who turned to Len Fairclough for help. When she was found murdered in his kitchen he was suspected until her husband confessed.

MAURICE JONES

· *Alan Moore* ·

1989–90 Property developer who demolished the Community Centre and Baldwin's factory to make way for new shops and houses. He sold one of the houses cut-price to his daughter Steph and her husband Des Barnes.

FLICK KHAN

· *Rita Wolf* ·

1990 Art student at Manchester Poly who shared No.7 with Jenny Bradley. Together they holidayed in France where she stayed, having fallen for a medical student.

JOANNE KHAN

· *Tanya Rodrigues* ·

1990 Flick's younger sister. She ran off to the Lakes with Steve McDonald but became disillusioned and returned home.

RALPH LANCASTER

· *Kenneth Watson* ·

1975–80 Owner of the Gatsby night-club where Rita was a regular singer. He made an enemy of Len Fairclough by taking every opportunity to lure Rita away.

JANICE LANGTON

· *Paula Wilcox* ·

1969 Ray's wayward sister. She lodged at No.9 and flirted with Len Fairclough while sussing out Dave Smith's wealth for her boyfriend Bob Neale. She helped Bob steal Smith's car and cash.

RAY LANGTON

· *Neville Buswell* ·

1966–78 Borstal boy Ray came to the Street to work for Fairclough and Booth, stole from the residents, attempted to rape Lucille Hewitt and was beaten up by Len Fairclough. He returned two years later a reformed character and was taken back on by Len. Ray lodged with Elsie Tanner but she objected to his sexual advances and he moved in with Len at No.9. In 1969, following his attempts to bed Mrs Audrey Fleming, he was paralysed in a coach crash. He regained the use of his legs six months later and in the meantime had become engaged to Sandra Butler. She ditched him when she found out he had continued his affair with Audrey. In 1975, he married Deirdre Hunt and two years later their daughter Tracy was born. The family lived at No. 5 until Ray left for Holland following an affair with waitress Janice Stubbs.

ELSIE LAPPIN

· *Maudie Edwards* ·

1960 The original owner of the Corner Shop. She retired to Knott End after selling the shop to Florrie Lindley.

IAN LATIMER

· *Michael Looney* ·

1986–87 Brian Tilsley's Australian cousin. He had an affair with Brian's wife Gail and was suspected of being Sarah Louise's father, but a blood test proved she was not his child.

NORMAN LEACH

· *Freddie Lees* ·

1973 Petty crook who blackmailed Alf Roberts and savagely mugged Bet Lynch.

NANCY LEATHERS

· Norah Hammond·

1961-62 Mother of Ida Barlow, grandmother of Ken. She lived with the family at No.3 before moving into an OAP bungalow.

BENNY LEWIS

· Jeremy Young·

1972 Owner of Rosamund Street's betting shop who was engaged to Rita Littlewood for one day before she dumped him for Len Fairclough.

GORDON LEWIS

· David Daker·

1981-85 Relief manager at the Rovers Return. He sacked Fred, Bet and Betty, but was seen off by Annie. After Annie's retirement he fought Bet for the manager's job. The regulars were so alarmed at the thought of him winning that they wrote to the brewery backing Bet.

FLORRIE LINDLEY

· Betty Alberge·

1960-65 Kind Florrie ran the Corner Shop, letting her customers believe she was a widow. In fact she was estranged from her husband Norman. She was unlucky in love – rejected by Harry Hewitt and Frank Barlow and led on by Tickler Murphy. In 1964, she suffered a nervous breakdown and left the Street for Canada shortly afterwards.

NORMAN LINDLEY

· Glyn Owen·

1965 Florrie's husband. He had a brief affair with Elsie Tanner before being reconciled with Florrie and emigrating with her.

TED LOFTUS

· Ted Morris ·

1969-78 Assistant at the betting shop under Dave Smith and Benny Lewis. When Hilda Ogden took ballroom lessons, he was her partner.

COLIN LOMAX

· David Jones · Alec Sabin

1961-72 Ena Sharples' grandson. He fell out of his pram when a baby and had learning difficulties as a result. In 1972, his son Jason was kidnapped from outside the Rovers but was recovered two days later.

VERA LOMAX

· Ruth Holden·

1960-67 Ena Sharples' downtrodden daughter. When her husband left her she borrowed Ena's savings, leaving her penniless. She died of a brain tumour in January 1967 after spending the Christmas with her mother.

MARTHA LONGHURST

· Lynne Carol·

1960-64 Cleaner at the Rovers Return and lifelong friend of Ena Sharples and Minnie Caldwell. She was the gossip of the threesome, and was always interested in everyone else's business. She occasionally rebelled against Ena's rule. In 1964, she made a play for wealthy Ted Ashley and was hurt when he ignored her in favour of Ena. She died of a heart-attack in the Rovers' Snug.

DOREEN LOSTOCK

· Angela Crow·

1961-63 Dizzy Doreen worked at Elliston's Raincoat Factory with Sheila Birtles and Christine Hardman before joining Swindley and Nugent at Gamma Garments. She rented the Corner Shop flat with Sheila and spent her evenings serving at the Rovers. She once dated Billy Walker and left the Street to join the WRACs.

DR LOWTHER

· Robert Scase ·

1982-87 Hilda Ogden's employer at Goldenhurst. Following his wife Joan's death he retired to the country with Hilda as his housekeeper.

MARION LUND

· Patricia Heneghan ·

1961 University librarian who had an affair with Ken Barlow and was his first lover. She was eleven years his senior.

ANDY MCDONALD

· Nicholas Cochrane·

1989- Andy moved to No.11 with the McDonald family in 1989 and soon got into trouble with twin Steve – they drove a JCB through the shop window. Andy did well at school but found his 'A' levels hard because he was in love with Paula Maxwell at the time. He went away to study Computer Studies at Sheffield but returned when he could not handle the work. He trained as assistant manager at Bettabuy under Curly Watts with whom he lodged at No.7. In 1994 he started a Combined Studies course at Manchester University.

JIM MCDONALD

· Charles Lawson ·

1989– Jim left the army (he was a Engineer in the Royal Signals) to buy No.11 and settle down. He tried (and failed) to hold down various jobs – TV repairman, security guard, motorbike restorer – before being employed as mechanic-chauffeur for Mike Baldwin. For a while he fancied himself as mine host when Liz was made manager of the Queens, but he blew his chances by hitting the boss. The McDonalds separated in 1993 and started divorce proceedings but they realized they had too much to throw away and became reconciled.

Andy McDonald refused to return to university just to please father Jim: 'You just want something to boast about, well let's face facts Dad, I'm just a failure – like you.'

LIZ MCDONALD

· Beverley Callard ·

1989– Pregnant at seventeen, Liz brought up her twins in a succession of army camps all over the world. She was delighted when Jim settled down in 1989 and bought No.11. She served as barmaid at the Rovers and the Legion before becoming manager of the Queens. Jim upset her by accusing her of having an affair with the area manager, and they separated for six months. During which time she took Colin Barnes as a lover. In 1992, her baby Katherine was born prematurely and died. She started work at Sean Skinner's betting shop in 1994, fighting off Sean.

STEVE MCDONALD

· Simon Gregson ·

1989– Andy's twin brother. He shone at school but dropped out without qualifications. Past girlfriends have included Joanne Khan and Victoria Arden. For a while he was infatuated with Steph Barnes but she made it clear she was not interested. He worked for Jim, at the café and at MVB Motors, before being taken on by Mike Baldwin at his print shop. In 1994 he took over the business himself, and surprised everyone by making a success of it with money borrowed from Vicky Arden and was torn between her money and faithful girlfriend Fiona Middleton.

JOE MAKINSON

· Brian Rawlinson ·

1961–70 Plumber Joe fell for Christine Hardman and comforted her after her mother's death. He was beaten up by Alf Roberts whose friend, Frank Barlow, wanted to marry Christine.

JACKIE MARSH

· Pamela Craig ·

1966 Newspaper reporter with whom Ken Barlow had a brief affair while married to Valerie.

RON MATHER

· Joe Lynch ·

1978–79 Taxi-driving boyfriend of Elsie Tanner. With Elsie he took a job in Torquay as a domestic servant, but Elsie finished with him after he turned a blind eye when the boss made a pass at her.

MOIRA MAXWELL

· Anne Castle·

1965-66 Disturbed woman who tried to kill Elsie Tanner, blaming her for her husband Bob's death.

PAULA MAXWELL

·Judy Brooke·

1992-94 Andy McDonald's sixth form girlfriend. She finished with him when they went to university – him to Sheffield and her to Manchester. He gave her holiday work at Bettabuy, and their affair was briefly rekindled after the boss Curly Watts failed to seduce her.

FIONA MIDDLETON

· Angela Griffin·

1993- Denise Osbourne's assistant at the hair salon. She started a relationship with Steve McDonald and lived with him at the flat about Jim's café,

CLARA MIDGELEY

· Betty Hardy ·

1965-66 Minnie Caldwell's friend who cleaned at the Mission when Ena holidayed in America. Clara fell for Albert Tatlock and proposed to him, but he refused to settle down.

FRANK MILLS

· Nigel Gregory ·

1985-86 Met Bet Lynch at a Blackpool hotel where he worked behind the bar. Having followed her to Weatherfield, he moved into the Rovers with her, where he helped out behind the bar. Bet later threw him out after he made a pass at Gloria Todd.

CHRISTINE MILLWOOD

·Julie Shipley·

1985 Designer who worked with Mike Baldwin to produce flying-suits. He tried to lure her away from her husband David, but she refused.

NEIL MITCHELL

·John Lloyd Fillingham·

1992-93 Denise Osbourne's second husband. He moved in with Angie Freeman but she threw him out because of his obsession with Denise.

PAM MITCHELL

· Prim Cotton·

1983 Editor of the *Weatherfield Recorder* who printed Ken Barlow's leaks about council cutbacks at the Community Centre.

CHARLIE MOFFIT

· Gordon Rollings·

1964-65 Comic at the Viaduct Sporting Club who lodged at No.5 with Minnie Caldwell. He gave up show business to be an insurance clerk, but eventually decided to return to the club circuit.

MEGAN MORGAN

· Sue Roderick ·

1989 Exotic dancer who moved into the Rovers as Alec Gilroy's housekeeper when he was separated from Bet.

VANESSA MORGAN

· Imogen Boorman·

1992 Assistant at Bettabuy who turned out to be daughter of the chairman, Lord Morgan.

BERNARD MORTEN

· Roland MacLeod·

1993-94 Vicar of St Saviour's. He became engaged to Emily Bishop but dumped her, unable to cope with her history of mental illness.

JIM MOUNT

· Barry Keegan ·

1965-66 Elsie Tanner's boyfriend from the GPO who lodged with the Ogdens.

TICKLER MURPHY

· Patrick McAlinney·

1964 Irish factory worker who tried to woo Florrie Lindley out of her shop. He trained Stan Ogden when he took up wrestling, but left the Street when Florrie became too serious about him.

DOUG MURRAY

· Brian Hibbard ·

1992-93 Mechanic at MVB Motors who stole Mike Baldwin's Jag and ran off to Germany. He tried dating Denise Osbourne, had a brief fling with Deirdre Barlow and was pursued by underage Tracy Barlow.

AMY NELSON

· Louise Duprey·

1993 Bettabuy assistant who fell for Andy McDonald. She was thrilled

N

when he accepted her illegitimate son Dominic and they became engaged. When holidaying in Trinidad she met Dom's father Errol again and decided to stay with him.

CECIL NEWTON

· Kenneth Alan Taylor·

1987–90 Managing director of Newton and Ridley, he gave Alec the tenancy and saw off Nigel Ridley's attempts to turn the Rovers into a theme pub.

WENDY NIGHTINGALE

· Susan Tebbs ·

1976 University graduate who left her husband Roger to set up house at No.11 with Ken Barlow, causing a scandal which threatened his job. After a couple of months she returned to Roger, unable to befriend any of the natives.

DEBBIE NUTTALL

· Gina Maher·

1981–82 Eunice Gee's daughter who lodged at the Community Centre with the Gees, upsetting Fed with her loose morals.

HILDA OGDEN

·Jean Alexander·

1964–87 Cleaner at the Rovers Return and the Street's main gossip-mongerer for over twenty years. Moved to No.13 with husband Stan, daughter Irma and son Trevor in 1964. Two other children, Sylvia and Tony, had been taken into care. She delighted in watching the downfall of those around her, especially neighbour Elsie Tanner and employer Annie Walker. In 1967 she suffered a nervous breakdown and disappeared wearing her slippers. She was found wandering the streets of Liverpool. Always aspiring to a higher standard of living, Hilda spent whatever she could on items such as an oil-lamp, cocktail bar and plastic chair. In 1976 she fell in love with a decorative mural, or 'muriel' as she called it, and used it as a backdrop on which to hang her three flying ducks, the middle one pointing downwards. She always regretted the way her children turned their backs on her – Irma emigrated to Canada, and Trevor only called when he wanted money. After Stan's death in 1984, she took in lodgers and busied herself looking after them. In 1987, she was attacked whilst attempting to stop a burglary and battled for life in intensive care. Shortly afterwards she left the area to live in Derbyshire as Dr Lowther's housekeeper.

'In darkest Africa they use a set of drums. Here we've got Hilda Ogden. I suppose that's civilisation.'

Renee Roberts

STAN OGDEN

· Bernard Youens ·

1964–84 The Rovers Return's most valued customer for twenty years, Stan was once publicly recognized by the brewery as their best customer and awarded a free beer a day for life. Stan was also one of the best customers at the local labour exchange. His varied careers included lorry driver, milkman, coalman, labourer, street photographer, scrap-metal artist, chauffeur, ice-cream man, Father Christmas and wrestler. In 1968 he bought a window-cleaning round and this remained his main source of income until his death. With his mate Eddie Yeats, Stan got into quite a few scrapes, many of them illegal, but was never caught out by the police. His finest hour came in 1970 when he rescued Minnie Caldwell from being held at gunpoint by murderer Joe Donnelli. During his work he befriended Mrs Regan at 19 Inkerman Street and then became the butt of the residents' jokes for the next fifteen years as they ribbed him and Hilda over his affair. Stan died in November 1984 following a long illness.

TREVOR OGDEN

· *Jonathan Collins* · *Don Hawkins* ·

1964-84 The Ogden's wayward son. He ran away from the Street after only four months in residence, taking with him money stolen from the neighbours. Nine years later the Ogdens tracked him down to Chesterfield where he lived with wife Polly and son Damien, having told Polly his parents were dead.

KAREN OLDFIELD

· *Sally Jane Jackson* ·

1980 Machinist at Baldwin's Casuals who went out with Martin Cheveski despite her police sergeant father's objections. She finished with Martin when he proposed marriage. She felt that at sixteen they were too young.

DENISE OSBOURNE

· *Denise Black*

1992- Hair-stylist who opened a beauty salon on Coronation Street, she divorced second husband Neil Mitchell and had a relationship with Ken Barlow. She gave birth to Ken's son Daniel in January 1995. In 1993, she was subjected to abusive phone calls made by Don Brennan.

DONNA PARKER

· *Rachel Davies* ·

1975-76 Con artist who allowed Alf Roberts to fall in love with her before conning him out of £500 to buy her own hair salon.

PHYLLIS PEARCE

· *Jill Summers* ·

1982- Widow Phyllis first appeared in the Street when she tracked down Chalkie and Craig Whitely to No.9. Her daughter Margaret had married Chalkie's son and was Craig's mother. Margaret had died of cancer and Phyllis needed to be close to Craig, the only family she had. Following Craig's emigration to Australia, Phyllis tried to get Chalkie to move in with her platonically, but he refused. Later, she set her sights on Percy Sugden and Sam Tindall, but both of them rejected her. For a while she served at Jim's café but was retired and became Des Barnes's housekeeper. In 1993, she won a poetry competition for a poem about her love for Percy.

BEATTIE PEARSON

· *Gabrielle Daye* ·

1961-84 Albert Tatlock's daughter, married to Norman Pearson, Beattie seldom visited the street or her father, unless there was a threat of her losing her inheritance. In 1971, she moved in with Albert, having left Norman. Albert made certain they were reconciled quickly.

VICTOR PENDLEBURY

· *Christopher Coll* ·

1982-92 Mavis Riley's pot-throwing admirer, or as Rita called him the 'Saddleworth Sage'. Energetic Victor whisked Mavis off on a camping weekend and asked her to live with him on a trial marriage. Mavis refused to compromise herself and did not move in with him. Victor proposed marriage in 1984, but by that time Mavis was engaged to Derek. In the 1990s Victor reappeared, the owner of a recycling plant, PPP. He employed Derek and married Yvonne, a Mavis lookalike.

ELAINE PERKINS

· *Joanna Lumley* ·

1973 Graduate daughter of Wilfred Perkins. She went out with Ken Barlow but dropped him when he became too serious.

WILFRED PERKINS

· *Wensley Pithey* ·

1972-74 Headmaster of Bessie Street School until his retirement in 1978.

P

Ken Barlow was his deputy and Wilfred despaired at the way Ken took up with the wrong women, including his own daughter.

LIONEL PETTY

· *Edward Evans* ·

1965-66 Ex-Sgt Major Petty bought the Corner Shop from Florrie Lindley. He upset the customers by trying to run it military style. When he went to live in Wales after eighteen months, the only one to really miss him was his dancing partner, Annie Walker.

SANDRA PETTY

· *Heather Moore* ·

1964-65 Local girl who fell in love with Dennis Tanner and persuaded her father Lionel to buy the Corner Shop so she could be close to him. She left the area when she realized that Dennis had no feelings for her.

ALICE PICKENS

· *Doris Hare* ·

1969 Pensioner who set her beret on Albert Tatlock. With her mynah bird, Kitchener, she lodged with Albert and nursed him following a fall. She charred at Dave Smith's betting shop and for the the Rev. James at St Mary's. Albert proposed but the vicar never arrived at the church to marry them. Alice thought it was fate and called off the wedding.

WILLIAM PIGGOTT

· *George A. Cooper* ·

1964-71 Local butcher and property developer. He attempted to bribe Ken Barlow to let his son pass an exam, and then blackmailed Emily Nugent into spying on his rival Len Fairclough.

NORMAN PHILLIPS

· *Ray Brooke* ·

1964 Manager of the Viaduct Sporting Club in Coronation Street.

GAIL PLATT

née Potter, prev. Tilsley

· *Helen Worth* ·

1975- With friend Tricia Hopkins she rented the flat above the Corner Shop and took a variety of jobs, from secretary to model. In 1976 she moved into No.11 with Elsie Howard and was nearly cited in a divorce case following an affair with sales rep Roy Thornley. She worked at boutiques Sylvia's Separates (with Elsie) and the Western Front (with Suzie Birchall, who became her room-mate). Gail married Brian Tilsley in November 1979 following a year's courtship. In 1986 Gail had an affair with Brian's cousin Ian Latimer and discovered she was pregnant. This led to the Tilsleys divorcing but they remarried in 1988 when Brian finally accepted Sarah Louise as his child. After Brian was murdered in 1989, Gail had an affair with Martin Platt, ten years her junior. Their son David was born in 1990, they married in 1991 and moved into No.8 Coronation Street later that year. Gail is part owner of Jim's café.

MARTIN PLATT

· *Sean Wilson* ·

1985- Martin first met Gail Tilsley when he was taken on to help work at Jim's café. He started an affair with Gail following an on-off relationship with Jenny Bradley. He moved in with Gail, and their son David was born on Christmas Day 1990. He married Gail in 1991. In 1992 he started training as a student nurse, and one of his classmates, Carmel Finnan, declared her love for him and nearly wrecked his marriage.

NICKY PLATT

· *Warren Jackson* ·

1980- Son of Gail and Brian Tilsley and the apple of Granny Ivy's eye. In 1987, he was kidnapped by Brian (his parents were getting divorced) and nearly ended up living in Ireland, but Brian realized he missed Gail too much. In 1994 Nicky began to resent stepfather Martin.

SARAH LOUISE PLATT

· *Lynsay King* ·

1987- Gail and Brian's second child, adopted by Martin in 1991. She once thought fairies planted sweets under Derek Wilton's 'magic' tree.

PATRIC PODEVIN

· *Franc Du Bosc* ·

1987 French student who fell for Jenny Bradley. He broke their engagement when he discovered she had been flirting with other men.

TANYA POOLEY

· *Eva Pope* ·

1993-94 Barmaid at the Rovers who had affairs with Des Barnes and his boss Alex Christie at the same time. When Alex found out he fought Des, and she

finished with them both. She ran off with Bet's boyfriend, Charlie Whelan.

HAROLD POTTS

· Russell Dixon ·

1992-93 Councillor who also worked as caretaker at Weatherfield Comp., making his junior Derek Wilton's life a misery.

WALTER POTTS

· Christopher Sandford ·

1963-64 Window-cleaner discovered by Dennis Tanner and launched as singing sensation Brett Falcon. His single 'Not Too Little, Not Too Much' was so successful that Walter had to leave his lodgings at No.11 to go on a European tour.

DAWN PRESCOTT

· Louise Harrison ·

1989 Receptionist at Alan Bradley's security shop. She alerted Rita to Alan's dark deeds after he had tried to rape her. She took a job selling flats at the docks and became Mike Baldwin's lover. They separated when her brother Robert conned Mike into buying Spanish land.

DEIRDRE RACHID
née Hunt, prev. Langton and Barlow

· Anne Kirkbride·

1973- First introduced as a dollybird sent to entertain Alan Howard by a business colleague, Deirdre soon fell for Billy Walker. They became engaged, but he then changed his mind so she married Ray Langton. Their daughter Tracy was born in 1977 and the following year the marriage broke up. Started work at the Corner Shop in 1980 and married Ken Barlow in 1981. Her affair with Mike Baldwin rocked her marriage, but it was finally wrecked in 1990 by Ken's affair with Wendy Crozier. Deidre was once a councillor. In 1994, she fell for waiter Samir Rachid whilst holidaying in Morocco. She paid for him to come to England and they married. Their happiness was shortlived as he died under mysterious circumstances in 1995.

SAMIR RACHID

· Al Nedjari ·

1994-95 Deirdre Barlow's third husband. He was twenty-one-years-old when he married her, she was thirty-nine. He died on his way to hospital to donate a kidney to Deirdre's daughter Tracy.

EDDIE RAMSDEN

· William Ivory ·

1989-90 Builder who fell for barmaid Tina Fowler. He proposed to her to find a mother for his son Jamie, but jilted her during her hen night when Jamie's mother Marie agreed to marry him instead.

MARIE RAMSDEN
née Lancaster

· Joy Blakeman ·

1990 Eddie's estranged wife who befriended Don Brennan while Eddie was serving a prison sentence for GBH. The Brennans tried to help her out financially, but she found them too interfering.

MAGGIE REDMAN
née Dunlop

· Jill Kerman ·

1982-94 Florist who fell for Mike Baldwin and had his son, Mark. She refused to marry Mike and instead wed an old friend Harry Redman. Together they stood against Mike's attempts to influence Mark's life. After Harry's death she started a relationship with Mark's teacher Ken Barlow only to find he was Mike's arch enemy. She was upset when Mark befriended Mike and Mike sent him to a private school. In 1994, she moved to Felixstowe to marry again, taking Mark away from Mike.

MARK REDMAN

· Thomas Hawkeswood, Christopher Oakes and Chris Cook ·

1983-94 Mike Baldwin and Maggie Dunlop's son. He was brought up thinking Harry Redman was his father and was amazed to learn from Tracy Barlow that it was really Mike. Mike paid for him to go to Oakhill Grammar School but he disliked Mike's interference in his life. He was relieved to move away from Weatherfield and Mike to start a new life in Felixstowe.

CONCEPTA REGAN
née Riley, prev. Hewitt

· Doreen Keogh ·

1960-75 First barmaid at the Rovers who married Harry Hewitt in 1961. She struggled to be accepted by Harry's daughter Lucille. Her son Christopher was born in 1962 and kidnapped months later. Concepta suffered a breakdown before he was found two days later. In 1964, the Hewitts emigrated to Ireland. They returned for Elsie Tanner's wedding in 1967, but Harry was killed and she returned to Ireland a widow. In 1972 she married a young mechanic, Sean Regan. In 1975 she visited the Street to see Bet Lynch off when she discovered Sean had made a pass at her.

MALCOLM REID

· Shane Rimmer ·

1988 Canadian who adopted Audrey Roberts' son Stephen. He visited the Roberts and begged Audrey to leave Alf for him, but she refused.

ANITA REYNOLDS

· Elizabeth Sladen·

1970 Barmaid at the Flying Horse who had an affair with Len Fairclough despite the fact he had gone to school with her father.

NIGEL RIDLEY

· John Basham ·

1989-90 Newton and Ridley executive who had an affair with Tina Fowler and tried to turn the Rovers into a theme park.

SARAH RIDLEY

· Carole Nimmons ·

1983-85 Newton and Ridley executive who made Bet Lynch licencee of the Rovers.

STELLA RIGBY

· Vivienne Ross ·

1985-93 Landlady of the White Swan and Bet Gilroy's friend/foe. She fell out with Bet in 1989 when Alec thought Stella's husband Paul had been having an affair with her.

BRENDA RILEY

· Eileen Kennally ·

1966 Ran the Rovers Return when the Walkers holidayed in Ireland. She saw off Ray Langton when he made a violent pass at Lucille Hewitt.

DAVID ROBBINS

· Jon Rollason ·

1963-71 Gamesteacher at Bessie St School who lodged at No.9 with colleague Ken Barlow. He moved into the flat over Frank Barlow's shop, but left after Ken's wife Valerie declared her love for him. After Val's death, he and Ken were reconciled and they started a jazz band.

ALF ROBERTS OBE

· Bryan Mosley ·

1961- Twice Mayor of Weatherfield, Alf started as a GPO sorter, working with Frank Barlow. Following the death, in 1972, of his wife Phyllis, he courted Maggie Clegg and was heart-broken when she married someone else. He became a councillor in 1968 and was elected Mayor in 1973, his Mayoress being Annie Walker. He lost his council seat in 1987 when Deirdre Barlow beat him, but four years later won the seat back and was made Mayor in 1994. In 1976, Alf had a relationship with canteen lady Donna Parker, but she ran off with his money. Two years later he married Renee Bradshaw and moved into the Corner Shop which she ran. He was in a coma and then suffered a personality change after a lorry crashed into the Rovers in 1979. Following this, he left the GPO to help Renee run the shop. Renee was killed in 1980 and he remained at the shop, marrying Audrey Potter in 1985. They lived at No.11, Coronation Street before moving to leafy Grassmere Drive. In 1994, Alf retired.

AUDREY ROBERTS
née Potter

· Sue Nicholls·

1979- Gail Platt's mother (she cannot remember who Gail's father was), she arrived in the Street to celebrate Gail's engagement to Brian and quickly settled in, flirting with the menfolk. Between boyfriends and jobs, she visited the Tilsleys, and for a few months in 1981 she lodged at No.11 with Elsie Tanner. That year she worked in the Corner Shop for Alf Roberts but ran off when he decided he wanted to marry her. In 1985 she returned, fed up with drifting through life, and courted and married Alf. Audrey has a son, Stephen, living in Canada, but turned down an offer from old flame Malcolm Reid to emigrate to Canada with him. She hated working in the shop and was grateful when Alf retired. In 1994, she was made Mayoress of Weatherfield and enjoyed buying new clothes.

RENEE ROBERTS
née Bradshaw

· Madge Hindle ·

1987-80 Supermarket checkout assistant who bought the Corner Shop with her life savings in order to provide a stable home for her brother Terry, but he soon left the Street to join the army. She fought Annie Walker in court and was successful in being granted a licence to sell alcohol. She married Alf Roberts in March 1978 despite her family's warnings that he was only after the shop. The couple decided to sell up and move to Grange before she was killed in a car crash in July 1980.

MICHELLE ROBINSON

· *Stephanie Tague* ·

1985 Andrea Clayton's best friend who went out with Kevin Webster. She went off him when he proposed marriage.

GERTIE ROBSON

· *Connie Merigold* ·

1974 Busybody who was employed as caretaker at the Community Centre, where she lived with nephew Gary Turner. When Gary left to become a professional footballer, she felt lonely at the flat and left to become resident housekeeper to Freda Barry at the Flying Horse.

HANIF RUPARELL

· *Ayub Khan-Din* ·

1993-93 Owner of Onyx Fashions who employed Angie Freeman as an in-house designer. He had an affair with Denise Osbourne, but backed off when she declared her love for him. She later accused him of making abusive phone calls but he had the perfect alibi – he was out of the country on his honeymoon.

TOM SCHOFIELD

· *Tom Halliday* ·

1965-73 Ena Sharples' great nephew from America. His wife Faye-Marie took a shine to Ken and Ena was shocked when Tom explained they had an open marriage.

BRENDAN SCOTT

· *Milton John* ·

1991-93 Bettabuy area manager who took redundancy to buy Alf's Mini Market. Renamed it Best Buys and transformed it into an olde worlde shope. He worked so hard he suffered a fatal heart-attack on the shop-floor in front of assistant Emily Bishop.

DEBI SCOTT

· *Lesley Clare O'Neil* ·

1993 Brendan's merry widow. Following his death, the former Miss Bettabuy was chased by Reg Holdsworth who wanted to buy the shop at a discount price. She eventually auctioned off the shop.

ELSIE SEDDON

· *Brenda Elder* ·

1986-90 Sally Webster's mother. Following the death of her violent husband Eddie, she moved to Scarborough and opened a boarding-house.

GINA SEDDON

· *Julie Foy* ·

1988-89 Sally's sister who moved in with the Websters at No.13 to escape her domineering father. She slept with Martin Platt behind boyfriend Billy Wyatt's back, resulting in a fight when Billy found out. She left the area with £1,000 from the insurance following her father's death.

JOSS SHACKLETON

· *Harold Goodwin* ·

1990 The man who claimed to be Vera Duckworth's father and the illegitimate grandson of Edward the Seventh. When he died in 1993, Vera spent all her savings on giving him a proper funeral.

ENA SHARPLES

· *Violet Carson* ·

1960-80 Caretaker of the Mission Glad Tidings until it was demolished in 1968. In the early days, she fought to uphold the Street's morals, taking on Elsie Tanner and Hilda Ogden. With Minnie Caldwell and Martha Longhurst and a glass of milk stout, she held court in the Rovers' Snug. Her family life was harsh because her vicious, criticizing tongue alienated her daughters Vera and Madge. She had one son Ian who had died as a babe in arms and she never remarried after her husband Alfred died in the Depression. In 1965, Ena inherited No.11 making her Elsie's landlady and she soon sold the house. For most of her life she struggled for cash and was once found guilty of shoplifting. Ena continuously took on those in authority over injustice – she organized a sit-in at an OAP hut to stop its demolition, and fought Laurie Frazer's plans to open a night-club in the Street. When the Mission was demolished she looked after the Community Centre but old age caused

her problems – she collapsed three times with heart problems. However, the Street's residents always closed ranks around her, fighting off those who tried to replace her at the Centre. Even mild-mannered Ernie Bishop brawled with a Councillor when he tried to evict her. In 1980 she went to stay with her old friend Henry Foster in St Anne's, and never returned.

LORNA SHAWCROSS

· *Luan Peters* ·

1971 Nurse who lodged at the Rovers for a couple of months and went out with Billy Walker. He was heartbroken when she left to marry someone else.

SEAN SKINNER

· *Terence Hillyer* ·

1994– Betting shop owner, Sean opened a shop on Rosamund Street and employed Des Barnes as his manager. Following his divorce from wife Lynne he made a pass at Liz McDonald, but she rejected him.

DAVE SMITH

· *Reginald Marsh* ·

1962–76 Cockney bookie who ruled as top dog in Weatherfield in the early 1970s, keeping the villains under control and protecting the interests of the residents. His on-off affair with Elsie Tanner lasted for ten years, during which time he also dated Irma Barlow. Although his main business concern was his betting shop on Victoria Street, he also owned Weatherfield County football club and for a while ran a hair salon. After fire gutted the warehouse on Coronation Street he attempted to open a cash-and-carry warehouse on the site, but met with too much opposition from the residents. He left to run a country club in Kennilworth with Blanche Hunt.

LILIAN SMITH

· *Rhoda Lewis* ·

1969 Dave Smith's estranged wife. He agreed to divorce her so she could marry villain Leo Slater.

JOHN SPENCER

· *Jonathan Barber* ·

1981 Local lad fostered by the Fairclough whilst his mother was in hospital.

EFFIE SPICER

· *Anne Dyson* ·

1968–69 Widow of a famous sports' journalist, Mrs Spicer moved into one of the maisonettes built on the Street and fell foul of her neighbour Ena Sharples who thought her a snob. Effie soon fell into debt and then left the area.

MARIE STANTON

· *Lois Baxter* ·

1976–77 Divorcee who made a play for Mike Baldwin when working as a machinist at his factory.

JEAN STARK

· *Rennie Lister* ·

1961 Machinist at the raincoat factory who rebelled against her strict parents to lodge with Christine Hardman at No.13. She had a brief fling with Jed Stone.

WILK STOCKWELL

· *Terence Longdon* ·

1981–82 Mike Baldwin's business associate who left his wife Doreen for Elsie Tanner. Doreen created such a fuss that an order was cancelled and Baldwins was put on a three-day week.

JED STONE

· *Kenneth Cope* ·

1961–66 Petty criminal who became a surrogate son for Minnie Caldwell. He came to the Street to entice Dennis Tanner back into a life of crime, but had a quick personality change to endear him into Minnie's heart. He was full of get-rich-quick schemes which always seemed to backfire, he ran a market stall, opened an auction room, a boarding kennels and stored old waxworks. His attempts at romance – with Jean Stark and Doreen Lostock – were even less successful than his business ventures. In 1966, he was arrested for handling stolen goods and sent to prison for nine months.

GARY STRAUSS

· *Callen Angelo* ·

1967–70 American army sergeant, and friend of Gregg Flint and Steve Tanner. He dated Lucille Hewitt and Bet Lynch during his stay in Weatherfield and left after Joe Donnelli's suicide.

PAULINE STRINGER

· *Patricia Browning* ·

1980 Supervisor at Baldwin's Casuals brought in by Mike to shake up the girls. They had a brief affair, but he soon got tired of her socialist values.

JANICE STUBBS

· *Angela Bruce* ·

1978 Waitress at Dawson's café on Rosamund Street who had an affair with Ray Langton and broke up his marriage.

SANDRA STUBBS

· *Sally Watts* ·

1988-89 The Rovers cleaner who struggled to bring her thirteen-year-old son Jason up single-handed. Her husband Ronnie tracked her down and beat her up before being seen off by the police. Sandra was gutted when Gloria Todd stole her boyfriend Pete Shaw, and left the Rovers to live with her mother when she feared Jason was mixing with the wrong crowd.

PERCY SUGDEN

· *Bill Waddington* ·

1983- Having driven a mobile canteen across the Western Desert, Percy attempted to organize the Street's residents into an army of residents fighting under his banner of Home Watch. Interfering and pompous Percy first came to the Street when he was made caretaker of the Community Centre. A widower (wife Mary had died of cancer in 1978), Percy had no children, but his niece Elaine stayed with him before marrying Bill Webster. Percy has always been attracted to Emily Bishop – she took him in at No.3 when he retired from the Centre – but she views him only as a lodger. Phyllis Pearce pursued him for years but he was never interested in her. In 1993, he proposed to Olive Clark. She turned him down but Maud Grimes accepted him. However, he finished with Maud when he discovered she had been unfaithful to her husband during the war. Percy retired from the Centre in 1988, since when he has served as a lollipop man and Bettabuy's Father Christmas.

'When you've prepared spotted dick and custard for 150 under heavy artillery fire and not allowed one lump in that custard, you can do anything.'

Percy Sugden

RITA SULLIVAN

née Littlewood, prev. Fairclough

· *Barbara Knox* ·

1964- The owner of the Kabin newsagents at No.10 made her first appearance on the Street as an exotic dancer at the Viaduct Sporting Club. Rita drifted from her dancing career into singing ballads and love songs in nightclubs and sleazy men's clubs. In 1972, she started a relationship with Len Fairclough, whom she eventually married in 1977. At that time she was calling herself Rita Bates, but later she revealed herself to be only Harry Bates' common-law wife. During her on-off affair with Len, she had relationships

S

'I, Rita, take thee, Edward John Sullivan, to be my lawfully-wedded husband.'

with other men, notably Ken Barlow, Jimmy Graham and Benny Lewis. In 1973 Len employed her at the Kabin and she started her working relationship with Mavis Riley. Her marriage to Len was stormy but together they fostered Sharon Gaskell. After Len's death in 1983, Rita shied away from men until, in 1987, she moved Alan Bradley into No.7. She twice refused to marry Alan (once outside the registry office when he tricked her to going to her own wedding) and eventually he turned against her, cheated her out of money and then tried to kill her. When he was released from prison, Rita suffered a nervous breakdown and took a job singing in Blackpool. He followed her, chased her, and was knocked down and killed by a tram. In 1990 Rita moved the Kabin from Rosamund Street to its present site and moved into a flat over the shop. She married Ted Sullivan in 1992 knowing he had a fatal brain tumour. He died a few months later, in her arms.

TED SULLIVAN

· *William Russell* ·

1992 Sweet salesman Ted retired from his job when he learnt he had only months to live. He courted Rita Fairclough in a whirlwind romance and married her in a register office. They had a few precious months together before he died watching Percy Sugden play bowls.

ARNOLD SWAIN

· *George Waring* ·

1980-81 Pet shop owner who married Emily Bishop when he already had a wife, Margaret. When Emily discovered he was a bigamist, he left her and suffered a breakdown, returning to force her into a suicide pact. She escaped his clutches and he was arrested by the police. In December 1981, he died in a hospital for the mentally disturbed.

LEONARD SWINDLEY

· *Arthur Lowe* ·

1960-65 Lay preacher Swindley was jilted at the altar by Emily Nugent. For years, Emily had been his assistant, at first his drapery store and then, when it was taken over, at the chain store Gamma Garments. Swindley, a pompous, selfish man lived in fear of Gamma boss Mr Papagopolous who had a habit of telephoning during a crisis – of which there were many. At the Mission Hall, Swindley had numerous battles with caretaker Ena Sharples, of which he never won a single one. In 1962 he stood for the local elections and came last in the poll. Eventually he left the area to work at Gamma House.

RON SYKES

· *Bobby Knutt* ·

1980-83 Brian Tilsley's boss at Sykes' Garage. In 1982 he went into partnership with Brian, opening another garage, but he soon lost interest and let Brian buy him out.

ARNOLD TANNER

· *Frank Crawshaw* ·

1961-66 First husband of Elsie Tanner, and father of Dennis and Linda. He divorced Elsie to marry Norah Dawson (she owned her own toffee shop), and in later life had to suffer his cantankerous father Wally living over the shop.

DENNIS TANNER

· *Philip Lowrie*·

1960-68 Elsie Tanner's wayward son came out of borstal in 1960 but soon settled down in an attempt to make something of his life. He tried various careers – salesman, warehouse labourer, taxi-driver, hair-stylist, auctioneer, builder's labourer, turf accountant – but he kept returning to his true passion, show business. Dennis worked for the Phillips-Frazer agency as booking clerk, talent scout, compère and even nightclub singer, but was too naive to climb the ladder of success. Women seldom bothered Dennis, although Sandra Petty fell in love with him and pursued him through 1965. He once dated two Swedish sisters, the Olsens, and hired his home, No.11, out to a nine-piece girl's pipe band. In 1968, he fell for cockney Jenny Sutton and, despite Elsie's opposition (she thought Jenny too much like her), they married in the May. Shortly afterwards the couple moved to Bristol where he found work selling hairdressing equipment. In 1973, Elsie visited him in Pentonville Prison where he was serving a sentence for swindling OAPs.

ELSIE TANNER
prev. Howard

· *Patricia Phoenix* ·

1960-83 The Siren of the Street throughout the 1960s, Elsie had a passion for men and got hurt by all of them. Her many lovers included Len Fairclough, Norman Lindley, Dave Smith, Bill Gregory, Laurie Frazer, Jim Mount, Ron Mather and Dan Johnson. Her relationship with Len lasted twenty years but, although he proposed twice, she knew she could never marry him as he was her best friend. She separated from husband Arnold after the war and struggled to bring up Dennis and Linda while entertaining her men friends. In 1967 she married American Steve Tanner who had been her wartime sweetheart. Unfortunately she soon discovered he was a selfish drunk and they separated. Three years later she married Alan Howard and he moved into her home, No.11, where they lived for three years – the longest time she ever spent with one man. When the marriage went through a bad patch they went to live in his native Newcastle, and in 1976 she returned home to the Street alone. In later years, Elsie struggled to keep glamour in her life but she found herself with sleazy one-night stands and dead-end jobs. When we first met Elsie she was working at Miami Modes in the Slightly Better Dress Department, a job she held down, on and off, until 1969. She also worked as a croupier, a model, a laundrette manageress, a florist, a receptionist and a salesperson. At her peak, she supervised checkers at the mail order warehouse and machinists at Baldwin's Casuals. For a time she ran Jim's café, but her last job on the street was working a machine in Baldwin's sweat shop. In 1983, Bill Gregory re-entered her life (she had had an affair with him in 1962). He whisked her off to Portugal to help run his wine bar and gave her story the fairy-tale ending for which she had always longed.

JENNY TANNER
née Sutton

· *Mitzi Rogers* ·

1968 Cockney who came to the Street in search of her hippie sister Monica who had been part of the commune staying at No.11. Jenny fell for Dennis Tanner and stayed on to be near him, working with him in a hotel. They married in May 1968 and moved to Bristol.

STEVE TANNER

· Paul Maxwell·

1967 American GI who returned to Weatherfield to court his wartime sweetheart, Elsie Tanner. They had a fairy-tale wedding and moved into a luxury apartment in Altrincham where the marriage broke up – he gambled and drank and refused to let her mix with her old friends. They left for America when he was posted home, but she returned to England after three months. Steve followed but never saw Elsie again; he was murdered by Joe Donnelli over a gambling debt.

WALLY TANNER

· George Betton ·

1966–68 Elsie Tanner's father-in-law who gave up the life of a tramp to live at No.11 and made a play for Minnie Caldwell.

ALBERT TATLOCK

· Jack Howarth ·

1960–84 Pensioner who was the original occupant of No.1 Coronation Street. He had served in the First World War and never tired of retelling famous battles to those who would listen. Although retired, Albert took a few jobs to earn extra cash – lollipop man, caretaker at the Mission, and Ena Sharples' assistant at the Centre. He spent two years living in Bury where he served as curator at the Lancashire Fusilier Museum. His wife Bessie had died in 1959 and his daughter Beattie seldom visited. During the 1960s his niece Valerie kept an eye on him and, after her death, her husband Ken Barlow took on the responsibility. In 1969, he nearly married Alice Pickens but called it off on the wedding day when the vicar was late getting to church. In 1973, he proposed to Minnie Caldwell, on the basis that they would save money on a joint pension. Minnie accepted his proposal but broke with him when she discovered he had got his facts wrong. His eightieth birthday, in 1975, was celebrated by the residents with a street party. The hardest thing for Albert to live with was the fact that one by one his old comrades died off. Eventually the old soldier died himself at the age of eighty-eight.

EDITH TATLOCK

· Clare Kelly ·

1969–78 Valerie Barlow's mother. Following Val's death she lived at No.3 with Ken and the twins, eventually taking the twins to live in Glasgow as Ken could not cope.

BRENDA TAYLOR

· Marlene Sidaway ·

1990–92 Mother of Kimberley and wife of GPO engineer Randolph. She objected to Kimberley's engagement to Curly Watts and did all in her power to split them up. She succeeded once but they found each other again.

KIMBERLEY TAYLOR

· Suzanne Hall ·

1989–92 Assistant at Bettabuy who fell for Curly 'Norman' Watts and tormented him by refusing to sleep with him until they were married. His lust drove her to break their engagement and she promptly gave her virginity to her cousin Adrian Gosthorpe. In 1992, she joined a computer dating agency and met Curly again. This time she did sleep with him but they separated.

EDDIE THOMAS

· Douglas Austin ·

1964 Len Fairclough's apprentice who helped build the Viaduct Sporting Club, he dated Lucille Hewitt but dumped her for Len's girlfriend, Joyce Lomax.

ROY THORNLEY

· Sidney Livingstone ·

1976 Married sales rep who seduced Gail Potter, taking her virginity, and then stood by while his wife cited her in their divorce.

BERT TISLEY

· Peter Dudley ·

1979–83 Ivy Brennan's first husband and father of Brian. Down-to-earth Bert worked in foundries all his life and never spent more than the odd hour in the pub, preferring to spend his spare time with his family. He was delighted when Brian married Gail and acted as go-between whenever Ivy fell out with her. He lost his job in 1980 and was unemployed for eighteen months. He suffered a mini-stroke and died shortly after being involved in an explosion at Brian's garage.

BRIAN TISLEY

· *Christopher Quinten* ·

1978-89 Mechanic and motorbike fanatic Brian moved to No.5 Coronation Street with his parents Bert and Ivy in February 1979. He quickly became engaged to neighbour Gail Potter and married her despite his mother's misgivings (he was Catholic, she C of E). Throughout his marriage to Gail, Brian enjoyed flirting and got too close to customer Glenda Fox and teenager Sharon Gaskell. Brian believed Gail's place was in the home and, following the birth of their son Nicky, he did all he could to stop her working at Jim's café. In 1981, he appeared in court after stopping a thug stealing from the garage till; the youth brought a charge of unlawful wounding, but Brian was cleared. When Gail had an affair with his cousin Ian Latimer, he divorced her, refusing to believe her daughter Sarah Louise was his. He moved in with Liz Turnbull, but his obsession with Gail and Nicky drove them apart. He was reconciled with Gail when he kidnapped Nicky and held him for four days. He remarried Gail in February 1988, but she never really loved him and he started seeing other women. He was stabbed to death outside a nightclub in 1989.

'You're like summat from the Dark Ages. Women should stay in their place, they're all right in the kitchen, in the bedroom, and that's about it.'

Gail to Brian Tilsley

SAM TINDALL

· *Tom Mennard* ·

1985-89 Percy Sugden's bowls rival who fell for Phyllis Pearce. She led him along to make Percy jealous.

GLORIA TODD

· *Sue Jenkins* ·

1985-88 Rovers' barmaid and Bet Lynch's bridesmaid. She became a regular behind the bar after the Rovers' fire, and became the subject of attention from Bet's boyfriend Frank Mills, Terry Duckworth, Jack Duckworth, Mike Baldwin and Alan Bradley. She had an affair with Alan, until she discovered he was also seeing Rita Fairclough. In 1986, she was reconciled to her mother who had given her away when she was four. She left the district with Pete Shaw, Sandra Stubbs' boyfriend.

BETTY TURPIN

· *Betty Driver* ·

1969- For over twenty-five years Betty has pulled pints at the Rovers and served her famous hot-pot to the regulars. She came to the Street to help her sister Maggie Clegg run the Corner Shop, living above the shop with husband Cyril. Jack Walker took her on at the Rovers and she served under all the licencees – Annie and Billy Walker, Bet and Alec Gilroy. Betty's dark secret was revealed in 1975 – Maggie's son Gordon was actually her's, his father being a sailor, Ted Farrell. Gordon accepted Betty as his mother and she often sees him and his son Peter. When Cyril died in 1974, she suffered a breakdown, but her friends helped her recover. She was mugged in 1982 and her arm broken. In 1994, she took over from Audrey Roberts as Mayoress of Weatherfield.

CYRIL TURPIN

· William Moore ·

1969–72 Betty's police sergeant husband who lived above the Corner Shop and policed the local area. He retired from the force in 1970, after assaulting a convict who had been terrorizing Betty. In 1974, he suffered a fatal heart-attack.

HENRY WAKEFIELD

· Finetime Fontayne ·

1985 Hilda Ogden's lodger at No.13. He left the area when his colleagues at Baldwin's discovered he was a strike-breaker.

ANNIE WALKER

· Doris Speed ·

1960–83 Longest-serving landlady of the Rovers Return, running it with beloved husband Jack until 1970, and then with the help of her barstaff up to her retirement in 1983. As the Street's snob she always saw herself as a cut above the regulars. Her finest hour came when she portrayed Elizabeth the First in a Street pageant, and her worst was when word reached the street that in the 1930s she had portrayed Lady Godiva. Her marriage to Jack was a solid one although she made several attempts to rouse him into passion. She tried to make him jealous by dating other men, including Lionel Petty, but Jack always knew no other man would put up with her melodramatic ways. When Jack died, she took on the licence of the pub and acted as hostess, while staff such as Bet and Betty did most of the work. For a while she struggled on at the pub, living alone, but in 1975 two youths threatened her when they raided the pub after hours. She was forced to take on a resident cellarman, Fred Gee, but she soon turned him into her chauffeur. She passed her driving test in 1977 and bought a Rover 2000 which became her most prized possession. She was heartbroken when Eddie Yeats reversed his bin lorry into it. Mayoress of Weatherfield and President of the Licensed Victuallers for five years, Annie was the ideal committee woman although her education, or rather lack of it, always let her down. She retired in 1983, going to live in Derby with her daughter Joan Davies.

'I can't help wondering where forty years have gone to. It seems like no time at all. They've been happy years for me, Billy.'

Annie Walker

BILLY WALKER

· Kenneth Farrington ·

1961–84 Son of Jack and Annie Walker, he was a trained mechanic. He refused to rot in the Street and spent much of his life in London, disappointing his mother by never marrying. After his father's death he returned

home to help run the pub, but his weakness for gambling led to Annie having to bail him out. When he started gambling with the pub's takings, she sacked him. In the early 1970s he ran the Canal Garage with Alan Howard and became engaged to typist Deirdre Hunt. The wedding was called off when they both had second thoughts. He ran a hotel in Jersey, returning home only when he needed money from Annie. Once he decided to take Deirdre back with him, but Annie blackmailed him into leaving her behind by threatening to withhold the £2,000 he needed to buy into a new hotel. When Annie retired, she paid off all his gambling and business debts but, in return, he was forced to take on the licence of the Rovers. He hated being stuck in Weatherfield and, after selling the pub back to the brewery, returned to Jersey.

JACK WALKER

· *Arthur Leslie* ·

1960-70 The much-loved genial host of the Rovers Return. As well as pulling pints, Jack served as mediator behind the bar, sorting out differences between customers and softening his wife's acid tongue. In 1967 he left Annie, briefly, following a row. He lodged with Albert Tatlock at No.1 but led Annie to believe he was living with Elsie Tanner. Jack was always disappointed in the way his children treated Annie – Billy saw her as an open purse and Joan considered her an embarrassment. In 1965, he suffered a breakdown when he was blackmailed by a man who had caught his ward Lucille Hewitt serving behind the bar when underage. The regulars came to Jack's aid by beating the man up in the Street. Jack died suddenly whilst visiting Joan in Derby in 1970.

GEORGE WARDLE

· *Ron Davies* ·

1985-86 Catholic rugby player who became engaged to Ivy Tilsley. Their plans to marry were cancelled when she discovered he was a divorcee and not a widower. He dumped her for Pauline Walsh, who was more accommodating.

SALLY WATERMAN

· *Vicki Chambers* ·

1983-85 Ken Barlow's secretary at the *Weatherfieeld Recorder.* She fell in love with Ken but was forced to fight her feelings because he refused to be unfaithful to Deirdre. She left for the *Gazette* after putting the nationals onto the story of Mavis Riley winning a second honeymoon when she had never had a first one.

DON WATKINS

· *Kevin Lloyd* ·

1983-84 Manager of the Graffiti Club who stole from the takings and eventually disappeared when boss Mike Baldwin became suspicious.

CURLY WATTS

· *Kevin Kennedy* ·

1983- One-time dustbinman and stargazer. Curly moved to the Street in 1983 when he lodged with Emily Bishop, his parents having moved to Crewe. He went into partnershp with Terry Duckworth collecting antiques, before taking a course in business studies which led to his employment at Bettabuy. Curly lost his virginity in 1988 to Shirley Armitage with whom he shared a flat above the Corner Shop. He proposed to her, but she was not interested in marriage. Kimberley Taylor, Raquel Wolstenhulme and Maureen Naylor were all sexual conquests from Bettabuy, but he lost his heart to design student Angie Freeman with whom he lodged at No.7. They spent two nights together, after which he declared his love, but she broke the news that, although he was her best mate, she did not fancy him. He bought No.7 in 1992. His engagement to Raquel Wolstenhulme ended when Des Barnes proposed to her. She told Curly she did not love him.

JOHNNY WEBB

· *Jack Smethurst* ·

1980-83 Eddie Yeats' binman pal. He lodged at No.13 for a while while Hilda Ogden was away. When she returned, his wife Maureen accused her of being his fancy piece. Hilda saw her off and then turned on Johnny.

BILL WEBSTER

· *Peter Armitage* ·

1984- Builder who rented Len Fairclough's yard from Rita and bought No.11 Coronation Street. He struggled to bring up his teenage children Kevin and Debbie before, in January 1985, he married Elaine Prior and settled in Southampton. He returned in 1995, his marriage over

DEBBIE WEBSTER

· *Sue Devaney* ·

1984-85 Kevin's younger sister. She left school with no qualifications to work at Jim's café and upset Bill by going out with a biker, Dazz Isherwood. She went to live in Southampton with Bill and Elaine.

ELAINE WEBSTER
née Prior

· *Judy Gridley* ·

1984-85 Percy Sugden's hairdressing niece who married Bill Webster.

KEVIN WEBSTER

· *Michael Le Vell* ·

1983- Mechanic who came to the Street after repairing Alf Roberts' car, he was taken on by Brian Tilsley and his family moved into No.11. When the Websters moved to Southampton, Kevin remained, lodging with Emily Bishop and Hilda Ogden. He married Sally Seddon in 1986, having dated Michelle Robinson first. When Hilda left, he and Sally bought No.13. They had two daughters – Rosie was born in 1990, and Sophie in 1994. Kevin is one of life's workers. Sally used to push him to buy his own garage but Kevin refused to consider it. He always felt uncomfortable with book-keeping and giving orders. As well as working for Brian, he worked for the Caseys and now Mike Baldwin. In 1993 he was fined £800 in court after being found guilty of corrupting the course of justice when he covered for Steve McDonald in a driving offence.

SALLY WEBSTER
née Seddon

· *Sally Whittaker* ·

1986- When Sally married Kevin in October 1986 she escaped from her violent, oppressive family and changed from a loud-mouthed, cheeky urchin into a respectable figure of the Street. Sally worked at the Rovers and Alf's Mini Market before becoming a registered child-minder. She gave birth to daughter Rosie in the back seat of Don Brennan's taxi, en route to the hospital. In 1993, tax inspector Joe Broughton attempted to lure her away from Kevin but she refused to break up her marriage.

JON WELCH

· *David Michaels* ·

1994-95 Hairdresser who rented a chair at Denise Osbourne's salon. He left when she rejected a pass he made.

CHALKIE WHITELY

· *Teddy Turner* ·

1982-83 Binman occupant of No.9 who looked after his grandson Craig whilst his son Bob served in the Merchant Navy. He was heartbroken when Bob took Craig to live in Australia. A five-horse accumulator gave him the money to visit Bob and he settled in Australia.

DEREK WILTON

· *Peter Baldwin* ·

1976- After a twelve-year courtship, Derek Bernard Wilton finally married Mavis Riley in November 1988. They had nearly married before, in 1984. A salesman by profession (now in stationery) Derek's lowest point was in 1992 when he took a job as junior caretaker at a tough Weatherfield School. Prior to marrying Mavis he was married, briefly, to Angela Hawthorne (now his boss).

MAVIS WILTON
née Riley

· *Thelma Barlow* ·

1971- Mavis came to the Street as Emily Nugent's friend from the mail order warehouse and stayed to become Rita's assistant at the Kabin, a post she has filled for over twenty years. Mavis is a very creative person, and met some of her boyfriends during artistic ventures. Potter Victor Pendlebury bought a cottage in Saddleworth and gave her a key, but as marriage was not on offer, she turned him down. Artist Maurice Dodds begged her to pose nude for him, but she refused as she had to consider her reputation. Her husband Derek is not in the least bit creative and many of their rows are caused by his insensitive attitude. Before marrying Derek, Mavis was very bitter about the way she was still single while Emily married twice. However, when she first got the chance to marry Derek in 1984 she felt she could not go through with it and it was a further four years before they married. Mavis has a pet budgie called Beauty.

RUTH WINTER

· *Collette O'Neil* ·

1966 Social worker who ran the Community Centre in the old Mission.

She won Ena Sharples' respect by standing up to thugs. Len Fairclough fell for her, but she left for Rome to marry her fiancée.

RAQUEL WOLSTENHULME

· *Sarah Lancashire* ·

1991– Miss Bettabuy 1991 left the area to embark on a modelling career only to return in tears after appearing half-naked in sleazy publications. She became the resident barmaid at the Rovers, making up for her lack of talent and intelligence by her ability to attract the male customers. Her boyfriends have tended to use and abuse her – Wayne Farrell the professional football who two-timed her, press officer Gordon Blinkhorn who tried to dominate her, and Des Barnes with whom she lived and planned to marry before discovering his affair with her colleague Tanya Pooley. She agreed to marry Curly Watts, but jilted him at their engagement party. One man who treated her well was Ken Barlow who gave her French lessons and boosted her confidence enough for her to take her modelling seriously.

EDDIE YEATS

· *Geoffrey Hughes* ·

1974–87 The Ogdens' binman lodger originally came to the Street on parole from prison to lodge with Minnie Caldwell, breaking his parole in order to have a date with Bet Lynch and was arrested at her flat. When he returned to the Street he helped Stan Ogden on his window round and began a friendship with the Ogdens which would last for years. With Stan he embarked on many get-rich quick schemes – hiring out a timid guard dog, brewing beer in the bath, selling beer from an ice-cream van on Sundays, renting out rooms at No.13 in Hilda's absence. In 1976, he redecorated the house but ran out of cut-price wallpaper, so introduced Hilda to the mural. Hilda refused to let him lodge at No.13 until he took a serious job, so in 1980 he settled down to life as a dustbinman. In 1982, he took up CB radio, called himself Slim Jim and fell in love with Stardust Lil. She turned out to be Marion Willis. They married in 1983. They moved to Bury to nurse her mother and their daughter Dawn was born in 1984.

'Slim Jim' and 'Stardust Lil' were handles adopted by Eddie and Marion Yeats.

MARION YEATS
née Willis

· *Veronica Doran* ·

1982–83 Assistant at the florist shop owned by Maggie Redman. She lodged with Elsie Tanner at No.11 while courting Eddie Yeats. The couple quickly brought forward the date of their engagement when Marion found out that she was pregnant. After they got married they moved away from the Street and went to live in Bury to look after Marion's mother, Winifred, who had suffered a stroke.

MIKLOS ZADIC

· *Paul Stassino* ·

1968 Hungarian demolition expert who oversaw the demise of the Mission Hall. He fell for Emily Nugent and introduced her to Communism.

Lists, Facts and Figures

A is for... ANIMALS

Pets have never featured heavily in Coronation Street, which makes the appearances of animals all the more noticeable. The most famous Street pet was Minnie Caldwell's cat, Bobby. In fact she had two cats, but the first disappeared in 1968 after six years walking the cobbles. Distraught Minnie took in a stray which she named Sunny Jim, but a few months later she renamed him Bobby. In 1973, Bobby ate Gilbert, a homing pigeon belonging to Albert Tatlock. Birds have played very important roles in the Street. Jack Duckworth inherited his pigeons from Chalkie Whitely when he bought No. 9 in 1983. He was devastated when a fox, named Freddie by nature-lover Mavis Wilton, ran amok in the backyard killing two of his birds. Recently, he spent a night on the rooftop attempting to rescue his favourite bird Fergie from Curly Watts' observatory. In 1980, Mavis found a budgie in her chimney breast and took him in, calling him Harry. she changed the name to Harriette when two years latter the bird laid an egg. Harriette died in 1990 of shock, during the move to No. 4 Coronation Street. A couple of weeks later, a bird flew into the house and Mavis kept it, only to discover it was a lost pet named Boris. As Mavis had grown attached to Harriette/Boris, Derek bought another budgie and returned it to Boris' owners, so Mavis had to rename him Harry. Sadly, Harry died in November 1994. Mavis had been horrified when, in 1983, Percy Sugden had attempted to mate the original Harriette with his own bird Randy. Recently, Percy was shocked when Emily Bishop revealed that Randy had died in 1988 and she had replaced him with another bird.

The first animals to appear on the show were whippets owned by Harry Hewitt. He swapped them for a greyhound, Lucky Lolita. Years later, Fred Gee and Alf Roberts bought a greyhound called Fred's Folly but it was not a runner. Nor was Harry's Luck, a greyhound acquired by Don Brennan, who promptly gave birth to six pups. Fury was the name of an Alsatian bought by Eddie Yeats to hire out as a guard dog. Her first and last position was guarding Len Fairclough's yard, because she was stolen with a load of lead piping. Bet Gilroy surprised husband Alec in 1988 when she took in an Alsatian called Rover. Alec distrusted the dog and paid a lad to claim the dog as his lost pet. The Duckworths had a miserable Christmas in 1990 because they spent three hours locked in their bedroom to escape Boomer, an excitable dog that Jack had bought Vera as a present. The dog made a grab for the turkey dinner and trapped its new owners upstairs while it wolfed the lot.

B is for ... BIRTHS

There have been seventeen births in Coronation Street, four of which involved babies who have never appeared. The birth of Tommy Duckworth was the first time viewers went into a delivery room, and Rosie Webster was born in the back of Don Brennan's taxi.

12.6.61 to Linda and Ivan Cheveski, a 7lbs 2½oz son, Paul.
6.8.62 to Concepta and Harry Hewitt, a 7lbs 3oz son, Christopher.
15.4.65 to Valerie and Kenneth Barlow, twins – 5lbs 3oz Susan Ida and 4lbs 11oz Peter.
20.11.68 to Irma and David Barlow in Australia, an 8lbs son, Darren.
21.1.76 to Trevor and Polly Ogden in Chesterfield, an 8lbs 6oz daughter, Jayne.
24.1.77 to Deirdre and Ray Langton, an 8lbs 4oz daughter, Tracy Lynette.
31.12.80 to Gail and Brian Tilsley, a 7lbs 2oz son, Nicholas Paul.
13.4.83 to Maggie Redman, a 6lbs 10oz son, Mark. In 1992, Mark's year of birth was changed to 1981 for the storyline.
23.5.84 to Marion and Eddie Yeats in Bury, a 9lbs 2oz daughter, Dawn.
25.3.85 to Caroline and Gordon Clegg in Wimbledon, a 7lbs 2oz son, Peter.
28.1.87 to Gail and Brian Tilsley, a

4lbs daughter, Sarah Louise.
24.12.90 to Kevin and Sally Webster, a 7lbs 5oz daughter, Rosie.
25.12.90 to Gail Tilsley and Martin Platt, an 8lbs son, David.
9.9.92 to Lisa and Terry Duckworth, a 6lbs 4oz son, Tommy.
4.11.94 to Sally and Kevin Webster, a 7lbs 5 oz daughter, Sophie.
4.1.95 to Denise Osbourne and Ken Barlow, an 8lb 5oz son, Daniel.

C is for... CREDITS

The end credits on Coronation Street have hardly changed over the years. Originally, the names of the cast were superimposed over the houses where the characters lived. For a time in the mid 1960s the names rolled over a picture of a gutter in a cobbled Street, but then switched to a smokey landscape of rooftops and chimneys. When Ken married Deirdre, the credits rolled over a selection of wedding photographs, and at the end of Emily and Ernest Bishops' wedding, they rolled over the images of Albert and Minnie walking down the Street while a steel band played the theme tune. The theme tune was written by composer, conductor, arranger and producer Eric Spear. He joined the BBC in 1939 and arranged an average of 150 shows a year. In 1952, he became famous for the theme 'Meet Mister Callaghan' which was played at the Garrick theatre, starring Terence de Marney. In 1960, he moved to Guernsey from Finchley and it was there that he wrote the theme tune which has become world-famous. The production team had sent him the first five scripts in 1960 and Eric in return sent a tape of himself playing the music on a piano. Eric Spear died in Southampton hospital on 3 November 1966.

D is for... DEATHS

Since May Hardman's demise in Episode 7, there have been sixty deaths in Coronation Street, including two budgies. Of these sixty-one, only twelve have been shown on screen, and twelve of the characters have never appeared. Ken Barlow has suffered the most – he has lost mother, father, brother, nephew and two wives.

31.12.60 May Hardman, *heart attack*
11.9.61 Ida Barlow, *run over by a bus*
4.7.62 Amy Carlton, *old age*
12.10.62 Colin Appleby, *car crash*
27.1.64 Susan Schofield, *run over by a lorry*
13.5.64 Martha Longhurst, *heart-attack*
18.10.64 Nellie Bailey, *cancer*
22.3.65 Alice Raynould, *old age*
15.9.65 Robert Maxwell, *heart-attack*
11.1.67 Vera Lomax, *brain tumour*
11.5.67 Sonia Peters, *crushed under rubble*
4.9.67 Harry Hewitt, *crushed under a van*
28.9.68 Steve Tanner, *pushed down stairs*
5.11.69 Reg Ellis, *coach crash*
8.4.70 David Barlow, *car crash*
9.4.70 Darren Barlow, *car crash*
30.60.70 Jack Walker, *heart-attack*
12.12.70 Joe Donnelli, *shot himself*
27.1.71 Valerie Barlow, *electrocuted*
18.9.72 Phyllis Roberts, *cancer*
7.5.73 Tom Schofield, *old age*
25.2.74 Cyril turpin, *heart-attack*
29.1.75 Lynne Johnson, *battered by husband*
9.7.75 Martin Downes, *car crash*
21.4.75 Frank Barlow, *old age*
1.10.75 Edna Gee, *burnt in fire*
10.11.75 Jerry Booth, *heart-attack*
21.2.77 Janet Barlow, *overdose*
17.8.77 Eddie Riley, *old age*
11.1.78 Ernest Bishop, *shot*
30.7.80 Renee Roberts, *car crash*
12.11.80 Monty Shawcross, *old age*
22.12.80 Arnold Swain, *mental illness*
4.7.82 Frankie Baldwin, *heart-attack*
18.5.83 Archie Crabtree, *stroke*
7.12.83 Len Fairclough, *car crash*
16.1.84 Bert Tilsley, *mental illness*
14.5.84 Albert Tatlock, *old age*
21.11.84 Stan Ogden, *old age*
3.6.85 Don Ashton, *drowned*
6.1.86 Pat Bradley, *run over by a car*
23.4.86 Ada Arrowsmith, *old age*
23.11.87 Joan Lowther, *heart-attack*
11.1.89 Eddie Seddon, *lorry crash*
15.2.89 Brian Tilsley, *stabbed*
8.12.89 Alan Bradley, *run over by a tram*
23.3.90 Harriette the budgie, *shock*
17.8.90 Peter Ingram, *heart-attack*
13.2.91 Amy Burton, *heart-attack*
5.7.91 Joyce Shaw, *heart-attack*
19.7.91 Tim and Sandra Arden, *car crash*
2.1.92 Katie McDonald, *premature baby*
9.9.92 Ted Sullivan, *brain tumour*
12.2.93 Lisa Duckworth, *brain damage*

5.5.93 Les Curry, *heart-attack*
20.8.93 Brendan Scott, *heart-attack*
8.11.93 Joss Shackleton, *old age*
25.3.94 Mandy Baker, *cardiac arrest*
4.11.94 Harry the budgie, *old age*
2.6.94 Samir Rachid, *blow to the head*

E is for... ELSIE'S MEN

During a row in 1984 with daughter-in-law Gail, Ivy Tilsley told her what she thought of her mother Audrey: 'She's had more men than Elsie Tanner, and she set a world record!' In fact, the number of Audrey's men friends never came near Elsie's list. Elsie remains the most courted Street lady:

1960-61 First husband Arnold Tanner
1961 Sales rep Walter Fletcher
1961 Police detective Arthur Dewhurst
1961-62 Chief Petty Officer Bill Gregory
1962 Bookie Dave Smith
1963 Builder Len Fairclough
1963-64 Theatrical agent Laurie Frazer
1964 Len Fairclough again
1965 Engineer Norman Lindley
1965 Solicitor Robert Maxwell
1965-66 GPO engineer Jim Mount
1967 Conman Percy Bridge
1967 Dave Smith again
1967-68 Second husband Steve Tanner
1968-69 Dave Smith yet again
1969-76 Third husband Alan Howard
1970 Bill Gregory again
1971 Personnel manager Dennis Maxwell
1977 Hotel manager Ted Brownlow
1978-79 Taxi driver Ron Mather
1980 Lorry driver Dan Johnson
1981 Engineer Wally Randle
1981 Businessman Bill Fielding
1982 Businessman Wilf Stockwell
1982 Conman Geoff Siddall
1984 Bill Gregory yet again

F is for... FUNERALS

Although there have been sixty deaths in the Street, the viewers have not been invited to many funerals. Residents have been seen to prepare for a funeral, with flowers arriving and everyone dressed in black, but glimpses of hearths or coffins have been few.

1961 Ida Barlow's funeral was attended by Frank Barlow, Kenneth Barlow, Valerie Tatlock, Albert Tatlock, Annie Walker and Esther Hayes.
1964 Martha Longhurst's funeral was attended by Ena Sharples, Minnie Caldwell, Leonard Swindley, Emily Nugent, Jack Walker, Annie Walker, Elsie Tanner, Frank Barlow and Harry Hewitt.
1971 Valerie Barlow's funeral was attended by Ken Barlow, Frank Barlow, Albert Tatlock, Esther Hayes, Irma Barlow, Ena Sharples, Minnie Caldwell, Beattie Pearson, Dave Robins and Lucille Hewitt.
1974 Cyril Turpin's funeral was attended by Betty Turpin, Maggie Clegg, Bet Lynch, Len Fairclough, Ernie Bishop and Emily Bishop.
1978 Ernie Bishop's funeral was attended by Emily Bishop, Ivy Tilsley, Suzie Birchall, Mavis Riley, Annie

Maggie Clegg comforts Betty Turpin at Cyril's funeral

Walker, Mike Baldwin and Elsie Tanner.

1980 Renee Roberts' funeral was attended by Alf Roberts, Daisy Hibbert, Hilda Ogden, Eddie Yeats, Bet Lynch, Betty Turpin, Mike Baldwin, Ken Barlow and Annie Walker.

1983 Len Fairclough's funeral was attended by Rita Fairclough, Sharon Gaskell, Mavis Riley, Elsie Tanner, Mike Baldwin, Emily Bishop, Fred Gee, Betty Turpin and Alf Roberts.

1984 Stan Ogden's funeral was attended by Hilda Ogden, Trevor Ogden, Billy Walker, Betty Turpin, Fred Gee, Ken Barlow, Mike Baldwin, Ivy Tilsley and Vera Duckworth.

1989 Brian Tilsley's funeral was attended by Gail Tilsley, Nicky Tilsley, Ivy Brennan, Don Brennan, Alf Roberts, Audrey Roberts, Kevin Webster, Sally Webster and Phyllis Pearce.

1989 Alan Bradley's funeral was attended by Jenny Bradley, Martin Platt, Kevin and Sally Webster.

1993 Terry Duckworth and Des Barnes nearly fought at the graveside when Lisa Duckworth was buried. Jack and Vera Duckworth, Geoff and Doreen Horten also attended.

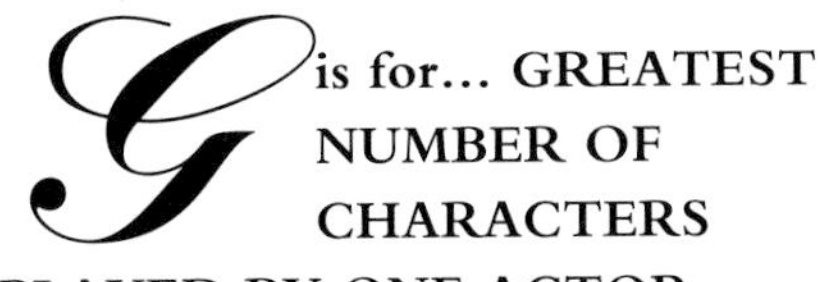

is for... GREATEST NUMBER OF CHARACTERS PLAYED BY ONE ACTOR

At the last count, 14 actors have appeared as five characters, including Roy Barraclough, George Waring and Bill Waddington. Peter Ellis and Alan Partington have played six characters. George Malpass has played seven. Brenda Elder and John Pickles have appeared as eight different characters, John playing mainly policemen and Brenda playing a variety of roles, from a shop lifter at the Kabin, to a loud mouthed employee at the Warehouse to Sally's mother Elsie Seddon.

H is for... HOTPOT

Betty Turpin has been serving hotpot at the Rovers since 1973 when Annie Walker put it on the menu. Here is the recipe:

BETTY'S HOTPOT

1½lb (675g) neck of lamb, cubed
1½lb (675g) potatoes, peeled and thinly sliced
1 large or 2 medium onions, roughly chopped
¾ pint (425ml) light stock or hot water
1 tablespoon Worcestershire sauce
1 bayleaf
1 tablespoon flour
1 oz (25g) dripping and 1oz (25g) butter
or 2oz (50g) butter
salt and pepper to season

Preheat the oven to 170°C/325°F/gas mark 5. Melt the dripping or 1oz (25g) butter over a high heat in a heavy-bottomed frying pan until the fat smokes. Seal the meat and continue frying until nicely browned. Remove the pieces from the pan to a deep casserole or divide among four individual high-sided, ovenproof dishes. Turn down the heat to medium. Fry the onions in the pan juices, adding a little more butter or dripping if necessary. When the onions are soft and starting to brown, sprinkle on the flour and stir in to soak up the fat and the juices. As the flour paste starts to colour, start adding stock or water a few tablespoons at a time, stirring vigorously to avoid lumps. Gradually add the rest of the liquid and bring to a simmer, stirring continuously, add the Worcestershire sauce and season to taste.

Pour the onions and liquid over the meat and mix well. Add the bay leaf.

Arrange the potatoes over the meat in overlapping layers, seasoning each layer. Dot the top layer with the remainder of the butter.

Cover the dish and place on the top shelf of the oven for 2 hours.Uncover and cook for a further 30 minutes. If the potatoes are not brown by this point, turn up the oven and cook for a further 15 minutes, or finish off under the grill, brushing the potato slices with more butter if they look too dry.

I is for... IN CHARGE – THE PRODUCERS

'I think the role of the producer on Coronation Street is an unusual one; it's not so much driving the programme, it's more steering it

H.V. Kershaw

Producers Reynolds and Pritchard, with the current writing team, including casting director, storyliners and archivist

away from problems,' says Carolyn Reynolds, Executive Producer. There have been twenty-five producers who have moulded the Street in the last thirty-five years.

Stuart Latham 1960-61
Derek Granger 1961-62 directed the first episode
H.V. Kershaw 1962-63 started as script editor on the programme
Margaret Morris 1963-64 had cast the original characters
Tim Aspinall 1964

H.V. Kershaw 1964-65
Howard Baker 1965 for many years a Street director
H.V. Kershaw 1965-66
Peter Eckersley 1966
H.V. Kershaw 1966-67
Jack Rosenthal 1967 wrote the award-winning Bar Mitzvah Boy
Michael Cox 1967-68
Richard Everitt 1968 was floor manager for the first episode
Richard Doubleday 1968
John Finch 1968-69 went on to create Sam and Family at War
H.V. Kershaw 1969-70
June Howson 1970
H.V. Kershaw 1970-71
Brian Armstrong 1971-72 became head of comedy at Granada
Eric Prytherch 1972-74
Susie Hush 1974-76
Bill Podmore 1976-77 went on to produce Brass and Brothers McGregor
Leslie Duxbury 1977 wrote over 300 episodes of the Street
Bill Podmore 1977-82
Bill Podmore, Executive Producer 1982-87
Pauline Shaw 1982
Mervyn Watson 1982-85 left to produce award-winning First Among Equals
John G Temple 1985-87 went on to produce Take the High Road
Bill Podmore 1987-88
David Liddiment Executive Producer 1988-92
Mervyn Watson 1988-91
Carolyn Reynolds 1991-93
Carolyn Reynolds Executive Producer 1993-
Tony Wood 1994 became head of comedy at Granada
Sue Pritchard 1994-

J is for... JILTINGS A number of the Street residents have nearly made it to the altar, but changed their minds at the last minute.

1964 Emily Nugent jilted Leonard Swindley at the altar.
1969 Gordon Clegg called off his wedding to Lucille Hewitt as she was trying on her wedding dress. Albert Tatlock and Alice Pickens called off their wedding when the vicar did not arrive at the church on time.
1984 Derek Wilton and Mavis Riley jilted each other.
1987 Alan Bradley lured Rita Fairclough to the registry office for a wedding which turned out to be her own. She jilted him on the steps outside.
1989 Eddie Ramsden jilted Tina Fowler during her hen party.

K is for... KEN'S WOMEN
Over the last thirty-five years, viewers have watched Ken Barlow fail in love time and time again.

Ken's first screen kiss – with librarian Marion Lund

At the end of the very first episode, Ken introduced his parents to a girlfriend and since then has not stopped courting or wooing.

1960-61 Student Susan Cunningham
1961 Librarian Marion Lund
1961-71 First wife Valerie Tatlock
1964 Exotic dancer Pip Mistral
1966 Reporter Jackie Marsh
1971 Receptionist Yvonne Marshall
1972 Rita Bates
1972-73 Shop assistant Norma Ford
1973 Graduate Elaine Perkins
1973-74 Second wife Janet Reid
1974 Unionist Peggy Barton
1976 Graduate Wendy Nightingale
1978 Chiropodist Sally Robson
1978 Unemployed Karen Barnes
1979-80 Third wife Deirdre Langton
1981 Yoga instructor Sonia Price
1984 Secretary Sally Waterman
1989-90 Secretary Wendy Crozier
1991 Café owner Alma Sedgewick
1992-93 Florist Maggie Redman
1994 Stylist Denise Osbourne

L is for... LONGEST SERVING

By December 1994, 3,800 episodes of the street had been broadcast. Below are the top twenty-one characters who appeared and how many episodes they clocked up:

1 **Ken Barlow** 2,389
2 **Emily Bishop** 2,102
3 **Bet Gilroy** 1,942
4 **Betty Turpin** 1,826
5 **Len Fairclough** 1,797
6 **Annie Walker** 1,746
7 **Rita Sullivan** 1,720
8 **Alf Roberts** 1,683
9 **Hilda Ogden** 1,647
10 **Elsie Tanner** 1,641
11 **Mavis Wilton** 1,564
12 **Deirdre Rachid** 1,525
13 **Gail Platt** 1,431
14 **Albert Tatlock** 1,322
15 **Stan Ogden** 1,246
16 **Mike Baldwin** 1,245
17 **Ivy Brennan** 1,205
18 **Vera Duckworth** 1,157
19 **Ena Sharples** 1,148
20 **Minnie Caldwell** 1,081
21 **Jack Duckworth** 1,020

M is for... MARRIAGES

There has been plenty of confetti thrown over the last thirty-five years, both in church and at the registry office. The first couple filmed saying 'I do' in church were Steve and Elsie Tanner, and the first time viewers saw a Street registry office wedding was when Dennis Tanner married Jenny Sutton. Many actors have appeared as vicars but one, Frank Topping, who as Rev. Smedley married Ken and Deirdre, was a vicar in real life. Does this mean that Ken and Deirdre are really married?

8.3.61 Jack Walker gave daughter Joan away when she married Gordon Davies.
1.10.61 Lucille Hewitt was bridesmaid when her father Harry married Concepta Riley.
20.6.62 Christine Hardman eloped with Colin Appleby.
4.8.62 Albert Tatlock gave niece Valerie Tatlock away when she married Ken Barlow.
19.10.63 Dennis Tanner was best man when Jerry Booth wed Myra Dickinson.
18.12.65 David Barlow eloped with Irma Ogden.
4.9.67 Elsie Tanner married Steve Tanner in Warrington.
29.5.68 Londoner Jenny Sutton wed Dennis Tanner.
15.7.68 Sixteen-year-old Audrey Bright eloped with eighteen-year-old Dickie Flemming.
22.7.70 Bet Lynch was a witness when Elsie Tanner became Mrs Alan Howard.
3.4.72 An Easter Monday wedding for Emily Nugent and Ernest Bishop.
29.10.73 Ken Barlow married his second wife, Janet Reid.
10.7.74 Betty Turpin watched sister Maggie Clegg marry Ron Cooke.
7.7.75 Deirdre Hunt married Ray Langton in a registry office.
20.4.77 Rita Littlewood married Len Fairclough, attended by bridesmaid Mavis Riley.
20.3.78 Alf Roberts married Corner shop owner Renee Bradshaw.
28.11.79 Mike Baldwin gave Gail Potter away when she married Brian Tilsley.
10.9.80 Emily Bishop unknowingly married a bigamist – Arnold Swain.
13.5.81 Rovers potman Fred Gee married Eunice Nuttall.
27.7.81 Deirdre Langton married Ken Barlow.

31.10.83 Eddie Yeats married pregnant Marion Willis.
9.1.85 Kevin Webster's father Bill married Elaine Prior, Percy Sugden's niece.
23.12.85 Gail Tilsley's mother, Audrey Potter, married Alf Roberts.
14.5.86 Ken Barlow gave daughter Susan away when she wed Mike Baldwin.
8.10.86 Sally Seddon wore peach to marry Kevin Webster.
9.9.87 Alf Roberts gave Bet Lynch away when she wed Alec Gilroy.
24.2.88 For the second time, Gail Tilsley married Brian Tilsley.
13.6.88 Jack Duckworth was best man when Don Brennan wed Ivy Tilsley.
9.11.88 Mavis Riley finally married Derek Wilton.
14.2.90 Steph Jones married Des Barnes.
8.8.90 In Portsmouth, Ken's son Peter Barlow married Jessica Midgeley.
5.7.91 Mike Baldwin married second wife Jackie Ingram.
27.9.91 Gail Tilsley married Martin Platt with her three children in attendance.
27.5.92 Terry Duckworth ran away after marrying Lisa Horten.
5.6.92 Rita Fairclough married Ted Sullivan even though he was dying.
19.6.92 Alma Sedgewick married Mike Baldwin in a registry office.
29.9. 93 After turning down Percy Sugden, Olive Clark married Edwin Turner.

Everyone loves a wedding

26.1.94 Maureen Naylor married Reg Holdsworth at St. Christopher's church.

28.11.94 Deirdre Barlow took Samir Rachid as her third husband.

N is for... NELLIE FAIRCLOUGH AND OTHER CHARACTERS WHO NEVER APPEARED

Nellie was the first wife of Len Fairclough, often referred to but never seen. There have been various characters over the years who have never appeared although they are referred to so often that viewers often think they must have seen them. They include Mr Papagolous, the boss of Gamma Garments – ever-present through his phonecalls to Swindley and Nugent; Alf Roberts' first wife Phyllis who died in 1972; Emily Nugent's Auntie May who lodged with her for over a year, banging on the ceiling; and the same ceiling-banging technique was used by Minnie Caldwell's mother who died in 1962 at the age of ninety-two. More recently, Derek and Mavis spent seven years talking about his first wife Angela Hawthorne; it was not until 1994 that she finally appeared.

O is for... OUTSIDE LOT

For the first eight years, the exterior street was built each week in the studio and filmed along with interiors. In 1967, when the train crashed off the viaduct, all the disaster scenes were still recorded in the studio. In 1968, producer Richard Everitt convinced the bosses that, after eight years of playing safe, they could afford to splash out and build a set outside. A disused railway yard near Granada was acquired and the Street, terraced side and new maisonettes was built. This location was feared by all the cast as it was built like a wind tunnel and was always bitterly cold, even during the summer months. It took months to build but filming carried on, using the old sets first then having brick frontages built on the houses. In 1981 a new site was chosen for the Street and it was carefully rebuilt – this time with a new house at No. 7 and a ginnel between the Rovers and No. 1. To build the new Street, 49,000 old bricks and 6,500 slates were used, and 29,000 bricks went into building the viaduct. To get an authentic finish, bricklayers used a special black mortar, mixed to the original Victorian specifications with an ash ingredient. The foundation stone of the new Rovers Return was laid by Doris Speed on 3 December 1981. The site was formerly home to three streets of back-to-back houses – Tickle Street, Camp Street and Garden Court. All the cast stood proudly by their doors when it was officially opened by the Queen in May 1982. The site is still used for location shots on the Street every Monday, and every other day it is open to the public as part of Granada's tours. Visitors will also see the original outside site, mocked up to represent a New York street.

P is for... PRISONERS

Terry Duckworth was to become a national hero after running away from custody during his wedding but he has not been the only resident to spend some time behind bars. In 1967, Ken Barlow was jailed for seven days for taking part in an anti-Vietnam demo. Eddie Yeats shared the same cell as Jed Stone in the 1970s, and in the late 1980s Alan Bradley spent some months at Risley remand centre before coming to trial. In 1971, Ernie Bishop spent three months stuck in a Spanish jail after he was arrested for taking photographs of semi-nude models on a beach. Other characters have had near misses: Mr Swindley was threatened with prison in 1965 for driving without a valid licence, and the following year Ena Sharples was found guilty of shoplifting but let off with a fine. More recently, Kevin Webster and Steve McDonald both feared they would go down for conspiring to obstruct the course of justice.

Q is for... THE MOST ASKED QUESTION

The most commonly asked question of the Street production office is: What was the name of Minnie Caldwell's cat? The answer is 'Bobby', although in fact Minnie had two; the first ran away in 1968 and she replaced him with a stray which she named Sunny Jim for three months before changing the name to Bobby as she was becoming confused.

Betty Driver and Fred Feast share a joke behind the bar

R is for... ROVERS' STAFF

There have been five licensees of the Rovers Return Inn – Jack Walker was the first and when he died, his wife Annie took over. She was followed by their son, Billy Walker. He did not want to stay and when he sold the pub back to the brewery, Bet and Alec Gilroy took over. Over the years, the pub has employed many workers. Some have come and gone in days, while others have lasted years:

Managers: Vince Plummer, Brenda Riley, Arthur Walker, Billy Walker, Glyn Thomas, Gordon Lewis, Fred Gee, Bet Lynch, Betty Turpin, Liz McDonald, Rodney Bostock.

Barmaids: Concepta Riley, Nona Willis, Doreen Lostock, Irma Ogden, Lucille Hewitt, Emily Nugent, Betty Turpin, Bet Lynch, Gail Potter, Dawn Perks, Arlene Jones, Diane Hawkins, Carole Fairbanks, Suzie Birchall, Kathy Goodwin, Maureen Barnett, Gloria Todd, Sally Seddon, Alison Dougherty, Margo Richardson, Tina Fowler, Liz Mcdonald, Angie Freeman, Raquel Wolstenhulme, Tanya Pooley, Jenny Bradley.

Barmen: Ivan Cheveski, Sam Leach, Jack Ford, Fred Gee, Wilf Starkey, Frank Mills, Jack Duckworth, Charlie Bracewell.

Cleaners: Martha Longhurst, Hilda Ogden, Amy Burton, Sandra Stubbs, Tricia Armstrong.

S is for... SHOP STAFF

The first words in Coronation Street were spoken outside the corner shop by retiring shopkeeper Elsie Lappin to newcomer Florrie Lindley. Since Elsie, the shop has been run by the following people and their assistants:

Dec. 1960 - May 1965 Florrie Lindley with Irma Ogden (April 1964-June 1965)

May 1965 - Jan. 1966 Lionel Petty with Irma Ogden (June 1965-Jan. 1966), Dennis Tanner (July 1965-Aug. 1965)

Jan. 1966 - April 1968 David and Irma Barlow with Hilda Ogden (June 1966 - Aug. 1966)

April 1968 - July 1974 Maggie Clegg with Les Clegg (April 1968 - June 1968) Ena Sharples (June 1968 - June 1970) Valerie Barlow (Sept. 1968 -Dec. 1969) Betty Turpin (June 1969) Irma Barlow (June 1970- Dec. 1971) Hilda Ogden (Oct. 1970) Janet Reid (Aug. 1971) Lucille Hewitt (Dec. 1971-March 1972) Norma Ford (May 1972 - Dec. 1973) Alf Roberts (May 1974 - June 1974) Mavis Riley (July 1974) Blanche Hunt (April 1975 - Jan. 1976) Tricia Hopkins (Jan. 1976 - May 1976) Gail Potter (Jan. 1976 - April 1976).

July 1974 - April 1975 Megan and Vera Hopkins

May 1976 - July 1980 Renee Bradshaw Roberts with Alf Roberts (April 1978 - July 1980)

July 1980 - June 1993 Alf Roberts with Deirdre Langton Barlow (Aug.

1980 - June 1993) Audrey Roberts (Dec. 1992 - June 1993) Sally Webster (May 1987 - Jan. 1992) Ivy Brennan (May 1991 - July 1991)

June 1993 - Aug. 1993 Brendan Scott with Deirdre Barlow (June 1993 - Aug. 1993) Emily Bishop (Aug. 1993) Nicky Platt (Aug. 1993)

Aug. 1993 - Jan. 1994 Alf Roberts with Deirdre Barlow (Sept. 1993 - Dec. 1993)

Jan. 1994 - Reg and Maureen Holdsworth with Maud Grimes.

T is for... TOP OF THE POPS

When the Street's Brett Falcoln released a single 'Not Too Little, Not Too Much' it shot up the charts thanks to Granada playing the track over the end titles as actor Chris Sandford sang. Before she joined the show, Sue Nicholls had a hit with 'Where will you be' and Bill Tarney and Liz Dawn both have successful singing careers. Bill's rendition of 'One Voice' rocketed up the charts. Betty Driver was an international singing star long before she became Betty Turpin. In the 1940s she became famous when she sang with he major dance bands of the day, and the song 'Sailor With The Navy Blue Eyes' became her theme tune. Amanda Barrie appeared in the 1960s musical *I've Gotta Horse* with pop idol Billy Fury. Barbara Knox cut an album in the 1970s called 'On The Street Where I Live', and Kevin Kennedy is now leading his own band, the Kevin Kennedy Band, after years of playing base guitar with northern bands. Davy Jones appeared in only one episode, as Ena's grandson Colin Lomax, before he grew up in America as one of the Monkees. The same applied to Peter Noone, who once appeared as Len Fairclough's son Stanley – he ended up singing with Herman's Hermits.

U is for... UNIVERSALLY FAMOUS

In 1971, Coronation Street entered the *Guinness Book of Records* in the biggest ever sale of a television programme, when a Canadian TV station bought 1,142 episodes. Tours are run from Canada to Manchester every year for devotees who spend ten days visiting everything to do with the Street. These tours are run by a couple, Michael Reynolds and Kathy Semple, who deal with all Canadian interest on behalf of the Street office. Canada is not the only country to fall in love with the folk from Weatherfield. In 1966, 50,000 people lined the streets to wave to Elsie Tanner and the Walkers during a tour of Australia. The Hawaiian island of Oahu (the setting for *Hawaii Five-O*) showed the Street at dusk and it was also a hit in Zambia. Ena, Annie and Co. have been subtitled in Scandinavia, Trinidad, Holland, Japan, Greece, Sierra Leone, Singapore, Spain, Thailand and Hong Kong. For a while, America viewed the Street, but it was never as successful as when showing in Canada. At the time of writing, the Street is being shown in Ireland, Canada and New Zealand.

'Eh Stan, did you know we're a hit in the Conga?'

V is for... VISITORS

Over the years, the Street set has played court to many visitors, from Her Majesty the Queen, to Prime Minister Margaret Thatcher who told Julie Goodyear that she had both a Newton and a Ridley in her cabinet. The first visitor was back in 1961 when Alfred Hitchcock popped into the Rovers, and in 1994 Norma Major visited. Other famous visitors include Dustin Hoffman, Howard Keel, Boy George, Diana Dors, Helen Shapiro and Laurence Olivier.

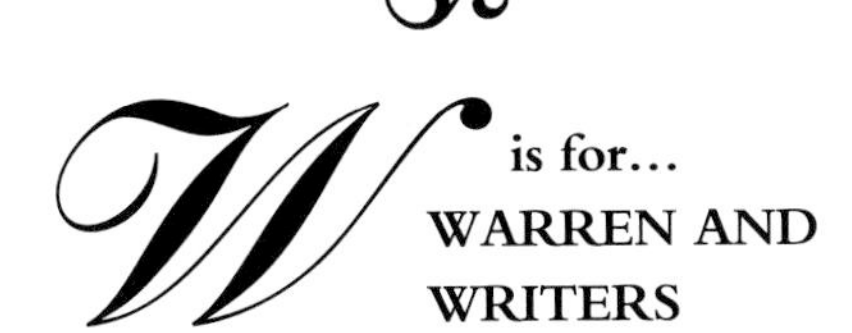

W is for... WARREN AND WRITERS

Child actor and model Anthony Simpson changed his name to Tony Warren and created Coronation Street. In 1994, he was proud to be presented with the MBE by the Queen in recognition and gratitude for giving the country the most important television programme the world has seen. Warren was twenty-three when he wrote the first scripts and continued to write for the programme, and and off, until 1968. In all, he wrote seventy-one scripts. Nowadays, he lives in Swinton, Manchester and is a best-selling author. He is also a consultant on the Street.

At present there are fifteen writers working on Coronation Street, and they are named at the beginning of his book under the dedication. Adele Rose is the longest-serving member of the team – she wrote Episode 40 back in 1964 and recently completed her 400th script. H.V. Kershaw joined the programme right at the beginning as script editor; he wrote Episode 15 after Warren had written the first 14 episodes. In all, Kershaw penned over 200 scripts from 1961 to 1988. Over the years, nearly 100 writers have come and gone. Harry Driver and Vince Powell wrote Episode 19 and continued to work together for the first four years of the show. Eventually, they left to act as comedy advisors to Thames Television. Jack Rosenthal, recently presented with a special Comedy Award, whose credits include *Bar Mitzvah Boy, Spend Spend Spend* and *London's Burning*, wrote 150 scripts for the Street. His friend Geoff Lancashire wrote seventy-four scripts in the 1960s and Geoff's daughter Sarah now features as Raquel. John Finch wrote episodes between 1961 and 1968 before creating the long-running series *Family At War*. Les Duxbury retired from writing for the Street in 1991 after writing over 300 scripts. Julian Roach wrote his first script in 1969, and John Stephenson joined the team in 1976. Together, they created Granada's hit comedy programme *Brass* and both have a string of credits to their name. They still write for the show along with Peter Whalley (creator of the BBC's *Castles*), Paul Abbott (creator of *Children's Ward* and producer of *Cracker*) and Frank Cottrell-Boyce (*A Woman's Guide to Adultery*). The Street also has an Australian writing for it – Patrea Smallacombe has written for soaps *Young Doctors, Neighbours* and *Prisoner Cell Block H*. Paul Abbott and Tom Elliott started work on the show as storyline writers, creating the structure for episodes and giving the writers guidelines on the thread of each story. There are currently three storyliners working on the Street – Gillian Creswell, David Millard and Marina O'Loughlin. For the last two years, the Street writers have won the prestigious Writers' Guild of Great Britain award for writing the Best Television Drama Serial.

Tony Warren

X is for... X-RATED SCENES

The producers, writers and actors of *Coronation Street* are proud to say that in the thirty-five year history of the programme there have never been any X-rated scenes. *Coronation Street* was created as a family drama and will always be viewed as such.

Y is for... YULETIDE CELEBRATIONS

In the early days on the Street, there was a tradition of putting on shows and pantomimes at Christmas. There has not been a Christmas show since Hilda Ogden blacked up as Al Jolsen in 1977 to entertain at the Community Centre. In 1962, the Mission Hall Players presented an original play *Lady Lawson Loses* starring Emily Nugent, Annie Walker and Kenneth Barlow. *Cinderella* was presented at the Mission in 1964, with Lucille Hewitt taking the title role. When the Centre players put on the same production in 1975 Tricia Hopkins starred. *Aladdin* was the 1968 panto with Hilda Ogden as Wishy Washy and Albert Tatlock as the Genie. Perhaps the most popular Christmas show was the one put on in the Rovers in 1972 – the 1940s show starred Rita Littlewood as Marlene Dietrich, Emily Bishop as Carmen Miranda and Bet Lynch, Betty Turpin and Norma Ford as the Andrews sisters.

Z is for... ACTORS NOW DEAD

When Arthur Leslie died in 1970, the cast of Coronation Street were shocked. His death was sudden, and he was the first of the Street actors to die. In the next twenty-five years many other actors have sadly passed away:

1974 Patricia Cutts committed suicide (Blanche Hunt)
1975 Frank Pemberton died from a stroke, aged sixty-two (Frank Barlow)
1975 Graham Haberfield died at the age of thirty-four (Jerry Booth)
1979 Fifty-three year-old Alan Browning died of a liver complaint (Alan Howard)
1982 Arthur Lowe suffered a fatal heart attack aged sixty-seven (Mr Swindley)
1983 Eighty-five year-old Violet Carson died in her sleep (Ena Sharples)
1983 Forty-seven year-old Peter Dudley died of a heart condition (Bert Tilsley)
1984 Jack Howarth died in his sleep, aged eighty-eight (Albert Tatlock)
1984 Christine Hargreaves died of a brain tumour aged forty-five (Christine Hardman)
1984 Bernard Youens suffered a fatal stroke aged sixty-nine (Stan Ogden)
1986 Patricia Phoenix died of cancer aged sixty-two (Elsie Tanner)
1986 Gordon Rollings died of cancer (Charlie Moffitt)
1987 Leah King died in her cot aged six months (Sarah Louise Tilsley)
1988 Margot Bryant died in her sleep aged ninety (Minnie Caldwell)
1989 Tom Mennard died of cancer (Sam Tindall)
1990 Lynne Carol died aged seventy-six (Martha Longhurst)
1991 Sixty-nine year-old Betty Alberge died (Florrie Lindley)
1992 Canadian Paul Maxwell died aged seventy (Steve Tanner)
1992 Seventy-five year-old Teddy Turner died at home in Leeds (Chalkie Whitely)
1992 John Sharp died on 26 November (Les Clegg)
1994 Ninety-five year old Doris Speed died in her sleep (Annie Walker)

Gone but never forgotten: Margot Bryant, Violet Carson and Lynne Carol

Acknowledgements

The author would like to express gratitude to the following people who gave interviews and helped with the production of this book. They all helped to make Coronation Street *a continuing success, from its conception to its thirty-fifth anniversary.*

Jean Alexander · Peter Baldwin · Judith Barker · Thelma Barlow · Amanda Barrie · Roy Barraclough · Ivan Beavis
Derek Bennett · Denise Black · Tracy Brabin · Elizabeth Bradley · Johnny Briggs · Susan Brown · Amelia Bullmore
Beverley Callard · Nicholas Cochrane · Chris Cook · Kenneth Cope · Pamela Craig · Angela Crow · Anne Cunningham
Catherine Cusack · Diana Davies · Elizabeth Dawn · Eileen Derbyshire · Veronica Doran · Betty Driver · Noel Dyson
Mark Eden · Tom Elliott · Edward Evans · Richard Everitt · Ken Farrington · Fred Feast · Julie Goodyear · Sandra Gough
Simon Gregson · Stephen Hancock · Doris Hare M.B.E. · Joan Heath · Malcolm Hebden · Sherrie Hewson
Madge Hindle · Geoff Hinsliff · Ruth Holden · June Howson · Geoffrey Hughes · Susan Jameson · Milton Johns
Meg Johnson · Kathy Jones · Maggie Jones · Kevin Kennedy · Bill Kenwright · Doreen Keogh · Anne Kirkbride
Barbara Knox · Sarah Lancashire · Charles Lawson · Michael Le Vell · David Lidiment · Philip Lowrie
Deborah McAndrew · Sally Ann Matthews · Reginald Marsh · Eileen Mayers · Philip Middlemiss · Heather Moore
Gareth Morgan · Ken Morley · Bryan Mosley · Jennifer Moss · Cheryl Murray · Chloë Newsome · Sue Nicholls
Caroline O'Neill · Daphne Oxenford · Denis Parkin · Lynne Perrie · Nigel Pivaro · Eva Pope · Sue Pritchard
Chris Quinten · Anne Reid · Carolyn Reynolds · Shane Rimmer · William Roache · Adele Rose · Jack Rosenthal
Alan Rothwell · Chris Sandford · José Scott · Patricia Shakesby · Kathy Staff · Doris Speed M.B.E. · John Stevenson
Jill Summers · Irene Sutcliffe · William Tarmey · Shirin Taylor · Bill Waddington · Ernst Walder · George Waring
Tony Warren M.B.E. · Mervyn Watson · John Wheatley · Sally Whittaker · Sean Wilson · Helen Worth

Bibliography

All My Burning Bridges, Patricia Phoenix. Arlington Books, 1974.
Coronation Street: The Inside Story, Bill Podmore. Macdonald, 1990.
Coronation Street: Twenty-Five Years, Graham Nown. Ward Locke in association with Granada Television, 1985.
I Was Ena Sharples' Father, Tony Warren. Duckworth, 1969.
The Importance of Being Percy, Bill Waddington. Boxtree, 1992.
Ken and Me, William Roache. Simon & Schuster, 1993.
Life and Times at the Rovers Return, Daran Little. Boxtree, 1994
The Street Where I Live, H.V. Kershaw. Granada, 1981.
Vera Duckworth: My Story, Liz Dawn. Blake, 1993.

INDEX

(References in *italics* are to picture captions)

INDEX